Robert Marshall Heanley

A Memoir of Edward Steere

Third Missionary Bishop in Central Africa

Robert Marshall Heanley

A Memoir of Edward Steere
Third Missionary Bishop in Central Africa

ISBN/EAN: 9783744754286

Printed in Europe, USA, Canada, Australia, Japan

Cover: Foto ©ninafisch / pixelio.de

More available books at **www.hansebooks.com**

A MEMOIR OF
EDWARD STEERE, D.D., LL.D.
THIRD MISSIONARY BISHOP IN CENTRAL AFRICA.

BY THE
REV. R. M. HEANLEY, M.A.,
QUEEN'S COLLEGE, OXFORD,
RECTOR OF WAINFLEET-ALL-SAINTS, AND HONORARY SECRETARY OF THE
UNIVERSITIES' MISSION TO CENTRAL AFRICA.

'Never anything can come amiss,
When simpleness and duty tender it.'
Midsummer Night's Dream.

LONDON:
GEORGE BELL AND SONS, YORK STREET,
COVENT GARDEN.
1888.
[*All rights reserved.*]

TO

THE MEMBERS OF THE UNIVERSITIES' MISSION,

PAST AND PRESENT;

ON EARTH, OR IN PARADISE;

WHOSE SELF-DEVOTED LIVES HAVE MADE OUR FAITH IN

GOODNESS STRONG; AND BEAR WITNESS, OF THE

LIVING POWER OF THE CHRISTIAN'S CREED,

TO THESE LATTER DAYS.

PREFACE.

IT is remarkable that, whilst Cambridge gave the first, and Oxford the second head to the Mission to Central Africa founded by the old Universities, the third was a distinguished alumnus of a new University, little more than fifty years old, and not attached by any special ties to the Church of England.

Nevertheless, it is pleasant to think that a son of the Church of England, entrusted to her care, has by his life and work ennobled the University of London.

This volume does not profess to be a record of such life and work. It is only a Memoir. It is an endeavour to catch, and to fix in print, a few glimpses of a great character. They are only glimpses of one, who, as the late Bishop Wordsworth of Lincoln declared, " Stood foremost among the missionary bishops of his age in special gifts, endowments, and attainments; in philosophical wisdom and meditative thoughtfulness, in ethical and metaphysical science, in sound Christian theology, in marvellous linguistic ability, joined with practical prudence, homely simplicity, indomitable courage, and universal sympathy; unflinching self-devotion, never-failing hopefulness and joy, and primitive holiness of life."

The compiler of this Memoir has sought, while his memory is still fresh, to enable Bishop Steere to show himself as he was in his speech, in his writings, and most especially in his actions (for in all that concerned himself he was the most reserved of men), so far as the materials entrusted to his hands permit.

"There is," Bishop Steere says in one of his published sermons, "a language that all can understand, that is to all most convincing, that has made more converts than any other. A loving, devout, self-sacrificing spirit, shining through the life, goes home to the hearts of all, and they cannot refuse to listen." It is with the confident expectation that his own life will thus speak to many that this Memoir is now given to the Church.

It only remains for us to tender our hearty thanks to those many kind friends without whose willing aid these pages could not have been written, amongst whom it is necessary to especially mention by name Mr. Hercules Brown, the Bishop's brother-in-law; Lord Justice Fry, his life-long friend; Mr. S. F. Palmer, the founder of the Guild of S. Alban; Archdeacons Hodgson and Maples; Miss M. Allen; the Rev. H. Rowley, author of "Twenty Years in Central Africa;" and last, but not least, the Rev. E. S. Lowndes, rector of Little Comberton, whose thoughtful suggestions have been of much service.

ROBT. M. HEANLEY.

The Rectory, Wainfleet-All-Saints.
Passiontide, 1888.

CONTENTS.

PAGE

CHAPTER I.
Edward Steere.—Birth and School-days.—Undergraduate of University College, London.—Lord Justice Fry's Letter (1828-1850) 1

CHAPTER II.
Law Student and Layworker—Essay on "The Being and Attributes of God."—Letters on the Schoolmen.—The Churches of Cornwall.—The Moral Influence of Pain.—The Joys of the Future State (1850-1853) . . 10

CHAPTER III.
The Brotherhood of S. Mary.—The Guild of S. Alban.—The Brotherhood of S. James', Tamworth.—Letters on Brotherhoods.—Admission of Novices.—The Responsibilities of Individuals.—The Duties of Superiors of Guilds (1853-1856) 28

CHAPTER IV.
Ordination and Clerical Life in England.—Curate of Kingskerswell.—Curate of Skegness.—Rector of Little Steeping.—Volunteers to go out to Africa with Bishop Tozer (1856-1862) 44

CHAPTER V.
Sails for Cape Town.—Journey up the Zambesi.—Settlement on the Morumbala Mountains.—Return to Cape Town (1863-1864) 58

CONTENTS.

CHAPTER VI.

The Island and City of Zanzibar.—Dr. Krapf, the Pioneer of Church Work in Eastern Africa.—Arrival of Bishop Tozer and Dr. Steere.—The Slave Trade.—Commencement of Mission Work.—Reduction to Writing of Native Languages.—First Efforts on the Mainland.—Return to England (1864-1868) 71

CHAPTER VII.

Little Steeping.—Plan for a Theological College at Lincoln.—Letter on Church Reform.—Speech at Church Congress.—Resigns his Rectory and Returns to Zanzibar (1869-1871) 88

CHAPTER VIII.

Bishop Tozer's Resignation.—Sir Bartle Frere's Embassy on the Slave Trade, and Memorandum on the Mission. Dr. Steere's Letter to the University of Oxford (1872-1873) 103

CHAPTER IX.

Work at Magila.—Purchase of the Old Slave Market, Zanzibar.—Foundation of Christ Church on its Site.—Dr. Steere Accepts the Bishopric.—Consecration.—Plans of Future Work (1873-1874) 116

CHAPTER X.

Death of the Rev. A. N. West.—Bishop Steere hastens his Return to Zanzibar.—Reinforcement of the Mainland Work in the Usambara Country.—Walk to Nyassaland. — Interview with King Mataka.—Return to Zanzibar (1874-1875) 135

CHAPTER XI.

Recollections of Bishop Steere by Archdeacon Maples (1875-1876) 158

CHAPTER XII.

Foundation of the Freed Slave Settlement at Masasi, on the Road to Lake Nyassa.—Serious Illness of Bishop Steere on his Return Journey, and consequent enforced Visit to England (1876-1877) 189

CHAPTER XIII.

The Bishop receives his DD. Degree from the University of Oxford.—Preaches the Ramsden Sermon at Cambridge.—Letter to the Secretary of the Prayer Union.—Speech on the Relations of Christianity and Civilization in Mission Work.—Returns to Zanzibar.—Archdeacon Hodgson's Recollections of the Bishop.—Progress of the Mission (1877) 200

CHAPTER XIV.

The Work outgrows the Income.—Progress in Zanzibar, and on the Mainland.—The Church in the Old Slave Market (1878) 218

CHAPTER XV.

Ordination of First Native Deacon.—Completion of Swahili New Testament.—Completion and Opening of the Slave Market Church (1879) 239

CHAPTER XVI.

A Walk in the Zaramo Country.—Appointment as Vice-President of the Bible Society.—An Outsider's Testimony.—A Large Arrival of Freed Slaves, and their Reception at Mbweni.—The Boys' School at Kiungani.—Mission Work in Town (1880) 255

CHAPTER XVII.

Daily Life in Zanzibar City.—Miss Allen's Letter (1880) 270

CHAPTER XVIII.

Finance.—S. P. G., and Special Funds 292

CHAPTER XIX.

Mohammedanism 305

CHAPTER XX.

The Work extends to Lake Nyassa.—Letter on Missionaries and the Civil Power.—Letters on Brotherhoods for Africa (1880-1881) 322

CHAPTER XXI.

Progress of the Mission.—The Bishop's System of Honorary Workers.—A Letter from Sir J. Kirk.—Converts from Mohammedanism (1881) 337

CHAPTER XXII.

Last Days.—Visit to England.—Return to Zanzibar, and Death (1882) 348

APPENDIX.

A Selection from the Bishop's Papers, and Letters of Counsel and Advice 361

ILLUSTRATIONS.

A Portrait of Bishop Steere . . . . *Frontispiece*
Slaves taken from a Dhow 78
The Boys' School, Kiungani 118
Exterior of the Slave Market Church, Zanzibar . . . 252
Interior of the Slave Market Church 356
Map of Eastern Intertropical Africa . . *At end of volume*

A MEMOIR OF EDWARD STEERE,

Missionary Bishop in Central Africa.

CHAPTER I.

Birth and Early Days.

EDWARD STEERE, the subject of this Memoir, was born in Charles Street, City Road, London, on May 4th, 1828, and baptized on September 7th, at S. Margaret's, Lothbury. The font in this church, was carved, it is said, by Grinling Gibbons, and by an interesting coincidence one of its principal subjects is the baptism, by Philip the Deacon, of the Ethiopian eunuch, the first African slave admitted to the freedom of the Gospel.

Edward was the only son, by his first wife, of Mr. William Steere, of the Chancery Bar, a man well known for his considerable legal attainments, and as a vigorous pamphleteer much in advance of the age, in urging various sanitary, social, and legal reforms.

At an early age he was sent to a day-school at Hackney,[1] under Dr. Alexander Allen, a good linguist and philologist, whose premature death

---
[1] To which then pleasant suburb his father had now removed.

in 1842 was a severe loss to his pupils. Of these days the Bishop wrote when in England for the last time :[1] "I am afraid I was not a very diligent scholar, but it always seemed to me that Dr. Allen taught me all that I ever learnt, and that was enough to float me through my degrees at College, and to give me a knack of dealing with languages, which has been invaluable in Africa." Dr. Allen's surviving sister describes Steere as "a bright merry-faced boy, whose ringing laugh broke out on the slightest provocation ; one not very proficient in games, but a very great favourite with the boys, who nevertheless often felt his remarkable powers of repartee."

On Dr. Allen's death he was removed to University College School, then under the able mastership of the late Professor Key, whence he passed to the College itself at the end of two years,[2] graduating at the University of London B.A. in 1847 ; LL.B. in 1848 ; and LL.D. in 1850, when he took the Gold Medal for proficiency in Legal Knowledge. The class lists show that he had amongst his colleagues and competitors several, who are, or have become known in the world—such as Sir J. Lister, the eminent surgeon ; the Right Honourable H. Matthews, M.P., the present Home Secretary ; R. H.

---

[1] To Miss Allen, the surviving sister of Dr. A. Allen.

[2] His home now, and for the rest of his London life, was at 14, Egremont Place, New Road, since swept away in the course of improvements in the King's Cross Railway Station. The solitary tree that long stood outside the station at the Euston Road end, was planted by Edward himself in what was then his father's garden.

Hutton, of "The Spectator;" Charles Crompton, Q.C.; Walter Bagehot, the brilliant writer on Political Economy and Biography; and two men now on the Judicial Bench, Lord Justice Lindley and Mr. Justice Wills. "It was in January, 1843," writes the present[1] Mathematical Master of Harrow, "that Steere and I entered the school the same day, and were placed in the same form; and as our way to and from school was the same, we soon became very intimate. My recollection of him is of a boy, somewhat stoutly built for his age, always dressed in black or quite dark clothes of a rather clumsy cut, with capacious jacket pockets, which usually contained a good store of almonds and raisins, or some other pabulum adapted to the wants of a schoolboy, and which on one occasion when he was my neighbour in a German class, led to the singular remonstrance from the master, 'Oh Hayward! Hayward! I hope you do not eat!'

"His face was not handsome, but there was a twinkle in his eye which told of latent humour, and it lighted up pleasantly in conversation. His views and opinions were expressed in short, sharp, incisive sentences, showing a good deal of wit, and much natural shrewdness.

"Steere did not specially distinguish himself in the work of the school, but I was impressed with the feeling that he had a much wider knowledge of subjects beyond the ordinary schoolboy range than the rest of our schoolfellows. He was never idle, but it was characteristic of him at school, and still more, I think, afterwards in the College, that he

[1] R. B. Hayward, Esq., M.A., F.R.S.

was always working at something different from what he should have been working at (according to ordinary rules) at the particular time. As one instance, I believe, he took up the study of Chinese, when his lectures in Classics, French, and German would have given him (according to ordinary notions) plenty of employment.

"I may relate one incident, which lingers in my memory, and illustrates his knowledge of matters familiar to very few school-boys. One day a pane of glass in the upper part of one of the school-room doors had been broken, and I was appointed with another boy to investigate the matter and report to the Head-master. Not wishing to get a schoolfellow into trouble, we had recourse to Steere, who drew up an admirable report, in good legal phraseology and with much circumlocution attributing the damage to the violence of Boreas, Zephyr, or some Son of Æolus, and engrossed it on legal foolscap. It was duly presented to our excellent head-master, Thomas Hewitt Key, who appreciated the joke, as from a window we saw him showing it to another master and laughing over it, and allowed the matter to drop."

This impression of Steere's character as a schoolboy is confirmed by the friends of the succeeding periods of his life.

"We were at University College together in the Senior Latin Class," says Mr. J. E. Hodgkin. "He used to sit between E. A. Leatham and myself. Dressed in queerest old-fashioned style, he was only equalled by the suave Home Secretary in the art of making the class misbehave with his quiet dry fun. And I was fonder of him than any other fellow."

But the fullest picture is that drawn by Lord Justice Fry in the following letter:—

"It was in the year 1849, or 1850, that I first made the acquaintance of the late Bishop Steere, an acquaintance which before long ripened into a friendship that was only interrupted by his death.

"When I first knew him, he had taken the degree of B.A. at the London University, and was studying for the Bar, chiefly, I believe, under the direction of his father.

"In every friendship, as Aristotle says, there must be some things ὧν ἕνεκα ἐ φίλουν. In our case the pursuit of metaphysical truth, especially perhaps on its religious and moral sides, was the keystone of our friendship.

"Upon so much we were agreed. But our points of view, especially on religious questions, were not identical.

"He was a decided High Churchman. I had been born and bred in Quakerism; and though not holding to all its doctrines or practices, I had a strong Quaker bent in me. He leaned more on authority, and the voice of the Church as the utterance of a collective conscience; I more on the private reason, and the individual soul.

"In our mode of arguing on any given theme, I recollect a difference too, which was the subject of discussion between us. He was inclined to gather together all arguments which he thought might lead anyone to believe in a conclusion that he held to be true; I inclined to reject all such arguments as did not convince my own individual reason.

"We differed therefore in many things, but I cannot remember that any harsh or unkind word ever came from him, and I am sure that the diversity of our sentiments never interfered with our friendship. I recollect that he maintained (whether rightly or wrongly I do not inquire), that the University College, London, was a good school for theologians, because it did not teach theology, but left the mind trained for inquiry, whilst unbiassed as to results. Again, I remember that he always maintained that in Church matters there were two views, and two only—the sacramental and the non-sacramental; and that the one logically resulted in High Church, the other in Quakerism.

"Our friendship, which began, I believe, at the Debating Society of the College, was continued at many discussions over the breakfast-table, or late into the night, on fate, free-will, and the other questions about which young men on whose minds are dawning the infinite problems of life, debate, and must debate, if they are ever to arrive at a working metaphysic for the rest of their lives. And there was a frequent interchange between us of such papers as we wrote, and a frequent correspondence, both then and in after years. After one long talk with Steere, I find myself adopting words from the Protagoras as expressive of the way in which I used him: Μοῦνος[1] δ'εἴ πέρ τε νοήσῃ, αὐτίκα περιὼν ζητεῖ ὅτῳ ἐπιδείξηται καὶ μεθ' ὅτου βεβαιώσηται, ἕως ἂν εὐτύχῃ.

[1] *Protagoras*, Steph. p. 348.—"But if a man 'sees a thing

"My recollection of his speeches at the Debating Society is that they were racy, humorous, with no effort at oratory, and that he rather liked to reduce his opponent to an absurdity, than affirmatively to support his own view. I think W. C. Roscoe, who wrote some good poems, was President when I first joined, then Walter Bagehot used to come, and was very striking with his great eyes and epigrams; Alfred Wills, now my colleague, came a good deal, and the Fowlers, one of whom afterwards sat for the Borough of Cambridge, and the other is still member for the City of London.

"Steere did not dislike the law, on the contrary, I believe that he liked it very well, though it was less congenial to him than philosophy, theology, or philology. Had he continued at the Bar, he would, I believe, have had a great chance of eminence. He took at the University the gold medal for the degree of LL.D., a safe evidence of considerable legal acquirements; he had great good sense, a quick ready grasp of things, a power of speaking clearly and forcibly, and without any tendency to rhetoric; a strong sense of humour; and above all, his mind naturally ran along the diagonal between reason and authority, a highway very much frequented by the legal intellect. If he had not chosen to take Orders, he might, to use the recent language of a distinguished writer, have ended 'ignominiously in large practice at the Bar.'

"He always considered that his legal training when he is alone,' he goes about straightway, seeking until he finds someone to whom he may show his discoveries, and who may confirm him in them."—*Jowett's Translation.*

was of much value to him in after life. During an evening which he spent at my house in June, 1882, just before his final return to Africa, whilst talking of the mischief done by Missionaries assuming jurisdiction over native races, he expressed his opinion that the justice of the chiefs was generally far better than that of the Missionaries, 'unless, of course'—with a merry twinkle of the eye—'they had been called to the Bar.'

"Steere had a more or less accurate knowledge of many languages, and he had a ready power of acquiring this kind of knowledge, a power which largely contributed to his usefulness in Africa. I believe that he read with more or less ease Greek, Latin, French, German, Italian, and Spanish, and that he had some acquaintance with Chinese. His knowledge of literature was very considerable, especially in the favourite regions of theology and philosophy.

"But somehow, he never seemed to me to possess the distinctly literary habit of mind. He thought more of the substance and less of the form than the literary student does; and he had in all he did (so it seemed to me), a certain want of finish or polish, which arose from his carelessness as to form. He rarely used the accents in writing Greek, and he was careless beyond most men of his stops and his capitals in writing English.

"That his religion was true, and was the deepest feeling and the strongest motive of his life, all that life shows. It was a religion of a masculine type; it never made him soft or sentimental; it never closed his shrewd eyes to the character, or the conduct of those with whom he was working; it never induced him to use enthusiastic or excessive language; it did not conceal from you his strong native humour, which gave a peculiar flavour to even his serious conversation; it scarcely hid a tendency, which would have been cynical, had it not been made Christian.

"I suspect that a casual observer would have thought him slightly dry and hard, and caustic, and would have failed to appreciate how warm and true was his heart. But with those he knew well he was a very delightful companion, cheery, simple, with at times a very arch interrogative smile, and at others a very hearty laugh.

"We greatly enjoyed a few days he spent under our roof during his visit to England in 1877, and his last visit, just before he sailed for the last time to Zanzibar, has left a most pleasant recollection behind it. He seemed in good spirits, was full of anecdote and fun, and I little thought when I said good-bye to him that we should meet no more on earth."

CHAPTER II.

LAW STUDENT AND LAY WORKER.

DR. STEERE was called to the Bar on June 7th, 1850, by the Inner Temple, and took chambers at 26, Chancery Lane, but he was more often to be found in the Reading Room of the British Museum, or the Lambeth Palace Library, studying some abstruse volume of philosophy or theology, than there. It was thus that he unearthed and printed some hitherto unpublished fragments of Bishop Butler.

"[1] The time was approaching for that almost romantic periodical emulation — the competition for the Burnett Prize. It is just a century since it was established by a benevolent but perhaps eccentric merchant of Aberdeen, who left a certain sum of money to accumulate, in order to afford a prize worth having at periodical intervals of forty years, to the writer, or rather two writers, of Essays on the Divine Character and Attributes, or the Evidences of Natural Religion.

"By an unwarrantable perversion of the founder's intentions these magnificent prizes have now been abolished, and the funds applied to the establish-

[1] "Blackwood's Magazine" for June, 1886.

ment of a semi-secularist lectureship." But at the time of which we write, the second of these periodical competitions was drawing near, and Dr. Steere was engaged in preparing for it.

The prize itself, with its agreeable accompaniment of £600, was ultimately awarded to the late Principal Tulloch; but Dr. Steere's essay on "The Being and Attributes of God"[1] was not only a remarkable production for a young layman of twenty-five, but still ranks as a solid contribution to the standard theological writings of the English Church. The enormous amount of illustrative matter freely gathered from English, Greek, Latin, French, German, Spanish, and Italian authors, and thrown into the notes in the published form of the essay, shows a range of reading as rare as it was wide and deep.

As a sort of relaxation, he took up that study of the art of printing which was to prove so useful in after days at Zanzibar; and having mastered its initial difficulties by the aid of a professional friend,[2] he set up a small press in his own rooms, from which, at various times, he issued little papers for the use of his friends.

[1] "A valuable book, which I venture to hope he will some day find time to re-issue, enriched with that deep knowledge of the natural heart of man, and of its growth under divine grace, which his almost unique experiences in Central Africa would furnish."—BISHOP OF SALISBURY, *Bampton Lectures*, 1881, p. 185. But his absorbing work as Bishop prevented this and other literary work. See his Advertisement to the 2nd edition of his "Persecutions of the Early Church" (Bell & Sons, 1880).

[2] The late Mr. C. Cull, Houghton Street, Strand.

During the Vacations he devoted much time to the study of botany and conchology, of which he gained more than a mere amateur's knowledge; and to forming a collection of rubbings from old brasses, in search of which he seems at one time or another to have visited nearly every part of England. But above all, this period of his life was one of incessant mental activity, and were we editing his correspondence we could enrich our pages with letters testifying to it abundantly. But the plan of this Memoir compels us to stay our hand. The difficulty really lies in making a selection. The following are extracts from a few of his letters addressed at this time to Mr. Edward (now Lord Justice) Fry:—

July 29th, 1851.

I have not read Chalmers' Life; I have only seen reviews and heard the fame thereof with my ears in periodicals. But from all these I gather that it was a life well worth writing, and a life well worth reading, and using to improve one's own conceptions of duty. There seems to have been something really like a conversion in it, and all that practical earnestness which makes up a Christian. His conduct in the Free Church schism was like him—ever earnest in what was practically right, but even reckless of patient striving to reform. He was like the Scotch Reformers, who got rid of what was wrong at all costs, and whose religion was and is a negation of falsehood rather than an assertion of truth.

I have sometimes thought that it is that unpardonable blasphemy of the Holy Spirit to deny that anything really good is good, to serve a preconceived end. It was very much such an act the Pharisees were then engaged in, and so I should not hesitate to say to such men as I understand Chalmers to have been, what a French priest said to Dr. Wordsworth, "Si vous n'étés pas du corps vous étés bien de l'âme." And this, being sorry that they missed the truth, not wavering in my own estimate of it, which I cannot do without denying my reason. See here my theory of charity, and ask yourself if those who hold all creeds indifferent are more really liberal perhaps not.

I think Dr. Chalmers was a very lovable Scotchman, but I confess I am not yet impressed with his greatness as a theologian.

September 19th, 1851.

I have been taking a run in ———shire, and staying at ————. Do you know the place?—planted, enclosed, and almost created by its owner, just now in its perfection, perfect of its kind always. He, enjoying for nearly eighty years perfect health, and wealth almost unbounded, is now so fallen that he cannot move himself, but is supported in his carriage by straps. His wife, like himself, till lately ever in health, has fallen into perfect mental imbecility, and the only person who can be said now to enjoy the beauty of the place is a lady, a stranger, who has established herself in the house as a friend and general confidante. The absence of family, which seemed the absence of care and burden, completes the desolation. And so it seems to me, that a place, which if it were mine would by its very beauty, I feel sure, lull every feeling in me of energy or longing for a better land, has within it as apt a lesson as may well be,—that man may plant and build, but it must be for another, and that far better is the recollection of good deeds and almsgiving, than the possession of the most costly and beautiful objects of mere natural production. Yet if one has any perception of loveliness in natural beauties, and their fascination, it will seem too true "how hardly shall a rich man enter into the kingdom of heaven."

September 23rd, 1851.

I suppose the danger of metaphysical theology, pursued to any great extent, is the tendency it may produce to place Christian perfection in knowing all mysteries; and in the same temper, supposing that because much more is known and understood, than the vulgar know, therefore what is not known and understood is false;—two manifestations of pride, despising others, and over self-reliance. I find an inconvenience in the habit of using technical terms; to take the commonest instance, "*a priori*" comes to be almost essential to the explication of one's ideas.

I am rather afraid of speculation in a retired individual who has no opportunities or occasions of very active practice; and one is very apt to leave off receiving facts as facts, and to begin to hold them only as one holds the theory of which they form a part, and so to modify one's belief in the facts as often and as readily as one modifies the theory—to argue unconsciously that the facts cannot be so, because then they would harmonize with a false theory, and clash with the true, for so we always deem our last conception.

I apprehend this is the way great thinkers come to talk such nonsense as they sometimes do. I believe the only remedy is to set the steady increase of personal holiness before one's eyes as the real object of life. Nothing proves more clearly how much hangs upon a very little distinction, than the attempt to give a reason for one's own actions, and to estimate their moral quality. . . .

I heard at Exeter that the present Bishop of that diocese, when Rector of Stanhope, made inquiries with a view to a life of Bishop Butler, and all that tradition had preserved of him was, that he was a tall thin man that rode about very fast on a black horse.

September 13th, 1852.

I am afraid I have misled you as to my conception of the delight in the beauty of nature, and of art too. To a certain extent I take it to be a natural feeling, very similar in character to the moral sense; like it, liable to be blunted, perhaps almost lost, by incautious handling, and, like it, essential to complete an excellent human nature.

Just as one gets moral jesuistry by casuistic subtlety, so one may get absolute indifference out of critical admiration. If the expression of any feeling be systematically repressed, or reduced to a matter of argument, the feeling itself is soon dulled, and so one may lose much enjoyment as pure and true as this of a love of nature's beauties, and get only some formal rules of taste, as bad a substitute as a casuist is for moral consciousness.

In truth, they will neither bear subjection to dry reasoning, nor, I imagine, will either come out untouched from the attempt to write a book upon them, or to talk much of them. They are like the bloom upon a newly-struck coin, essential to a good specimen, but soon lost by handling.

I have been thinking that something of this kind is true of the intellect,—that there is an instinctive appreciation of truth, which may be lost by too much logic, especially in attempting to prove quasi-self-evident propositions, and which, when lost, leaves the individual a sceptic or credulous, according to his disposition. Is this so?

August 2nd, 1853.

I suppose there is no doubt on any system that there are other souls like ours, and if so matter may remain as the medium. I take it to be clear that matter in itself can be no object, even of its own creation, being wholly incapable of perception, comprehension, and enjoyment; and perhaps from this may be derived one of the best arguments against its perpetuity, or self-existence.

It seems to me every day more and more clear, that the world must be regarded as a school, in which our concern is to gather instruction and make improvement, without dwelling upon the lot and condition of others, except so far as they may afford opportunities for our own advancement, and that the only point of view in which we may expect to comprehend and habitually contemplate with advantage, the external world, is in its relation to ourselves as moral and sentient beings. On any other basis we are likely to feel the view too awful, and so miss its benefit.

On your other point I have more objection to make. I do not think you regard the Pagans from any real point of view. They were brought up in a religion. They did see Deity in all things. They could only come to that dark state of doubt you describe by a voluntary course of rejection. I do not believe the religion of the world has at all materially changed since the earliest times of which we have any record. The great mass of mankind, those, that is, who have been distinguished neither for devotion nor impiety, have always held, and held it material that all should hold, that there is something of Deity governing the universe, that there is a state of rewards and punishments after death, and that any man who is remarkable for impiety and injustice will certainly then be punished, and I believe that I may add that popular belief has never assigned any definite limit to the continuance of those rewards and punishments.

Certainly the early education of a Greek brought Deity much closer to him than any but a very religious education does to us; and in Pagan times as now, but a very, very few were philosophers, or theosophers, and men generally cared but little for any deep system, though they jealously defended the formal profession of some religion.

I wonder how you came to be so deep and loving a student of real philosophy—I wish you were quite consistent in it. I wonder whether it was suggested by the example, and encouraged by the sympathy of others. It is a very curious subject, this divergence of tone and temper among men, and one which lies very much at the bottom of all possible knowledge of human nature, and has no doubt a close connection with that deepest of problems, the moral character of man, with what is, in the language of theology, Original sin. And yet, as far as I have ever heard, we are all in the dark about it still. Is it so?[1]

August 26th, 1853.

I have just had a note sent me from the diary of the son of Bishop Wilson of Sodor and Man, dated Dec. 23rd, 1737, relating of Butler, that he preached before the king on being bettered by afflictions, which affected him so much that he

[1] We may be permitted to refer our readers to the Bishop's "Sermon Notes" for fuller thoughts on this subject.

asked for the sermon, and said he would do something very good for him. Quaere, was a fair copy made of that sermon, and is it now in existence? If you are ever in the neighbourhood of Lampeter don't omit to look in and see whether Butler furnished his books with marginalia. If he did, however, I have no doubt they will be found to have been shaved half off in rebinding.

August 27th, 1853.

I should be exceedingly happy to help you if I could, but to tell you the truth I know next to nothing of Bacon, and never yet comprehended what was the great thing he did for philosophy.

The truth is that the schoolmen wished to assume nothing, and so they spent their costliest labour upon elaborating what a modern would assume without scruple, or perhaps wholly disregard. And, again, they wished to express themselves in a manner wholly incapable of misapprehension, and with the dimmest notion of language tried to make that most uncertain of all things absolutely certain, and then spent yet more time in settling all the niceties of logic into the greatest possible nicety of mood and form.

And then, poor men, they took the Bible as always true, and Aristotle as generally so, and quoted him out of barbarous versions at third hand; and when you have untied all these knots I can say nothing of their philosophy in other respects; but their theology was an effort to demonstrate, *a priori*, in the strictest manner, the absolute and eternal truth, and necessity of the whole of Middle Age religion.

Thus of the works that I have looked into, more than half is mere settling of preliminaries, and of the rest some is palpably false, some seems wholly useless, much is so interwoven with a web of logical subtleties, which it gives one the headache even to think of, as to be scarcely, if at all extricable, without material damage, and some rests at last on a dictum of Aristotle far from self-evident, and I suspect very often used in a manner he hardly dreamt of.

I have a great idea that Bacon, like most of his followers, left off the pursuit at the first attempt or so, in unutterable and insuperable disgust, and thought for himself freely, and popularly, and therefore sensibly and intelligibly. Yet there is a kernel even in this theology which those who think the truth in its smallest quantity worth the largest possible amount of labour will be much pleased with.

I do not think there is much extra-theological philosophy. Their scientific knowledge has all been long since superseded, and is so expressed as to require no small industry and ingenuity to get at. I suppose the "Opus Majus" of Bacon's great namesake Roger is the most important of any not directly theological work now accessible, and in their zoology, and geography, and so forth, they fell into the mistake of supposing that the ancients had expressed themselves with as trustworthy a degree of logical accuracy as the Doctor Resolutissimus himself, and quoted them accordingly. If you will let me know any particular point on which you find the schoolmen referred to, I will endeavour to find it out, or I will make you an abstract of some book of note, such as the great keystone of scholastic theology, Peter Lombard's "Liber Sententiarum."

I think of making an effort to comprehend Aug. Comte's "Philosophie Positive," but to tell you the truth, I find the works of infidel writers so exceedingly dull, and their systems and arguments so obscure and transitory, that I rather thought it better to avoid any direct reference to any particular system, and not neglecting to make myself acquainted as far as possible with the grounds and difficulties which have been the real source of unbelief, to write[1] with a view to forearm believers for all time, more than to refute the unbelievers of this, when there seems to be nothing opposed to us but a cloud of ungraspable mysticism.

I imagine that the source of much practical carelessness is the having at some time started a difficulty and found no

[1] This is in reference to his Essay on the Being and Attributes of God.

answer. A philosopher would from this begin to doubt other men to be careless.

Oct. 3rd, 1853.

I have certainly been wandering. I went first to Westbury in Wiltshire and saw there its White Horse and Bratton Castle on the downs, said to be the very Danish camp to which Alfred went as a minstrel, and certainly a strong position if only there had been water easily procurable. In Westbury itself I was quite astonished at the abundance of springs pouring out everywhere, as well as at the contemptible little watercourses which are made to work the cloth-mills.

Thence by coach from Warminster to Salisbury, not an unpleasant ride, though Salisbury plain is rather monotonous in its border line. I got out at Bemerton to see George Herbert's church, and felt so horrified at the skylights in the roof, and the pews, and the gallery, that when I got into Salisbury I bought some note-paper and wrote an indignant letter to the "Guardian," which I see ultimately got inserted.

I never saw so disappointing a Cathedral as Salisbury, with which I renewed my acquaintance. You may find its whole portrait in works on cathedrals, so that when you get there you have nothing new to see. There are some fine elms, though, in the Close. Thence by rail to Portsmouth, and never met with a more confused junction that that at Bishopstoke, but it was Wilton great sheep fair. Thence to Brighton, to me who think London dull, the very dullest place in mundane creation. Thence to Lewes, and so to the hospitable roof of a distantish relation just under the South Downs, far superior in every respect as it seemed to me to those near Westbury. And so, sometimes playing with a cockatoo, sometimes wandering about over the Downs, or hunting for those modest little Sussex churches, or vainly trying to make myself useful in the hare and partridge-butcher line, or other such like employments, the time slipped away and I slid back into dingy, stopped-up London. I say stopped-up, for they have closed Chancery Lane, and Fleet

Street, and Judd Street, and have got half Parliament Street up, besides other countless stoppages more beyond my ken.

The whole tract of country is poor, both in architecture and in monumental remains. I never saw the inside of Wells cathedral, I should like to do so some day. I have only seen of Wells and Glastonbury what could be seen in riding through on a coach-top. Glastonbury is peculiar in many respects. I have too keen a perception of present evils, however, to see without regret the ruins of places so consecrated to piety and learning. The three hundred years seem to have wiped out the recollection of their abuses, and I want to think of them as their founders thought. There is a parish church at Glastonbury with a very fine Somersetshire tower. Curious subject that of localisms in architecture. You have entirely hit my idea of the Braintree case. Cornwall you are aware is a congeries of dissent, for which there are long scores against divers civil and ecclesiastical magnates, and belongs rather to the family of Wales and Man than to England proper. As to what you say about the churches, I should think it probable that the idea of land or sea marks *had* been entertained by their builders, unless there should seem ground for thinking that the sea had chased away the village, or some mansion or manor house had formerly stood where the church now alone remains, which are the common ways of accounting for a divorce between the church and the village in Southern and Eastern England.

But I think I noticed in the Isle of Man, and in the map of Ireland (and Cornwall might historically be of this family), that the churches and villages seemed to have been sown broadcast by different hands, so as to lie together only by accident, or for reasons of after convenience. I do not know how this is to be accounted for, but I would suggest that Christianity in these countries is much older than it is in England, so much so indeed as probably to have antedated the parochial scheme, whence it would happen that churches would be built on the scene of a miracle, or near a recluse's cell, or as they seem almost to have been once in the Isle of Man, one to so many acres ; and then the parochial division, when introduced, would fix upon these old strangely placed chapels for parish churches, and give them a district somewhat heedlessly; and antiquity might operate in yet another way, by giving increased scope for displaying the contrast between church immobility and village changes, for I suppose nothing but the extremest inconvenience would ever move a church.

Again there might happen, what has, I believe, often happened in England, that a chapel in a thinly populated country, might at first have no true village attached to it, or indeed contained in any part of the neighbouring district, but afterwards a village or town might be developed in some extreme corner, and claim that chapel for its parish church.

It is to be added, that in the dearth of monasteries in very early times, if a man made a vow, he used to build a chapel, instead of founding a monastery, and so many out-of-the-way future parish churches might be founded.

In England all this was different, for Christianity came into a settled country, which has never since materially changed its local characters, evidence of which may be seen in the fact that in England we hardly ever find a village taking its name from its church, and when we do we can almost always see a reason in the modern growth of the village.

But in the Isle of Man every parish is Kirk-something; nearly every other in Wales, Llan-, or Eglwys-somewhat; and[1] not a few in Cornwall Lan- or Eglos-, or Saint-somebody; which proves, I suppose, that the churches preceded the present villages.

Oct. 7th, 1853.

I should very much like to know what a direct moral influence is. I suppose there is such a thing, and I hope it is not presumptuous to believe that one does sometimes feel a direct moral influence from the Holy Spirit, when some sin

---

[1] About 103, including S. Endellion, in the entire county; fourteen out of twenty-one in Pyder hundred; and nine out of twelve in Trigg hundred.

seems to become impossible, seems to part off from us by a gulf we feel we can never pass. I hope too, that without unnecessary self-excusing one may believe that sometimes one feels a direct moral influence exercised against ourselves, when one slides into sin without any consciously active volition, or even with a consciousness of its guilt, and a conscious desire not to fall into it. Of course Pain has no such direct moral influence as this. The nearest approach to it is perhaps in pre-occupying the attention so as to make the application of the mind to any volition at all impossible, or difficult; but even so this pre-occupation has no distinctive moral character.

The central direct effect of pain seems to me to be, that it compels a recognition of individuality. We increase our pleasures by society, but we must all suffer alone. Suffering cuts us off from all external things, and drives us back upon ourselves, "what is all without us to this one gnawing pain within?" Thus in suffering we see the man, it brings out sharply all the strictly intellectual goodnesses and badnesses of his character. If ever a man is peevish and short-tempered it is when he is in pain; if a man is ever calm and patient we see it in his moments of suffering; if a man is given to cursing and swearing, he shows it in the gout; if he is given to pray, his sick-bed is hallowed by it; if he lived in excitement he takes opiates, and tries to read exciting books, whenever he cannot be entertained and have his attention distracted by the presence and conversation of others. When one suffers much, this individuality, this disregard of external motives becomes fixed, and forms part of the character. Thus it is, I believe, universally true that persons in habitual ill-health, or suffering, are either very kind and gentle, or very selfish, and violent, and unfeeling. Thus too, I am inclined to account for the fact that we are accustomed to see very repulsive characters described as crooked, and diseased, in mind and body, and yet to think and read of saintly characters as suffering much and dying early. I believe both to be true to nature, and due to the intensifying effect of pain upon the moral character.

Few of us have any real sympathy with persons of a disposition very unlike our own. We know what we like, and if we desire to serve another, we think of him as more or less desirous of the same things. Thus sympathy sometimes becomes troublesome and annoying, though it may be sincere, and we would rather be without the effects of what is yet real kindness. Thus two persons of uncongenial tempers will live together more happily, if they be actuated by pure motives, without rather than with any very strong affection; and if also their uncongenialities have not been developed by pain, and are not called into action by the sight of it.

A slave, they say, makes the very worst of masters, and similarly a sick man ought to make the very worst of nurses, yet it is not so in fact.

However, there indubitably are instances of persons, who are and think themselves confirmed invalids, who are the very most unfeeling persons conceivable. I suppose that this may be traced to a certain shallow self-sufficiency, which thinks that having itself suffered pain, this other sufferer must be relieved by what would have relieved that, sometimes thinks that it showed more patience when it suffered more, and I suppose one who has suffered very much has a natural impulse to despise less excruciating pains.

Yet a person in robust health never realizes what sickness is.

Thus I am brought back to my old idea of the simply intensifying effect of suffering. One who is patient and considerate when personally in pain, will be patient and considerate to another; one who is impatient, and exacting then, will be hasty and unfeeling now. I may add that one who is apt to exaggerate his own misfortunes, will be sure to underrate those of another.

What then shall we say of pain generally? I think, at present I can only think, that since men are seldom deliberately and self-originatedly evil, and if they suffer much, their internal nature comes out sharply, most men become more kind and sympathizing by suffering much, as undoubtedly all become better able to appreciate what illness is.

Again the influences brought to bear upon a sick person are generally those of kindness and religion, to which last, in the absence of the blinding effect of strong and immediate worldly passions, he is peculiarly sensitive.

More than this, we then learn to estimate truly the value of quiet, unobtrusive gentleness, and to see our pursuits and longings in a clear moral light, especially if our pain be in any way an effect of our own evil-doing. For I am apt to think that the feeling, that there is something wrong in our physical structure, has very much to do with our conception of wrong in its more abstract sense.

If contemplation be, as I have no doubt it is, the first step to reformation, then pain, which induces or compels it, must be useful.

Generally, I take it, suffering makes the unsettled and the good better, but only renders the bad worse.

I hope I may have suggested something to you. I have written these thoughts down as they occurred to me, and await better instruction at your hands.

Did you ever read Maitland's Eruvin? I think you must like it.

Oct. 23, 1853.

I do not know how we can adopt physical theories of another life, or attempt to explain in such a manner as to be even to human comprehension, wherein the joys or pains of such future existence may consist. Yet it seems to me that we have a very definite revelation of what are the essential points of that happiness. Your unsatisfied power of enjoyment has its object clearly propounded ; human nature is imperfect, insufficient to bring satisfaction to itself. Now we read in the Bible that the cause of this unsatisfaction is our separation and alienation from God, to be remedied by a union so close, that it is described as a partaking of the Divine nature.

Well, here is the joy of the future state ; can it be wrong to speculate upon this? But revelation does not leave us here, it talks of palaces, and gold, and emeralds, and most physical of all, of actual bodies. Can it then be wrong for us to imitate our revelation, and speculate upon the joys of a future state according to the pattern there set us? But further, is it possible to imagine that the real joys and pleasures of earth are not *intended* to be to us prophecies and foretastes of the joys and pleasures of the blessed?[1] Our ideas of pleasure, happiness, and enjoyment are derived from these, and we are promised what these give us.

Earthly happiness is given us to incite us to seek heavenly, it must therefore have some likeness to, or congruity with it, else the promise of future happiness would not mean what the words express.

Again, we are told that the joys of heaven exceed all we can imagine. What then? Are we to say that we may not dream of any definite kind of happiness because that will exceed all we can dream of? Or should we not rather try, by supposing all that gives us most pleasure magnified a hundred-fold, to stir up in ourselves a longing for the place where they shall be realized?

I doubt whether the greater part of mankind can ever have a real earnest longing for a state of happiness of which they never attempt to realize a symbolic representation.

Our Lord excited the Jews to desire heaven by comparing it with the rule over two cities. I am afraid that if you tell men that it is worse than useless for them to strive to picture to themselves the joy of heaven, you tell them in effect to regard those joys with cool curiosity rather than with warm, earnest longing.

I suppose that physical sensations and mental sensations are always separable, and that our true way of imagining future happiness is to take the mental emotions caused by the most pleasant physical sensations, and imagine them in greater strength apart from the physical sensation.

I cannot tell why men are so afraid of allowing the bodily nature any share in their ideas of perfection. It is as much God's work, and a part of them, as their intellectual nature

---

[1] I say real pleasures, to distinguish them from those of mere nervous excitement, such as games of chance, and lust, which when analyzed do not appear to contain any real pleasure.

is, and perhaps not essentially more changeable or corporeal.

There is great danger of religion becoming an abstraction, indeed practically the men of the world regard their present nature as occupied properly with earthly things, and think of God and heaven as incomprehensible, and not proper subjects of any realizing meditation.

The result is that they seek this world's goods with all their might, and hope that they shall gain heaven as a sort of bye end, with which their actual thoughts and pursuits cannot have any strict or immediate relation.

If you say that we cannot comprehend what pleasure is, you contradict yourself. If you say that heavenly pleasures are essentially different from anything we have an idea of, you negative the actual idea of their being really pleasant, without supplying any other, and this seems dangerously akin to the doctrine that the temporal is certainly good, the eternal doubtfully so.[1] For men know what pleasure is, but there are few who can really long for what they have no idea of. And if all men, especially if carnal and vicious men, cannot long for the joys of heaven, then must the whole argument, to induce to a virtuous life from the consideration of its rewards, fall to the ground. And I am afraid that it is the fact that the general apathy about eternal happiness has arisen from its having been described as a mere inconceivable abstraction, something talked of in words, as immeasurably superior to all we can conceive, but never presented in such a shape as to realize to the mass of mankind any idea at all of actual pleasure.

I do not think that all speculation on things unrevealed is evil. I think some is useful, if not necessary. Indeed all human science is but the construction of a theory to reconcile and account for appearances, the appearances only being real, the theory and the science pure speculations.

If this be right and useful in natural science, I think we

[1] " Shall you be happier in this world we *can* see, by despising to-day and looking up to the clouds ? "

" I don't know about the unseen world—the use of the *seen* world is the right thing, I am sure ! "—*Thackeray's Letters.*

may not condemn it in theology. Such a speculation is that, which enquires how a state of waiting for judgment could be one of change or progress, without physical or material accidents. Indeed, as we find that the best way of teaching what is natural and real is very often to begin with the imaginary theory (and this has been true even where the theory afterwards turns out false), so I imagine human theories may be of use in theology, only we must not make them articles of faith.

Thus it is, I think, revealed that there is an intermediate state: for ought I know prayers for the dead were commanded by our Lord: well, then, can it be wrong to strive to find a theory upon which you can suppose these prayers to be useful? For myself, I have felt, that without some such theory of the lesser practical matters of Christianity, it is difficult to be a practical Christian, though one might confess an abstract doctrine.

CHAPTER III.

THE GUILD OF S. ALBAN.

THE fearful sanitary condition of the homes of the poorer classes in London had attracted much public attention about this time. And the inquiries which caused this movement had brought again into prominence the still more startling heathenism which prevailed amongst them, notwithstanding many efforts of good and wise men to make head against it.

To a really thoughtful mind the physical destitution, and want of sanitary appliances, were absolutely as nothing compared with the spiritual destitution, and the absence of healing for the soul, which existed side by side with them.

In the urgent and bitter cry that arose from these starving souls, Dr. Steere heard a call from God to which he could not but respond.

There is a passage at the end of his essay on the "Attributes and Being of God," written about this time, in which he seems to drop the essayist, and strike for us the keynote of his own life.

"Let us consider the horror of a painful, lonely, lingering death—the death of an outcast, loathly and infectious, dying in the full consciousness that his own acts, against the entreaties, the warnings, nay, to the hurt of his dearest friends, driven from him only by his own persevering wickedness, have brought him to it, and try to feel and know that that was and naturally is our state ; let us put ourselves in it, and feel its certain anticipations till its awfulness is clearly before us, and then let us picture to ourselves a life the most joyful and smiling, with prosperity and a good conscience, friends and youth, and health and riches, and unmingled happiness, and let us recollect that far above all this is that state of joy and everlasting felicity Christ's Blood has purchased for us.

"Consider what gratitude we should owe to any man who had so changed our fate, then let us remember the agony and death by which we have been redeemed, and finally in reverent awe, yet full of awful love, let us contemplate the nature of our Lord, His incomprehensible Majesty and Godhead, and all earthly things will fade and crumble from before us ; our hearts will be lighted up with that fire of love, which can accomplish all things, and we shall almost long for some difficult and painful task, to show what we can do for Him who hath done so much for us ; and when we learn that He requires of us only that which will most certainly secure our present happiness, only to value goodness to our fellow men above unnecessary worldly possessions, to imitate Him without His agony; can we hesitate? Can we draw back? Can we refuse to serve Him? No! no! it is impossible, for the love of Christ constraineth us, His love to us while we were yet sinners—and flowing from that as its cause and root, our love to Him, our glorious and ever blessed Saviour."

This living conviction soon shaped itself to action, and we find him writing,[1] "What can we do? What we must do is to assist the distressed; teach the ignorant; help the weak; reclaim the lost; this is what God requires at our hands, and what He requires He will enable us to perform. How then can we do it? First, by remembering and acting on the recollection, that our brethren are committed body and soul to our keeping, that as the destruction or salvation of a sinner is the greatest crime, or the noblest reward of virtue, so the uppermost thought with us should always be, how can I so live as to best perform this trust? There need be no fear of our interest and theirs coming into conflict, for both alone are to be secured by obeying the will of God.

"This is our first duty, and the effect of one pure, holy, self-denying kindly life, has often far exceeded those of most eloquent and most learned books.

"But besides our own life, there is active missionary work to be done—work that requires the whole energy of mind and body of those engaged in it, work the most trying, wearying, and at first, in seeming, thankless to any but a pure zeal for God, that can be discovered, the actual probing of the wounds of misery and ignorance and vice, the going into their festering depths and there endeavouring to begin their cure.

"For this we must have missionaries trained in, and for the work, and given to it heart and soul: all

[1] To Mr. S. F. Palmer, founder of the Guild of S. Alban.

cannot so work, how then can such men be found and supported?

"The men are found; those who have felt and realized the call of God to labour for His glory, have formed a society for carrying on this very work, already in several places have they done what their time and means allow. Several of them are now desirous of living together in a collegiate manner, intending to spend their lives in labours of love and charity, desiring only such a maintenance as may enable them to work most effectually.

"They propose to settle themselves in a destitute district, where the parochial clergy shall need and desire their assistance, and such a district has already offered itself. The brethren hope that they may have a house given them, after which they estimate that they can be supported at an annual expense of only £20 for each member, and are willing to commence operations as soon as £60 a year is secured."

The "Brotherhood of S. Mary," which is here referred to, had been formed on September 1st, 1853. In a letter written some years afterwards Dr. Steere says:—"It originated with a few young men belonging to the congregation of S. Matthew's, City Road, London, who feeling strongly the danger to themselves of personal activity without constant intercession and prayer, met together for the purpose of united devotion, and hoped also by means of their offerings to be able to make donations to such Church works as they found ready to hand. In May, 1854, however, having heard of the now famous Guild of S. Alban, founded about two years previously by Mr. Shirley Palmer, a surgeon at Birmingham, and having very carefully discussed its formation and objects, they agreed to join it in a body, on being admitted to it as a distinct, self-governing brotherhood.

Thus the London district of the Guild, of which Dr. Steere was appointed the first " Steward," had its origin in this brotherhood, consisting at first only of its eight members, and three probationers, admitted at their first meeting. Their first work was the bringing fifty-five children to Holy Baptism at S. Matthew's Church on Whit Monday, 1854.

To the infant Guild Dr. Steere's learning, ability, and energy were simply invaluable. Much of its actual printing was at first done by his own hands at his private printing press; he edited its monthly Magazine from its commencement in 1856 to within a few months of his departure to Africa; to him also the Guild was mainly indebted for the preparation of its "Offices," and he was largely concerned in the revision, which brought them into their present form.

And if, moreover, as we believe, the Rules and Constitution of the Guild not only preserve the high tone of early devotion, but meet practically and efficiently the difficulties and needs of the nineteenth century, it was the sound common sense, the legal training, the clear intellect, and wide sympathies of Dr. Steere, which largely contributed to so happy a result.

"No one of our brethren," says a companion [1] of

---

[1] Dr. J. W. Lea, the well-known writer on Ecclesiastical subjects.

those early days, "was ever a more conscientious worker, no one, perhaps, ever set before himself a higher standard of work or responsibility; no one was more intensely and entirely in earnest; and at the same time, few if any were ever more ready to rejoice in the least true work done by any of the brethren. We well remember one of the earliest occasions of our meeting him in London. We were alone together, and he had just been reading over some reports of the members' work. He took up one and said, 'that is not a bad week's work for a *probationer.*' Simple and kindly words, and in themselves perhaps nothing more. But there was a something in the way of his saying them that could never be forgotten, as though he were feeling that probation was but the beginning; and that, with advancing grades, higher responsibilities would ensue, and still more earnest labour be required; and this, not with any special reference to the individual probationer whose report had given occasion to the remark, but rather as a quiet recognition of a great principle."

"One other illustration of his genial brotherliness and sympathy with the smallest attempt to do good may be permitted. We were just starting a little mission-room for occasional services in a somewhat forlorn hamlet near our house, and it chanced that Brother Edward Steere came down to see us on the day when we were busy in putting up some very simple hangings, &c., round the walls. Though only there for a few hours, he threw himself into the work with as much energy as if it had been a special undertaking of his own, working like an ecclesiastical upholsterer nearly all the time, and subsequently, to our surprise, and indeed rather to our discomfiture, writing a kindly little notice of the thing, which, as Editor, he put into the next number of "Church Work."

For some little time all the members of the brotherhood had business occupations which took up most of their day, but in the autumn of 1854, Dr. Steere having come into the possession of about £1,500 by the death of an uncle, severed altogether his connection with the Bar, gave up his chambers, and took rooms in the midst of those to whom he had devoted himself, at 23, New Union Street, Moorfields,[1] working under the direction of the late Rev. W. Denton. Like S. Dominic he sold his books to feed the poor, and like him he would have said if remonstrated with, "How can I peruse dead parchments, when living and breathing souls are perishing?"

But he evidently had not yet found his full voca-

[1] The following lines, taken from a Report of the Westminster sub-district of the Guild, throw an interesting sidelight on this period of Dr. Steere's life, and may also afford some little encouragement to those who are apt to think that the success of a Guild consists in the largeness and publicity of its meetings :—" It was in the summer of 1854 that a few members of the congregation of S. Barnabas heard of a certain meeting to be held in the City by some men, who called themselves the 'Guild of S. Alban.' We, four of us, walked to the place of meeting, the schoolrooms of S. Bartholomew, Cripplegate, expecting to find a room full of talkers, moving and seconding resolutions, and of course carrying them unanimously. Judge of our surprise at being ushered into a small, dirty-looking room, with scarcely any furniture and some four or five young men, looking very gloomy and disconsolate, presided over by one a little older

tion. Practical as his mind was, there seemed to be a sort of restlessness in it, feeling after and stretching forward to something dimly longed for but not yet clearly seen. He was being trained for his life's great work. Thus we find him writing to Mr. E. Fry about this time:—" I was wrong in saying that this life is all I want. I mean that it supplies so sufficiently the checks and incentives which are not to be found in public life that I suppose it would be folly not to be satisfied." And again a few lines further on, " It may seem paradoxical, but I am inclined to think that it is really pride which lies at the root of the feeling which comes at times, the best men have said, over all of them, that the future opened to Christians is one of too much greatness and too high privileges for them to dream of as ever possibly to come to themselves. They say, and I suppose one must believe it, that when a man has learnt to do and be nothing

and equally mournful in aspect. All were listening intently to a Catechetical Lecture of S. Cyril. The reading ended, a few words were interchanged respecting the visiting an old and poor parishioner. An offertory of a few shillings was collected, and after a little strained conversation with those present, we departed grievously disappointed, and expressing our fears that nothing would come out of that.

" But somehow or other some of us found our way thither again, one of us several times, and in spite of all the dulness we soon saw that there was a definite earnestness and living reality at bottom. At last, after some consideration, we requested the Steward (Dr. Steere) to come down to us one evening, and meeting in the room of one of the clergy we talked over the Constitutions and plan of the Guild : the result of which was that five of us applied for admission, and so the Sub-district came into existence."

of himself, he will perceive that God can in him be and do all things."

And so it was not surprising that as the work of the Guild grew in extent and importance, and he was compelled more and more to take the part of a leader in it, he should feel more and more strongly the need of some quiet home, where, to use a favourite expression of his in later years, its members might "cultivate repose." He dreaded for himself and others the loss of that deep inward peace, which comes only of meditation and prayer, and without which, as the foundation, no lasting spiritual work can be done : he noted with delight the successful revival of sisterhoods in the English Church, and desired to promote a like revival of brotherhoods, feeling that here was work to be done for God which could not be done so well in any other way.

Several places were suggested for such a home, and finally he purchased the old ruined chapel of S. Edward, otherwise "The Spital," near Tamworth, together with a few acres of ground adjoining, and early in May, 1855, opened it with two or three brethren of the Guild as his companions, under the title of the "Brotherhood of S. James."

His success, however, did not equal his expectations, and better so; for the great work he was destined, under God, to accomplish in central Africa has amply compensated the Church at large for the failure of the far narrower design he had formed when he took up his anchorite-like abode in "The Spital" at Tamworth. Doubtless too, the experiences he now gained of the daily difficulties of community life, though on the smallest scale, were of inestimable value in aiding him to provide against their recurrence in that wider sphere at Zanzibar. For so it often is, that where at the time one sees nothing but failure and sorrow, in after years as one looks back one can clearly trace how the Father's hand was bringing order out of seeming disorder, and leading us "by a way which we knew not" to a more perfect end; whilst for others there can surely be nothing more helpful, than to see a good man recover himself from a thorough and painful failure.

The following letters will show how high his aims were, and how honestly he endeavoured to carry out those aims at Tamworth. One can hardly read the pithy letter on Brotherhoods without being reminded of S. Francis of Assisi's rejoinder to some fidgety members of his own brotherhood who wished to go barefoot, "Change your brains, but keep your shoes."

A Brotherhood[1] is, after all, but a society of units; men do not become devils, any more than they do saints, by joining a guild or brotherhood. What the brethren are, that the brotherhood is; if they be calm, sensible, active men, the brotherhood will possess these qualities; if they be dreamy, reckless, idle, and fond of littlenesses, the brotherhood will be but a nest of dreamy, ridiculous projects, which, in all probability, the brethren themselves will look back to in after life with regret or amusement.

Let anyone, then, who loves and admires holy Confraternities, inquire of his own conscience, what it is that makes them holy and admirable, and then strive earnestly himself to become a model brother.

If he does this, he needs little more than patience to realize what he admires and longs for; but if a brother

[1] Written for the Guild S. A.

admires midnight matins, and he himself gets up with difficulty between seven and eight; reverences fasting and fears to spare one of four good meals a day; honours the fervour that attends the sick and dying, but trembles at a cold wind, and always has the headache in a bad smell; dreams with delight of singing out of illuminated breviaries, but has not the zeal and perseverance himself to learn to know one note from another, or to draw so much as a turn and a straight line;—such a brother's brotherhood must be a ridiculous failure; its decorations will be tawdry and in bad taste; its singing will scare away inquisitive listeners; it will be the home of talk, a nest of mare's eggs, the scorn of the worldly, the regret of the pious, and the worst stab to the cause it was fondly intended to promote.

But it would not be the joining in a brotherhood that made the men silly; it would be as little able to do that as to realize for them the abstract thing they lazily conceived that it ought to be.

Our opponents are bound to show us a set of sensible men made foolish by joining a brotherhood, before they have a right to brand all such bodies with the stigma of folly, or to raise a hue and cry against them as wicked inventions of the devil.

There is one way, and one way only, of convincing men; let a brotherhood be real, let it be active and useful, and you will have no need of arguments to defend it; but, if it be none of these, men would answer a mathematical demonstration of the benefits and excellence of such institutions only with a derisive laugh, or an impatient exclamation.

The Spital, Tamworth, Nov. 13th, 1855.[1]

Madam,

I have just heard in an indirect manner that you disapprove of the proposals made by your son about joining our community here, and as I wish above all things to avoid any secresy, I hasten to write to you on the subject. I have received a letter from a clergyman, and one from himself on

[1] To Mrs. W——.

the matter, to both of which I have replied, not urging him to join us, but setting forth simply some of the benefits and many of the disagreeables he will be likely to meet with here. I shall feel deeply obliged if you will favour me with the grounds of your opposition, that I may be the better able to judge whether I ought, or ought not, to refuse to treat with him any further.

The case, as it presented itself to me, was briefly as follows.

I heard of one who wished to give himself to God's service, rather than to seek a good position and standing in life, who felt himself called to obey literally our Lord's precepts to forsake all, and follow Him, undeterred by the hardships he would have to encounter, and unregretful of the little comforts and easinesses he would leave behind.

I supposed, and what I have just heard confirms my suspicion, that there would be many infirmities and imperfections mixed up with this intention, as there are with all the best purposes of every one of us.

But, for myself, I have chosen rather to serve God in obscurity than to apply myself to the pursuit of worldly distinctions, I cannot therefore but sympathize with all who profess a desire to do the like; indeed, how can anyone hesitate as to which is the nobler prize to aim at, a heavenly crown of everlasting glory, or the fading splendour of the highest worldly wealth and station?

Some may, perhaps, be able to gain both, but I fear they are few indeed. Which would you yourself choose for your son, that his pious life should intercede for you with God, or that his earthly position should shed a transitory lustre on your declining years, and leave no trace of good in the long ages of eternity?

Pardon my speaking so boldly: I feel bound to do so, in order that you may be able to appreciate the point of view from which I see the proposal of any to join us.

I have done a bold thing in opening my house to such—a thing so bold, that nothing but the sense of imperious duty could have justified it to myself.

If you are afraid that any unsteadiness of character, and tendency to extremes in practice and opinion, are injuring your son's character, allow me to suggest that the most effectual way to correct these, is to allow him, among us, to feel and know that the stern realities of human life cannot be gilded over by any profession, and to find that mere vagaries of thought will not give anyone strength to bear the continued trials incident to any really devoted and earnest life.

I expect that some will come to us, who are really called to a life of self-devotion, and I should feel that I was sinning against God if I did not encourage all such to live up to the very highest point of their vocation; some I suspect there will be, who will find sooner or later that they have mistaken the feelings of the moment for the settled purpose of a sober mind.

I shall have done them the greatest possible service if I have been the means in God's hands of bringing them to a truer knowledge of themselves, and sending them back into the world free from that vague longing for an undefined something that they cannot have, which is eating the heart out of the efforts of not a few young persons, and unfitting them for sober diligence and actual usefulness.

If your son belongs to neither of these classes, I shall ever remember your kindness in undeceiving me; if he is in either state mentioned, I think you will see, that, however your own wishes may lead you, I am doing neither a wrong nor an unkind thing to him or to yourself in not absolutely refusing his admittance. Asking your prayers that God may direct us all aright in this and all our doings, I am your very obedient servant, &c.

To a prominent member of the G. S. A.[1]

A—— expects to find rest in the Roman communion, *because* he intends to yield up his own judgment entirely to Mr. Oakeley, or someone else; he would find just as much if he yielded it up to Mr. Stuart, or to Dr. Cumming, or to anyone else that comes first.

We have each of us a responsibility as to the side we will

[1] Mr. A. C. Crickmay.

choose, which we find a burden as soon as we begin to see things in the doubtful state in which they really are.

It is a strong temptation to most of us to throw ourselves into a party, or the personal following of somebody, and leave off thinking about right or wrong any more.

We cannot, however, so shake off our responsibility, any more than a man who shuts his eyes is not to blame when he runs into mischief.

The true course, if we feel ourselves incapable of holding our own, is to make no public demonstration whatever, but to devote ourselves to the cultivation of personal holiness.

A man may be saved who holds some false doctrine, no man can be who does not act up to the light he has.

I fear that A—— is singularly incapable of forming an independent judgment, and that he greatly deludes himself if he thinks the rest he longs for, anything else than an escape from the labour of thinking.

He avoids anything like reasoning, and rests upon mere feeling. Feeling is often a good guide in action, but it is an exceedingly insufficient ground to decide about sound doctrine upon.

I take it, heretics have generally been people who saw some abuse or irreverence in the Church, and therefore set themselves to frame a scheme of doctrine which should correct it.

It is not shifting from one communion to another that can give a man real peace, it is the cultivation of the gifts of God's grace, especially of charity, and humility, which will lead to that.

To the Same.

Do you not think we ought to take special notice in ourselves and in our brethren, of our several tempers? I am sure it is very proper for a Steward of a district to know his men: there are people who will do anything under one course of treatment, who will do nothing at all, and blame you for their idleness, under another.

Every Steward and Master in the Guild must learn, first of all, not to quarrel with his tools. After all, the men who join us are for the most part mere tools, very indifferent ones sometimes. There are a few workmen here and there, but generally we must try and find something to keep our tools bright on. Some are soft and cannot do hard work; some are cross-grained, and break if we try to do with them the very thing they were made for; so we must put the soft tools to look like useful ones—the worst of them will do at least to give an appearance of numbers to those without; and for the brittle ware we must show them deference, and persuade them to do a little, ever so irregularly, and ever so much less and worse than they are capable of, and we may hope that in time they will do better.

Every man we have may be useful in bringing us new members, and in practice we have often found the worst men bring us the most useful helpers. It will be a great worry and trouble and annoyance to our superiors to avoid despairing, or being offended, or to find means of seducing men into usefulness; but in God's service we ought not to shrink from these things. I do not think that anyone ought to leave his post because the men under him will not work. If they were resolved to do nothing, less would not be done than if they had never joined the Guild at all, and we must learn to look upon the idleness of inferiors as our fault in not finding appropriate work for them, or in failing to persuade them to exertion, not theirs in being idle and obstinate. It does not matter how bad a man is, we must strive to make him better; it does not matter how long we have striven in vain, we must strive on till we succeed, or he leaves us; we must never quarrel with anybody, we can do no good by that.

I believe that the fault of our age is a too great longing after activity; let men work, by all means, everywhere, but let the Steward remember that he is doing a more certain benefit when he improves the temper of one of his inferiors by his own moderation and kindness under trying circumstances, or improves himself in patience and fortitude, by bearing up against misfortunes and ill-usage, than when he secures to the Guild the credit of some active home missionary, or unwearied school-teacher, or even successfully carries out some scheme of external beneficence.

It seems to me that our Society will always be a kind of sieve that men will work in for a year or two and then leave. Our problem is how to make the best of them whilst we have them.[1] We are doing God's work, and " if God be for us, who can be against us ?"

Here too is a characteristic touch from a letter to Mr. E. Fry, December 7th, 1855 :—

The most interesting person of the Middle Ages, seems to me Peter, the venerable Abbot of Cluny, holding the scales between Bernard and Abelard, opening his doors to the condemned, and pleading for him that he might not be compelled to go to Rome, and then, after his death, sending his remains to Heloise with a letter full of kindly feeling. And his whole life squares with these doings. The Abbot of a rich old house, defending its customs against the Bernardine fervour, and yet bidding his monks not hate nor despise the new order, a man, who, having the intention of writing against the Mohammedans, began by procuring a translation of the Koran ; a very personification of mild, dignified good sense, and learned Christian feeling.

[1] We believe that this "*sieve*" theory is confirmed by Dr. Benson's experience at Cowley. "It is the third year that will try you."

CHAPTER IV.

Ordination and Clerical Life in England.

DR. STEERE had been repeatedly urged, especially by the Revs. W. E. Bennett, and Prebendary W. Gresley, both intimate friends, to seek Holy Orders, but had as constantly refused; partly because of the very high standard of the priestly life held by him, and his humble estimate of himself; partly because of his conviction of the pressing need there was for lay-brotherhoods, and his proved value to the Guild of S. Alban; and partly because he felt keenly the slight cast upon his University [1] by the terms upon which alone the Bishops would then accept its graduates as candidates for Orders.

But with the closing of the "Brotherhood of S. James" at Tamworth his thoughts were once more led in this direction, and he put himself in communication with Dr. Phillpotts, Bishop of Exeter.

That prelate had lately endeavoured to restore the order of Permanent Deacons, chiefly with a

---

[1] A correspondence into which he had entered with Dr. Phillpotts so far back as 1852, was broken off by him upon this ground.

It is no slight triumph for the University of London that it should have given a Bishop to the one Mission which peculiarly belongs to the older Universities.

view to the ordination of schoolmasters in country parishes. Such men, if advanced to the Priesthood at all, were to serve in the Diaconate for at least five years, and during that time were not licensed to preach, but only to "assist the Priest in Divine Service, and search for the sick, poor, and impotent people of the Parish."

It is to the credit of the Bishop that after the brilliant examination passed by Dr. Steere he consented in his case to lessen the time of probation to two years, but he firmly refused to license him to preach at all during that period, and thus the curious irony occurred that in the parish of which he was the licensed curate, one of the rising theologians of the day was kept silent, whilst, when on a visit to the diocese of Lincoln, he was freely permitted by its Bishop (Dr. Jackson) to preach it might be three times a day.

It is perhaps, however, to his enforced silence at Kings Kerswell that the Church at large owes his "Account of the Religious Society in England in the Eighteenth Century," his "Early Christian Persecutions," reprinted in 1880, and above all, his valuable "Introductory Preface," to Bishop Butler's "Analogy of Religion," which he prepared in 1857, having shortly before brought out an enlarged and greatly improved "Index."

But how humble was his estimate of his own powers will be gathered from two letters written on the subject to Mr. E. Fry:—

October, 12, 1857.

That little edition of Butler's "Analogy" is not out yet, and I have had a note asking whether I thought a short analytical preface would be useful to students. I suppose it would, but I do not think I see deep enough to make one. I feel the shallowness of my reading daily more and more, and have neither the books, nor the vigour to keep it up, still less to deepen it.

And again :—

I have been many times thinking over the subject of a preliminary dissertation to the "Analogy," but the more I think of it, the more am I overwhelmed with a consciousness of my appalling ignorance, and insufficiency.

When I look at it seriously, vistas of thought seem to open up, but all ending in mist ; believe me, too much leisure is worse than too much work, and indeed I have lately been so languid and unnerved, that I have felt equal to nothing.

To us these two letters seem to contain a parable of Dr. Steere's life. So humble that he distrusted his own powers of doing, and therefore shrank back from the undertaking, but so faithful to his sense of duty, that once seen to be a duty, he did it with all his might, just as seventeen years later he held back from accepting the Bishopric of the Universities' Mission, but once having accepted it threw his whole strength into its duties till death took him at his post.

He was ordained Deacon in the cathedral church of Exeter, on Sunday September 21st, 1856, and licensed to the Curacy of King's Kerswell, near Newton Abbott, Devonshire, then in the incumbency of the Rev. C. A. Fowler.

There was but little scope for action in so small a parish, and the wet, warm climate was very trying to one never constitutionally strong, and it was an acceptable change when in 1858 he was invited by his friend, the Rev. W. G. Tozer, then Vicar of Burgh-cum-Winthorpe, to come to his aid in Lincolnshire.

Under date of Easter Eve, 1858, he writes to Mr. E. Fry :—

I think it is now quite settled that I am to go into Lincolnshire at Trinity Sunday, to take charge of Skegness and Winthorpe, two little parishes on the sea-coast. I am hoping much from the more bracing nature of the climate. I have had a violent attack of influenza, which has left me weaker and more languid than ever.... I do feel the happiness of being in the country, except when I am longing for books, sometimes I feel so helpless for want of them that I quite wish myself back in town again; but then comes a bright day, or a fresh cold one, and I look northwards to Dartmoor, and southwards across Torbay, and I feel that no man in England lives in a pleasanter locality. ... It is extremely gratifying to see the move towards earnest religion now becoming general. I feel myself quite lazy and old-fashioned. I often think I have not a spark of Missionary zeal, being too anxious to feel my way cautiously, to throw myself heartily into a movement; but this is greatly owing to my languid state of bodily health, and the wretched divided state of this poor parish. I am going to serve under a man who shrinks from nothing, and succeeds in everything. Give me your prayers.

Dr. Steere was accordingly admitted to Priest's [1] orders at Lincoln, and the sole charge of Skegness, together with the curacy of Winthorpe, on Trinity

---

[1] It is said that some of the candidates were inclined to look down upon the quiet, self-contained, comparatively elderly-looking man, and one remarked after the Butler paper : " Let me give you a hint, if you are ploughed by the morning's paper. Get the edition with an Introduction by a man called Steere, and if you know that, you are sure to get through next time." "Yes," quietly replied the Author, " I have some acquaintance with the work."

Sunday, 1858. He married a few weeks afterwards Miss Mary Beatrice Brown, of Barton Hall, King's Kerswell, a daughter of a well-known old Devonshire family. Their union was never blessed with children.

The now popular seaside resort of Skegness was then a mere straggling village with a population of about 200 souls, chiefly fishermen.

There had been no resident rector for many years, and one service a Sunday, conducted by the vicar of a church five miles away, who occasionally visited the place during the week, was all the pastoral aid that had been provided till within a year or so of Dr. Steere's appointment.

But he was not a man to be easily discouraged.

I have been very well received, [he says in a letter to Mr. E. Fry,] and have no reason to be dissatisfied with my reception or progress. There are, of course, inconveniences in all places, and my great difficulty here is that the church is too small, and lies away from the village, with nothing but a marsh path to it, so that evening services are not to be attempted. I am thinking of having prayer meetings and lectures in the schoolroom, but that is not central, and is at best a poking little hole. If I were rector, I think I would try to get the church rebuilt. There is now a Wesleyan chapel placed exactly where the church ought to have been, I wish we could change places. I have just raised £9 for an harmonium to steady our singing a little, which will be enough, I hope, to purchase a good second-hand one, and am now trying to get a little money for maps, &c., in the schoolroom; it is very badly provided in these matters, and with moving and other expenses my own spare cash is very low indeed. We have had several wrecks on the coast in the last few weeks, and I have buried two bodies cast on shore here.

It was at this time that the writer of this Memoir

first came to know Dr. Steere. He was then quite a lad, living in the next parish, and his first distinct recollection of him is a very characteristic one.

The church was so damp that the harmonium could not be left there during the week, but was carried to and fro every Sunday.

There were several wide ditches, spanned only by a narrow plank, to be crossed on the way, and to meet the difficulty he had fixed large handles to the sides of the instrument, through which poles were run, and the whole carried sedan-chair fashion.

We used to watch him bearing one end, and encouraging the sexton at the other when they came to the ditches, whilst he slily hinted that a washing would do the man no harm, but took very good care that he should not fall in. The firmset mouth, and the humorous twinkle of the eye can never be forgotten. The face was certainly not of the type which is ordinarily called "devout," but one could not be with him ten minutes, without feeling that one could trust him for ever, a *downright shirt sleeve man, and a real Bible parson,* as one of the fisherfolk graphically put it.

Those who will turn to the paper on Wesleyanism, given in the appendix, will not be surprised that though his ministry in Skegness extended over little more than a year and a half, yet his memory is still warmly cherished there, and by none more warmly than by Wesleyans. And though at his first coming one said, "We comes to church in the morning to please you, Sir, and goes to chapel at night to save our souls," there were not a few who learnt from him "a more excellent way" in those short months.

Early in the Autumn of 1859, he received the offer, and accepted the rectory of Little Steeping, a small out-of-the-way parish at the foot of the Lincolnshire Wolds, about eight miles inland from Skegness.

"It[1] may be that education and love of travel have to some extent weakened the popular misconception that to live in Lincolnshire means little short of floundering in a swamp, and shivering with ague. The day will doubtless come when people will be awakened to the fact that Lincolnshire enjoys one of the healthiest climates in the kingdom; that, in a drive across the Wolds, a landscape meets the eye surpassing in beauty the scenes familiar to the south countryman amid the Hampshire downs; that the geology of the county is full of interest, from the oolite ironstone, and red chalk of the hills, to the submerged forests of the coast; whilst the church architecture vies with that of any county in Great Britain."

And yet Steeping (Doomsday Book, "Steveninge," the low lying meadow), might in itself well answer to the old misconception of the county. True, that to the West, a few miles off, the wolds rose sharply up against the sky; northward lay a well wooded undulating tract: eastward one looked across the rich marshes and the Wash, to the red cliffs of Hunstanton; whilst to the south, beyond the Holland towns, stood out the beautiful and

---

[1] Streatfield, "Lincolnshire and the Danes," p. 1.

stately tower of Boston church, that grand old parable in stone, commonly called "The Stump," with its 365 steps, fifty-two windows, and twelve pillars, portraying the Christian "stump" or walk; each day one step higher, each Sunday a fresh light upon the path, each month supported by an article of the Creed.

But in itself Little Steeping was a dreary place. Remote from the high road, its inhabitants looked on outsiders as "foreigners," and it is on record that a mother complained of her daughter, who by some chance had taken service in London, and there learnt the smoother speech of the south, that she "could not speak English" when she returned home.

Such was the parish upon the charge of which Dr. Steere had now entered, according to that irony of our parochial system by which[1] the best man of the day may, for ought we know, be perched on the top of a Wiltshire down, or buried in the clay of a North Devon parsonage, fifteen miles from a railway station. It is scarcely to be wondered at that Dr. Steere should say to Mr. E. Fry, "You never saw some things so hopeless, and yet there are some things hopeful too. The immorality of these country villages in various ways is simply incredible, and I am so little fitted either for an example or a teacher, that I scarcely know whether to run away or stay." And yet, as the saintly Bishop Wordsworth[2] reminds us, these difficulties

[1] Rev. S. Baring-Gould, "Post Mediæval Preachers," p. 59.
[2] In his Introduction to Vol. I. of Bishop Steere's "Sermon Notes" (Bell and Son, 1884, p. xi.)

and drawbacks were not without their compensating advantages.

"They produced in him a spirit of moral and intellectual independence, and courage, and of indifference to worldly influences. He was left at leisure to commune with himself and with God, in quietness and solitude for several years, and to hold silent converse with the natural elements of earth, and sea, and sky. Elijah and St. Paul were trained for their prophetic and apostolic work by solitude in a wilderness. S. Chrysostom was prepared for his priestly and episcopal career at Antioch, and at Constantinople by four years' retirement and meditation in a monastery, and two years in a hermitage.

Bishop Steere had the benefit of a somewhat similar solitary discipline, when he devoted himself to the study of Holy Scripture, and to meditation on things eternal, and to spiritual ministrations to his flock, and to faithful watchfulness over them, and to diligent preaching of God's Word. His Sermons, of which the notes remain, were delivered for the most part in those two small country parishes; and they show his high sense of the dignity of his sacred calling, and his scrupulous regard for the few and simple people committed to his care."

Here is a picture of his life at Steeping, drawn by his own hand in October, 1861.[1]

I am going steadily on, making a very little work go a long way, and finding plenty of occupation as my own schoolmaster, choirmaster, bellringer, sexton, architect,

[1] Letter to Mr. E. Fry.

painter, gardener, and so forth, as one must be if one has large desires and a small income.

I am very glad to say that I have now gone on since Easter with my three Sunday services, with ease to myself, and so far as I can judge with satisfaction to the parish.

I had a day set apart for a Harvest Thanksgiving; Matins at eight, Litany at twelve, and Evensong with sermon at seven. There was a good congregation at Matins, and an overflowing one in the evening. I am now arranging with three of my neighbours for a periodical exchange of duties, to begin with the second Sunday in each month. We hope that this will be a relief to ourselves, as we all have three services, and three sermons every Sunday; as well as a pleasant change for our congregations.

There lie before us as we write, the notes of the sermon preached by Dr. Steere at Little Steeping on the first Sunday of the year 1862. In it he recapitulates the chief things that had been done for the parish in the two preceding years. In that short time a rectory house had been built; the churchyard set in order (chiefly by his own hands); the church itself had been lighted and warmed, cleaned and painted; the chancel floor had been relaid, and new seats provided; the school-house new fitted, and the school itself risen from an average attendance of eighteen to sixty, several now coming in from other parishes; whilst a new site had been secured for a better schoolroom, which might also be available for meetings, etc. And, lastly, the night-school [1] had averaged twenty-four throughout the winter, the whole population being little over three hundred.

[1] See an excellent letter on "Night-schools" in the Appendix.

He then proceeds to press with all his force a warning that this outward progress would only be positively mischievous unless accompanied by inward growth, contrasting the death of a fairly well-to-do parishoner, which had followed on a public-house brawl, with that of a poor old widow, hard by, whose constant exclamation, whatever happened, had for years been "Bless the Lord."

Speaking of his sermons at this time one of his neighbours said, "Steere certainly had not many books, but it always seemed to me that he never really needed those he had. He had an extraordinary power of tearing out the vitals of any book he read, and packing them away in an orderly fashion in his memory, ever ready for instant use, as occasion required. I remember his saying one day that he must leave me as he had his next morning's sermon to prepare, but he was back again in no longer time than the actual writing down of the notes, from which he always preached, could have taken. Yet the sermon, which I heard, was positively crammed with matter. Indeed his sermons at that time, more especially his morning ones, were more like very thoughtful readings from a book of meditations than sermons proper. He grew far more eloquent and impassioned in after years; at this time his manner was somewhat that of a barrister pleading his case, and his delivery rather monotonous."

And now at last, though he did not as yet fully know it, came the call to that great work in which he was to glorify God, not by his life only, but by his death also, as one of the noblest pioneers of

African civilization and Christianity in this or any other age.

The Central African Missionary Bishopric, vacant by the death of the saintly Mackenzie, was offered to the Rev. W. G. Tozer.

A friend,[1] who was staying at Little Steeping at the time, adds, "We were talking over the offer together at luncheon, and Dr. Steere had just stated that he should advise him to accept it, when Mrs. Steere looked up and said, 'You had better go too, Edward, to take care of him.'

"'Do you wish me to go?' he replied. She answered at once in the affirmative. 'Very well, then I will.'" And so when Mr. Tozer came to discuss the matter, he found not merely an adviser, but a companion of his venture.

As Dr. Steere put it himself in a speech delivered long afterwards, "It seemed to me an unworthy thing to send one's best friend into the middle of Africa and to stay comfortably at home oneself, so I volunteered to go with him for a year or two and see him settled."

Thus quietly and simply, as becomes the follower of Him Who went about doing good, and the world knew Him not, Dr. Steere went forth to devote his life to the work of making a Christian nation out of a part of what is still degraded Africa.

The following letter to his still older friend[2] carries on the story to the time of leaving England.

---

[1] Miss Campbell, Sleaford.   [2] Mr. E. Fry.

The Palace, Chichester, 17 Dec., 1862.

I had hoped to have called upon you long before this in Lincoln's Inn, and talked over my African expedition.

I have not resigned my Rectory, but go out on leave of absence for a time, not being willing to give up one home until I am sure I shall find another. I have given up my house to a Curate, who will I hope prove a good one, and as to the remainder of the income, I have laid out a scheme for little improvements about the parsonage and church, which will exhaust it for I think at least five years to come.

Mrs. Steere I have established with one of her sisters in a house in Kingskerswell. She could not go out at present, and would not unless I had found a reasonably comfortable state of things on the Zambesi, which I suspect is not likely to be secured until another year or two is passed. It struck us both when we heard the first hint of Tozer's appointment that it was very desirable he should have friends about him, and singularly enough the same idea had occurred to Charles Alington, about whom Tozer and I had agreed, that he was the one man in our neighbourhood that we should most care to take with us, so that we are going to transplant the same little circle of friends which was so pleasant here to our new scene on the Shiré (pronounced Shirray). I have sent off by this post a copy of the last Report of the Mission Committee, which will put you in possession of the history and present state of the undertaking. I am now at the end of a little tour of meetings, and on Friday night I hope to get from this place *viâ* Portsmouth and Salisbury, to Kingskerswell, which will be my address till after Christmas.

I justify my going on two grounds. The first, that the necessities of the African population are incalculably greater than those of the English, the one being necessarily ignorant in spite of all they can do, the other actually ignorant only because they have no will to be otherwise. The second reason is that I think one is bound, if one has the opportunity and ability, to give practical proof that one does reckon one's calling as a Christian priest something higher and more engrossing than a comfortable house, and easy-going quiet. I confess I should be ashamed to read our

Lord's words about forsaking houses and so forth, if I had refused, when I had so clear an opportunity, to do the thing which He recommended. A thousand unforeseen events may yet occur to bring me back again or to take me away altogether, but as to this last I have satisfied myself that the dangers of the climate are much exaggerated, and that upon the whole one deserves very little credit for facing all that it is at all likely one will meet with, though one may hope that people at home will feel one's going a call to them to do a little more in their own proper vocations. I shall yet hope to see you before we leave England.

CHAPTER V.

To the Zambesi and Back.

THE early history of the Universities' Mission to Central Africa has been so fully and so well told, that it is only necessary here to note the chief facts connected with it.[1]

In 1857, Dr. Livingstone appealed to the Universities of Oxford and Cambridge to make Central Africa—then and still the stronghold of the accursed slave trade—the place of a special effort for Christ, and for His kingdom of Christian freedom.

In 1859, the Mission was accordingly undertaken by the four Universities of Oxford, Cambridge, Dublin, and Durham, the two latter being added at the suggestion of the Bishop (Gray) of Capetown.

In 1861, the first body of volunteers, headed by Bishop Mackenzie, landed in Africa.

In 1862, news arrived in England of the almost unexampled combination of untoward circumstances, war, famine, and pestilence, which had resulted in the death of the devoted Bishop Mackenzie and three of his noble fellow workers. The

---

[1] See especially the Bishop of Carlisle's "Life of Bishop Mackenzie" (G. Bell and Son), and "Twenty Years in Central Africa," by the Rev. H. Rowley (Wells-Gardner).

Mission thus crippled called for instant succour from home, and doubts were even expressed whether it could continue to occupy that part of the country, which at Dr. Livingstone's advice had been first chosen. This latter question was left to the new bishop to decide, in what way we shall presently see.

The Rt. Rev. William George Tozer, under whom Dr. Steere was now for the second time about to work, was a man of extraordinary energy and power of influencing others.

The joint parishes of Burgh-cum-Winthorpe, of which he had had the charge since 1857, measured about six miles by four on the map, with a very poor scattered population of 1,600, and an endowment of only £90 a year; whilst the two churches were more than four miles apart.

During that time he had built a master's house for the school at Burgh, and provided a site and buildings for a school at Winthorpe, beside placing an organ in each church.

And yet more, the day school at Burgh being in a thoroughly disorganized state he conducted it for many months himself, till it became quite re-established; whilst at Winthorpe, which had had no school at all, he gathered together a flourishing day-school, and a Sunday school attended by nearly every child in the parish.

But his greatest work at Burgh was the night-school, numbering about 150 young men, nearly all of whom came forward unsolicited as candidates for confirmation, many becoming consistent and devout communicants. It is still talked of at Winthorpe how many hundreds took part in the great school feasts, and at Burgh how Mr. Tozer found time to nurse, with his own hands, through a dangerous fever, a boy for whom an attendant could not be found.

The neighbourhood of so vigorous a worker naturally acted upon Dr. Steere, and helped to correct that "natural tendency to over-cautiousness," which he himself deplores in more than one letter. It has been justly observed, that the dedication of the church at Burgh to SS. Peter and Paul was not an unsuitable one, in that the two men who worked together there, and afterwards at Zanzibar, were not without resemblance in character to those two great apostles.

Bishop Tozer's consecration took place in Westminster Abbey on the Feast of the Purification, 1863, a day which will be ever memorable in the Annals of the African church, as the day also of the consecration of the first Bishop of the Orange River Free State.

He sailed as soon as possible to join Dr. Steere and the Rev. C. A. Alington, who had preceded him to the Cape by a few weeks, and on April 20th the whole party, including four mechanics from Lincolnshire, and Mr. Drayton, who had gone out from S. Augustine's College, Canterbury, some little time before, left Capetown for the Zambesi River on board H.M.S. "Orestes," Captain Gardner most kindly placing his own cabin at their disposal.

They reached the Kongone mouth of the river on May 9th, but were not able to land until the 19th, owing to a severe storm, during a lull in which Dr.

Steere was as nearly as possible drowned, having gone on shore with the captain at Quillimane, bearing important government despatches for Dr. Livingstone. In returning they got into a most dangerous surf on the bar, and were all but lost.

The news they brought back was most disheartening. Two more of the former Mission party *dead*—Mr. Scudamore, and Dr. Dickenson; the former almost the mainstay of the Mission, and the latter most invaluable as a medical man. News so disastrous decided them to land as soon as possible and push up to the rescue with provisions and reinforcements.

On landing they at once proceeded up the river to the Portuguese settlement at Mazar. Their progress and mode of life on the way are thus described by Dr. Steere in a journal letter to Mrs. Steere.

Mazar, June 11, 1863.

Here we are, all together again, after having got perhaps a third of the way to Chibisa's.

On the 3rd of June we loaded our four canoes, and prepared to leave behind Drayton, Richard and Tom, when next morning another côche, *i.e.*, large-sized canoe, arrived, which enabled us all to get forward together, leaving only a third of the goods behind.

The large canoes had ten men each, the smaller eight, in all sixty-four working blacks, and about a dozen more of us in one way or another.

The côches all ran on shore the first bank they came to, and when we got to Tangalane they were so far behind, we had to stay and sleep there. We slept in a half-thatched building, which is to be a storehouse, and were cautioned against going out at night, as there were "tigers and lions" close by.

In the morning we found the côche people making palmetto

ropes to tow their boats by in difficult places, and beating the bark off poles to punt by, and could not get them off in at all reasonable time, so we shifted our party into Mesquita's and Alington's canoes, so as to be able to keep in advance and get our meals together. We had a sharp shower before starting, and it rained off and on most of the day. The "Orestes" people had given us an old tarpaulin which we found most useful in the whale boat, covering all but our heads, which the Bishop's umbrella sufficed for. We passed at last by a narrow channel into the main stream, which is here called the East Luabo, and soon after landed at a kraal, on the right bank. Here we were shown into a half-unroofed hut which served to protect us from the pouring rain. There was a fire under another hut, most of them being built with an open under-storey to lift them above the floods, and the fowl houses are lifted up in the same way to keep out some of their enemies. The chief was a thin old man with a very little grizzly beard.

On the morning of the 6th we had better weather, and got into the main stream of the Zambesi, which is the tamest and dullest conceivable, banks of sand, and great reed-like grass, six, eight, ten, or twelve feet high. The boats keep along the shore and run aground very often; the water is very thick and yellow, and shoaly in every part of its broad channel. There are islands of all sizes, so that it is hard to say when you can see all the river at once. We saw many large birds, some looking at a distance like men stalking along about the sandbanks. There were a number of hippopotami swimming about, and we saw two or three alligators, one an enormous beast, seemingly as large round as an ox, and probably at least eighteen feet long. We dined on the beach, and slept on a sandy island in the open air. They always sleep on islands to avoid lions and leopards; and in the dusk, just before landing, Mesquita fired at an animal on the mainland, which they said was a very large lion. Next day it came on to rain, and that not in bucketfuls but in waterspouts, and we were all tired and wet when we landed, at a kraal called Chueza. Here they dealt very kindly by us, clearing for us the largest house in the place, which belonged to the bachelors of the village, who leave the parental nest rather early, and live in a house in a sort of community till they marry. It was hung round with drums, bags of seeds, which they use as music, a sort of accordion made of metal tongues tied to a board, or inside a gourd, and struck by their fingers. There also hung their dress coats, in the shape of a very full, and very short skirt of grass or palmetto leaves. The rats kept high carnival all night, and the rain made a bog of the whole village, drains not being African institutions; but in spite of it all, we were exceedingly comfortable. The morning was tolerably fine, and they helped us down to the boats again. We landed, and dined about 1 p.m. at a little kraal called Canharica, on a high piece of land on the bank of a narrowish branch of the river. We were all struck with the exact resemblance to the hills at Skegness. We could see a long way over a country all sand, with short hard grass, and here and there a bush or a very stumpy tree. That night we lodged all together in a hut, about five feet high in the highest part; it was quite full of fleas and mosquitoes; our curtains protected us from the one, but Drayton and Mesquita, who tried to do without, were almost eaten up. The name of the place was Kufambo. Next morning we got off at 8 o'clock, and found the current stronger than ever. Part of the way they dragged us by a rope from the shore, and the rest they punted us with poles. The paddles would not have kept us from drifting down. They punt along very fast, much faster than I expected. The whole look of the canoes seemed to me very Egyptian, like the boats in hieroglyphics.

Mazar was, we were told, only a few hours from this, so we sent a messenger on at once to Alington, who had preceded us by a few days. I saw the letter go off, in the charge of two men going at a trot, and armed with bayonets fastened on sticks. Meanwhile we dined on bananas and biscuits. They have a way of sprinkling the bananas over with flour and drying them in the sun, when they taste something between figs and raisins; they are sometimes boiled up in honey, and then are very like toffee. It was dark long before the canoe came up with Richard and Tom. We went down to the landing place and got a fire made, and shouted as soon as we heard the song of the paddlers, and heard them sing some old Burgh tunes, but when they landed they said they had not heard a word of our voices. The crews often sing, generally a sort of "lulleelah! lulleelah! lulleelah!" kind of sound; but some almost like negro melodies, with a quick recitative and chorus. Very often the men on one side sing a measure, and those on the other come in with a note or two, like a minute gun, at regular intervals. Sometimes they clap their hands on the blade of the paddle between each stroke; sometimes they knock the handle of the paddle on the gunwale of the boat.

We were all very glad to sleep in what might really be called a house once more. The Bishop had the host's bedstead, I slept on the floor in the same room, and Drayton and the two men in another. The house was up at daylight, and we had a cup of tea handed to us in the verandah, but Paolo, our host, only having four cups, had to wait for his own till one of us had finished.

We saw in his farmyard almost everything one could wish in the way of live stock, pigs, hairy sheep, goats, fowls, turkeys, ducks, and Zambesi geese. Breakfast was served at eleven o'clock: first a sort of dinner, then tea with milk and sugar, biscuits, and bananas. In the middle of it Alington came in with young Manuel Vianna, a lad of thirteen, who is in sole possession and authority at Mazar.

It was finally resolved that the Bishop and Alington should push on to the Mission station at Chibisas', whilst Richard Harrison and I should go down to Quillimane to see the Portuguese governor, and then visit the Morumbala mountains, lying near the confluence of the Shiré and Zambesi, to see whether they afforded a suitable site for a Mission station.

Sad news again awaited them. The deaths of Mr. Scudamore and Dr. Dickinson were confirmed. Mr. Procter and Mr. Rowley were both so reduced by sickness as to render their leaving the country immediately, a matter of absolute necessity. Adams and Blair, the two mechanics, had also suffered much, the former having had upwards of 100 attacks of fever in less than three years. Mr. Waller was the only one of the party who was in fair health.

The land was desolated by war and famine, hundreds and hundreds of people had died of starvation, sheep and goats were not to be had nearer than Tete, and Dr. Livingstone was going out of the country; what should be done for the best?

Under the circumstances, Bishop Tozer decided on moving the Mission down 200 miles nearer the coast, to some high lands, the Morumbala Mountains, taking with him twenty-five native boys, mostly orphans; of the rest of the natives, the greater number preferred remaining at a distance from the Portuguese. All the arrangements for the move were soon made, and before many weeks the Mission was fairly settled in its new locality. Mr. Procter and Mr. Rowley had in the meantime left for England; and Dr. Steere, and the rest of the new comers, had rejoined Bishop Tozer.[1]

Here is Dr. Steere's picture of life on the Morumbala Mountains, in a letter to the Bishop of Lincoln (Dr. Jackson).

                Chicama, Morumbala, October 2nd, 1863.

We are all now hutted in round straw huts, with a centre post, varying from 12 feet to 14 feet across inside the walls.

---

[1] It is a deeply interesting fact, and due to the credit of the African that it should be mentioned, that when, twenty-two years afterwards, this country was re-occupied by the Mission, the graves of its pioneers were all found to be carefully tended and kept free from overgrowth by the loving hands of the natives.

The men we hired to build them came and offered to *tie* houses for us, every portion being fastened with the root of a kind of convolvulus, which is very tough and stringy. We begin by clearing a spot of all roots and weeds and fixing in a circle of poles, each with a small fork at the top. A circle of twigs tied firmly together is laid in these forks by way of wall-plate. Then the centre post is put in and slender rods laid to it to form the roof. Four or five rings of twigs firmly tied to these rafters give them something of the strength of a dome. Then split bamboos are tied round the circle of poles at intervals of about a foot from each other, leaving a space for the door, and then the house is tied. For this work we pay two men two yards each of calico. As yet, however, we have only a sort of basket-work skeleton, and it costs just double as much to get the house clothed with grass. The grass is set upright against the bamboos and others are tied to them through it, and so the walls are completed. The door is nothing but a sort of loose shutter made in the same way.

The huts would be charming if the floors were not so dusty, and we could have any chimney beside the door, or any window that would let in light only ; and if the mist and wind did not feel free to come through the grass walls in so many places.

In hot weather they are really pleasant, and we are gradually finding out how to fortify them against the other inconveniences. We are very fortunate in having had so rainy a June and July, as otherwise the grass would nearly all have been burnt before our arrival. As it is, we see immense fires everywhere in the low country, and one rushed up a part of the mountain about a mile from us some days ago, with a sound which reminded us of a railway train at home.

The church is to be a grand edifice, 35 feet long and 11 feet wide, with a south porch and a round east end. It is now in the skeleton stage, and I have been buying grass as fast as people bring it, at six bundles for a yard, till we have quite a rick of it ready to complete the new cathedral. We should have been very well pleased with our situation were it not for the clouds, which drive along the top of the mountain with a fierce wind and drenching mist. It is curious, however, that we have less wind than we had at the foot of the mountain, and much less than there is at a hut we built as a resting-place about a third of the way up. But the mountain is a paradise compared with the valley of the Shiré, which, as you look down into it, you see to be nothing but a wilderness of stagnant water. The poor Glasgow weavers who were to make a home there were very wise to stay in Scotland. Our goods were all carried on men's heads up more than 2,000 feet of very steep climbing. The most cumbrous thing we had was the little harmonium. Several tried it, but all declined; and it came up finally in three burdens, the Bishop himself having taken it to pieces. It was a noticeable instance of the honesty which seems to us to be a characteristic of the natives, that one very heavy box, which had proved too much for its bearer, was found in the bush with the cloth we had given him lying upon it.

Several of the Portuguese who have visited our house at the landing-place have had thoughts of ascending to our settlement, but they all agree in not only giving up the attempt, but in declaring it a thing so impossible that all hope of accomplishing it must be given up, unless, indeed, they could find men to carry them up in their macheelas, which we know that no men could do. There are more difficult ways up from the Shiré, but we have not yet heard of an easier. Nothing can be more beautiful than the weather is sometimes, but its uncertainty exceeds the uncertainty of England.

We have not been able to do much with the language as yet. For myself, I have found abundant occupation as treasurer and storekeeper.

I do not suppose that many would agree with me, but I am almost disposed to wish the Mission continued here, merely as a protest against the notion that the English Church can never do anything beyond the influences of an English-speaking nation. I should gladly see English Missions as common in the colonies of foreign powers as foreign missions are in our own dominions. It seems to me a suicidal mistake to admit that Romanists are so far in the right that their veto ought to exclude any Missionary efforts of our own, when we know that the sole cause of that veto is that we preach the truth in its verity.

A residence of a few months, however, at the new station showed that it would be quite impossible, for many reasons, to make it the permanent head-quarters of the Mission. Early in 1864, therefore, it was determined to leave that part of Africa altogether for a time, and to attempt to reach the interior from some other point. With this view, the whole party left the Zambesi for the Cape. After staying there some weeks, and fully discussing the various plans which suggested themselves, it seemed best in every way to make Zanzibar the starting-point for the interior; and a favourable opportunity occurring of obtaining a passage in a man-of-war, the Bishop and Dr. Steere at once started for that place, Mr. Waller adding one more to his long list of good services to the Mission before returning home by bringing the orphan boys down to the Cape, and there finding suitable homes for them. There being no immediate occasion for the services of the rest of the party, they also returned to England.

It must not be supposed, however, that there was any real breach of continuity in the aim and history of the Mission at this time.

Just as the Douglas, carrying the Bruce's heart to the Holy Land, desperately threw it into the thick of the fight, knowing full well that his knights would be sure to follow where it led the way, so the grave of the martyred Mackenzie, the first Missionary Bishop sent forth by the English Church in modern days, has been the lure for the heroic efforts which have ever since been made to reach the tribes for which he laid down his life. Bishop Tozer, after a prolonged personal survey of the work on the Shiré, determined upon a different method of pursuing that work, but it was all one work. He and Dr. Steere made up their minds that the best way in the end would not be to attack the interior directly as before, but by a gradual process, slower and more sure.

Native teachers must be trained and educated at some central spot. When this had been accomplished, the work would not have to depend on the lives of a handful of white men to whom the climate had hitherto proved so disastrous. Lake Nyassa should be approached from an entirely new starting point, but Lake Nyassa was still the ultimate object of their labours.

There has lately been growing up a feeling amongst many at home, which has more than once found public expression, that it would be well to translate the relics of Bishop Mackenzie to the great church raised by the skill and perseverance of Bishop Steere on the site of the old slave market in Zanzibar.

But Bishop Steere would have opposed any such plan with all his might, as directly contradicting the plan of his life's labours. "Do not call my church in the slave market the Cathedral," he frequently said; "it is Christ Church, Zanzibar. Please God, we will build our Cathedral on the shores of the Nyassa some day."

And though he has not lived to do that, he was spared to send his Missionaries on from Zanzibar to pave the way, and to give his approval to those plans of work which at the present time are being so bravely and so wisely carried out by the Mission on Lake Nyassa itself.

CHAPTER VI.

THE ISLAND OF ZANZIBAR.

"THERE were brave men before Agamemnon," as the old Roman poet sings, and Bishop Tozer was not the first missionary who trod the streets of Zanzibar.

It is to the Church Missionary Society that the honour is due of being the pioneer in the work.

It is true that there are ruins of a Portuguese castle at Mombas, the port at the foot of the hill on which the present Church Missionary Society station is placed, with an inscription upon it dated 1639, which speaks of a tributary king of Jara; and Portuguese missionaries may have gathered a "first-fruits" 250 years ago, but all traces of their occupation have perished long since.

In 1842, Dr. Krapf, an excellent man and able traveller, having been refused permission to work in Shoa, turned south, and after a perilous voyage arrived at Zanzibar, where Capt. Hamerton, the then British Consul, introduced him to the "Imaum of Muscat," Zanzibar being then still a part of that kingdom, from whom he received permission to extend the blessings of Christianity to the heathen tribes of the interior.

He settled at Mombas in 1844, and later on at

the healthier station of Rabbai on the hills above that port, where he was joined in 1846 by Mr. Rebmann, a missionary equally able and devoted with himself. They took interesting and important journeys to the interior, and astonished the scientific world at home by announcing the discovery not only of thickly populated districts, but of two mountains covered with perpetual snow.

Their work amongst the natives was slow, but in the meanwhile their efforts to master the languages, especially the Swahili and Kanika, were persevering and sagacious. A Swahili and Kanika dictionary was transcribed in " 595 quarto pages," and a tentative translation of the New Testament into Swahili was made.[1]

[1] In an article in the Bible Society's " Monthly Reporter " for July, 1882, Bishop Steere says of Dr. Krapf :—

" Bible translation, like geographical discovery and almost everything else in the recent history of East Africa, owes its beginning to Dr. Krapf, who was sent into East Africa some forty years ago by the Church Missionary Society. Within a very short time indeed the Doctor had collected vocabularies in a great number of the Eastern languages, had compiled a dictionary and grammar of the Swahili or coast language, and had translated into it nearly the whole of the New Testament, and a great part of the English Prayer Book. Having settled near Mombas in the Nyika country, he translated St. Luke's Gospel into that language, and compiled a dictionary and grammar. Of all these works a small part only was printed. The Swahili and Nyika Grammar, the Prayer Book, St Luke in Nyika, and a comparative vocabulary of five languages, were almost the whole that he himself saw through the press.

" In the year 1864 the Universities' Mission came to Zanzibar, and we began at once to inquire about the language. All the Europeans told us that Dr. Krapf's books were of no use at

Mrs. Krapf died at Mombas, and his bereavement seemed to summon Dr. Krapf to fresh exertions.

"Tell the committee," he wrote home, "that there is on the East African coast a lonely grave of a member of the mission, connected with your Society. As the victories of the Church are the stepping stones over the graves of many of her members, you may be the more sure that the hour is at hand when you are summoned to work for the conversion of Africa from the East."

Such was the man whose linguistic labours laid a foundation, on which Dr. Steere was to erect a fair structure, and whose spirit of devotion to the cause of his Master he had caught when he landed at Zanzibar.

The Island and city of Zanzibar was represented by Burton, the traveller, as a most unhealthy place, so much so, that "English husbands who want to get rid of their wives might easily do it, if they gave them a trip for a few months to Zanzibar."

But "the wonderful activity of Sir John Kirk through so many years of consular employment,

all, and indeed we found them very little help. Not because he had misconceived the language, but because he had been to some extent misled by a pedantic clique of so-called learned men in Mombas, who induced him to accept as pure Swahili an over-refined kind of dialect, scarcely or not at all intelligible to the mass of the nation, and, further, because of a singularly confused style of writing and spelling, so that these works were of scarcely any use to a mere beginner.

"We started, therefore, almost independently, and in about five years' time produced our first translation, that of St. Matthew's Gospel, written by myself and revised by the help of several natives."

the hard work of the merchants, and the athletic sports in which the Europeans constantly engage, all combine to shew that Zanzibar is worthy of a better name as a residence for Europeans."

Such is the verdict of Mr. James Thompson, the well-known author of several works of travel in Central Africa, a verdict confirmed by many others.

The following description of Zanzibar is in Dr. Steere's own words, written in 1869, and if we modify the statements about the personal authority of the Sultan of Zanzibar, which has been curtailed of late by the new-born colonizing zeal of Germany and Portugal, the picture is as true now as then.

It has been asked why Zanzibar should have been made the headquarters of the Central African Mission. The answer is simply because it is the capital of Eastern Africa. There is no town which has the least pretension to dispute such a title with it between Port Natal and Aden. One may almost say that it is more than the chief town, it is the only really large town and great centre of trade for all that immense coast, 2,000 miles in extent, and the vast countries which lie behind it.

Traders from Zanzibar have even penetrated to the Atlantic coast, after traversing the whole interior. It is not unusual for men to go out with goods, and travel for many years, buying and selling in different places, until they have accumulated enough to return as comparatively rich men. I was asking once how far some districts I had heard of might be from the coast; the answer was an account of a trader who went there; his son was not born when he left, he was able to run alone by the time the place was reached, and was between twelve and thirteen when his father returned to Zanzibar.

Nor is the town less important in a political point of view. Its ruler has admitted authority over all the coast from Cape Gardafui to Cape Delgado. His power in the interior is of a less determinate kind, but he has a Governor even at Ujiji on the Tanganyika Lake, besides which he can bend any tribe he pleases to his wishes by stopping their trade, which must start from or pass through his coast dominions.

One result of all this is too important to be passed by in silence, it is that the language of Zanzibar—the Swahili—being the official and trade language, is everywhere more or less understood ; so that if one has mastered the Swahili he is at home everywhere, in every tribe he will find some who can act as interpreters, and who can at once open to him the intricacies of their own tongue.

What other marks could distinguish a place as fitted for the head-quarters of a Mission save such as these, which make this town the actual head-quarters of trade, of government, and of language?

The actual position of the town may be well brought home to us by supposing London to stand where Cowes does on the Isle of Wight. The mainland is always visible, and many boats pass across to it every day—a distance of about twenty-eight miles, the Island being a little more than twice as large as the Isle of Wight.

The town itself shows a long front of square white houses, built of stone. The whole aspect of the place from the sea is more Italian than African. When we land however, the scene changes ; there is no street practicable for wheeled vehicles, very few are more than ten or twelve feet wide, and in many places there is no proper street. But as it is the law that everyone who builds a house should set up his scaffold on his own land, there is generally about a yard left outside the walls, and the six feet that thus intervene between the houses make the street.

The greater number of houses are built only of mud and stud, thatched with the cocoanut leaf. They are divided by internal partitions into a number of small rooms, but have no light except from the door ; as for smoke, it finds its way through the thatch promiscuously. There are some chief thoroughfares, and some streets of shops, which are merely small stone houses with the front of the bottom story taken out, and are therefore quite open to the street ; these are frequently protected by an awning of cocoanut leaves, which is very annoying in wet weather, as you have no room to walk, except either under the drip of these leaves, or exactly in the middle of the path, where the rain-water is running in a stream. Not that the negroes feel so much annoyed as the Europeans do; for you may often see a man stand under the spout of a stone house and take a shower bath, or even take off his clothes, and wash them in the rain water, and put them, or rather *it*, on again to dry. No picture of a street in Zanzibar would be complete without two or three cows or a bull, of a small breed with humps, wandering about in search of something green. All the cattle of this part of Africa have humps, so that when we first showed our boys a picture of a cow, they said "That's not a cow; where is the hump?" These cattle are excessively tame; I only heard of one which, having taken an antipathy to Europeans, was shut up by its owner, not lest it should hurt the Europeans, but lest they should hurt it, which, in the eyes of its owner, a heathen Indian, would have been the greatest of calamities.

There are very few open spaces; the largest is what is called the Great Market, close by the Fort, a square-walled enclosure with a few round tub-shaped towers. Here, between nine and twelve, daily, every kind of fruit and vegetable is brought in on men's heads in immense quantities—oranges, cocoa-nuts, bananas, sweet potatoes, pine-apples, casava-root, but especially (in their season) mangoes, which are often carried in a sort of basket called a *chimney*, five or six feet high, and not a foot and a-half across, dressed out with green leaves and flowers.

The chief remaining open space was (at this time) the Slave Market. Such, then, is the town of Zanzibar, in a climate where winter and summer are hardly marked by any difference of heat or the length of the day, the thermometer seldom standing far from eighty degrees in the house, and the sun always rising and setting within twenty minutes of six o'clock.

There are never storms, nor even a really high wind, for more than half-an-hour or so at a time. The strongest marks of season are the rains, the less in November, the greater in April, or from March to June. These occur when the wind is uncertain; from December to March it blows from the north, from June to October from the south. After the great rains comes the cold season, in June and July, when the thermometer sometimes goes down to seventy degrees, and sets everybody shivering. In such a climate one can understand how people come to lose count of time, and forget how old they are.

Bishop Tozer and Dr. Steere arrived at Zanzibar in August, 1864, and were most kindly welcomed by Colonel Playfair, the English Consul, who took them into his own house. In the course of a few days, however, through the instrumentality of Colonel Playfair, the Bishop was able to make an arrangement with the Sultan for the occupation of a large house facing the sea, to be devoted permanently to the purposes of the Mission.

Zanzibar, at this time, was the seat of a vast unblushing trade in human beings. For many years there had been a treaty between the British Government and the Sultan of Zanzibar forbidding the export of slaves to foreign countries, and English men-of-war cruised on the coast to intercept slaving vessels; but the slave trade flourished, nevertheless. Writing of this period, Dr. Steere said:—

I hope one may never see again such sights as one used to see almost daily when we first landed in Zanzibar—the miserable remains of the great slave caravans from the interior, brought by sea to Zanzibar, packed so closely that they could scarcely move, and allowed nothing of food on the voyage but a few handfuls of raw rice passed round to be nibbled at. It is said, sometimes, that our efforts to stop the slave traffic have increased the sufferings of the slaves during their transit, but it was simply impossible to increase the misery of this open and unrestrained traffic between Kilwa and Zanzibar. Even as it was, the least delay caused a large proportion of deaths, and the parties of slaves that were led from the custom-house to their owners' houses presented every form of emaciation and disease, till it seemed impossible that they could support themselves, if only for a few minutes longer. There were even some who were left lying at the custom-house, because it was doubted whether they would recover at all, and the traders would not pay the duties till they knew. Beyond even this, we have found some yet alive, left upon the beach by the sea, into which they had been thrown as the dhow neared the harbour, because they were already past all hope of recovery.

The Arab is almost always an indifferent, though rarely a cruel master, and the waste of and recklessness about human life, in every part of the transit of slaves from their homes in the interior to their Arab masters' houses, would have seemed wholly incredible, had we not seen with our own eyes so much, and found the testimony of all who have seen anything, agreeing so completely.

The usual course of the trader when he wished to get his human commodity beyond the Zanzibar territory, was to take a pass to some place within the Sultan's own dominions, pay the customs duties (and this tax on slaves formed a considerable portion of the Sultan's income), make presents to the Sultan's favourites to prevent awkward inquiries, and then using the pass as long as it was of any use, make his way to Arabia. But sometimes the trader endeavoured to evade the customs, and sometimes instead of buying slaves he stole them, and then it not unfrequently happened that the Sultan would seize and burn his vessel, take the slaves and distribute them as presents amongst his friends. An incident of this kind happened just as Bishop Tozer and Dr. Steere arrived at Zanzibar, when the

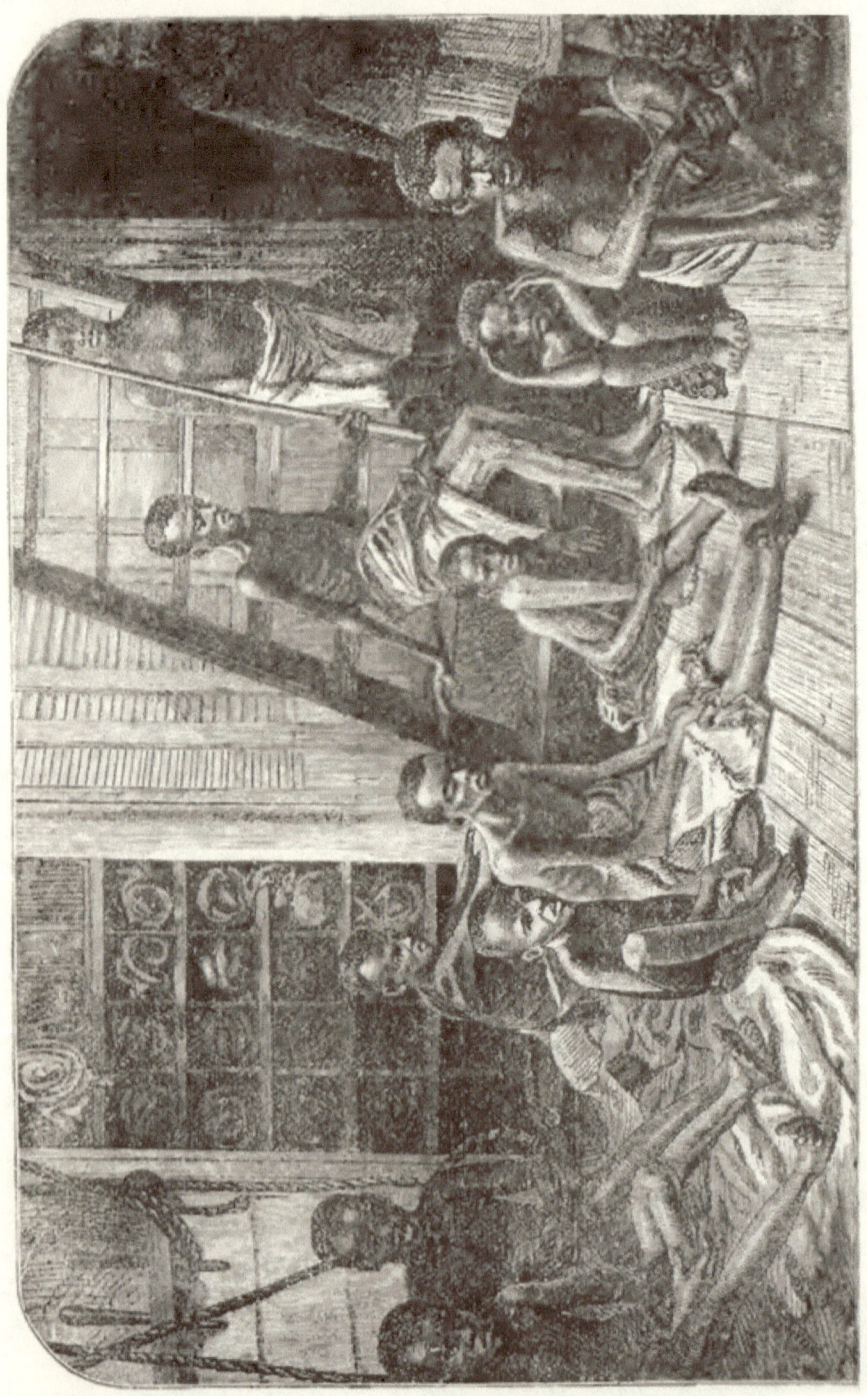

Consul suggested to the Sultan that it would be a graceful act to give some of the boys into the charge of the Bishop, who had just been to pay him a complimentary visit, and the Sultan gave him five. With these boys Bishop Tozer commenced afresh the attempt to bring the Gospel to the regions of Central Africa. Realising keenly the difficulties in the way of a conversion of the natives through the agency of European missionaries only, he resolved, from the native materials he had in hand, and from others that might come to him, to raise up a native ministry, and to entrust to it, in the main, the work of extending Christ's kingdom amongst the tribes of the interior. Until additional aid came to him from England the Bishop devoted himself to the education of these boys with that object in view; and Dr. Steere, being more than most men qualified for that branch of the work, gave especial attention to the study of the Swahili and other languages, and, setting up the first printing press that had been seen in Zanzibar, began, with the aid of some of the boys, to publish and circulate for correction and criticism, the translations that he made.

In a speech delivered at Oxford some years afterwards, in speaking of this period of the history of the Mission, Dr. Steere said:—

> Now if you can imagine yourself standing opposite to five little black boys, with no clothing save the narrowest possible strip of calico round their middles, with their hands clasped round their necks, looking up into your face with an expression of utter apprehension that something more dreadful than ever they had experienced would surely come upon

them, now that they had fallen into the hands of the dreaded white men, you will feel our work somewhat as we felt it. And then, how are you to speak, or they to answer? You have not one word in common. Yet these are the missionaries of the future. When any one tells his friends in England that our plan is to educate native missionaries, people say it is a very good plan, and no doubt in a few years we shall see great results. But when you come to begin with the actual pupils, you will see that it is not a work of a few years, but rather, as life is in Africa, of several lifetimes. So having no other way at hand, we began to teach them the English alphabet and to read our common school reading-cards. We found them sharp enough, and soon began to make way towards a mutual understanding; then we added other pupils from vessels taken by the English men-of-war, and a few brought to us by their friends. Our plan was not to bring in such numbers as that we might be overwhelmed by a mass of heathenism, but to try and give a Christian tone to our first scholars, and then to bring in a few, time after time, so that they might catch the rising spirit. Thus our school grew on, and soon we were joined by some lady helpers, and a girls' school was formed after the same manner.

It was not long before even the natives perceived that our boys had an air and a bearing such as their old companions never had. It was their Christianity beginning even so soon to show itself, as sound religion must, in their ordinary speech and bearing. We had taught our children that white men might sometimes be trusted. They have told us since that their impression was, the first night they slept in the house, that they were meant to be eaten.

In the extract from this speech, the results of a long time of work are given in a few words; but something of the mere manual labour which it entailed upon Dr. Steere may be gathered from a letter, in which he is evidently describing his own experience for the benefit of the many, who have but a dim notion of the practical realities of mission work in a country like East Africa.

There are several classes of persons who are apt to offer themselves, or to be pressed to offer themselves, as missionaries, who will find no welcome, and ought not to be accepted.

These are, first, young men who merely want to get ordained easily ; and next, discontented people who have never found a congenial employment or congenial spirits at home ; next, failures—who believe that they can do exceedingly well some things which they have never tried, but who have never done well anything they have as yet attempted. Then people who want a new start in life, especially people who have fallen into some sin, or in some way ruined their home character and prospects. It is incredible what grievous sinners their friends think fit to represent Christianity to the heathen, and how very prone people are to think that they will be able to teach others what they have never learnt themselves. To these classes may be added the merely helpless and the fanciful, especially such as think that missionary work can be done without risk or discomfort, and are disheartened or disgusted very speedily, or who, on the other hand, think all care and precaution unworthy of a missionary spirit, and thus become a constant anxiety to their friends, and very generally discredit the Mission by sicknesses and deaths, due to nothing but their own folly.

Mission work differs from home work in its universality. It is impossible to confine oneself to one branch only. One cannot be merely a preacher, merely a school-teacher, or merely a student of languages.

There will be a house to build, and accounts to keep, and land to cultivate, and servants to teach and superintend, and all these works *must* be done, and done well and carefully. Whatever comfort is wanted, whatever necessary must be provided, the missionary himself must scheme it out, and must himself see it procured.

It not unfrequently happens that a young man comes out with the idea that secular work is somehow unnecessary or unbecoming, and so he throws a double burden on the older missionary, who has to provide everything for him and to occupy many weary hours in securing leisure to his subordinate. Of course the result cannot be satisfactory to either party. The younger man is disgusted at the secularity of his senior, and the senior still more disgusted at the selfish, ignorant indolence of his assistant.

It is not uncommon for a person to join a mission in the expectation of escaping home cares, who only finds out the mistake by some domestic catastrophe brought on by inattention. A very favourite form of missions now is that of a home or school, and it is easy to picture to oneself such a life as that of a schoolmaster in England. But even this is more than some imagine, who think of the missionary, and of themselves in that character, rather as a sort of visiting clergyman. So the drudgery of teaching their letters to little children is found very irksome ; still, it must be done, and so of all the routine of a mere school.

Then the school-house has to be built, or repaired, and the missionary will fare badly who does not use his own wits about the way in which it had better be done. It has to be kept clean, school furniture may have to be extemporized out of local materials. Order must be kept, but with the recollection always that the children are under no sort of obligation to come, unless school work is made pleasant to them.

They will probably have very dirty ways, and school offices must be arranged and kept cleanly by the constant personal oversight of the missionary himself, who will find probably no one willing to help him in so disagreeable a business.

Where orphans or boarders are taken, all these cares increase, and the dormitory, the kitchen, the sick room, and the back yard, the buying of food, and the washing of the children and their clothes, will occupy as much thought, and more time, than any of the matters usually printed in missionary reports, or spoken of on missionary platforms.

Thus they went forward with the work, and Dr. Steere was preparing to return to England in the summer of 1866, when Bishop Tozer was seized with a serious illness, which drove him home for the benefit of the voyage, and for a complete change and rest.

Dr. Steere accordingly remained in charge at Zanzibar, being shortly afterwards reinforced by some welcome additions to his staff, including the Rev. C. A. Alington, who had formed one of their party before the move to Zanzibar.

Hitherto the work of the Mission had been chiefly preparatory; little could be attempted outside the walls of their own house until some knowledge of the prevailing languages had been acquired. Dr. Steere's well-trained philological talents had been from the first employed in dealing with this difficulty.

He soon succeeded in constructing a Swahili handbook, based in some degree on the grammar and vocabulary of Dr. Krapf, whose labours in this direction have been already mentioned; and aided by two learned Swahilis, "who allowed me to spend every Saturday morning in questioning them about their language, and to whom I owe all that is best in my knowledge of African tongues."

He also reduced the dialect spoken in the Usambara country, a little north of Zanzibar, and now the scene of the Mission's most successful labours, to writing; and produced a Shambala grammar, which, with the help of the native boys attached to the Mission, he printed himself.

As soon as the difficulty of the language had thus to some extent been removed, it was determined to make the first attempt to start a Mission on the mainland ; for the Bishop had never allowed the promising field of labour in Zanzibar itself to divert his thoughts from the steady prosecution of the original design of the Mission, and all that was being done in Zanzibar was with immediate reference to future work on the mainland.

At last, in August, 1867, Dr. Steere felt that the time had come to make an effort in this direction.

The districts of the mainland most accessible from Zanzibar, and recommended as suitable for the establishment of mission stations, were the Usambara country, about fifty miles from the coast, the Jagga country, about 150 miles inland, and the Lake Nyassa country.

In the natural order of events it seemed that, other things being favourable, the Usambara country should be first occupied ; and Mr. Alington, accompanied by Vincent M'Kono, one of the Mission boys, and a Swahili from the coast, proceeded to Vuga, the capital of that district, to seek permission to settle there.

Kimweri, the king, was at first suspicious, and afraid that Mr. Alington's request for permission to build harboured some deep design upon his country ; and when he finally gave him leave to erect a mission-house at Magila, it was upon condition that it should not be built of stone, so as to serve as a fort. Nevertheless, his kindness and generosity did not fail, and when Mr. Alington left him he desired him to return soon, and he would send bearers to the coast to meet him.

It is interesting to note that so long before as 1848, Dr. Krapf, when passing through this district, had cut a Cross upon a large tree, in the full assurance that it would some day be won for the kingdom of Christ. So it is, that "men labour, and other men enter into their labours."

Meanwhile, in Zanzibar itself a good deal of intercourse was kept up with the Arabs, to whom Dr. Steere's learning, humility, and dignified reserve was especially attractive. Here and there in our letters occurs an incidental mention of it. One or two such notices may be of interest as giving an insight into his daily life, and showing that he let no opportunity slip of leading them also to the truth.

The inversions of our European customs are very curious; not only do people take off their shoes instead of their hats, but it is the highest praise you can give anyone to say that he is a *slow man with a cold heart;* a man, that is, who is neither hot nor hasty in his temper, and whose heart is like a piece of ice, the most delightful and refreshing thing you could easily think of. It is a fundamental rule of good breeding not to do what will make yourself or anybody else hot; you must walk slowly, and keep as cool as you can.

If you meet anybody, or find anybody sitting on your baraza, you say, "Are you well?" to which the invariable answer is, "I am well," after which you go into the question of ailments. Even if you are dying, you must begin by saying, "I am well," and after that explain your fears and feelings.

When the subject of health is exhausted, you must ask after the news; "What news?" to which the answer is "Good." This is for the sake of the omen. If you ventured to say "Bad," you would throw all your hearers into a state of dread and horror. So you must say "Good" first, and then qualify its goodness in any way you may deem necessary.

Again, among the Mohammedans it is held profane *not*

to introduce the name of God into everything you say; and, if there is a pause in the conversation, someone will put in an ejaculation, such as " God is great !" and then the conversation goes on as before, and so the rudeness of sitting looking at one another is avoided. . . .

Dr. Rebmann came in one day in April, and said he had met Hassan bin Yussuf on the way, one of the men to whom we gave an Arabic Bible. He found him intelligent and inquiring, and well acquainted with his New Testament. Since then, one of the Sheikh Moheebin's grandsons came for a Prayer book. The copies we had of the Pentateuch by itself were much prized. They are all gone. A little Arabic tract, called " The Treasury of Faith," of which two or three copies were sent us from Bombay, has been much inquired about. . . . .

Abdul Aziz called and asked for an explanation of the statement that man was made "in the image of God," which shocked them. I wrote and sent him an explanation in Swahili. . . . .

Sometimes one of them will visit the Mission chapel, and take note of the proceedings. Thus, on Christmas Day, Shaaban bin Tayib was present at the service, and reports of it in this wise : " He thought our words were very good, but our manner of praying much lacking in devoutness.". . . .

No one at home can judge of our difficulties, [writes another member of the staff,] French, German, Portuguese, and Swahili are all wanted here ; so *without Dr. Steere we should be lost—he speaks all.* It is fortunate his learning and patience equal one another, he is a wonderful man. After a hard day of teaching the boys, and printing, and writing, and accounts, he comes quite fresh to give me a Swahili lesson after tea, and goes on till Ali comes to give him a lesson in Arabic.

Bishop Tozer returned to Zanzibar in July, 1868, accompanied by two clergymen and a young layman ; and in the following month Dr. Steere sailed for England, Mr. Alington returning to the mainland the same day.

Thus the two years for which Dr. Steere volunteered had grown to six before he could be spared; and even now, in leaving Zanzibar, he did not cease to work for it. He brought home with him in MS., or roughly printed at the Mission press, a grammar and dictionary of the language, several parts of the Bible translated, and other helps in the work, such as portions of the Prayer book, and sundry school books, for the purpose of revision and publication in England.

In those four years he had won the respect of men of all classes in Zanzibar.

One of the most learned [he says in his account of Zanzibar, published in the following year] wrote me a sort of valedictory address, and sealed it with his own seal, that I might always have an evidence of the respect and esteem in which he held me. Another, a schoolmaster, who happened to be out of town when I was making my farewell visits, heard of it at the last moment, when I was actually embarked, came down to the shore with a friend, borrowed a boat, and rowed himself off to take leave of me. I will mention but one thing more; it shall be a polite speech of the Chief Vizir's when I was taking leave, who said he could only bear the parting in the hope that, in getting our grammar and dictionary printed in England, I might be building a bridge over which the thoughts of Zanzibar might pass to England, and English learning and wisdom find their way to Zanzibar. And perhaps our own wishes could hardly have been expressed more neatly.

CHAPTER VII.

IN ENGLAND AGAIN.

THE opening of the year 1869 found Dr. Steere writing from Little Steeping to Mr. Edward Fry: "I have come home as well as ever, after nearly six years out, and four of them spent in Zanzibar in the enjoyment of first-rate health. This was, in fact, what kept me away so long from home, as I could least be spared.

"The Bible Society is printing a Gospel for us in Swahili, and I have a very copious vocabulary to arrange and print. I think I have more than a year's work before me."

He worked unceasingly at this at all spare times, and following the lines of Dr. Krapf, he may be said to have founded the literature of Central Africa. Nay more, experience on the West Coast of Africa, the story of the English Bible, and of Luther's Bible, warn us that when the language of a country is still in flux, it will settle down and gravitate round the translation of the Bible. Therefore, humanly speaking, the lines of the Swahili language are laid down for ever by Dr. Steere's Biblical work.

The Swahili language can now be acquired by

any person of ordinary intelligence who will master the handbook and dictionary brought out by Dr. Steere, and since enlarged by Mr. Madan, upon whom his linguistic mantle seems to have fallen.

Events at home had not the while stood still. Bishop Jackson left the Diocese of Lincoln on succeeding to Archbishop Tait in the see of London, and Dr. Christopher Wordsworth was consecrated Bishop of Lincoln soon after Dr. Steere's return to his old parish. The influence of that eminent prelate was not long in making itself felt in his diocese. The Education Act of 1870 led to energetic discussion and action all over the country, and the new Bishop availed himself in many ways of the powers and experience of Dr. Steere.

Before noticing a very remarkable paper from Dr. Steere's pen, written at the request of Bishop Wordsworth, we can pause a moment to look back and contemplate his career.

An active Churchman and Guildsman in London and at Tamworth, a clergyman in Devonshire and Lincolnshire, his experience thus gained had been succeeded by six eventful years on the Zambesi, and in Zanzibar as a Missionary.

His powers, intellectual, linguistic, literary, and theological were all the while growing and ripening.

The editor of Bishop Butler's works had gained a more than theoretical knowledge of self and men, which he was able to use as an instrument; the ever-busy Missionary had gained a readiness and directness of speech. He had at the same time a patient way of his own, which served to carry through (*perficere*) all kinds of varied work when taken in hand, whether physical, mental, moral, or spiritual.

Added to this he had a singular largeness of heart and robust breadth of view, and he possessed a downright energy of action, combined (gift most rare) with unfeigned personal humility. One of his neighbours at this time photographs him thus: "Steere always seemed to keep himself in the background, and said very little; but somehow or other, one always found oneself doing what he wanted, and wondering afterwards how one could ever have thought of doing anything else."

When Dr. Wordsworth came to found his Theological College at Lincoln he naturally turned to Dr. Steere for advice and aid, and though his proposals were too bold and sweeping to meet with full acceptance then, they show so noble an ideal of Church life and of the Ministerial office, and present so much living truth which may yet be of service to the Church, that we do not hesitate to insert a large portion of them here.

> In considering whether any and what sort of theological College should be attempted at Lincoln, it would very much simplify the matter if we could point to any college already established which would serve as a model on which ours could be formed. I believe we all feel that no such model is now in existence. The first idea of the older colleges was that the ordinary education given at Oxford and Cambridge should be supplemented by a year or two's theological study. This scheme has broken down under the burden of expense and delay which it imposed upon the candidates. There has been added to it a sort of grudging admittance of non-graduates

which seems to me to have no great effect in any way. I think that a college like those at Wells and Chichester and Salisbury might do some good, but I could never feel any enthusiasm about it. I think that the whole system of preparation for Holy Orders has hitherto begun at the wrong end. A young man wishes to become a Priest, he calculates the expense of a University course, he is met everywhere by examinations and restrictions, and has to struggle through them all in order to be admitted to an unremunerative profession. All this has a tendency to shut out the modest and retiring, and to sift into the Priesthood only the pushing and self-conceited. Of course I do not refer to those who have a certain income awaiting them to which they must make their way through any difficulties, even through the responsibilities of the cure of souls to which the income is attached; with them it is a mere question of so much time, trouble and money to be laid out as an investment which is to procure them so much money in return. But it is a great evil that our arrangements should seem to declare that a man who has not interest enough to be pretty sure of getting a benefice has no business in the Priesthood. Nor again is it right that a man should be compelled to push himself into so awful a responsibility as that which belongs to a Priest. The burden ought to lie upon the shoulders of those who are to reap the benefit. Now if we look upon the benefice as the substance, and the cure of souls as the accident, no doubt a man ought to bear all the expense and trouble involved in fitting himself for the benefice. Then the substantial benefit which results from the settling of a Priest in a parish is that he gets a good income. When it is stated thus nakedly the whole business is evidently as shocking a perversion of the objects of the Priesthood and of the parochial system as it is well possible to imagine. Certainly in theory the object of settling a Priest in a parish is that the parishioners may be benefited by his labours. If so, who ought to be at the expense of his training? Manifestly the parishioners. Every single item of his preparation has its effect upon them for good or for evil. When we pull up the root of all evil out of our thoughts it is evident that we ought to look out the best man among us and give him the best training we can, and then make him our guide and pattern. I conclude, therefore, that, in the ideal Church, the expenses of clerical education would be borne entirely by the laity, and, by a similar process of reasoning, that the whole Church would be on the watch for the wisest and purest souls everywhere that they might be in a manner compelled to take the oversight of this business. I know very well that we are not likely to see such a state of things in perfection in our day, and that the laity will probably be slow to see their true interests, but it is exactly on such points that it is our duty to lead them. I abhor the idea of a theological college, where a man goes and pays fees in order that he may learn to preach so well, and manage his parish so much to the satisfaction of everybody, that he will be sure, before long, to get a good living given to him. I want to see a college which shall invite within its doors the teachable, whoever they may be, and give them, at the expense of the Church at large, for the benefit of the Church at large, the very best guidance and instruction which can be obtained for them, and I can hardly conceive a higher calling in life than that of a man who should give his whole time and thought to the training of such youth without desiring any pay, beyond his bare food and clothing, nor any reward except the fruit of his endeavours. There is a very vague and general dissatisfaction now prevailing throughout the Church, and I believe the cause to be that, from beginning to end, the Gospel has been smothered and perverted by worldliness. I am afraid that I may be thought visionary and unpractical, but I am sure that it is no use putting up a fine building on a rotten foundation. It is upon such principles as those I have stated that I think we ought to come to the consideration of the business before us.

The first point to be considered is what we want, the next how we are to get it. We want to compensate for the apparent diminution of the religious character of the education given at the old Universities. We want to supply a training for those who being otherwise fit for ordination have not, for some sufficient reason, taken a University degree. Incidentally we want to make our noble cathedral and its endowments more directly and generally useful. But I think we want a great deal more. We want a cheaper clergy and we want a higher style of clerical character. The average country clergyman is very far indeed from being a model Priest. It was the perception of this which gave the first impulse to the idea of founding theological colleges. Country parishes are by no means universally well served. There are a great many churches where only once on one day of the week matins or evensong is said and a hymn or two sung, both more or less indifferently, and a sermon is delivered, which is a model neither of eloquence nor of zeal, and that is all the worship of God, and all the public instruction which the parish gets. There are places where the clergyman is very rarely seen, except at the time of the Sunday service. There are parishes where a clergyman is legally resident, but for the spiritual good of the parish he might as well or better be away. What proportion of our parish Priests are leading lives that can be called, in any real sense *saintly?* And yet we are called to be saints, and the Priest ought to be a pattern to his flock. Such considerations as these make one regard clerical education as a very different matter from the mere getting up of a certain amount of theology, or even the acquiring a certain familiarity with parochial work. It makes one feel, too, that there has been a radical defect in the training which has given us the most honest and manly clergy in Christendom, but nothing more. We want a great deal deeper and sounder theology, and, still more, we want personal holiness and an unworldly spirit. It is not the popular clergy who are the strength of the Church, its real defenders are those who compel respect by their lives, and who are manifestly actuated by a higher spirit than the mass even of the community. We all want raising, and must all strive and pray that our successors may be better than ourselves. Then again we want a cheaper clergy. The average income of an English benefice is little over £200 a year, and an average English clergyman cannot live comfortably on less than £400 or £500—and can easily spend £1000 in merely maintaining his position. In order to get out of this difficulty, country benefices are coupled together, often in strangely unreasonable ways, and there is such a demand for gentlemen possessed of private means that there is the greatest possible difficulty in procuring them. The Ecclesiastical Commissioners are now engaged all over England in building architectural traps for them, in the shape of parsonages which no one possessed of no private means could ever afford to live in. Would it seem credible, if we were not so familiar with it, that it is a sort of axiom in the Church of England that the religion which more than any other exalts the poor and depreciates the rich, can be best and most effectively preached by gentlemen possessed of private means? Surely such a notion ought to be hissed out of the Church as speedily as possible. A parish Priest with £200 a year is richer in almost all cases than four-fifths of his parishioners. In the eyes of God a labouring man and a peer of the realm are each just one soul and no more. Are they each just one soul and no more or no less in the eyes of an average English clergyman? If we look into the New Testament as to which is most likely *a priori* to go to heaven, we find that it is the peer who stands at a disadvantage. And yet in choosing our clergy we strive to secure the rich man's son and absolutely refuse the labourer's. Christ did not so choose His Apostles, nor does the Roman Church so choose those Priests of hers who have carried off so many of the richest and wisest out of our very midst. It is true that a gentleman is *ceteris paribus* a better Priest than a man who has no breeding. Just so Saint Paul had a wider influence than Saint Peter. But how? By keeping up his position? Not at all, but by giving up more and equalling himself with the lowest. Similarly, in the opposite extreme, where the clergyman's relations with the poor are of a patronizing character, the born gentleman knows how to do it, and the poor will take it from him; but then his advantage begins in this world and ends there. We forget too often that what pleases everybody and goes smoothly is, very often, doing no work at all. Methodist preachers make enemies as well as friends, but they do act strongly and have an influence which is really felt. The great objection that literate clergy do not know their places and expect more than their due, arises mainly, I believe, from the paucity of their number, and would disappear if it were understood that a Priest might be of any class in society, and claimed the respect due to a Priest, but not necessarily the position of a so-called gentleman. We can never supply all the old parishes, still less can we form all the new ones that are wanted, until we can get preachers who can live on the average income of those under their charge. It is just the case of the employment of native agency in missions over again. The most obvious way is clearly to take men of the most numerous classes of the community and train them first as good Christians, and next as efficient preachers of the Gospel. How absurd it is to suppose that one thin stratum of society can supply Priests for the whole community, yet this has practically been the rule of the Church, and a sense of it has so pervaded all ranks of the people that the Priesthood is not thought of as a career for their sons by any who do not, at least in their hopes and wishes, belong to that particular stratum. I think, therefore, that we ought now not merely to tolerate, but actively to smoothe the way of access to holy orders to members of all and every class. We have to undo the effects of a long policy of exclusion. Our scheme of clerical education is incomplete unless it take up members of each class at the point at which they have to choose a calling. This is done abroad by taking young men at an early age into a diocesan seminary. We might do it by offering evening classes and private tuition, by means of which aspirants might fit themselves for admission to the regular theological college. Once there the first aim must be to cultivate and develope every Christian grace, and stamp a character of thorough self-denying holiness on the soul of every student. In subordination to this, his mind should be supplied with a sound theology and led to choose those particular fields of study most congenial to it. His physical education should go on at the same time, so that he may learn to sing in time and tune, to articulate well, to read and speak freely and distinctly and with moderate and appropriate action. He may be able, and in Lincoln, surely, would be able, to help in good works in some part of the city, but I do not think that this should be any part of his college course.

The object of a college is to make him fit to minister and to teach. Actual experience can hardly be acquired by a layman, and there is very great danger of a student's forgetting, in the bustle of a town parish, that the salvation of souls, and of his own first of all, must be his great object in life, and that salvation does not come of man's activity, but of God's grace. The hands and minds of many active clergymen are full of very secular kinds of work, which will make them popular, and may attract their people and possibly purify their amusements, still leaving them as really ungodly as ever. Penny readings and cricket clubs are very good things, but they are not clerical work. It is not difficult to forget God, even in works for God. I for one distrust the effect of plunging a young man, who has had no special devotional and theological training, into the bustle of a large parish—by way of special preparation for Holy Orders. I think the chaplain by far the most important officer of a theological college, or diocesan seminary, just as I think that a habit of devout meditation is perhaps the very most necessary of all qualifications for the Priesthood. A theological student learns nothing of any value until he has learned to be in the world and not of it. I wish I could believe that, under the present system, the great body of the English clergy had learned this lesson. Next for our theological tutors or lecturers; we ought not to be satisfied until we have found men who have made or will make some particular study the one chief work of their lives. In every department of our manufactures we find that men are obliged to take one particular thing and give their whole attention to that in order that the completed production may be perfect; and so, I think, it is with Church History, Biblical Criticism in its several branches, the sacred languages, and other such like departments of theological work. It must be remembered that just in proportion as you get a man whose whole soul is in his study, you get a man who will not need the attraction of a large income, nor be easily tempted to leave his place by the offer of preferment at a distance. If the college is to be a school of self-denial, its heads must begin by being examples of it themselves. The head of a theological college who makes a good thing of his headship will turn out men intent upon making a good thing of what they undertake, which means that their work will all be corrupt, and robbed of half its value. The example of Canon Woodard's schools shows us what sort of inducements would furnish our theological colleges with their best principals and professors. A work of this kind must be carried on by men who will work for the work's sake, not for the hope of making themselves a name and ultimately securing a good income. . . .

It is of the greatest importance to secure to the College the warm approval of the Bishop, and the Chapter for the time being, and we may well trust to God's care the preservation of the Institution, if it be a valuable one, whosoever may be by His permission in authority, with the confident hope that if it works to His glory it will be safe ; if not, who could wish to save it? I do not think that we ought to attempt the formation of anything like a committee, for the supervision or defence of the College.

In a letter written to Mr. E. Fry he adds:—

I am inclined to think that absolute perfection is unattainable in any parochial system, but that the Parish Priest should be in relations of comparative equality with the largest number of his parishioners.

In our locomotive days especially, the higher classes will very easily gather themselves into special congregations, perhaps around the town clergy, who would find, and do find, that in order to work their whole charge satisfactorily, they must have a poor man's church as well as a rich one's.

I think, however, that I see more than a probability of lay-preaching on a large scale, and it may be that we shall so meet some of our chief wants. Still the all but total exclusion of poor men's sons from holy orders must be a vast evil, and the placing a gentleman in charge of every parish is a waste of power, and a real hindrance to progress.

The Theological College Committee are not inclined to venture on such a bold course as I should prefer, but they are anxious for something in what I conceive to be a right direction. I am afraid of the right being watered down into the practicable, and by the effort to make it practicable, becoming impracticable as well as worthless.

And again, a few weeks later :—

I have been lately journeying about the neighbourhood speaking for Missions. My own panacea in this matter is a Society of Missionaries, all bound to go wherever they may be sent, and all provided for out of a common fund. The only restriction I should be inclined to impose, would be that no one possessed of private means should be admitted.

Again, writing to another friend on the subject of Church Reform, he says :—

I am for root and branch reform in our good old Church of England, but the Reformation we need is the reformation of churchmen.

I am for reform on the Primitive model. I should like to see an English Bishop who could say, "These hands have ministered to my necessities." I should like to see a very rich young man, who had sold all that he had, and given to the poor. I should like to hear of people who had lost their life for Christ's sake, not as rare wonders, which make good people hope their own sons will not take a Missionary turn, but as very much a thing to be expected of a Christian, and a special subject for all his friends and relations to rejoice in.

There is a story in the "Arabian Nights" of a man who went among the people of the sea, and one day hearing a great rejoicing, asked what it was. "Oh," said his sea companion, "someone is dead." "Indeed," said the landsman, "we always mourn and lament." "Is that true?" "Yes it is." "Well then, you get out of the sea, and never venture here again, for I see that you are only infidels after all."

What is the use of our saying and singing that we long for Paradise, and all the while carefully keeping out of the shortest way to it?

There are many people who are tired of the monotony of being rich, and who like to picnic, as it were, among good works, just as there are others who are tired of the monotony of being safe, and climb untried mountains in order to avoid it. There are very few who would like to become actual

Alpine guides, going over the same road hundreds of times, with people of every shade of the disagreeable; and dependent on them for food and clothing.

So, even amongst the clergy and religious ladies, there are but a few who really desire to do good, and nothing else.

It is a very nice question of conscience how far a man, who leaves his cure because his wife is ill, can suppose himself one of those who are exhorted to leave everything for Christ; or how far a man who spends nearly half the endowment of his cure in taking himself to Italy every year, can show that his summer visits are worth so very much to his parishioners.

When I look round I see so very many things, which are very respectable, and yet very rotten, that I scarcely know where to begin.

Perhaps it will be the best to begin at the bottom. Why don't our poor go to church? Because they are proud and self-indulgent? The vices of the rich are but reflected upon them. A communist is a communist because he cannot bear to think that any man is above him. And what was the vice of an ambitious old Spanish grandee? that he thought himself anybody's equal, and could not bear to have anybody above him.

What is the special vice of the rich? That they spend very nearly all they have in some way or other on themselves.

The British workman almost surpasses them in selfishness. Find how a well-paid workman spends his wages; they are very soon gone, and self, self, self is the chief item; after all, he is a very conscientious man if he does not look out for something out of the shop, under the name of waste or perquisite, which will in some degree make up to his wife for the money spent in beer, which he drank and she did not; unless indeed the perquisites are all devoted to an exclusively man's supper.

Just as among Religious Orders it is the lay portion and the servitors who are the best Christians, so among our workmen it is for the most part the wife, and not the husband, who is ready to do a good turn for a neighbour, and who is really poor.

It is no wonder then that the wives should take to

Christianity better than their masters. The slaves did so in the early ages.

It so happened that the Church Congress of 1871 was held at Nottingham, then in the Lincoln diocese. One of the subjects for discussion was the relation and duty of the Church to the slave trade, and few of those who were present at the meeting will ever forget the feeling that was roused by the closing words of Dr. Steere's speech, expressing his conviction of the only method by which slavery could be overcome.

The question before us is, What is the duty of the Church in regard to the Slave Trade? It is, of course, to put an end to it altogether. But how is it to be done? It is to be done only by the evangelization of the African nation. I, for one, will not lean upon an arm of flesh. It is not to be done by firing cannons indiscriminately into the dhows, killing the slaves at the same time as we kill those who hold them in slavery. It is not by such means as these that we shall put an end to slavery. We must go to that which is the fountain-head in the interior of Africa, and do the work which was done when slavery in Europe was put down. So we must go into Africa, and put down slavery there. There is merely one fact with which I will illustrate this. Those slaves set free by Dr. Livingstone—of whom you have heard just now—were not going down to the coast, to be exported to Arabia, or to America, but going up into the interior, to be trafficked with there; so that when we deal with the slave trade, we must not only draw a cordon round the coast, but we must go and grapple with it in the interior, or we shall never get rid of it.

For this work we look to the Church to supply men who will come forward and devote their lives to the eradication of that which has acquired so vast an influence as this horrid slave trade. It is because Englishmen are lukewarm about the whole matter that the slave trade continues as it is.

When one sees the power that is thrown away in our country parishes in England—men of distinguished ability sent to minister to sixty or seventy people, to rust and be wasted for want of something to employ their powers—can one help feeling that the system must be utterly mistaken that can put such men in such places? When one discovers that it is the rich endowments which draw so much of our ability and energy into such positions, one feels that the army of the Church of England cannot go on to conquer, because it has found its Capua in our country parsonages. It is not from the large towns that we call for men to do this work, but we call those who are wasting their energies in small places amongst two or three farmers and their labourers. We call upon them to join in the work of making a Christian nation out of what is now degraded Africa.

Indeed it was plain to all that he had left his heart in Africa, and when the next mails brought tidings of Bishop Tozer's enfeebled health, and of a terrible visitation of cholera, which had swept away some ten thousand of the inhabitants of Zanzibar, and not spared the Mission House; the feeling that had found utterance in his speech at Nottingham deepened into a conviction of a special call from God to himself.

It was no ordinary trial for a man of affections so warm as Dr. Steere, to "forsake" not only his country, his flock, his friends and kinsfolk, but his wife also. But Mrs. Steere had bravely consented to his former sacrifice, and now she bade him God speed on his second venture, and quite intended following herself, accompanied by a sister.

We may add that the idea was not definitely abandoned until some years afterwards, when delicacy of health, ending, alas! in disease of the brain, rendered it impossible. It is a fact, we believe, that the poor lady twice prepared for her journey, and only gave it up when in sight of the sea and the steamship.

Thus Dr. Steere had the pain of living on without the companionship of his wife; for himself he had at last found the true vocation for which God had so long, and in so many ways, been preparing His servant—"the devotion of a lifetime to the eradication of the slave trade, and laying deep and wide the foundations of an indigenous native church in Central Africa."

I am off to-day, in the "Abydos," I believe, for Zanzibar, [he wrote to Mr. E. Fry on February 8th, 1872]. I have been in a great hurry at the last, because the merchants are so jealous, that they will not let the news that they are sending out a ship, get wind until the mail before is gone, lest their rivals should hinder their buying a cargo cheaply.

The Livingstone Search Expedition is going in the same ship, and I am in a sort of a sense appended to them during the voyage, as instructor in languages.

I am going out to complete the translations. I feel that I have special powers for that work, and if I see that the Mission can go on without me I shall come home again, time enough to see you, I hope, on the woolsack, if it should so long exist. Mrs. Steere will for the present live in Spilsby, close by my old living, which I have just resigned.

Give my kind regards to Mrs. Fry, and remember me in your prayers.

CHAPTER VIII.

Bishop Tozer's Resignation.

THE "Abydos" arrived at Zanzibar on the 17th of March, 1872, and writing on the 25th, Miss Tozer, who had also come out to stay a few months with her brother, says :—"We arrived at the very nick of time, when every one was worn and harassed by a wet season, and by the utter absence of home news. The rains are still constant, and we have thunderstorms daily, and no sun; quite curious weather, and it has been going on so for the last two months."

This weather was the prelude to a terrible hurricane on April 15th, which wrought fearful desolation in the town, and throughout the island of Zanzibar. This was the more extraordinary, as Zanzibar is out of the ordinary line of hurricanes: they seldom come so near the Equator, and in Zanzibar none had ever been known.

The Mission suffered severely. The house was unroofed, the out-buildings ruined, the entrance gate and sea-wall thrown down, the front rooms, including the chapel, were filled with sand and water; the garden, which the day before had been filled with cocoanuts, palms, bananas, and stately rows of aloes, was swept bare of every tree, and filled with planks, stones, and wreckage of all kinds.

After this terrible disaster there naturally followed a period of great depression. All the Europeans fell ill, Dr. Steere had the worst attack of fever he ever experienced, the children connected with the Mission were so sickly that many of them died. Mr. Pennell, one of the saintliest of men, whose life was an exemplification of self-sacrifice for Christ's sake, died; Bishop Tozer's health broke down completely, and he left Zanzibar. For a time he stayed at Seychelles; from thence he came to England, and finding that his health did not sufficiently improve to warrant him in returning to Zanzibar, he resigned the headship of the Mission in April, 1872.

By the death of Mr. Pennell and the departure of Bishop Tozer, Dr. Steere, who was now the only clergyman left at Zanzibar, was in charge of the Mission. "It seemed," to use his own words, "as though we were come to the last extremity." But he set to work vigorously to repair the damages caused by the hurricane; and in October 1872, he wrote:—

We are looking anxiously forward to the time when our new buildings shall be ready for occupation, and the dormitories swept away by the hurricane shall have been replaced. At present we are dreadfully overcrowded.

Khatibu came across from Morongo the other day. He asked me eagerly when we were going to reoccupy Magila. He told me that the wars in the Shambala country consequent upon the death of Kimweri were at an end, all parties having given up fighting from sheer exhaustion. Magila does not seem ever to have been the scene of actual war, and our house and goods have been scrupulously respected. One effect of the desolation of the interior has been an increase of the population round Magila.

The people, who cherish a vivid recollection of Mr. Alington, and who had evidently a great love for Mr. Fraser, are all asking when the white men are coming back to them. You will readily imagine how much I longed to do something, especially as our sub-deacons are now old enough and men enough to be sent to actual mission work. It seems also desirable to move off the elder scholars, so that little offices of trust may be given to the younger lads, who are rapidly following them. Francis Mabruki had expressed a strong desire to be sent to Magila, the Bishop having always laid before the sub-deacons the prospect of their going sooner or later to some station on the mainland.

I could not, however, send him alone; so I asked Mr. Speare,[1] our English sub-deacon, in whose solidity and steadiness I feel the utmost confidence, whether he would be willing to go. He told me that he should like very much to do so, especially if he might look upon it as his own sphere of work, so that if he goes home, as before long he ought after five years' residence here, he might consider Magila as the home to which he was to return, and the Shambala Mission as the work for which he was especially to qualify himself.

Under the circumstances I could not have desired anything better than this. Then I found that John Swedi, the other native sub-deacon, would like to go also. Thus a plan seemed to shape itself that Speare and Francis Mabruki should go up first, and look at the land, and get the house and place in order, and when they reported all ready, that John should follow with the wives and children. (Francis and John were married to two of the young native Christian women that had been trained by the Mission.) Thus the two native sub-deacons would permanently occupy Magila, and Mr. Speare would spend most of his time there.

[1] See "The Story of a Suffolk Boy." S.P.C.K.

It was determined to put this plan into execution, and all preparations being completed by October 8th, on the morning of that day all the Europeans and five of the native African lads came in to an early celebration of Holy Communion, when Dr. Steere gave an address to those about to leave. His words are so good that it seems well to preserve a portion of it in this record.

Brethren, you are going on the noblest errand on which it is possible for men to go. You are sent as God's messengers to publish His acts and explain His counsels. The more completely you can forget yourselves and remember only Him, so much the better will your work be done. God has looked with compassion upon the sinful and the miserable, and sends you to tell them that He loves them. God has sacrificed Himself, left His Glory, taken a human nature, and in that nature suffered and died, that He might be able to deliver men from sin and hell.

He sends you now to tell them what He has done for them. If none will receive your message, still God's part has been done, and you will have done yours if you have faithfully declared it. You will not be asked at the last day, How many professing converts have you made? but, Have you faithfully declared the whole counsel of God? Let this be your purpose, and let nothing hinder you from it. Let there be no attempt to soften or conceal your message. . . Do not expect immediate success. It is better to work slowly than hastily, and I shall not be disappointed,—and you must not be so,—if you seem for some years to preach and teach in vain. Darkness, as old it may be as the flood, is not likely to be dispelled quickly.

You will, as often as you can, openly read and explain the written Gospels. You will teach the prayers, and hymns, and psalms, to those who may be willing to learn them. In regard to your own outward demeanour, you will take care to avoid all reasonable ground of offence. You must not be proud and self-reliant, but must be ready to suffer wrong rather than exact your extreme rights. Follow, as far as you can, the customs of the place and people. Quarrel with no one, however much you may be provoked. Treat no one with contempt. Never use violence or hard language. Be moderate in eating, drinking, and sleeping. Remember in all things the character you bear, and seek to do as Christ would have done in your place. Try to understand the thoughts and difficulties of the people you live amongst. Try to put your message in such words, and deliver it in such a manner, as may make it most intelligible and most acceptable to your hearers.

Do not be afraid to say out all you have to say; but do not, if you can help it, say it in such a way as to provoke blasphemy. Do not grow weary in well-doing; God is with you; and though you may see no result, your labour is not in vain. If you find yourselves in danger from war or tumult, do not be in a hurry to escape; if your people stay it will be best for you to stay with them. Even in the extremest danger God can save you. Set your faces steadily against all superstitious fears; however strong evil spirits may be, God is stronger.

If you should ever be in danger because of your religion, look upon that as a special honour, and do not shrink from meeting it. In any case, whether from disease or violence, do not fear death; for what men call death is really the gate of peace and joy to all true Christians. But our prayer for you is that you may live long and happily, and have such success that you may be counted amongst those who, having turned many to righteousness, shall shine as the stars for ever and ever.

Meditate upon these things, and look continually up from earth to God in heaven; and so may God's presence, and God's blessing be with you abidingly.

Little by little the Mission work at Zanzibar began to revive.

And then came the event which will be a turning-point, not only in the history of our Mission, but in that of East Africa

—I mean the embassy of Sir Bartle Frere. England had heard of what Livingstone had seen, and so many others had described, and the nation was moved to do something. At first the Arabs refused to make any change. As they put it, their fathers had had slaves, and their grandfathers had had slaves, and Ishmael had slaves, and Abraham had slaves, and society was inconceivable without them; so there must be slaves, and if so, there must be a slave trade.

The Sultan of Zanzibar holds no legal position in the State, but is merely the strongest chief, who represents the whole body to the outer world so long as he does not offend his great men, and, as he truly said, without their consent he could do nothing. So Sir Bartle Frere left the work to another messenger—the English admiral—who came to Zanzibar with six men-of-war, and to show that we were all of one mind, the French sent two men-of-war, and the Americans one.

Then the Arabs had another meeting, and looked upon the ships; and some said they would go back to Arabia, but at last they agreed that it would be best to consent to whatever the English wanted, and the treaty was signed.

This treaty put an end to all juggling with passes by forbidding all carriage of slaves by sea, and it ordered the closing of all the open slave markets in the coast towns. Thus a very heavy blow was dealt to the slave trade in East Africa; what its whole effects may be we have not yet had time to see, but they are great already.

Sir Bartle Frere, however, did not confine himself to his negotiations with the Arabs; he examined the country himself, and amongst other things, he made himself personally acquainted with the work of the Mission.

The following information with respect to the Mission was given to Sir Bartle Frere by Dr. Steere:—

The Universities Mission has had under its care, since its arrival at Zanzibar, seventy-eight boys and thirty-two girls, in all 110 children; of these, all except five boys were released slaves, fourteen of the boys were taken out of the dhows by Seyid Majid (the previous Sultan), and put by him under the care of the Mission; two boys and one girl were procured by Europeans (not British subjects) residing at Zanzibar, and given by them to the Mission; the rest were all taken by English men-of-war. Nineteen children have died; three of the girls are married; two of the boys are sub-deacons—one is at Magila station, the other is preparing to go there; one old scholar is chief assistant in the printing office, another is employed about the Mission premises, one is engaged as servant to Bishop Tozer, four are in service in the town of Zanzibar, three are engaged as pupil-teachers in the school, four have in various ways turned out badly. Forty-two boys and twenty-two girls are now in the schools.

In an official report on the subject of liberated slaves Sir Bartle Frere remarks:—"The missionaries have laboured at Zanzibar to train selected lads for school teaching and for pastoral missionary work, giving for this purpose a good deal of attention to both English and the native languages.

"In both respects they have been successful; a fair proportion of the pupils have a useful knowledge of English, and all have learned to read and write their own language, or at least Swahili, the general language of the coast, in English character, in a manner which has hardly been attempted by other missions, and which leaves little to be desired.

"This is mainly due to the labours of Dr. Steere. He has furnished anyone who can read English with the means of thoroughly mastering Swahili, the most generally useful of East African languages, and greatly facilitated the acquisition of three others commonly spoken by slaves.

"Very excellent work, in these languages and in English, is turned out at the Mission press, the whole being composed, set up, and printed by negro lads and young men.

"It is difficult to over-estimate the value of Dr. Steere's labours in these two branches of mission work; and nothing seems wanting in either, than to continue and extend what has been so well begun.

"In the benefits of both, as most important auxiliaries in the suppression of the slave trade, and in the general civilisation of East Africa, the Government partly participates. It is to this Mission also that we must, for the present, mainly look for a supply of well-educated interpreters, able to read and write both English and Swahili.

"Judged as a whole, for secular purposes, such as the disposal of liberated slaves, the main defect of the Mission seems to me to be the want of more industrial teaching in mechanical arts or agriculture; many even of the best selected lads have absolutely no capacity for intellectual acquirement, by means of reading and writing; and I have heard of 'lamentable failures,' so called, simply because a boy who was quite willing to work in the fields for his living, but had no capacity for any but bodily exercises, ran away from his lessons.

"If I might presume to advise the Bishop[1] and his missionaries, I would introduce a far larger industrial element into their schools. Every one

---

[1] At this time the fact of Bishop Tozer's resignation was not known to Sir Bartle Frere.

should learn a trade, a mechanical art of some kind, or sufficient of agriculture to support himself. The teaching might be such as a good native artisan, or mechanic, or cultivator could impart; to which might be added, tentatively and with caution, instruction in European methods, and the use of European tools, which are not invariably adapted to African habits and necessities. Every boy should, I think, be taught to make himself useful in building a hut, in cultivating, in managing a boat, and mending his own clothes and shoes, and nets and fishing-tackle, &c., after the native fashion, with European improvements only when clearly seen to be better than native ways.

"Elementary instruction, sufficient to read and write in their own language, might probably be imparted to all; but only the apter pupils should be required to learn English."

Sir Bartle Frere's hope was to find in the Mission the means of disposing of liberated slaves, and he saw that Bweni, or Mbweni, might be utilised for that purpose, to the extent at least of providing for the temporary reception of any batch of liberated slaves which might be brought in, pending adjudication or awaiting decision—a hope that was destined shortly to be realized.

There is still a vague, unavowed feeling in the minds of many churchmen that mission work among the heathen of foreign lands is something essentially different from mission work among the untaught and irreligious of our own country; that a Missionary, who, after a season of labour in the mission field returns to work at home, has thereby in some degree "looked back after putting hand to the plough;" and that earnest and zealous men,[1] who wish to devote some two or three years to the foreign service of the Church, had better stay at home altogether.

We need not to argue against impressions, which, though they may still influence the action of a few, rarely now take the form of opinions held by thoughtful or influential men.

The Church at large has now generally recognized the fact of the great similarity between the work to be done in the darkest regions of heathendom, and the neglected districts of our own country; that, as in England, so in foreign heathendom, there is no talent so great but that it may be worthily employed in the Church's service, no talent so small that it can be superfluous or useless in aiding the work of the Church.[2]

Still it is as well to put on record the deliberately formed view of the practical Missionary, as shown in the letter written by Dr. Steere in answer to the request from Sir Bartle Frere "for something to send to Oxford."

---

[1] We trust that no second person can anywhere be found to follow the author of "The English Church in Other Lands," (Longmans, 1886, p. 205), and deliberately sneer at such, as actuated by "romance and adventure."

[2] The above paragraphs are mainly taken from a valuable pamphlet on Eastern Africa as a field for Missionary labour by that honoured statesman, who "found Scinde a desert and left it a garden," and in the midst of political cares never forgot that the most precious thing England could give her Colonies was her Faith;—the late Sir Bartle Frere, G.C.S.I., K.C.B., D.C.L., "Eastern Africa," pp. 95, 96.

Zanzibar, 22nd June, 1873.

When you ask what the University might do specially for the Mission one is inclined at first to say,—everything. Men, money, and interest are our great wants. I do not think that we want so much individual men, who will devote their lives specially to the one work of Missions in East Africa, as we do a general flow of men backward and forward, so that a knowledge of the country and its people may be diffused at home, and fresh minds apply themselves continually to the great problems which have to be solved.

There is a narrowness of view, which can scarcely be avoided by one whose whole life is spent in one kind of work, and that in one special locality.

Missions are often spoken of as though they were a thing apart, altogether unlike home work. For myself, I do not understand that anything more requires to be done for the heathen than has to be done for each generation of Englishmen; men are not born Christians, they have not instinctive knowledge of the truth. We see among the heathen merely what man without the Church of God has come to be, and what he is always tending to be, even in what men fondly call Christian countries.

One great value of Missions, both at home and abroad, is that they compel men to distinguish between the Christianity, which is a mere swimming with the stream, and that which is really a thankful use of the gifts and grace of God. I think every parish priest would be the better for some actual knowledge of heathenism.

If such ideas as these could be well put forward at the University they would naturally lead to what I should like our friends there to undertake; and that is a systematic recommendation to the young men who year by year are looking forward to Holy Orders as their vocation, that they should spend a year or two, at the very beginning of their course, in the work of some Mission, and as we are here, we should wish that it might be ours.

There is, or might be, an interval of a year or two between the degree and ordination, which could well be spent in work here, perhaps in something like Minor Orders. Young men travel over the world for the sake of knowing what it is like, it would be better worth while to study one set of people thoroughly, as a Missionary must.

I think it is folly to ask a man in England,—"Will you devote yourself to Mission work in East Africa?" when his ideas about East Africa are probably a mass of errors, and those about Mission work not much better. Let him come for a year or two and see what it all means, the time would be usefully employed for himself as well as the Mission, and no one need lament over his going, as though he were running unusual risks, or permanently severing any home ties whatever.

If he finds his vocation here, well for him and well for us. If he does not, well for him, and for us also. He will have gained an insight into his own capacities as well as into our work. He will diffuse correct ideas at home, and we shall have the benefit of his independent and intelligent criticism, a thing which Missions generally are very much in need of.

I do not think there would be much difficulty in procuring Deacon's Orders in England for anyone coming out here upon the understanding that he should be cordially received at home, whenever he returned, bringing good testimonials from the Missionary Bishop.

First, then, I would ask our friends to take care that no one should go to Ordination from the University without having the opportunity of spending a year or two with us distinctly offered to him, and its acceptance, if necessary, pressed upon him by such arguments as ought to have most weight in each special case. The Bishops approve very highly of the plan by which a rich town parish charges itself with the assistance of a poor one; they ought by parity of reasoning to be ready to encourage each his own diocese to send help to some Missionary diocese, and to reckon work done there as work done for themselves.

Another special thing the University might do for us would be to take care that our native college should be well supplied with good teachers.

This is a most necessary thing, and one for which the University might well make itself responsible. Let it be understood that the University Committee undertakes to keep the native college supplied with two or three really valuable men, not necessarily any one of them to stay any great length of time, but that matters may be so arranged that each one may be relieved when he desires to return. Now that we have a monthly mail, passages can be obtained so as to hit exactly the time when the vacancy will occur, and the Committee will of course be in correspondence with its nominees, and will always know how they are succeeding, and when they will be likely to want a change.

I hope, by the aid of such men as the University could well spare us for a time, our investigations into the languages, traditions, opinions, and affinities of the tribes to which we minister, may be conducted in a much more complete and scholarly manner than one could possibly expect from men wholly and merely Missionaries.

If these proposals seem unpractical, or in addition to them, the University Committee might very well and usefully find and maintain one or more Missionaries, whose work will be then specially the work of the University, and may excite a personal interest, which sometimes proves very valuable.

I have spoken chiefly about men, because it is exactly in the presence of men engaged in studies congenial to Church work that our Universities consist. I have no fear that if men be forthcoming anything else will long be wanting.

CHAPTER IX.

Dr. Steere Succeeds Bishop Tozer.

A FEW extracts from Dr. Steere's journals and letters will carry on the history of the Mission to the time when he was called to succeed Bishop Tozer as chief pastor thereof.

March, 1873.—Mr. Karn's arrival is an immense advantage to the Mission. He is working well (as a schoolmaster), and is taking a warm interest in the boys.

Speare is come down from Magila. He seems to be doing very well, and looks to a school for children, and conversations with the natives who gather round him wherever he goes, as his chief present objects. Benjamin Hartley (a young layman who had not long before joined the Mission) is to go back with him.

April.—I think we may reckon that for £1,500 a year spent here we could keep the two schools going, and two mainland stations. Of course there will be proportionate expenditure at home, which will raise the amount to £2,000: indeed we ought to aim at £3,000, which would allow some margin for growth. The Kiungani establishment may be set down at sixty mouths, all told; that at Shangani at twenty-five, and that at Magila at about ten. This last is now being put upon its permanent basis. The sub-deacons are to feed and clothe themselves and their families out of their salaries, the Mission paying passages, house-building, and items not of a personal nature.

We have finished printing Mr. Pennell's translation of St. Luke's Gospel, and have now in hand the Book of Kings.

May 10th.—Our new recruits, Revs. J. Midgley and A. N. West, have arrived, and we are as yet in the first joys of meeting.

Since the departure of Bishop Tozer from Zanzibar up to this time, Dr. Steere had been without any clerical coadjutor. A little later he writes, showing how much his heart was set upon mainland work to the South as well as to the North :—

Do not hesitate to send out any one who is at all promising, and we will make the best of him. My thoughts are full of Kiswara or Lindi as a starting-point for the Yaos and the Nyassa. Gilbert M'Gwenda came back in the Natal mail with a very good character from his master; and as they wanted another, Vernon Baruti has gone down this voyage with him. The Natal people seem so eager for labourers that they would carry off the whole town, if they could, to work on their sugar plantations.

Now that the slave trade is become more and more a matter of small smuggling, we must look to the mainland stations for our supply of scholars, and this makes me increasingly anxious to multiply them.

We must also, I think, be content with a class of Mission priests in whom self-devotion takes the place of learning. If I were bishop I would offer special facilities to earnest men wishing to join us; admit them at once as sub-deacons; then make a thorough knowledge of the Bible, and a good acquaintance with some native language the conditions of deacon's orders; and so after some years, during which a few sound standard theological works had been thoroughly digested, admit them to priest's orders. We want all the well-taught men we can get, but we want a great many more besides. We are also in great need of some ladies who would really master the language, and lay themselves out for the benefit of the townspeople.

July 23rd.—Mr. Midgley left us on the 7th to take charge of the station at Magila. There remains one thing that we must do here, and as speedily as may be, and that is to set up a mission church in the town with regular vernacular preaching. For this purpose I am trying to secure the site of the old slave market, now closed. We shall then cover the ground here well, though spread out very thinly.

At Magila there is just now an accumulation of force which only waits for the coming of another priest to divide itself and form another station.

Mr. Midgley's first impressions of Magila seem to have been very good. He writes: "Anything more charming than the site of this station it is, I think, impossible to imagine."

The people gathered together in crowds to welcome the missionaries, and there were many natives listening during their first service. They found the country along their route much more populous than it had been, and fresh cultivation going on everywhere, especially about Magila. The people gave them most readily the best accommodation they had to offer.

Our work is going on very briskly. The boys are visibly improving under Mr. Karn's teaching, and Miss Fountain and Mr. West are taking good care of the girls. S. Speare leaves by this mail. He is of the greatest value to the Mission, especially as the first fruits of Bishop Tozer's Mission Pupil scheme. I hope very great things from him, if he gets well through his two years in England.[1]

I have just bought 1,000 young palm-trees for Mbweni. If they do well they will be very profitable. At Kiungani I am planting orange-trees along the paths.

I find that they are beginning to use our words, and to study our translations, at the French Mission (at Bagamoyo, on the coast of the mainland). I came upon Frère Marcellin the other day, sitting under a bush and working away at our St. Matthew, and Père Etienne was most glad of a copy of our hymns which I showed him. I always make a point of

---

[1] S. Speare never returned to Zanzibar. He was preparing himself to do so, but died at Burgh, Bishop Tozer's old parish, before his preparation was finished; we are happy to think that he was ready for his call when it came.

THEOLOGICAL COLLEGE AND BOYS' SCHOOL, KIUNGANI.

To face p. 118.

sending them copies of what we print, and so I hope in time to get them more and more for fellow-workers.

August 28th.—We held our feast on the 25th. Mr. West is just returned from a trip in H.M.S. "Shearwater." They found Kilwa a small, poor place, and all about it full of bones and skulls. The slaves were being marched thence up along the coast. He had a day's walk along the shore, and was everywhere treated with the greatest kindness.

The site of the old slave market was purchased by Mr. West, and made over to the Mission. Dr. Steere was not long before he made use of this site as the place of all others from which to preach deliverance to the captives. We have heard it said by one of those who accompanied Bishop Mackenzie that when they first met Dr. Livingstone at the mouth of the Zambesi River, in 1861, one little incident made his heart sink within him. In answer to an inquiry about the native languages, the old traveller said, "If you men have sufficiently reduced the language in *twelve years* so as to be able to preach to the natives, you will have done good work." The prophecy was a curiously true one, as the following details show:—

December.—Last evening, the First Friday in Advent, I held our first preaching at the slave market in a mud-house. The boys and girls came in. I preached, and we sang the Advent Hymn and said the Litany, all in Swahili. The townspeople were shy, and did not come inside till we had well begun the Litany, when twenty or more entered in a body, headed by the Imam of a mosque, who is a neighbour of ours, and by way of being friendly, he said they were very good words that he had heard, and not so very different from what he himself thought.

Our preachings in the mud-house prosper. The arrangements are primitive, and necessarily as simple as possible. Two large poles prop up the ridge of the roof, and we have put some mats on the floor. The east wall is marked by a large print of the Crucifixion nailed up in the middle of it. A good deal of light comes through the thatch as well as by the door and light-holes. Last Friday, when we arrived, we found a good many people waiting for us, and while we were singing the hymn they came in and filled the lower part of the room. Miss Fountain counted eighty of the townspeople, so that if I can only hold them we promise very well.

I am making a little mud bench under the eaves in front, which are very deep, so as to be able to sit there and talk to all comers. I hope to arrange to spend Fridays there, and, if it can be managed, that the boys and girls should meet there on Sunday afternoons, I should then be able to speak to them and the people both at once. I should hope that Mr. West's zeal for a church will rouse everybody to do more in other ways for us.

The last open slave market in the world has just been closed. It has been closed by the direct influence of the English nation, roused into sympathy by the details of the suffering caused by that odious traffic. And what is there that ought to be put in its place? Instead of hatred, love; instead of hardened and hardening selfishness, generous self-devotion; instead of forced labour, gratuitous help; instead of the narrowest worldliness, a holy religion.

It is not enough to suppress slavery, if there is nothing to put in its place. The Mohamedan, slave-dealer as he is, teaches his slaves that there is one God. If we are so superior to him that we cannot tolerate his customs, what are we to put in the place of his grand though cold monotheism?

We must put in its place that which has delivered ourselves out of slavery, the teaching of Christ.

To set a slave free to starve is poor charity, to leave him in ignorance is no better.

In place, therefore, of the old slave market, and on the very spot where men and women have been from time immemorial bargained for like cattle, we intend to set up a church, where Christ, the Saviour of slave and free, may be preached, and the Sacraments, which bind together men of all colours and races, may be fully administered.

The great zeal of the English nation against slavery is a standing puzzle to the Eastern mind. It really proceeds from the fact that we feel the equality of the whole human race before God, and resent as an injury done to our own flesh and blood the cruelties inflicted upon other men. We feel this because we have, more or less, taken in and made our own the great fundamental principles of Christianity. But how are Arabs and Negroes to guess at this if we suppress our religion, and hide the true source of our actions?

If we want credit for being honest we must be honest, and proclaim, as worthily as we can, the religion which has made us free.

There is nothing so contrary to slavery in the natural mind of the English nation as to have hindered it from being in times past the most active of all slave-dealers. The change is due to the awakening, first of individual consciences, and then of the national conscience as a whole, to the awful contradiction between our professed belief and our old habits.

The people of Zanzibar are now full of doubts and suspicions as to our motives. What answer can we give them except the proclamation of the glorious liberty which is in Christ Jesus, and the setting forth of that light which has filled so many evildoers with shame, and has begun at last to shine even in that darkest corner of the whole earth—the Eastern Coast of Africa?

The congregation of eighty soon grew into one of one hundred and fifty, which included the representatives of many nationalities,—Indians, Persians, Comoro men, Swahili of the coast and of the town, and some pure Arabs, as well as pure up-country negroes.

In the meantime the building of a permanent church was taken in hand and prosecuted with such energy, that on Christmas Day the first stone was laid by Captain Prideaux, acting Consul-General, amid a great concourse of natives and most of the European population.

We sang "Jerusalem the Golden," and I said some prayers and made a short address. The church is to be named Christ Church. There was some slight fear of a row among the Mohammedans, and certainly the way in which they came to hear us, and the interest they manifest in what I say, is most unlike what we might have expected from them. One cannot help feeling how much mission work is really thrown upon England by the marked way in which the people here prefer an Englishman, and listen to him rather than to any other European. I myself overheard a woman telling some country friend of hers that our custom was to read and preach, and then we all fell upon our knees and prayed God to be merciful to us sinners. Standing almost alone, as I do here just now, the Epiphany epistle [1] was strangely affecting when it came to me to read.

In connection with the church we propose to establish day schools for the townspeople, who are very anxious to have their children taught, many adults also offering to pay liberally for instruction. In addition to this we hope to have a dispensary, of which the consular surgeon is willing to undertake the management.

The New Year, 1874, opened auspiciously with a wedding, for on New Year's Day Vincent M'kono was married to Elizabeth Kidogo, and went to live at Kiungani, where he acted as a sort of usher out of school and general superintendent.

Early in the year also Juma (or Chuma, as he is now called), who had accompanied Dr. Livingstone throughout his last travels, and to whom it was owing that the doctor's body was brought down to the coast, who also was a *protégé* of the Mission

[1] Galatians iv. 1-7.

when it was in the Zambesi districts, was added to the number of those connected with the Mission at Zanzibar.

The events of February were some of them sad. Mr. Midgley suffered so much from fever at Magila that he much feared he would have to give up—a fear that was soon after unfortunately realised. Francis Mabruki, one of the sub-deacons, lost his infant child, he being at Zanzibar when it died. Writing upon this to a friend who had been kind to him when he was in England with Bishop Tozer, he says:—"I thank you, indeed, for your kindness in sending poor Flory the things. She is not now with us, but gone up, and has been called by God who made her. Poor child! When I was in Zanzibar spending the Christmas a letter came to me, and I read it, and saw the sad news of the death of my child. Whenever I think of her last little hand-shaking with mine, and her last loving kiss, my tears flow down. God bless the little thing! It is good that God has taken her away from this sinful world into a glorious kingdom."

Mr. Hartley, a schoolmaster, also came down from Magila to spend the Christmas at Zanzibar, and near to Morongo, on his return journey, he met some Arab slave-dealers who were on their way from Kilwa with two gangs of slaves. Some words seem to have passed between him and them, and then shots were fired on both sides, and Hartley was severely wounded. The people at Morongo put him on board a dhow, which happened to be in the harbour, and sent him across to Zanzibar.

At the end of a week he was going on so well, in spite of the number and severity of his wounds, that Dr. Steere hoped to be able to send him home by the steamer in March, but lock-jaw supervened, and he died on the 15th of February.

Then came an offer of thirty-four slaves—men, women, and children—that had been taken from a dhow by H.M.S. "Briton." The offer was accepted, though Dr. Steere wrote upon this occasion:—

> I am so overwhelmed that I know not how to turn. The females are unfortunately all grown women, who must have work now, and husbands as soon as may be. I am very glad to have prepared the way for a settlement of girls at Mbweni, where there will be work for all.
>
> The house at Mbweni is nearly ready. It stands on the top of a gentle rise from the sea. The upper floor has two long rooms over the schoolroom and temporary chapel, and two small ones over the stores and porch. We have a good water-tank, which will be an inestimable benefit. We begin our village with seven grown men and fifteen women.

At this time Dr. Steere was again alone at Zanzibar, for Mr. West had not intended to work permanently at the Mission, and, after staying at Zanzibar a few months, returned, as had been arranged, to England. Nevertheless, it will be seen from the records of this chapter, that the Mission had not only recovered from the state of prostration in which it was at the time of Bishop Tozer's departure, but that its sphere of operations had been greatly enlarged.

The number of children connected with the Mission had been greatly increased; an asylum for released slaves at Mbweni, which is about four miles from Zanzibar, had been established; religious services and preaching in the town of Zanzibar itself had been commenced; the old slave market had been purchased for the site of a church, and the church was so far advanced that at Easter it was completed to the first stage of eight feet all round; and finally, the work at Magila had been carried on without any break in the operations for many months.

It was most fitting that when Bishop Tozer's resignation was accepted, the bishopric should be offered to Dr. Steere, for no one had rendered such great and valuable aid to the Mission as he, and of all men he was best qualified for the post. For some time, however, he steadfastly refused to accept it. Writing to the Rev. J. W. Festing he says:—

> Bishop Tozer tells me that he has determined to send in his resignation as head of the Central African Mission, and that I may very possibly be thought of as his successor. I write therefore at once, to say through you to the Committee, that I am not willing to accept the appointment.
>
> I have many reasons for such a determination of a private as well as of a public nature. I think, for instance, that it would be a very grave reproach to the old Universities, that a Mission started under their auspices should be committed to a stranger, who has no connection with either of them. Again, I cannot shut my eyes to the fact that the Mission has hitherto been mainly supported by the friends of Bishop Mackenzie, while he lived, and afterwards by the friends of Bishop Tozer. It would be a most imprudent thing on the part of the Committee to appoint a man who has no friends, and under whom, therefore, the funds of the Mission would be likely to sink to a very low ebb; indeed, I am afraid that the people who are really and primarily interested in the

benefit of the East African negro are too few to be exclusively relied upon.

I should, however, be far less swayed by such arguments as these, if I did not feel that there were other reasons behind, more personal to myself. In the first place, I do not possess some of the essential elements of a Missionary character. I can be very friendly with Negroes and Arabs, and can learn to use their language, and enter into their modes of thought, mainly because I am content to accept them as my teachers rather than to put myself forward to teach them.

This disposition enables me to be useful to the Mission as an interpreter of European thought to Negroes, and of Negro thought to Europeans, but it makes it very necessary that the head of the Mission should take a more decided line.

In the next place, I have no reason to think that I should succeed as the head of a small body of people, such as this Mission must consist of, but all my experience goes to prove that I should not.

In the last place I am conscious of a certain want of steadfastness, which might be very injurious to the Mission, were I in a position in which I should not only have to regulate myself, but to be at once bridle and spur to all the rest.

I should recommend the Committee to select a man who has taken a good degree at either Oxford or Cambridge, who has zeal in abundance (he will learn discretion here), who has a large personal following, and who is as young a man as the Canons allow.

Robust and active men are not likely to have so good health here, as men of a quiet character, and a sound, though rather tender, constitution. Patience and large-heartedness are the two most necessary moral qualifications.

There is one more point to which I must draw your attention. Bishop Tozer has very largely contributed to the expenses of the Mission from his own private purse. He has thus spent, at the least, £400 a year, which has not appeared in the accounts. This ought to be known, both on his account, and on my own. It should be known, to his credit, that he is leaving Zanzibar a far poorer man than when he came to it; and, unless it is known, I shall appear o be spending £400 a year more than before, even if I do no more than is now being done.

So far Dr. Steere. But what those on the spot who saw and knew his work felt, may be gathered from the letter written to the same member of the Committee by Sir Bartle Frere, in February, 1873, when Dr. Steere had for some time been the acting head of the Mission.

I have seen a good deal of Dr. Steere, and am much impressed by his ability, and energy, and by his extraordinary fidelity to his Diocesan.

I took the liberty of asking him the reason of his having said that he could not accept the vacant see. He said that there were many other reasons, which he did not specify; but that the one reason, which, to his mind, was paramount and conclusive, was his having urged Bishop Tozer to resign.

Were the see vacant, and were I Pope or Emperor of Zanzibar, I should disregard his refusal and nominate him, but his unspecified reasons may be stronger than the one he mentioned, and, perhaps, the see may have been already filled up.

I have no hesitation in saying that if nothing else had been done by the Mission beyond the publication of Dr. Steere's works on the languages of East Africa, the money expended would have been well laid out. It is not easy to convey an idea of the difficulty attending the examination of such dialects, and their reduction to forms, which admit of the language being learnt in the ordinary method with grammar and dictionary.

But with the means he has provided in his "Handbook" and "Tales," any one might acquire enough of the language to be independent of an interpreter in a few months. The language is a very soft, pleasant-sounding tongue, and will carry one along at least 700 miles of coast, and a long way into the interior. It is also a good foundation for other dialects, as Italian is for French, or Spanish.

I think Dr. Steere's plans for the future, as far as I understand them, are very sound, especially as regards putting out an offshoot on the mainland. He does not propose, by any means, to abandon this Island.

Someone, however, of lower rank than a Bishop, ought at once to come out to help Dr. Steere with the current work. He has far more to do than he can manage without risk of breaking down from sheer exhaustion. A single man now, may be better than three a couple of months hence, and, now that there is a regular monthly mail to Aden, very little preparation is needed, you can send for everything as it is required.

And so it was, that under urgent pressure from those both at home and in Zanzibar, Dr. Steere at last yielded, and, having arrived in England on August 4th, 1874, he was consecrated in Westminster Abbey, on S. Bartholomew's Day, the 24th of the same month.

Whilst in England, Bishop Steere was actively engaged in pleading the cause of the Mission, and the mention of this reminds us of a remarkable thing that happened in the course of his rounds, and will serve as an apt illustration of his power of winning men.

He had been announced to speak at a meeting in a certain northern town, which shall be nameless, and from some cause or another, only three persons were present. The chairman proposed to adjourn. "No," said the Bishop, "these people have come to hear about Africa, and I will not break faith with them," and the meeting went on as usual. Hardly was it ended before one of the three men came forward and said, "My lord, you little know what you have done for me to-night. I came here believing that Bishops, especially Missionary Bishops, were all humbugs, and I came to make sure of it. You have taught me not only to believe in Bishops, but what is far more, in the power of Christian faith and self-denial. I humbly beg your pardon, and beg you to accept all that I have in my purse for your work." It was £25. "So," said the Bishop, as he told the tale to his organizing secretary, "never despise a small meeting."

During the last three months of 1874 Bishop Steere was almost every day preaching or speaking on behalf of the Mission, setting forth what was being done at Zanzibar, and what his plans and aims were for the future. When at Oxford, after describing the efforts that were being made for the children, he said:—

But then, when one feels that something has been done, there naturally arises a longing to do more; and the first thing that suggested itself was the desire to do for the adult slaves what we had been doing for the children. Now, the Arabs say of our efforts to suppress the slave trade, that we are in want of hands for our sugar plantations at Natal and Mauritius, and, being strong at sea, we find it the cheapest plan to take the slaves and send them to work for our planters. What is done, is far too much of this sort; for to take an African away to a strange country, and apprentice him for a term of years to an Englishman, for whom he will be compelled to work much harder than he ever would have worked for an Arab master, is the strangest possible way of giving him his liberty; yet this is what we do. It is a reproach to our English Government that we give five pounds a head to the men-of-war's men for every slave seized by them, and then refuse one penny for the benefit of the released people. Children, infirm, sick, whatever they be, no schools, no refuge, no hospital, not even a temporary allowance, scarcely any food, are provided. No wonder the Arabs disbelieve our talk about philanthropy.

But what the State will not, the Church must do; and I should be ashamed to hint that this Church of England was not rich enough and liberal enough to do all that is required. Many individuals, many congregations, many schools have come forward to help us in our work for the children by maintaining each one or more of our orphan scholars. In like way for the adults—we must feed them, and clothe them, and maintain them until they get strength and heart enough to work for themselves. An Arab always reckons the first year of a new-come slave as a loss. At first body and mind are so broken that there is not strength if there were will, nor will if there were strength. We must teach them to trust us, and we must try to set, not the body only, but the spirit free also. Nothing yet has ever uprooted slavery except Christianity. Nothing else will destroy it in Africa. Nothing else will destroy it in a man's heart. You may knock off his fetters, but ships of war and soldiers can never make him really free.

Just as the outward life of an African is full of fear and uncertainty, so his inward life is all fear and uncertainty too. The East Coast Africans are not idolaters; they all believe in God, but they think of Him as too great and too far off to care individually for them. Their whole thoughts are full of evil spirits and malicious witchcraft. A man gropes his way through his life, peopling the darkness round him with fearful shapes, and on the continual look-out for some omen, or for some man who, as he supposes, knows more than he does of the invisible world, to give him some faltering guidance. His life is dark, his death is darker still. His friends dare not even let it be known where his body is laid, lest some evil use should be made of it. No man in the whole world has more need of inward strengthening and comfort, and no man in the whole world has less of it. To talk of giving such a man what he wants most, by getting a few years of work out of him, and then sending him adrift among the dregs of a colonial town to die, as he very often does prematurely, of some disease engendered by the change of climate, is surely ignorance, or folly, or worse.

If, on the other hand, we can give him a new home in his own land, in which his freedom will be assured to him, and he will be taught lovingly to use it as a Christian, and so in the very face of his oppressors to be a living witness of our charity and our faith—a Christian freeman instead of a heathen slave—then we need never fear that our motives will be misconstrued, or our good intentions perverted. It was with the thought of founding such a home that Bishop Tozer bought our land at Mbweni, and when we began to recover from the effects of the hurricane I bought more, and Mr. West, out of his own means, added more; and we have now the beginnings of our Christian village of freed men there, not more than fifty perhaps as yet, but waiting only your approval and your liberality to expand into its due proportions.

Then again, when we found that the old slave market in Zanzibar, the last in the world, was to be used no longer for its old abominable purpose, for what should it be used? The evil spirit was driven out, what spirit should dwell there? The English State had done its part, it remained for the Church to do hers. What place could be so appropriate for the preaching of the gospel of liberty as this, where liberty had been so long unknown? So our good friend West came forward and purchased it for God. There is now the church, already showing its fair proportions, and the schools, already filled with scholars, and the hospital waits only for English alms to build it.

We did not begin to raise the material church without laying first the foundations of the true Church. I began my vernacular preaching in the old slave market, and soon the room was filled to overflowing with listeners, and the tracts and papers we were able to print were eagerly snatched from my hands. Africa is ready, if only England be ready too. Look on the two pictures—rows of men, women, and children, sitting and standing, and salesmen and purchasers passing in and out among them, examining them, handling them, chaffering over them, bandying their filthy jokes about them, and worse scenes still going on in all the huts around ; and then, in the same spot, see instead the priest and preacher, the teacher, the physician, the nurse, the children, crowding to be taught, the grown men coming to hear of God and Christ, the sick and suffering finding help and health. Look at these two pictures, and is it not a blessed and a glorious change, and is it not worth a life to have made it possible?

But all this is only on the very edge of our work. Bishop Mackenzie's grave is some three hundred miles inland, and he only touched the coast regions. Beyond and beyond lie nation after nation, until the mind is overwhelmed by the vastness of the work before us. How are these nations ever to hear the good news that we have to tell them? The first starting of this Mission seemed a great undertaking, but its scale was altogether inadequate to the work. We want such a Mission to each of the great nations, and why should we not send one? Because Englishmen are poor? Or are English Churchmen too few? Be it so, then here are our native scholars—the cheapest and the best helpers that we could have for this work. Some of them are now preaching and catechising, some are busy in our school-work, and many more would be able to help in our inland mission.

My plan is to cut up our work into manageable portions. I think we may take it for certain that we have not to do with broken fragments of tribes, or with little petty groups of people isolated either by distance or language one from another. There seem to be nations, it may be several millions each, speaking the same language, and occupying countries which are to be measured hundreds of miles in either direction. Our East Africans are not nomads, dwelling in a wilderness or a desert, but settled cultivators who would gladly remain for many generations in one place. Each of these nations ought at least to have its own church, and its own bishop and clergy.

As our preparation for this, we propose to send up first a small party of a few men of good judgment, to make acquaintance with the chiefs, and look through the country, to find the healthiest, most acceptable, and most central spot on which to make our chief settlement. As Africa is now we shall have to fix the site of future cities, as the monks did in England, and the English missionaries in Germany. People will soon gather round us, and, if we choose our place well, there they will remain.

First of all, we will set up a great central school for the people of that language, and then whilst preachers go out from it to reach every part of the tribe, we will send up, as they can employ them, artificers and workmen who will teach the natives all that our civilization can give them. Thus a centre of light and life will be formed, and from it that whole people may be enlightened.

We have such a centre begun at Magila for the Shambalas. We are forming a party to go up and work amongst the Yaos, the Ajawa of the early days of the Mission, who now hold all the country in which Bishop Mackenzie made his first attempt.

Between the Yaos and the coast there is one great nation —the Gindos, who are for the present altogether disorganised by the ravages of the Maviti. We must try to plant a station amongst them. Then there are the Zaramos and the Zegulas, near the coast, the Nyassas and Bisas on the other side of Lake Nyassa, and the various tribes up to and beyond the Nyamwezis, all and each ready to receive us, and would gladly have us amongst them.

But how is such a work is this to be done? It is a question which you and I can well answer if we will. The question is not how can it be done, but, who will join in it? We have had hitherto four or five workers, we want twenty or thirty at the very least. We have raised hitherto some £2,000 a year, we want £10,000 for such a work as we ought to do. I do not think money will be wanting where work is actually being done, but I mean to leave the raising of money entirely to those in England who desire the good of Africa. I have very much more upon my mind than I can well attend to, of actual mission work. I shall render a full account of how all moneys are spent, and will take care that they are made to go as far as possible; but I will not accept the post of head collector, or attempt to organise a scheme for supporting the

Mission. If we are starved for lack of funds, the fault will lie with those who stay at home, and not with those in Africa. Every one, whose heart is touched, is, by that very fact, bound to help and gather help. The Propagation Society will receive money for us, and those who write to me in Zanzibar will have an answer. I do not ask people to help me, I ask them to feel the call from God to do something for Africa, and by me, or by any other agency they like, to do it.

We have a continent to work upon where chaos still reigns, both in the social and the spiritual world. We have the reproach of ages of cruelty and neglect to wipe out. We have the key of the gate of heaven, and millions are waiting for us to open to them. Christian men and women, come yourselves and help them. If you cannot come, seek out and send your best and dearest, that their glory may be yours. If you have money, give it; and that not in little driblets, but as God has given it to you. Do not wait to be canvassed, but canvass others yourselves. Above all, send your hearts with us, and, as you stand in spirit on the edge of that great continent of darkness, do for it with all your might whatever the whispers of God's Spirit may suggest.

CHAPTER X.

RETURN TO ZANZIBAR AND WALK TO NYASSALAND.

WHEN the bishopric had been accepted by Dr. Steere, the Rev. A. N. West had returned to Zanzibar to take charge of the Mission for six months.

Till within a fortnight of his death he had seemed remarkably well, and wrote in November, 1874, pleading for the extension of the operations of the Mission, and hoping that he might be able to remain in its service.

He died, however, quite suddenly on Christmas Day, and Bishop Steere received the news by telegram from Aden, on January 25th, just before his advance guard of new fellow-workers sailed under the leadership of the Rev. E. S. Randolph. Writing to Mr. Randolph the same evening, the Bishop says:—

> We have as yet no particulars, but we know how uncertain his life was at all times. The souls of the righteous are in the hands of God, and perhaps such a day, and in such a work, he would himself have chosen.
>
> Death had been very near him under very different circumstances, and he lived with the thought of it before him. It is a very heavy loss to us, and I scarcely know as yet what to think.

The first question for me is whether I am not bound to break off all engagements, and go out by the next mail to join your ship at Suez.

Luckily, there is time to telegraph a few lines of comfort and promise. I need not ask your prayers for the work, and especially for me, to whom all things seemed yesterday so full of unalloyed promise; but our work on earth is action and not lamentation, specially not for the blessed.

The Bishop finally decided to go overland to Brindisi, and so to catch up Mr. Randolph at Suez, and left England on February 11th, 1875.

He was present that very afternoon at a large meeting at Cambridge, and slipped away quietly as soon as he had finished his own speech to catch his train, few even of those upon the platform being aware till after the meeting why it was that he had left.

At this point in the life of Bishop Steere it is difficult for the writer of a Memoir to draw the line between the main facts of his life, and the story of the Mission of which the Bishop was now the head, and it may be added, the heart and the soul. He proceeds to the best of his power to state concisely the events which followed Dr. Steere's consecration to the bishopric. With much to try him and weigh him down, the next few years were perhaps the brightest and happiest of his life.

Bishop Steere arrived in Zanzibar early in March, and he had scarcely settled himself to work when he was offered a cargo, which he accepted, of forty-eight slaves of all ages.

In April, the Rev. J. P. Farler and five laymen arrived; in May, the Rev. C. A. James and another lay-helper; and in June, the Rev. Forbes Capel.

The Bishop was now surrounded by a staff more numerous than had yet mustered at Zanzibar, sufficient to enable him to strengthen and extend the work of the Mission.

Accordingly on July 7th, the Bishop, the Rev. J. P. Farler, and Messrs. Bellville, Beardall, and Moss, with Acland, one of the native readers, and five or six boys from the Mission house, started for Magila, of which Mr. Farler is now Archdeacon.

Francis Mabruki, the native deacon, had been sent on in advance to get things in order, the station having been for some months unoccupied.

"We made a good passage," wrote the Bishop, "and had a pleasant walk, everyone on the road asking us, Is it peace?"

"As soon as our arrival at Magila was known, we had swarms of visitors, several head-men offering us useful gifts.

"We found Mr. Midgley's house quite habitable, and the main road up to the house, which he had made in good order.

"The day after our arrival, Farler and I climbed up to the top of the nearest mountain, and surveyed the country, and talked over our plans. We saw villages too many to be counted, and in all nooks of the mountain-side little groups of huts and plots of cultivated ground."

Such was the humble commencement of the second attack upon the African mainland, in the Usambara country, now so flourishing and prosperous a centre of work.

Having established Mr. Farler and those who were to be associated with him at Magila, the

Bishop returned to Zanzibar, and began to make preparations for his journey to the Nyassa country, with the view of finding suitable positions, among the Yaos, if possible, for mission-stations, and a very hearty anniversary festival of the Mission was held on St. Barthlomew's Day, thirty-eight converts being baptized; Chuma and Susi[1] were among the guests at dinner.

Shortly before sunset the cemetery was consecrated. Hymns were sung in procession round the ground,—"When our heads are bowed with woe," at starting, and "Jesus lives," at the conclusion.

Flowers had been placed by loving hands on the graves of the departed members of the Mission.

The idea of planting a village of freed slaves in the centre of Africa, was one which had been first promulgated during Bishop Steere's recent visit to England; it was hailed with enthusiam by those who bore in mind the lines originally laid down by the supporters of the Universities' Mission. There was a universal desire to see one more attempt made to reach the tribes surrounding Lake Nyassa, and it was curious to note how, when Bishop Steere roughly sketched out his plan of action, public opinion had eagerly risen to meet his suggestion half way. Feeling the importance of the step he was about to take, Bishop Steere's preparations for the expedition were made with the greatest deli-

---

[1] Susi was Chuma's companion during Dr. Livingstone's last years of travel, and they brought the great traveller's body from Lake Bangweolo to Zanzibar, and attended the funeral in Westminster Abbey. Chuma died in 1883. Susi was baptized in Christ Church, Zanzibar, in 1886.

beration and care. He omitted nothing that was likely to ensure success, though only experience could prove what was really most needed. An extract from a letter written to the "Guardian" by the Bishop, shows the spirit in which he started on the Nyassa expedition :—

By the time this reaches you I shall be, if God will, well on my way to the Lake Nyassa with the companions England has sent me. They are, as was said of English soldiers, the best in the world, but very, very few. By the end of the year we shall be preparing for a second expedition. I, or rather not I, but Christ our Master, asks for volunteers, especially clergymen and medical men, for His great work in this centre of grief and darkness. We are going in faith: we have not yet the funds to justify us in attempting so much; but England is full of money, and there are many who could singly give us all we want for any one station. I will not make any boasting as to what we intend, but whatever becomes a Christian and an English Churchman that we each hope to do. While we thus go inward to reach if possible the source of that flow of blood, which has so long desolated Africa, we leave here on the coast the home which we have formed for those whose old homes have been hopelessly destroyed,—I mean our settlement for released slaves. The work grows upon us: we have now nearly 250 who have no support except the charity of England administered by us: of these far the larger part are children, but there are some ninety adults, who want a new start in life and Christian teaching. We must have land and buildings and personal help, and we want (say) £2,000 to enable us even now to meet the case as we ought. The Church Missionary Society are at work on a grand scheme at Mombas, and we would gladly maintain a friendly rivalry with them; at least, we hope our friends will not let us lag far behind; ten times more than we both can do is wanted for the work of this Continent. We have touched the feelings even of the Mohammedan coast men, and we ask the means to deepen and make permanent the impression. This is the account a native woman was overheard lately giving to a companion, of our preaching in the old slave market in Zanzibar: "They go into town and read and preach, and then they fall on their knees and say, 'God be merciful to us sinners.'" Who would not like to have a share in such work as ours?

Three or four days after the consecration of the cemetery, the Nyassa expedition left Zanzibar in one of the Union Company's mail steamers, and was landed at Lindi on the second day afterwards. The Bishop was accompanied by the Rev. C. A. James, Mr. A. Bellville, and Mr. Beardall, the party whom he hoped to place in a permanent station at Mataka's town near the Lake, with about twenty Zanzibar porters under Chuma and Susi. They were well received by the Governor of Lindi, but instead of aiding them, the people of Lindi hindered them by vexatious delays, and by promises that were never intended to be fulfilled.

Dreading the effect of inaction on his companions, the Bishop sent them on two little exploring journeys, but Mr. James returned unhappily so seriously ill from his exploration, that the Bishop could only send him on to Zanzibar, accompanied by Mr. Beardall, for advice. He reached Natal, but a bright and promising career ended abruptly in his early death.

The party being thus broken up and the season rapidly advancing, the Bishop had to determine what to do himself, and decided to push on alone. "I thought it due to our friends at home that I, at all events, should see the country, and open the way for another expedition. I was anxious, too, that the coast men should not have a triumph over us, as that would have made any future journey still more difficult. Even so, it was not till the 1st of November, a full month too late, that I was able to make a real start. I had about forty men as porters under the command of Chuma as captain of the expedition, and two coast men, said to have great experience as guides. These last turned out to be merely expensive ornaments, but Chuma was throughout the soul of the expedition, and success without him would have been all but impossible."

The Bishop continues :—" The coast settlements end at Ching'ong'o, some ten or twelve miles from Lindi. Thence we plunged into a thickly grown forest, and after a long morning reached Lake Lutamba, a fine sheet of water about five miles long and two or three wide, with high, wooded hills all round. We were now fairly in the Mwera country, and stopped at a village close by the Lake.

"We were nine days of slow travelling in passing through the Mwera villages, which lie along a fine range of high hills, with many spurs and sub-ridges, in general direction north and south. Thence we passed to our first stretch of uninhabited forest, and were six days before we emerged upon the belt of villages near the Rovuma.

"The Mwera forest is very level, and most part of it wet at the wet season, and very scant of water at the dry. We were passing just at the driest time, and had to arrange our marches so as each night to encamp near water.

"There is something very solemn in these huge forests. The men have a superstition against shouting and singing as they do at other times, and the bare feet make no tramp, so that the only sounds one hears are when they pass the word to avoid a stump, or a stone in the path, or an elephant's footmark, which means a round hole a foot or so across, and deep as may happen, or, most to be shunned of all, a line of ants across the path.

"The approach to the Rovuma is marked by the sudden rising of enormous masses of granite rock, often of grotesque shapes, and seemingly strewed about by accident. The country we had passed had not always been so bare of people; it forms part of the great waste made by the raids of the Maviti and Gwangwaras. We found the first village we came to inhabited by Gindo fugitives from near Kilwa, who, being timid folk, are terribly bullied by an otherwise insignificant Yao chief named Golilo. They begged us to make him a present, lest he should revenge our not doing so on them.

"As we passed on we heard that a coast caravan had kidnapped one of the villagers—the first trace of the slave trade.

"By the roadside I saw an iron furnace, hollowed out of an ant hill. It was not at work, but there was some ore close by prepared for smelting, of which I got specimens. The smelters are Makuas, but the Mweras are the best smiths.

"We had just crossed a broad dry river-bed, when we met what we took at first for a caravan, but it turned out to be a fugitive chief and his followers who had fled from the other side of the river. They told us that the Gwangwaras were out on a raid before us, that some hunters in searching for game had seen them and given the alarm, so they were fleeing they could not tell whither.

"We went on to a village of some three hundred houses, under a Makua chief. Livingstone had seen the same people on the other side of the Rovuma; their chief Makochero had moved to this place.

"From Makochero's we came to the Rovuma.[1] It was then at the lowest, and at the spot without much current, the whole bed studded with rocks and sand-banks and reedy islands. It was fordable in many places and nowhere deep. A more unpromising stream for navigation could hardly be; for some distance a little higher up no water was visible, only a waste of rocks and the sound of water rushing between them. We were three days more passing up the north bank, and crossed two large rivers, still flowing very low, which drain respectively the forest wastes that were once the Gindo and the Donde territories. We crossed at a place where the river was broad and still, but covering its whole bed, and looking more like the great river it really is. The water was nowhere more than three feet deep, and mostly but little

---

[1] It was in March, 1861, that Dr. Livingstone brought Bishop Mackenzie in the *Pioneer* for five days up the Rovuma, hoping to ascend much nearer to Lake Nyassa. Had the party had a smaller boat, and been able to get 100 miles further up the river, and found the road thence well open to the Lake, the Mission would probably have commenced its work on the East instead of the South of Lake Nyassa. Who can tell with what results?—See "Memoir of Bishop Mackenzie," p. 258.—ED.

above the knee. The men walked straight across, and I was cleverly ferried over a little higher, where there was more current, in a very small canoe."

Having crossed the Rovuma, the Bishop entered the Yao forest, and pursued his journey unmolested, but through a country from which the alarm of war seemed to be rarely absent. After journeying for several days, a large caravan, exporting tobacco and slaves, was met, the leaders of which informed the Bishop that he was five days from Mataka's, his destination, that the road was clear, but that he would find no more villages. This was serious news, for his provisions were nearly exhausted; so that before he and his followers arrived at Mataka's, they were not only very tired but very hungry also.

When nearing his journey's end the Bishop writes:—" The night after crossing the Luatize we soon got good fires and a plentiful supper, and woke the next day on a good specimen of a May morning, bright and fresh and sparkling. This beginning of the rains is the spring of the tropical year, the trees are coming into fresh leaf, flowers are everywhere showing themselves. Among the brightest at this time were the gladioli, scarlet, white, lilac, puce, lemon, and orange. No one in Yao land need fear to want flowers about Christmas.

" We were now close to Mataka's villages, and slept in one of them on the night of the 8th of December, having made twenty-seven full days of travelling, the remaining eleven being days and half-days of rest and provision-seeking. We rounded a great mass of granite rising some five hundred feet nearly perpendicularly, and were immediately in cultivated land.

"We stopped at a village on the brow of a hill, where lived Nyenje, sister's son to Mataka, and, therefore, by Yao customs of inheritance, his next heir. He gave us a goat, and we revelled in abundance.

"The view from Nyenje's house is very fine; it looks down a broad valley, from five to ten miles wide, fringed by fantastic craggy hills, and studded with villages and towns, several of them with three or four thousand inhabitants. All these are Mataka's subjects.

"The morning after our arrival at Nyenje's, we were all refreshed and in good spirits, and started early for Mataka's own town, with flags flying, a small gong making its music, and every man's gun loaded, to fire in honour of the chief. Besides, the evening before they had all had 'their backs straightened'—a necessary operation at the end of every job in Africa—by a present of a red cap each.

"We crossed two narrow valleys, and round the shoulder of a great hill came upon the broader one in which, in a town called Mwembe, Mataka has now for a good many years resided.[1] One saw the effect of this prolonged residence in the more careful cultivation, and the utter absence of trees. The Mwembe valley is as bare as any part of England,

[1] It is not a little interesting that at this very time the "Ilala," the first steam-boat that ever rode upon the Nyassa, was making her trial cruise under the charge of Gunner Young. Had the Bishop gone a little further he might have seen it with a good glass.

and the great hills around are largely cleared. Everything here is planted in ridges, which enables the people to bury the grass and rubbish as a sort of manure, and prevents the plants from being stunted by the baking of the dry season, during which the clayey soil becomes dry and hard as a stone.

"On entering into Mwembe, we blazed away a good deal of powder, and the town turned out in force to look at us. It was a new thing to me to see a genuine town crowd in Africa. Livingstone reckoned about a thousand houses in Mwembe, and it has not since diminished.

"The people have made a curious compromise with their old custom of moving away from the place when anyone dies. They build a new house close to the old one, and ridge up the clay and rubbish of the old walls into a small plantation of Indian corn. Every spare plot is planted, so that after the rains the town must look like a sea of green, with house-roofs floating upon it."

Mataka made the Bishop very welcome, and offered him the choice of two houses; and afterwards sent him presents. He professed to be quite willing to let missionaries settle at Mwembe, but afterwards preferred that they should settle nearer the Lake Nyassa, at Losewa. He declared that he only sold criminals into slavery, but it was certain that he sold his own slaves, and, when he could get them, the people of Makanjila, his great enemy.

The Bishop stayed at Mwembe about a fortnight, explaining "our plans and wishes, he says," "as widely as possible, and speaking as I could about our great work. Some evidently believed not a word of what I said, some heard with more or less of interest, all promised me a welcome if I returned. I found that I could make myself understood very frequently in Yao, and that, though full of deficiencies, the collections for a handbook of the language printed for us by the Christian Knowledge Society was as a whole very correct and useful. Mataka's women guessed all the enigmas at the end, and brought their companions again and again to hear them.

"It seems to me morally certain that the Yaos will be Christians or Mohammedans before very long, and I think the question will turn a good deal upon which is the first to write and read their language."

The Bishop hoped to have gone down to the coast lightly burdened and very quickly, but his men, finding that he had but few burdens, bought such a quantity of tobacco for themselves that they were more heavily laden than before. The Yaos use their tobacco almost exclusively in the form of snuff, but in Zanzibar it is specially valued for chewing, and commands a higher price than any other sort. There is no legitimate commerce between the Yaos and the coast except in tobacco and bhang, and a very little ivory, the elephants being nearly all killed off. This want of other trade is probably the chief reason why the Yao chiefs cling so firmly to their slave traffic; the opening up of some new commerce would be the surest way of destroying the trade in human beings.

The final start from Mataka's villages was made on December 22nd, and the Rovuma was reached on the 1st of January. The river was unusually high, and overflowed all the adjacent lowlands; but it was crossed on January 7th at a place where the river flows in one channel, and is in breadth and current like the Thames at Westminster when the tide has begun to run out strongly. Two days more brought the party to the Mwera forest.

"It rained now," says the Bishop, "nearly every night and a few days, and we rushed through the Mwera forest, making two days less than in going up, chased by thunderstorms, which generally burst upon us just before sunset, by which time we were hutted in and prepared for them.

"Here we saw some of the horrors of the slave-trade, as we were close behind a caravan which had left in each day's journey one or more of its number cruelly murdered by the roadside, and the very last day before reaching the villages we came upon a man lying in the path in the very act of dying of hunger and fatigue. He was far beyond all help, and we could only watch his last sighs.

"Surely if there can be a holy war it would be one against a traffic which bears such fruits as these. If we had the means to hire and feed some hundred or two of men, to clear and plant, and build, and defend themselves if necessary, I think this line of trade at least might be finally closed; but it would be madness to attempt force unless one had ample means, and at least the passive support of the English Government."

In his journey the Bishop met nine caravans

representing from 1,500 to 2,000 slaves, and possibly some 10,000 for the whole year.

On January 16th the party was again among the Mweras, for whom the Bishop confesses a great liking, and who are a simple, quiet people, scarcely touched at all by coast influence, but no stay was made among them, as food was scarce and rain plentiful; and on January 21st the party walked again into Lindi, in very good condition, having been thirty-one days on the road from Mataka's, twenty-five of which were full days of marching, and the remaining six, days of resting and buying of food.

The Bishop heard of a shorter route to the Rovuma from Lindi which was even more level, but the coast men did not use it for fear of a Yao chief, who was said to be a captain of a band of robbers.

The country through which the Bishop passed has been the scene of terrible destruction during the last twenty years, and whole nations have practically disappeared. The Yaos are now in every sense the strongest in mind and body as well as in numbers.

The Mweras are even less united, every little group of huts being independent.

Concluding the account of his remarkable journey —remarkable in the way it was undertaken and carried out, and remarkable also in its results—the Bishop says:—" Old traders say that the road from Kilwa to the Nyassa used to lie entirely through an inhabited country where food of all sorts was fabulously abundant. East of Kilwa lay the Gindos, and south of them the Mweras; east of both these the Dondes, and then, on the lower Rovuma, Matambwes, and on the upper and along the Lake, Yaos. South and east of the Lake, Nyassas, and east of them again the Bisas, who were ardent traders, and used to send down caravans of their own to Kilwa.

"The great disturbers of this state of things were the Maviti or Mazitu, a Zulu army sent on an unsuccessful expedition, which, instead of returning to be decimated, went north, and found a new home round the north end of the Nyassa, where they plundered and burnt in all directions, even sending an army against Kilwa itself, and for the time stopping all trade. They were not great slave-dealers, but used to cut off the left hand of such captives as they did not kill. I saw many were thus mutilated.

"It is said that during the suspension of trade, some people called Magwangwara, from near Lufiji (of whom the Mission were to hear more in the future), came to Kilwa to ask why no cloth now came to them, and being told of the Maviti, promised at once to clear them out of the way, which they did so effectually that the Maviti are no longer dreaded. But the Gwangwaras, having felt their power, became still worse destroyers than the Maviti had been, and all the more so because they found that slaves were valuable merchandize in the eyes of Kilwa men. Their custom is to incorporate the more likely of their captives into their own tribes, the rest they offer for sale, and if they cannot get a good price they kill them. The

scattered remnants of the Gindos and Dondes were
an easy prey, and for a time the Zanzibar market
was full of Gindo slaves. The smaller Yao chiefs
could offer but little resistance, and though the
Gwangwaras have never ventured to cross a large
river, or to attack a village in the mountains, they
soon found they could easily cross the upper
Rovuma in the dry season, and so the country to
the north as well as that to the south of the river,
lay open to them. The few remains of the Gindos
flee backward and forward as they hear of the
approach of their dreaded enemies, and the few
Dondes left have generally taken to the trade of
thieving.

"The stoppage of the Kilwa slave-trade would
take away the motive of these Gwangwara raids,
and the existence of a city of refuge under men
bold enough to give them two or three crushing
defeats, would teach them not to treat their neighbours as cattle to be driven at their will. Now,
however, strong thieves get gunpowder as the price
of slaves, and the peaceable are deprived of their
only means of defence.

"The coast trade itself, in anything like its present dimensions, seems to be scarcely twenty years
old, corresponding, in fact, to the growth of Zanzibar as a centre of commerce. Yet it must have
been once of great extent, or Kilwa could not have
been the important city which the Portuguese
found it.

"In the Yao language there are a few words
which point to the old commercial relations with
the coast, especially the name for coast people,

which is merely the Arab name for Christians; this seems to show that at the coming of the Portuguese there was Arab influence enough among the Yaos to give them an Arab name. The trade died in their hands, and only in our own days is returning to its former importance. The same conclusion may be drawn from the vague acknowledgment of one God by all the nations between the great lakes and the sea. This is just the remnant of Mohammedan teaching which might be expected to survive, when that teaching was first forcibly suppressed at the fountain-head by a professed Christianity, and then allowed to wither away into forgetfulness, nothing really remaining except a distaste of visible idols.

"It is only on the young men of the present generation that Mohammedanism is beginning to exert a powerful influence, and this just in proportion as they are struggling into some kind of civilization. It is therefore much more felt by the principal Yao chiefs than by the smaller, or by the less advanced Mweras."

The Bishop returned to Zanzibar early in February 1876, having been detained some days at Lindi. His joy at having returned safely from his successful journey to Mataka's was sadly damped by the news of Mr. James's death, and by finding that of his clerical staff only two remained, Mr. Randolph at Zanzibar, and Mr. Farler at Magila.

Miss Marsh, also, who had not long joined the Mission, and who was proving most valuable in training the native girls, died of fever.

The bright hopes of settling on or near Lake

Nyassa were thus doomed to disappointment. The time had not yet come. To add to his troubles, at this time, Mr. Farler came to Zanzibar very unwell, but after some weeks of rest and medical care, was able to return to Magila.

The work of the Mission, under the direction of Mr. Randolph, had, happily, flourished in all its branches, and with the arrival of Miss Allen, since so well known, hospital work was begun.

Industrial occupations were largely developed in 1876. Laundries were established at Kiungani and Mbweni. At the carpenter's shop the quantity of work done had greatly increased, and gardening operations were commenced.

But the great event of the year was the official attack on Slaving. In April the Sultan of Zanzibar, influenced by the observations which the Bishop had made in his journey to Mataka's, and the vigorous efforts and representations of Dr. (now Sir John) Kirk, the English consul, issued two proclamations, one forbidding the sending of slaves by land from Kilwa to the north, and the other prohibiting the bringing down of slaves from the Nyassa districts.

"These," remarked Bishop Steere, "are the first steps towards a complete destruction of slavery itself. We have printed these proclamations in Arabic, English, and Swahili for distribution, and our work (*i.e.*, the printing) gets much praise from all quarters. It is the severest blow that has yet been aimed at this iniquitous traffic."

Some attempt at rebellion against these decrees was made at Kilwa by the people engaged in the slave-trade, but with the assistance of H.M.S.

"Thetis" it was promptly suppressed, and the chief instigators of it were brought prisoners to Zanzibar. The slave-trade was thus diverted and made more difficult, the first step to its suppression. It was not long before the Bishop's need of more clerical aid was supplied. In March the Rev. Chauncy Maples, accompanied by two laymen, Mr. C. Yorke and Mr. J. Williams, sailed for Zanzibar; and a few months afterwards Mr. W. Percival Johnson, a graduate of University College, Oxford, who had gained distinction both in the schools and on the river, joined the Mission. Mr. Johnson was ordained soon after his arrival at Zanzibar. In June, in company with Mr. Maples, the Bishop visited Magila, and found the Mission thriving. Mr. Farler had not only shown great zeal and wisdom in direct missionary work, but had also developed a power of giving medical help which had raised him high in favour with the natives.

In order to do justice to the scenery and features of the Usambara district, in which Magila forms the Mission headquarters, we refer our readers to Mr. Thomson's picturesque description of the country. "[1] Our path," he says, "led us into a perfect little tunnel. Picture to yourselves a circular space two hundred feet in diameter. Round it plant the densest forest you can realize. From every available point in the circle of trees hang manifold festoons of creepers, binding the branches into one unbroken mass of foliage. Fill the interstices between the trunks of the trees with greenest shrubbery. On the clear space build a number of mud huts, thatched

[1] "To the Central African Lakes and Back," pp. 45, 52.

with grass, and of all shapes—square, round, oval, composite—not one to be the same as another. Add some life to the scene by throwing in a few negroes, goats, and hens, and you have before you the little village of Madanga. Such is the normal type of village."

"We found Magila situated in a charming and populous district at the base of the mountains of Usambara. As we were eager to get some glimpse of the country we had come to see, we resolved in the afternoon to ascend to the top of a prominent peak which rose behind the Mission Station.

"It was a somewhat hard climb up three thousand feet, but the labour did not lessen the enjoyment. The whole mountain was covered with rich forest, with the exception of a few cleared spaces, where a number of natives had taken up their abode for greater security, and down its side dashed a succession of cascades half hidden by huge ferns and bananas. Imagine the pleasure of meeting among the former a number of old friends, notably the bracken.

"On Monday we began our march into the glorious Usambara mountains. It was indeed a marvellous forest. Every tree is a veritable giant, rising with bare trunk, as if struggling for the free air of heaven, to a height of from seventy to a hundred feet before branching, and then forming a parachute-shaped crown, through which the rays of the sun in vain attempted to penetrate. Little less gigantic than the trees were the inevitable creepers. None of your slender convolvuluses, or passion flowers, or ivies; but massive fellows, thick as a man's thigh, and two or three hundred feet in length, hanging aloft from tree to tree, or wriggling and twisting up their stems. Everything was strange, and grand, and colossal."

"The chapel," writes the Bishop, "is a small building, or rather room, of corrugated iron, with a thatched roof overhead to protect it from the sun. The house is a large square mud and stud erection, standing in a sort of terrace made of large stones, which Mr. Midgley collected and arranged with a strength and skill which is very wonderful. How he moved some of the stones we could scarcely imagine. The deep eaves make a wide, cool corridor all round. Here morning prayers were said and I preached. In the afternoon the *Dies Iræ* was sung as a Litany, and Francis Mabruki catechized and addressed the people.

"We had many and long talks about the work, and saw Mr. Farler's patients, who came in crowds daily for medicine and advice; and heard his classes, which he conducts with the help of Francis Mabruki and Acland Schera. Mr. Farler is very skilful in employing them as interpreters and exponents, and so they themselves are benefited by their share in the work.

"He pays daily visits to the neighbouring villages, and makes long excursions as he has opportunity. The reputation of his cures and his preaching has extended far and wide. Among the catechumens are several men of importance, and all the rest are friendly."

While at Magila the Bishop confirmed five lads from the school at Zanzibar, only one of the six who had come up with Mr. Farler having failed to satisfy him of his earnestness, and admitted eleven catechumens, who had all given up wearing charms and using spells, and were already known as followers of the Mission teaching. In giving the result of his observation, the Bishop says: "The only opposition to be met with is the Mohammedan influence. The whole country, which may roughly be defined as that north and east of the Pangani River, seems quite ready to give a friendly hearing to all we have to say, and with good men, and enough of them, I see no reason why it should not all become Christian."

CHAPTER XI.

Archdeacon Maples' Letter.

A FEW weeks before the visit to Magila detailed in the preceding chapter, the Rev. Chauncy Maples, now Archdeacon of Nyassa, had arrived in Zanzibar, and perhaps this will be the best place to insert the "Recollections of Bishop Steere" kindly contributed by him to this Memoir.

"It is to me a pleasant and congenial task to place on record some reminiscences of Bishop Steere. Nor do I find it difficult to call to mind and note down many recollections of one whose gifts were so brilliant, whose individuality was so marked, and whose genius was so versatile.

"Indeed his was one of those characters that never fail to stamp upon the minds of all those who come in contact with them such an impression as, while life lasts, is never likely to fade; a character, in a word, as far removed from commonplace, and as superior in most respects to those who moved around him, as it would be possible to find anywhere amongst contemporary Englishmen.

"My first acquaintance with the Bishop began with a correspondence I held with him shortly after his consecration, in connection with my wish to join the work, over which he had been called to preside.

"I wrote from Oxford, and begged for an interview at his earliest convenience. He in reply mentioned a time when he expected to be in Wells, holding a meeting, and preaching there.

"This was in the autumn of 1874, though I have no note of the exact day or month, when in answer to his letter, I went down to Wells to see him. The meeting was held in an ancient crypt which, I believe, now forms a part of the Bishop's palace.

"I remember well my first impressions of Bishop Steere's personal appearance as he sat behind the Bishop of the Diocese, while the latter was introducing him to the meeting in an opening speech.

"I first thought how very unlike any Bishop I have ever seen he is, and struggled against a feeling of disappointment at what seemed to me then his insignificant and plain appearance. A closer scrutiny, however, quickly dispelled these first impressions, as I scanned more diligently the strongly marked features of his massive face.

"Comeliness, it is true, there was none, an unusually long upper lip, and large straight mouth combining to impart a rigid severity to a countenance, which, while it not unfrequently was lit up with an expression of singular sweetness, could not with any truthfulness be spoken of as handsome.

"But if his face lacked beauty, it was easy to trace in it something far more indicative of the great qualities of its possessor. Firm will, indomitable resolution, and force of character were, I could see, all written as plainly as possible about his mouth

CHAPTER XI.

ARCHDEACON MAPLES' LETTER.

A FEW weeks before the visit to Magila detailed in the preceding chapter, the Rev. Chauncy Maples, now Archdeacon of Nyassa, had arrived in Zanzibar, and perhaps this will be the best place to insert the "Recollections of Bishop Steere" kindly contributed by him to this Memoir.

"It is to me a pleasant and congenial task to place on record some reminiscences of Bishop Steere. Nor do I find it difficult to call to mind and note down many recollections of one whose gifts were so brilliant, whose individuality was so marked, and whose genius was so versatile.

"Indeed his was one of those characters that never fail to stamp upon the minds of all those who come in contact with them such an impression as, while life lasts, is never likely to fade; a character, in a word, as far removed from commonplace, and as superior in most respects to those who moved around him, as it would be possible to find anywhere amongst contemporary Englishmen.

"My first acquaintance with the Bishop began with a correspondence I held with him shortly after his consecration, in connection with my wish to join the work, over which he had been called to preside.

"I wrote from Oxford, and begged for an interview at his earliest convenience. He in reply mentioned a time when he expected to be in Wells, holding a meeting, and preaching there.

"This was in the autumn of 1874, though I have no note of the exact day or month, when in answer to his letter, I went down to Wells to see him. The meeting was held in an ancient crypt which, I believe, now forms a part of the Bishop's palace.

"I remember well my first impressions of Bishop Steere's personal appearance as he sat behind the Bishop of the Diocese, while the latter was introducing him to the meeting in an opening speech.

"I first thought how very unlike any Bishop I have ever seen he is, and struggled against a feeling of disappointment at what seemed to me then his insignificant and plain appearance. A closer scrutiny, however, quickly dispelled these first impressions, as I scanned more diligently the strongly marked features of his massive face.

"Comeliness, it is true, there was none, an unusually long upper lip, and large straight mouth combining to impart a rigid severity to a countenance, which, while it not unfrequently was lit up with an expression of singular sweetness, could not with any truthfulness be spoken of as handsome.

"But if his face lacked beauty, it was easy to trace in it something far more indicative of the great qualities of its possessor. Firm will, indomitable resolution, and force of character were, I could see, all written as plainly as possible about his mouth and chin, while the merry twinkle of the eye revealed the fine play of wit and humour, which I afterwards found so notable in him. And last, though not least, the overhanging brows, and the broad forehead told unmistakably of the keen intellect and mental power he had already turned to such good account in the service of the Mission.

"He spoke for about an hour, and told in simple, straightforward language the story of the Mission from its foundation. Yet, although there were no rhetorical adornments about the speech, no vivid colouring, no striking appeals to the imagination and emotions, I can unhesitatingly say I have never, before or since, listened to a speech in which earnestness, simplicity, and true eloquence were so happily blended.

"At its close I was introduced to the Bishop, and in a few kind words he thanked me for coming forward to join his band of workers, and bade me God-speed. The next day he addressed the students of the college, and spoke of what used to be known amongst us as the 'three years' system,' urging them to send forth some of their number to cast in their lot with us. We parted that day, and the next time I saw him was in S. Paul's Cathedral, when he occupied the pulpit at one of the winter Sunday-evening services, and was pleading there on behalf of the Mission.

"It was then that I noticed for the first time some of the main characteristics of his preaching. He was wont to close his eyes, and, in entire independence of all MS., or notes, would pour out his thoughts in one continuous flow of calm, unimpassioned language, rarely pausing to begin a new train of ideas, never at a loss for a word, and never changing one.

"Monotonous as was his voice, its very monotony seemed a harmony well suited to the invariably even progression of the thought and ideas worked out in each sermon.

"When dwelling on eternal verities, and even when treating of them most dogmatically, it was wonderful how convincingly and clearly he was able to set forth the didactic element in the dogma, bringing home to the conscience and the heart the higher mysteries of the faith, in language at once most lucid and most forcible.

"Many, I think, will have felt how powerful those sermons were to impress upon the mind the thought of all doubt and difficulty, and misgiving, finding their resolution in God's revelation of Himself through His Word. Such a sermon as that in the first series of his published 'Sermon Notes'[1]— entitled 'Christ the great I Am'—abundantly illustrates this particular point.

"I saw the Bishop many times between December, 1874, and February in the following year, at 31, Euston Square, where, at that time, when in London, he usually resided.

"On one occasion he invited some six or eight of us, who were about to join him in Africa, to have tea and spend the evening with him.

"He seemed then abounding in health and good spirits, and put us all at our ease at once by his

---

[1] Second Edition, G. Bell and Sons, London, 1886, (p. 127).

kindly, cheerful manner, and his quiet fun; talking with us all in turns, and drawing each one of us out in his own clever way.

"One of the party, somewhat given to pedantry, managed to introduce into the conversation some allusion to Pizarro. 'Ah,' said another, who has long since laid down his life in Africa, 'Pizarro, Pizarro,—one of Dickens's characters, wasn't he? But I am so stupid at remembering names!'

"At this we nearly all manifested a disposition to giggle, though anxious not to do so for fear of hurting one whose character merited and had won the respect of us all.

"Bishop Steere immediately came to the rescue, seeing how discomfited the poor fellow was beginning to look, and said humourously, 'Ah! J—— I don't think we are likely to see the shades of Mr. Pickwick and the conquerors of Peru hob-nobbing together, are we?' This little sally, so opportunely ventured, and so adroitly answering the ludicrous question, without drawing attention to the ignorance, or aberration of memory that had begotten it, prevented any further awkwardness, for it enabled us to give vent to our laughter, by turning it into another channel, while the Bishop quickly went on to some other subject of conversation, having effectually laid the ghost of Pizarro for the rest of the evening.

"Soon after this the Bishop was recalled suddenly to Africa by the news of Mr. West's death, and when I next met him, it was in Zanzibar at the beginning of May, 1876.

"At that time he was living at the boys' school,

Kiungani, going in on Sundays and Thursdays to Mkunazini (the town house), to celebrate there, and to conduct the Sunday-evening service in English, for the European residents in the town.

"Every day he used, soon after breakfast, to repair to the printing-office, where he remained till nearly noon, revising and correcting proof-sheets of his various Swahili translations, setting up the type himself not unfrequently, and often sewing together the pages of the little pamphlets and tracts, which were handed to him wet from the press.

"Tradespeople in the town would occasionally send in bills and prospectuses to be printed, or Seyed Burghash would require a *menu* card arranged and printed. At the time of which I am speaking, Bishop Steere used almost invariably to attend to these cards and prospectuses himself, so anxious was he that everything done in the printing-office should be done well, and that nothing should issue from it but what would be creditable to us.

"After the midday meal he would bring a whole pile of freshly-printed matter into the general sitting-room, and handing round a few needles and some thread, would soon begin stitching together the tracts and books with a rapidity we vainly tried to equal.

"Then, as he plied his needle, and we laggingly followed the example of his industry, he would encourage us to ask questions on matters linguistic and missionary, for which he was always ready with a wise and satisfying answer. In the afternoon he would again take his place in the printing-office, where he stayed until after school hours were over.

"In the evening he nearly always walked into town to inspect the church-building, and to give the clerk of the works and the chief masons directions for the morrow.

"Here, too, he was in his element, as he climbed from part to part of the gradually rising edifice, here shifting the measuring lines for a string-course; there helping to adjust the centreing for a window, or an arch; there, again, ordering the demolition, and re-erection from its base of a pillar, which, when almost at the height where it would have been topped by its capital, had begun to wander from the perpendicular.

"On these occasions, visitors would often look inside the church, and were glad to have pointed out to them by the Bishop the details of its construction.

"I remember one of these visitors happening to be a certain officer from one of H.B.M.'s cruisers, who had obtained a disagreeable notoriety in Zanzibar for his dictatorial manner, and habit of laying down the law on every subject, in total disregard of his own ignorance.

"Bishop Steere took good-humouredly all the disparaging remarks he made on the building, the while watching his opportunity to silence him quietly. After a time our officer remarked, in his most superior and lofty manner, 'Of course you are aware that the ancient Greeks were careful never to make the lines in their architecture quite straight, and that is why all modern buildings, not following this rule, fail so egregiously in their effect.' 'Indeed,' answered the Bishop at once, 'I was not aware of it; but if it be so, we can satisfy the most fastidious Greek taste in this respect in our church here, for my native workmen have never been guilty of building anything in a straight line yet, and are not likely ever to do so.'

"Towards the end of June, the Bishop planned a visit to Magila, proposing that I and another should accompany him thither. Before the day of our start, he went to Mbweni, and there held the first adult baptism that took place in the Mission, at which some eight couples were baptized. Walking back to Kiungani in the evening, he spoke of the happy event of the day, saying that a day like that was ample repayment for the years of anxious preparation and trials that had gone before it.

"I think it was the next day that we started for Magila. We embarked on a dhow from a point a few miles north of the town, and becoming becalmed soon after we had sailed, lay awake for hours to enjoy the bright moonlight of the tropical night, now listening to the Swahili tales which the sailors were telling each other, and now again conversing on a variety of subjects, in which the Bishop's interest vied with my own.

"It was then that I first discovered his fondness and taste for music, shown in his real appreciation of those of the works of the great masters with which he was acquainted.

"I remember humming over for him at his request some of the chief airs from Mozart's operas, a particular favourite being the bass solo from the Zauberflöte, — 'In these holy shades,' which he spoke of as affecting him to tears, whenever he heard it. Of his musical taste I shall have something more to say presently.

"Another subject we discussed, I remember, was S. Paul's shipwreck, and I was astonished to find that, although he had not read the famous little book by Smith, of Jordanhill, he seemed to have discovered for himself as much as is to be found in the pages of that exhaustive work, 'The Voyage and Shipwreck of S. Paul.'

"And this was characteristic of him, for though in his later years he read little, he never seemed to be behind the thought and ideas of the age, for lack of what new books could tell him. He was more independent of such aids to information, and to the expansion of the mental faculties, than any man I have ever known, so that one never felt inclined to say, 'This man reads nothing,' although to have said so would have been merely to state what was the fact,[1] so far as my observation extended.

"The Bishop's kindness and consideration for younger men were apparent on our walk from Pangani (the landing-place for the Usambara country), to Magila, for he would not allow me, as one not yet used to the climate, to carry a heavy bag of dollars which we were taking up to the

[1] A friend of the Mission, who heard the Bishop preach in Christ Church Cathedral, Oxford, on his visit in 1882, states that the sermon pointed out in a masterly way the best methods of answering modern sceptics. The seeming contradiction is perhaps best explained by referring to the Bishop's own statement in a letter to Lord Justice Fry, page 18, line 30, of this Memoir; and by the comments of an old friend, page 54, line 8.

station, and which we did not like to trust the porters with. He cheerfully slung the bag across his own shoulders, and trudged off in front of us all.

"In the villages where we stopped for the night, he preached informally to the throng of people who came to stare at us, admirably adapting to their dull apprehensions, such truths about God and the soul as were best calculated to set them thinking, and to rouse their consciences. We reached Magila early in the morning of Trinity Sunday in time for the Bishop to preach the sermon at matins. Many of the principal natives were brought up to him afterwards, for all of whom he had a friendly greeting.

"We stayed at Magila rather more than a fortnight the Bishop being in radiant spirits all the time, in consequence, I think, of the evident success of Mr. Farler's work.

"In the forenoon of each day he was busy translating S. John's Epistles, and by way of varying his task, he showed us how to plait grass for thatching, not being satisfied with the way in which the houses were being roofed at Magila at this time.

"His way of showing how it was to be done, was to sit down with bundles of grass all round him, and a supply of bark-rope, and then work away for several hours at a stretch himself.

"No one could fail to bend himself to the work, with such an example before him, however mean an occupation grass-tying might have seemed previously.

"Wherever Bishop Steere saw anything to be done, he invariably did it, without waiting to consider whether it was within his province, and utterly refusing to regard anything as beneath his attention.

"Thus it was, that to us who knew him, it seemed as natural to see him plying a chisel, or hammer, or a needle, as to see him celebrating the Holy Mysteries, or preaching to a native crowd. Like S. Wilfred, he could show the natives how to do their own particular work better than they knew how to do it themselves, and could help them to improve the natural resources of their country. Like S. Athanasius, he was able to turn from one occupation to another as easily as if each fresh labour to which he gave himself, had been his own especial study.

"I am myself inclined to think that his claim to be regarded as a great missionary rests rather on his aptitude in this respect—his readiness to turn his brain or his hands to any work—than on any power of helping forward the conversion of individual souls, such as has distinguished other great missionaries, but which no man knew better than the Bishop himself, could scarcely be predicated of him.

"He was very conscious[1] that it was this last gift that had been denied him, and both to me and to others, constantly and very humbly mentioned it.

"Sometimes he would say, 'I know I am of use here as Bishop, it is true that I can do some things, and fulfil some duties better than others of the staff, but I am no missionary in the real sense of the word. A missionary is one who has the power

[1] See his own words when declining to become Bishop, page 125, line 32, of this Memoir.

of bringing souls one after another to Christ, of showing them their sins, of breaking down the barriers that gird their hearts against all religious influences, of creating in them a sense of their own true need. I can't do that. X is a missionary, and Z in his way is a missionary, too. I am not one.'

"Yet, if much that he said to this effect was undoubtedly true, it may be questioned whether *we* can venture to deny to him this name of missionary, when we consider his devotion in the Master's service, his unflagging energy, his brave example, his inflexible determination to dare and do all that was possible to be done, his self-sacrificing zeal, his dauntless faith.

"Perhaps it was because he was so well aware of his own inability to bring what powers of spiritual sympathy may have been latent in him, to bear upon individual natives with whom he dealt, and because of his true humility, that he always rated as the gift that makes the real missionary, just that one which did not belong to him.

"During our visit to Magila the Bishop employed a part of each evening in teaching some of us the Arabic alphabet, as it is used by Swahili people when writing their language.

"When we took our departure, and on our walk down to the coast, he spoke with enthusiasm of all that was going on at Magila, and I remember his saying, 'In another few years, if things go on as they are now, Farler will have all the Bondei people at his feet, and the whole tribe will be converted to Christianity.' It is interesting to note after the lapse of ten years, the progress that has been made towards this keenly longed-for result.

"On our return to Zanzibar the Bishop resumed his occupation of translating, printing, and church-building, and within the next few months, brought out in Swahili the Epistles to the Philippians and Ephesians with great diffidence, owing to what he felt to be one of the great difficulties in rendering S. Paul's language, namely, the paucity and poverty of the prepositions in the vernacular of Zanzibar.

"He expressed himself agreeably surprised one night after evensong, when a lesson from the former of these Epistles had been read, to find that 'it seemed almost intelligible,' but he attributed this approximate intelligibility to the way in which R—— had read it. He used to say at that time, that he would much rather not *publish* his translations of the Bible at all, and that he only did so lest others should translate and publish, who were not so well equipped for the work as he was.

"He considered Swahili very inadequate as a language for rendering the subtleties of even New Testament Greek, and never ranked his own translations highly. He was conscious too, of writing unidiomatic Swahili, and often alluded to this.

"I have it in writing from him that if he thought people were likely, when learning to speak and write Swahili, to rely upon his books and translations, he should wish them all burnt.

"The genius of the language, he said, would be found exhibited in the Swahili tales, which from time to time he collected, and wrote down just as he heard them; but that Swahili was such as could not be made use of in translations, not because it was ungrammatical, or vulgar, for he was very far from allowing that, but because of the sheer impossibility of imitating its peculiar style, and terse rapid idiom.

"'All that I can do,' he said, 'is to write the language with grammatical correctness, but the genius of the language must not be sought in any translations that I have published.'

"Towards the end of September, the Bishop began making active preparations for his second journey on the mainland, intending to take with him a body of the Mbweni released slaves, in order, if possible, to restore them to their own country in the neighbourhood of Lake Nyassa.

"On S. Michael's Day he held his first ordination, on which occasion Mr. Johnson was admitted to the diaconate, and I to the priesthood. A few days afterwards, he and Mr. Johnson, and a party of some thirty couples from Mbweni left Zanzibar for Lindi on the expedition which was to result in the founding of the Masasi station.

"The story of this memorable journey, and of the planting of the released slave colony among the Masasi hills is sufficiently told by himself in his little pamphlet, 'The Christian Village in Yao-land.'

"Perhaps on no other occasion had he such full opportunity of calling into play his many abilities, as during the march up to Masasi, and the month he spent there.

"He showed the natives how to build, with his own hand he laid out the gardens, measured the roads, planted the first trees, planned out the houses, varying these labours with incessant interviews with chiefs, visitings, parleyings, instructions, making friends everywhere, and imbuing all around him with the same spirit and energy which he was himself throwing into the work.

"He was never idle for a moment, and his busy hands and mind knew no rest during those eventful weeks.

"In the press of other work, his favourite study of the languages was not forgotten, nor his task of translating allowed to be in abeyance.

"Yet all this time he was far from well, and when a few days before Christmas he left Masasi, to return to Zanzibar, he had so severe an attack of fever that he became utterly prostrate, and but for the timely aid rendered him by Captain Boys, of H.M.S. "Philomel," who a week or so later picked him off the dhow near Kilwa, too weak to take any nourishment or to sit up, he in all probability would not have survived to reach Zanzibar.

"Towards the end of January, 1877, he was brought back to us, and for some days it seemed doubtful whether he would rally, or be sufficiently restored to be put on the mail steamer for a voyage home, so weak and exhausted by fever was he.

"The turning-point, however, came, for when, after he had been hovering between life and death for some ten days, the news of the death of Mr. Moss at Mkunazini, one of the younger members of our staff, was brought to him, he quietly observed, 'Then I think I shall recover, for God will not take two of us away at this time.'

"From that day he got better, and to our joy, when the time came for the mail to leave for England, he was well enough to go on board. I do not think he ever quite recovered from the effects of that fever, and probably his illness after his first walk to Mataka's had previously sown the seeds of that chronic state of ill-health, which lasted till his death, and which, in spite of his manful efforts not to let it interfere with his daily labours, could be traced in him ever since the year 1876.

"Since February, 1877, I saw but little of Bishop Steere, and on the only two after occasions when we met—namely, in April, 1879, and in August and September, 1880, Bishop Steere seemed to me an entirely different man from the Bishop whom during a great part of 1876 I had lived with, and who then had taught me so much, and allowed me so large a share of his intimacy.

"It was in my first year in the Mission, the last half of the second year of his episcopate, that I gathered from him his views and opinions and teaching on a variety of matters in the free converse and intercourse I then enjoyed with him.

"He was, as I have already said, in his later years more of a thinker than a reader, but his great mental power, and his deep and searching knowledge of human nature, caused his opinions and views to have an independence and originality worthy of profound consideration, nor did one ever feel in his case that ignorance of what had been written by others lessened the value of his opinions on subjects that are confessedly the most difficult for the human mind to fathom.

"Much has been said by those who knew him of Bishop Steere's 'dry humour.' To my thinking he excelled rather in sparkling wit.

"Certainly when amongst friends, and in the unrestrained conversation of the circle in which he moved, it was his racy wit rather than dry humour that abounded.

"Often in the form of withering sarcasm he would employ it with most telling effect, when he deemed the occasion demanded it, as when he wished to administer a well-merited rebuke; and few who have come under the lash of his powerful sarcasm would care to renew the risk of a second scourging.

"Woe to the luckless wight who, in his presence, ventured to transgress the bounds of decorum, to utter any profanity, or to act in a way unbecoming a Christian gentleman. Such a one never escaped.

"I remember once at a large dinner-party given by one of the principal European residents in Zanzibar, the Bishop being present, a young officer from one of H.M.S.'s cruisers who had been boasting of his prowess in dhow catching, and who had recently taken a cargo of slaves, many of whom had been consigned to the care of the Mission, stretched across the table, and, with an air scarcely less impudent than it was patronizing, exclaimed, 'Well, Bishop, have you thrashed those young niggers into Christians yet?' All heard the question, or maybe the Bishop would have been content to have passed it by in silence. As it was, he felt it deserved a public rebuke, so he said at once, 'That is not one of our methods, but I am thinking that if the experiment were tried upon young upstarts in the Navy, the service might begin to improve a little.'

"The language of indignant sarcasm could scarcely have gone further, yet none who were present thought that the Bishop had given the young man a severer castigation than he had deserved, although, as one remarked afterwards, 'We felt as if we had been whipped all round.'

"It must not be supposed that the Bishop ever wielded the powerful weapon he knew so well how to use, save for the discomfiture of those whom he saw to be perverting the truth, or speaking or acting irreligiously.

"Conscious, as he could not but be, of his powers in this direction, he was careful not to put them forth, save when he felt the occasion to be a grave one, and when he knew his character, as one who watches for the souls of men, to be at stake. Then indeed he would fearlessly launch forth the shafts of his remorseless sarcasm, in utter disregard of what might be thought of him, either by those who came under, or those who witnessed, the chastisement inflicted by his unsparing rod.

"But the scathing sarcasm he was wont to employ for confounding gainsayers was but one phase of his ever ready wit.

"Many are the times when in congenial company I have heard his conversation flow on in a perfect stream of witty epigrammatic sayings, as he lit up with inimitable touches of original humour each subject as it arose. It is true to say of his conversation 'on such occasions, as was written of Goldsmith by the friend who so lovingly inscribed his epitaph, *nihil tetigit quod non ornavit.*

"Many, I think, will remember the telling use he would sometimes make of a pun—that humble element of wit, which, from its abuse by would-be wags, has long since fallen into scarcely undeserved disrepute.

"One story will serve to illustrate the freaks his wit would sometimes play with this now much despised artifice in joking.

"The arrival each year of the admiral for the time being of the fleet that cruises in Eastern waters was the signal for Zanzibar to put itself *en fête*. Dinner-parties and receptions were the order of the day. At one of these dinner-parties the admiral—noted for his good stories and his jollity—happened to be placed as *vis-à-vis* to the Bishop, the two sitting on either side the hostess. The old adage, 'When Greek meets Greek then comes the tug of war,' was amply illustrated on this occasion, for the Bishop was on his day, and was not to be outdone by the Admiral.

"Stories of strange doings and adventures in and about Africa fell thick and fast from the Admiral, always matched by others, equally extraordinary, from the Bishop.

"At last it was the latter's turn to narrate, and he told a marvellous tale, on the authority of some ship's captain, of a huge ape that had been seen in the interior, whose strength and stature, and surprising achievements, threw those of the gorilla entirely into the shade. As he descanted at length on the feats of the wonderful animal, making the story more amusing by his assumed appearance of faith in it, which most of the party, who knew the Bishop, understood quite well, the Admiral, whose attention was rivetted, opened his eyes wider and wider, and at the conclusion of the story asked in all seriousness, 'And do you really believe all that? Do you think it *can* be true?'

"The Bishop looked at him for a moment, and seeing that the question was asked seriously, said at once, 'Why, my dear Sir, how can I disbelieve it? The captain came down to me with the *tale*.'

"'And did you with your own eyes really see the creature's'—but before he could finish his question the company, no longer able to restrain their laughter, were convulsed, and the Admiral was soon good-naturedly joining in the mirth provoked by his own defeat.

"Amongst his acquaintances in Zanzibar, Bishop Steere numbered not a few of the native grandees, Arabs and others. With these he was always a favourite. His courteous manners, which he knew well how to adapt to the Arab ideas of etiquette and propriety, gave him an *entrée* to their houses, which in various ways proved very useful, and I think not a few, had they been brave enough to face martyrdom for the faith, would have entered themselves as his catechumens, and placed themselves in his hands for definite Christian instruction.

"During the time he had to spend at Lindi, in 1876, he became very intimate with the Arab coterie there, and to this day he is spoken of in that town with marked respect, which, when the Arab disdain for all who are not of their faith is taken into account, is not a little noteworthy.

"I have already said that the Bishop was fond of pointing out that he himself had no claim to be called a missionary. However this may be, certainly no one knew better than he did how to advise others to set about missionary work.

"A letter which he sent up to J—— and myself when we were beginning to conduct the affairs of the station at Masasi, contained an excellent epitome of what should be a missionary's work and duties in a purely heathen district.

"The letter itself is unfortunately mislaid, but some of the advice given therein is well worth reproducing here. He warned us that it was a cardinal mistake of many missionaries to keep too much to themselves, and besought us to be ready to lend a willing ear to all, and to be the servants as well as the friends of all, to keep our lives open before the people as much as possible, so as to dispel the more quickly all misunderstanding and suspicion on the part of the heathen around us. He said that the work of studying languages, collecting vocabularies, compiling dictionaries and grammars, was well enough in its way, but should by no means occupy a missionary's first thoughts, or be allowed to take up a principal part of his time, which, he said, ought to be given to visiting and preaching in the villages.

"Attention, he told us, was to be given to the body; sufficient rest must be taken, and some pains be bestowed on the preparation of food which should supply proper nourishment.

"He said we were to try in all cases of grievous wrong-doing on the part of outsiders towards ourselves or our people, to get their chiefs to recognize the wrong and punish it, but that we were not to press the matter if they refused to act, or to be anxious to revenge the injury, remembering always St. Paul's words as a check upon any such desire, 'Why do ye not rather suffer wrong?'

"No doubt in other parts of your Memoir the subject of Bishop Steere's doctrinal views will be dealt with, but since his reserve on these, as on many other subjects, was very great, it is possible that what I have to say on some of them, gathered as it is from private conversations he held with myself, may be unknown to others.

"Although the Bishop was, as is well known, a thorough-going and uncompromising High Churchman, he was far too deep a student of theology to sacrifice his own independence of thought to party cries, or to accept without profound conviction of their truth, based on careful and original study, the doctrines and tenets of the school to which he thus belonged.

"Thus, when he had occasion to express his belief as regards Eucharistic doctrine, in language so different from the terms in common use would he set it forth, that some were inclined to doubt whether he held in full, and unreservedly, the real presence of our Lord in the Blessed Sacrament. No one, however, possessing sufficient knowledge of the subject, and who is also aware of the profoundly philosophical mind of Bishop Steere, can doubt what his belief was when he reads the letter written to a former head of the school at Kiungani when about to celebrate the Sacred Mysteries for the first time there.[1]

"The Bishop was of opinion that there was a danger lest many, fervent in adoration at the Holy Eucharist, should incline to the error of directing their worship rather to the Presence of our Blessed Lord than to His Person; thus he insisted strongly that a Presence, as such, ought not to, and indeed cannot, be worshipped.

"He was careful, too, to draw attention to the *mode* of the Presence in the Eucharist, noting always its supra-local character.

"He feared lest some might even be led to adoration of the *Res Sacramenti*, and to substitute it for that adoration of the Person of our Divine Master in Heaven, to which His mysterious Presence in the sacred elements is intended to lead us.

"He believed that many were apt to adore the Blessed Sacrament in forgetfulness of the fact that Christ's Human Nature ever remains *literally* in heaven, however spiritually present in the consecrated creatures of the Bread and Wine. Unless this fact were constantly insisted on, he said, people would soon begin to draw away their devotion and their worship from what should be their sole object —namely, our Blessed Lord Himself, and His Humanity only as taken up into union with the Divinity in His Personality as the Eternal Son of God.

"Christ, Who is to be adored in the Holy Eucha-

[1] See appendix.

rist, is not to be thought of, or looked for, as *localised* in the consecrated elements. If, indeed, we are careful to direct our worship to Him as a Divine Being, we cannot thus localise Him; His Presence must therefore be a supra-local one, and we worship Him in the Eucharist because of His mysterious Presence. So far as we can employ so finite a term as *local* in treating of the mystery of the Presence of Him Who is Infinite, we must say that Christ in heaven alone, at the right hand of God, is *locally* present, and there alone may we safely offer Him worship.

"Bishop Steere fully held the important distinction between *reverence* and *worship* with regard to the different modes of the Presence of the Second Person of the Holy Trinity, however little he was inclined to accept as a part of Catholic truth that fallacious distinction between our Lord and His Body and Blood with which an able writer has made us familiar, and on which is sometimes based the reason for denying Eucharistic adoration to be sanctioned by the Church.

"It must indeed be said that, with regard to ritual, he was slightly inconsistent; for though insisting that the Holy Eucharist, as the greatest act of Christian worship, requires, in order to its celebration with becoming dignity, such accessories as a more or less elaborate ritual supplies, he himself not only preferred to celebrate in the very plainest manner, but was also somewhat impatient if others showed signs of introducing any advance upon his own usage.

"I have already said something of his preaching.

How striking his sermons were, is, I think, abundantly shown in the volumes of 'Sermon Notes' that have already been published. Bursts of eloquence there were none, and he would have despised all rhetorical artifice; yet where can one find an eloquence more touching, or a more stirring appeal to the deepest emotions of the soul, than in the sermon preached at Burgh when the news reached that quiet Lincolnshire village of the death of the Rev. Lewis Fraser, in 1870, at Zanzibar.[1] Surely no better funeral sermon was ever preached, for surely there is none in which the death of a saint is more powerfully set forth as an incentive to self-devotion, or more convincingly shown to be the greatest glory to which a man can attain.

"The want of stability in so large a proportion of our converts, as they grow up into manhood, was a great source of grief to the Bishop; and he constantly referred to it, though always adding that we must be content to see much of our work amongst the first generation of Christians apparently bear no fruit.

"He considered that the weakness of the native African character, and the lamentable want of backbone and moral resolution that distinguishes it, was not to be remedied by pressing upon the converts the *habit* of Confession.

"He strongly held that the evil was aggravated whenever a frequent recourse to private confession was urged as a remedy, and steadily insisted that, as a basis for the building up and strengthening in

---

[1] "Sermon Notes," vol. i. p. 60.

their souls the power of resisting temptation, confession was not to be relied on in the case of these people.

"He had, he said, seen it so greatly abused, and so readily adopted by many of them as a mere *opus operatum*, which they had got to regard as an easy method of getting rid of the burden of sin at any time. This feeling, he believed, helped to lessen their fear of committing sin, and caused them to be more careless of running into temptation; and so confession, which besides being effectual to procure forgiveness of past sin, is also designed to strengthen and increase the power of those who are struggling against temptation, became in this case a snare, and only served to develope and enhance their natural weakness of character. Thus, while Bishop Steere was very far from denying himself to anyone coming to him with the proper dispositions, I have known him constantly refuse to hear the confessions of natives, so impressed was he with a sense of the wrong use they were prone to make of the sacrament in question.

"Nor ought anyone who is aware how deeply he felt his responsibilities with regard to the soul of each one of his flock to dare to question his wisdom in acting thus, or to hint that he was denying a means of grace to those to whom he ought to be ministering it.

"Anything that savoured of the nature of compulsion, or of over-pressing of confession upon our native converts *en masse*, was to him distasteful in the highest degree; and he strongly objected to sermons which advocated it in such a way as to represent it as essential to the health of the soul.

"'Let the natives be taught about confession individually,' he would say, 'and use your own discretion, directed as it will be by God, if you go to Him for guidance, as to when, and on whom, and in what measure you should press it. Confession is a medicine for sick souls, and a potent one, but all sick persons cannot always take medicines, and there are times when they must be withheld.'

"Those who have had a long experience in dealing with Africans, and who have seen children grow from boyhood to manhood under their charge, will, I think, be more inclined to agree with the Bishop's views than those who can only judge of them *ab extra*.

"It must be understood that I have said nothing as regards his teaching of private confession generally, but only as connected with the native converts in our Mission schools and establishments. It should be added that it was in confession in one aspect only, if a very principal one, that he recognized a danger.

"Bishop Steere was not one to water down the definite teaching of the Catholic Church on any doctrine, least of all what she has ever been careful to inculcate on one of such vital importance as confession. Nor would he be contented with a mere theoretical view of the subject. Not only was he the most practical of men, but as a Priest and a Bishop his greatest pains were bestowed on endeavours to carry out in his daily life the injunction contained in his favourite motto, 'Now it is required in stewards that a man be found faithful.'

"I have already mentioned that Bishop Steere read but little during the few years of his episcopate, though at the earlier period of his life he must have studied deeply, at least in one branch of literature, as his knowledge of the schoolmen and their writings, shown in his book on the 'Existence and Attributes of God,' attests. Conchology, mediæval art, architecture, liturgic lore, were all subjects with which he was something more than superficially acquainted, and were all tastes that he was able to turn to account in Africa.

"He had also a great love for music, without, however, professing a correct ear. I have known him to sit down to a harmonium, and play on that dismal and unpromising instrument a hymn-tune with feeling and expression such as many a trained musician could scarcely have equalled. He had not, however, made any scientific study of music, and I must demur altogether to a statement I have seen made somewhere in print since his death, to the effect that the Bishop "knew how to alter a hymn-tune to suit the Swahili words without spoiling it." So far from this being the case, he failed egregiously in his attempt to do so; and this is less odd than that, possessing so much true musical taste, he should have essayed so hopeless a task.

"I should prefer to say of Bishop Steere that he was possessed of great linguistic ability, rather than to speak of him as a great linguist,[1] for, with the exception, of course, of Latin and Greek, he was versed in no ancient tongues. Hebrew he had never found time to study, nor was he sufficiently acquainted with it to make his Old Testament translations from the original. Of Arabic also he knew but the elements in 1876.

"Linguistic ability no doubt he had in abundance, and this it was that enabled him to bring to perfection the reduction of the Swahili language, and to do so much for the neighbouring and kindred tongues. Others, doubtless, will testify to his labours in the vernacular of Zanzibar. I will here only add what I know to have been his opinion with regard to a language on which, before his consecration as Bishop, he bestowed a great deal of attention. He told me that he considered he never knew Swahili properly until he had studied Yao, which study he described as having thrown a flood of light upon the language which chiefly occupied his time.

"He said he was prepared to recognize Yao as an older, and in many respects a far superior language to Swahili, though he added that he did not think his ear would ever be able to follow its rapid sounds, or allow of his learning to speak it.

"It was from Yao phonetics that he borrowed so much when illustrating the transmutation of the letters in Swahili; and he spoke in high praise of

---

[1] Compare with this the judgment of his lifelong friend, Lord Justice Fry, p. 8, and the silent evidence of the notes in his essay on the "Existence and Attributes of God," *passim.—Ed.*

Yao as able to hold its own in entire independence of a bulky vocabulary from a neighbouring tongue, which Swahili, on the other hand, had not been able to do.

"The obvious difficulties in the language in question were just such as served to stir up his interest, and provoke him to grapple with them. In the year 1879, when talking with him on this favourite piece of linguistic study of his, he spoke with great regret of having been obliged to give it up in favour of labours that had more urgent claims upon his time, encouraging me to work all the harder at it, as he knew he should never be able to return to it again.

"From fear of trenching upon what others had better means of knowing than myself, and of what they are likely to say, I forbear carrying these recollections of our late chief any further.

"But writing them here on Lake Nyassa, in the heart of the continent for the sake of whose regeneration he devoted his great gifts, and finally laid down his life, I cannot but add my testimony to the truth of the verdict that has long since been passed upon him by the Church at home, and say that the name of Bishop Steere will ever stand out conspicuous in the long roll of Christian heroes who, from the first ages of Christianity until now, have laboured as missionaries for the extension of Christ's kingdom upon earth; who, amid trials innumerable, and privations and disappointments manifold, have, by the power of the Holy Spirit working in them, risen superior to all, manfully fighting on to the end; and who are now enjoying a foretaste of that everlasting rest in God which, perhaps, they have done more than all others to render precious, and more than all others to win."

CHAPTER XII.

THE FREED SLAVE SETTLEMENT AT MASASI.

IT was not until the end of September, 1876, that the Bishop was able to take up the work connected with his expedition to the Nyassa country, referred to by Archdeacon Maples in the preceding chapter; then he began to make preparations for another journey with the view of finding a suitable position for some of the freed slaves living at Mbweni.

On the 16th of October he left Zanzibar, accompanied by the Rev. W. P. Johnson, Mr. Beardall, four of the old scholars from Kiungani, Chuma, seventy porters, and fifty-five of the Mbweni people, viz., thirty-one men and twenty-four women, including two girls who accompanied their mothers. Some of these last people were baptized, all had been under Christian instruction, and they had as native leaders John Almasi and Sarah Lozi, one of the best of the baptized couples.

Besides the necessary personal luggage, and food for the journey, the Bishop took with him five draught oxen, a donkey, and a cart that had been made in the Mission workshop. He carried on also towards its original destination the portable altar table taken out by Bishop Mackenzie, but left by him at Cape-town, which was brought on to the Zambesi and then to Zanzibar by Bishop Tozer. Captain Crohan of the "Flying Fish" kindly towed the dhow in which the Mission party had stowed themselves to Lindi, where they arrived on the 18th.

It took nearly a week to hire the necessary additional men, to buy food and to get it prepared for use on the way, and to distribute the guns and axes and hoes, and so forth. Everybody from Mbweni had a hoe, and every man an axe, in view of the clearing that it would be necessary to do.

This was a very different party from that of the year before, when the Bishop's companions broke down, and the people of Lindi did all they could to hinder his journey. Now all seemed equal to the occasion, porters offered themselves in any numbers, and a caravan of nearly two hundred was formed.

On the 25th a start was made; but before the end of a week it was found necessary to leave the cart behind, for though the oxen pulled well, and the men worked well, the forest was so thick, and so matted together with old thorny creepers, that it would have taken months to clear a road through the first belt of woods, beyond which the way is clearer. So the animals only were taken on, to make sure whether the tsetse fly, whose bite is fatal to them, was in the path.

"I had satisfied myself," says the Bishop, "in my first journey, that there was an easier way through the hill range, and so we now followed up the line of a small river, the Ukeredi, which flows into Lindi harbour. We walked on for ten days through a famine-stricken country, and then emerged upon a district of plenty. On one of the most inland spans of the coast range, some eighteen hundred feet above the sea, lies a mountainous district called Masasi, well watered, fertile, untouched by war, which seemed to us all a paradise in comparison either with what we had passed, or with what lay beyond it. More than a hundred and fifty fowls and a great number of pigeons were killed in our camp the night of our arrival.

"Directly I got to Masasi I had a sort of deputation from the Mbweni people to say:—'Here we are among our own people, here is no fear of war, here is food in plenty, here let us stay.'

"Not to decide rashly, I made all the inquiries I could about the road in front, and having satisfied myself that the famine before us would make a forward journey scarcely possible, I accepted this as the voice of God, and determined to plant the colony at Masasi.

"We found that our party was consuming food at a rate we should find it difficult to supply. We sent off, therefore, first the packages we had in charge for *Livingstonia* (the station of the Scotch Mission established at the south end of Lake Nyassa), and our present for Mataka, to keep alive an interest with him.

"A party was next sent to the coast to fetch up the fifty loads we had been obliged to leave behind This reduced us to our Mbweni people and a small working party from among the porters, including a mason who had often worked for us in Zanzibar.

"I had a very interesting visitor the day after

our arrival at Masasi. Very early in the morning a man came with a fowl, who said he had come to see us because long ago he had been set free by the English, and they treated him so well that when he heard of our arrival he took a fowl as the best thing at hand for a present, and set out to come and see us. As he was more at home in Yao than in Swahili, I called Chuma, and we made out that he had been in one of the parties set free by Dr. Livingstone and Bishop Mackenzie at the same time with Chuma himself. He had wandered about a good deal, and was now settled on the mountain. He afterwards brought his little daughter to see us, and said that as soon as he could, he would come and join us altogether.

"Next day came another man, who owed his freedom to our consulate at Zanzibar; so we had some friends already.

"We determined upon the site of a new station, and then got permission from a chief named Namkumba, who is a great smelter and worker in iron, to settle on the place we had chosen. We made presents of calico and brass wire and ornamental cloths to Namkumba and to a number of his relatives, and then began to clear.

"We marked out first a site for our own house on the top of a rising ground looking out in three directions between great rocky hills over the plain country beyond. Then we marked out a road forty feet wide, leading directly down to the water. Along each side of this road we marked out lots, fifty feet wide, running back to the rocks on either hand, so as to contain something less than half an acre each, and gave our people their choice of them. This was a trial for the temper of the men who had come up with us. We had not been altogether without a fear that they might scatter off among the native villages, or perhaps sit down and expect to be fed; but our fears vanished in a moment. They at once entered into the spirit of the village, and began without delay to build and to cultivate. In little more than a fortnight every couple had a house up on their allotment, a house for fowls, and perhaps for pigeons also; and before I left most of them had completely cleared and planted their home closes, and were at work in the adjoining forest clearing fresh ground for their chief grain crops.

"We wanted to make the church something better than our houses. The granitic rocks round us scaled off in such conveniently flat pieces, that the idea of building with them, using the earth from an old ant-hill for mortar, immediately occurred to us. Among our porters was a mason who had worked for us in Zanzibar, and he soon set to work. So we put up a chancel, or rather sanctuary, of stone, with a great thatched nave before it, and our village was then complete.

"Let us try to describe the spot as it is now. Our own house is laid out as an oblong, with circular ends, twenty feet wide, and seventy-six feet from end to end. One end, which commands no view, is walled round as a store-room. There are three bedrooms, each twelve feet by ten, and the other circular end is half open and used as a dining-room. A passage leads through to a back-yard and kitchen, and a large verandah, about forty feet by ten, is to serve as a public room in front.

"Standing in the verandah you look down a road, forty feet wide, to the water. This is about 500 yards long, and falls at first gently, but afterwards more rapidly. This is the High Street of the village, and the cottages lie in order on either side. Looking across the water the land rises again, and one can see a village on the slopes about a mile off. Still farther, rise two great mountains of granite blocks, with a sort of saddle between, over which a higher peak appears, probably 1000 feet above us; the level of our house, so far as we could judge by the barometer, being about 1800 feet above the sea. The base of this great peak is about four miles away. Turning to the left, the clearings now enable us to look out (nearly to the east) over a wide plain, to the far-off coast ranges. Still farther to the left, our gardens are bounded by a well-wooded rocky ridge, about 100 feet high, and perhaps 300 yards long, with a bold cliff to the eastward. Behind the house, to the south, is a wide opening, showing the great rocks near the Rovuma, some near and sharp, others fading away into distant shadows, the flat forest horizon bounding all. Due west is the grandest of all our rocks— three great masses, lying, as it seems, loosely one on another, each nearly a hundred feet thick, and broken masses beside them fringed with trees, all crowned by one huge block, enamelled with orange and grey lichen. The morning and evening effects on these great rocks are strikingly beautiful. Then a rather narrow cliff, shut in by broken rocks and trees, opens a view to the north-west of the endless forest, with its sea-like horizon. Some great single blocks, perhaps forty feet high, bound our gardens to the north, and then a glimpse, showing us the sides of the various summits of the mountain itself, brings us round to the door again.

"When the men came back from Lindi they brought us, as a present from the chief Arab there, a great many young plants of orange, lemon, mango, guava, and jack fruit-trees, besides some choice cocoa-nuts for planting. Thus we were able at once to fringe our roads with the best fruit-trees of the coast.

"I stayed a month at Masasi, till all matters had arranged themselves, and in returning to the coast I had the opportunity of opening a fresh work, by which I hope we may hereafter supply our central schools with the best possible material for raising up our future native ministry. Several of the sons of chiefs along the road asked me to take them down to Zanzibar, to see something of our work, and learn something of what we had to teach. They came down, and they were very attentive, and learnt much in a short time. Two of them did us good service on their return; for when I had gone down, the neighbouring chiefs had been wondering much among themselves what could have induced us to come and settle in the country; and some suggested that I was to return soon with soldiers and enslave them. Then some said,—Let us burn their village before they get too strong. Just at this moment the two young men came back, and not only did they give up all thought of burning our houses, but they sent down a fresh party of pupils."

Directly after reaching Lindy, the Bishop succumbed to a very severe attack of fever. Providentially, Captain Boys, of H.M.S. "Philomel," fell in with the dhow in which he had started for Zanzibar, and taking him on board, tended him with the greatest assiduity, so that the worst of the danger was past before his arrival. But as it was impossible to keep quiet in the midst of the work at Zanzibar, the Bishop yielded to the solicitations of Dr. Robb, and sailed for England at the end of February, 1877. The extreme fatigue and anxiety of the two Nyassa expeditions had told on even the Bishop's calm temperament, but he had gone about his work as usual, abating nothing for the sake of health, and taking no notice of what was plain enough to others, that he was far from being as strong as usual.

He wrote an account of Masasi to the "Guardian" of February 7th, 1877, enclosing a strange and interesting letter he had just received from an old scholar who had left them some time ago, and who they never thought would do them much credit. This was a proof of the good seed which was being sown broad-cast through Africa, bearing unexpected fruit. How many more such cases must there be of which we shall never hear?

Nantagala, April 23rd, 1876.

My dear Bishop,

Let thy heart be turned to thy servant, and let me have favour in thy sight, therefore send me Swahili prayers, and send me the big black Bible. I want slates, board, chalk, that I may teach the Waganda the way of God. I been teach them already, but I want you to send me Litala Sundi, that he may help me in the work of God. Oh! my Lord, pray for me. Oh! ye boys, pray for me. And if thou refuse to send me Litala Sundi, send John Swedi.

Your honour to the Queen, and my honour to you,

J. SCOPION,
(*alias*) DALLINGTON MAFTAA.

I am translating the Bible to Mtesa, son of Suna, King of Uganda. I was with Henry M. Stanley, together with Robert Firuzi, but Robert is gone with Stanley, but I being stop in Uganda translating the Bible.

Thus, says the Bishop, "We may claim the credit of being *the first* in Uganda, though we have no wish to hold it against the 'C.M.S.'"

It is sad to find him ending his letter with the words, "In spite of all our successes, the Committee tell me I must drop some of my present works, for they cannot find money for them. It is very hard."

And while the Bishop is on his journey to England we may pause to take a short review of the work up to this date.

How plainly can we, even at this stage, trace the leading of the Divine hand. Driven from the fever-stricken Zambesi, where the Mission had been separated from its resources by thousands of miles, it found its infant life aided by willing hands and hearts in the Royal Navy, and at the Zanzibar Consulate.

The slave trade, which had already fatally crossed its path, provided the very condition of its useful existence in the supply of re-captured natives from the interior.

The establishment of the Mission draws English attention to the accursed traffic, and a first great step to its abolition is the consequence.

On the very site of the now abandoned slave market, in the very heart of the great Mohammedan city, rises a noble English Church, surrounded by the dwellings of Christian worshippers, a centre from whence great enterprises set forth in hope, and towards which they bend again their thankful steps.

The lessons of caution, learnt by sad experience of ruined health and premature death, are gradually learnt.

The call to labour amongst the tribes adjoining the Zanzibar territory trains the native teachers for their work, and prepares the way for the establishment of outposts in the direction of Lake Nyassa.

No sooner are those steps taken than men from the Universities begin to respond to the call which aroused them years before by the lips of Livingstone, and English athletes contend on a nobler arena than at home.

Christian colonists trained at headquarters make permanent settlements.

Linguistic difficulties disappear under the effect of the laborious years spent upon them by Bishop Steere, and the Gospel is heard by "every man in his own tongue wherein he was born."

Roads are commenced. Trade is about to follow on its track. Christianity and civilization are marching hand in hand to Lake Nyassa. "So," to quote words of Bishop Steere, "it is with the business of our lives. In due time we shall reap if we faint not. It seems that we have sometimes a hard winter, and sometimes a bright spring time, but God rules over all, and the harvest comes at last."

CHAPTER XIII.

VISIT TO ENGLAND.

THE Bishop reached England on April 20th, 1877, much the better for the voyage and a month's stay in Algiers, where the Mission has many friends. He took out a few days rest in his own home at Spilsby, and then threw himself into a round of sermons and meetings that lasted, with little intermission, till his return to Africa in September.

We ventured one day timidly to suggest that he had come home for *rest*.

"My dear fellow," he said at once, "don't you know that the railway companies will never mend their ways till they have killed a director or two; perhaps if the clergy kill a missionary bishop they may seriously consider the utter rottenness of the deputation system;" then very gravely, "How would one desire to die, if not in the active service of one's Master?" And so it was all through, whether he was quietly toiling at the translation of St. John's Gospel in his own room, or carrying on some intricate discussion with University professors; whether he was preaching to a highly cultured congregation at St. Peter's, Eaton Square, or addressing some simple village meeting; whether he was sitting in a West-end drawing-room, or working with his own hands in the mud of a brickfield,[1] or amidst the shavings of a wheelwright's shop; one could not but perceive, during this visit, how it was to him—all one work—the doing the duty of the hour in the immediate service of His heavenly Master, Who, coming on earth to redeem mankind, did not disdain to prepare Himself for that Ministry in the carpenter's shop at Nazareth; and to wash the feet of His disciples when it was His Father's will, and if this be not of the essence of the life of the true missionary, we know not what it is. The Universities were not slow to do honour to their representative missionary; he was appointed "Ramsden Preacher" for that year at Cambridge, whilst Oxford had the privilege of conferring her D.D. degree upon him; and as he proceeded along the crowded floor of the Theatre, amidst the tumultuous plaudits of the graduates and undergraduates[2] alike, one could not but think of the day when his great African predecessor, Dr. Livingstone, had been received in a like fashion in the Senate House at Cambridge, and uttered the memorable words, "I shall return to Africa and die there; but *I leave it with you* to see that the door I have opened for Christianity and civilization shall never be closed."

[1] See page 203.
[2] Someone from the gallery called out "*Bos incomparabilis*" as he went up to receive his degree. As he came back Dr. Steere quietly observed, "I suppose I ought never to dislike *American* slang again."

Of the Bishop's many wise utterances[1] during this visit to England, there are three which must find their place here as containing matter of lasting interest to the Church at large : his letter on "Intercession" to the Secretary of the Mission Prayer Union; his "Conception, as embodied in the Ramsden Sermon, of the proper work of the great Missionary Societies;" and his statement of "The relations of Christianity and Civilization in Mission work." Another feature of his visit is thus described by his brother-in-law, Mr. Hercules Brown, who writes :—

"Steere came to stay a few days with us just before he went abroad the first time. I was at home then too, and having been a musketry instructor for five years, he requested me to instruct him, as it might be useful. I therefore set to work, and, much to my surprise, he picked the whole thing up in about an hour. I afterwards had a long letter from him, thanking me much for what I had taught him, and the good service I had therefore done the Mission, as he could now show his men how to clean guns and put locks together almost as well as he could, and the little information imparted had, upon several occasions, enabled him to kill and keep off wild animals on his way up country.

"When he was over again, in 1877, and sitting in my library one night, he suddenly said, 'I want to

---

[1] A valuable paper on Mohammedanism will be found in the Report of the Church Congress for 1877. The Bishop had left England before the session commenced, and it was read for him by the Secretary.

be building out there; you set me up about guns, can you help me about bricks?' Strange to say I do know something about the process of making, the sort of clay required, &c., and so I took him next day to a regular brick-making place, and we went thoroughly into the whole matter; he quite won the heart of the manager by his practical questions and the way in which he insisted on working himself[1] at every part of the process that was at all possible; I do not know what use he made of it in Africa afterwards, but he said it would help him greatly."

The Secretary of the Mission Prayer Union reminded him one day, when in his company, that he had asked him for a few lines to send round to the members of the Union, and had not yet received them.

The Bishop called for a sheet of paper and wrote off the following letter *currente calamo.* It shows not only marvellous power as a matter of logical arrangement and composition, and a firm, comprehensive grasp of the Mission in its manifold work and needs, but it contains, if we read it aright, the essence of many a prayer to his Master, as the great Bishop wrestled in intercession for his Mission and its varied interests and surroundings. It takes thus a special place in his Memoir. It is a photograph of the Missionary Bishop on his knees, in his closet :—

[1] Just as in the same year we found him in his shirt-sleeves in a wheelwright's shop in Lincolnshire, " finding out what was the matter with the wheels we make at Mbweni." " I see now," he said, " we make them too well."—ED.

Exmouth, 19 July, 1877.
To the Secretary of the Universities' Mission Prayer Union:—
My Dear Cator,[1]

I am very sorry to have been so much occupied that I have hardly had time to collect my thoughts since I landed, but I have been anxious to tell you how much we depend upon the help of the Devotional Union. It is scarcely possible for one who has not been alone in a heathen land to understand the full value of the intercessions of the Church at home. We should be few and weak indeed without the help and sympathy of the great Church at home. One feels in Africa how much depends upon God, how little is really in the power of men. What one knows and can provide for is as nothing compared with what one does not know and cannot guard against. We have most of us felt how impossible it was for us to see far enough into the inner life of those under our charge to be sure that we were always doing and saying for and to them what was clearly wisest and best; and so much more is it the case where all is strange and different from our own old situations and experiences. Thus the children and people under our care demand your special intercessions. Their words to us may be misunderstood, their modes of thought are very hard to discover and sympathize with; and so when we have done all we can, there is very much more which we cannot do; but God has reserved all that to Himself. Pray for our people, then, that the defects of our work may be supplied, and especially that the young may be kept from temptation, or rather strengthened against it. They are specially prone to misconstrue our intentions, and to suppose that we mean in some way to make a profit out of them, and therefore are apt to feel as though liberty meant freedom to disregard our teaching. The younger are exposed to many temptations which we never hear of, as is so generally the case even at home, much more with us; the elder have in an unusual degree the temptation to throw off all authority and plunge into the idle amusements

---

[1] The Rev. W. Lumley B. Cator, Eakring Rectory, Newark, from whom copies of this letter may still be had.

of the bad world around them. Pray, therefore, specially for those who are growing up that they may choose wisely their work in life, and specially that God would put it into the hearts of an increasing number to devote themselves to the work of teaching their own countrymen. For those who are out in the world, ask that they may be kept from the great sins, of which drunkenness and impurity are the chief, by which they are surrounded. For those who are teaching, that they may have the graces of sincerity and holiness, and may become examples to those who hear them. For those who are married, that they may be constant and loving, and that their children may grow up in the faith. For those who come to us as only just delivered from slavery, that they may learn to use their freedom as the freedmen of Christ.

Do not forget either the Englishmen not of our Mission with whom the people of this land have to do. Thank God for the help and comfort we and ours have from so many of them, and for the rest, that God would give them the good thoughts and pious wills which as yet they have not.

The rulers and people of Zanzibar require your prayers, that they may learn to do their duty in all things, first as they already know it, and then that their eyes may be opened to see the duties of which they are as yet unconscious; and then the great continent beyond needs to be prayed for, that wars and strife may cease, that robbery and violence may come to an end, that a desire may spring up in the minds of all to know the truth and do the right, that their own sins may come to their remembrance and be repented of, that they may seek their Redeemer and long to hear what God has given for their instruction and deliverance. Especially that the people around Magila and Masasi may be drawn to the preaching of the Gospel, and may be made to understand and accept it; that those who are now deaf to it may hear; that those who are doubting may have the gift of faith; that those who have accepted the faith may never forsake it; that the baptized may lead new lives; that the communicants may have the full participation of Christ; that the sick and afflicted may be strengthened and comforted; that the perverse and wandering may be brought back; that the dying may be received of the Holy Angels; and that all may have a merciful judgment at the last day.

You will not, I am sure, forget us, and we want your prayers for our health of body, for sound wisdom and discretion, for light to enable us to see the wants of those about us, and how to meet them, for good words to say, and a heart to beat in unison with our work and our preaching. Especially pray for mutual love and concord among ourselves, that we may learn to think more of the virtues and graces of our fellow-workers than of their defects, that we may never strive for our own rights and authority, or intrude our own opinions and practices into the work committed to another; that we may be very slow to take offence, and always answer unkindness and injustice by special kindliness and unusual acts of self-denial and self-forgetfulness. That God would be to us each all-sufficing in Himself, and compensate us for the loss or want of congenial society. That we may all live and die for our work's sake in Him, and may all be helpful to one another, and that with us or without us, by us or as He will, yet still that His name may be glorified, and His Church may grow and increase until all the fulness of the land has been gathered into it. And so may God have you all in His holy keeping.

MISSIONS AND MISSIONARY SOCIETIES.[1]

To speak of our Missionary Agencies, I cannot think that either we receive our information in the best way, or that our great Societies have yet settled into their proper station.

The history of our Mission work is now gathered from the reports of missionaries themselves—they are what men say of themselves. Here is first of all a snare and a trial to the missionary himself. What a grand scope for a vain man to display himself, what a sore temptation to exaggerate, to say not what one knows but what one hopes, to talk of and therefore after a while to think most of what will pay in England, rather than what will most solidly benefit one's own people.

[1] Ramsden Sermon, 1877.

A good missionary is himself the most touching, the most interesting thing about his station, and what he is himself is the most powerful instrument for working upon his surroundings. Of all this we can ordinarily hear nothing, the good, conscientious man reports duly the round of his outward duties, and rarely trusts himself to speak of his hopes and fears, his encouragements, or his depression, because his mind is not set upon them, but on the result which is to follow them.

He cannot draw a picture of his own soul to be printed off in the Society's penny monthly.

Bishops, where they have time for it, can, and sometimes do let in the light upon hidden work, and give us a fair view of what is doing, but they, too, are interested parties, and the burden of worldly cares is upon them also. Thus it is that in mere despair of getting impartial testimony, men are driven to trust to the casual reports of travellers, who came perhaps to a station tired, and in ill-health, and found the natives unwilling to leave their cultivation to help them unless they were well paid.

In the book they publish, the mission will be described as uncomfortable, and badly managed, and the people as idle and uncivil. The gossip of an Indian station, and the strange tales that get currency in the ward room of a man-of-war are to many minds the only true account of mission work. The remedy would be easy enough if the great Societies would let their travelling secretaries travel sometimes among their missions, and so enable themselves to tell not merely an extract from the published reports, but a tale of what their own eyes had seen, and their own ears heard. We are ready to welcome all publicity, and are afraid of nothing that is true. You may pay us by results if you will, but then you must send us competent inspectors to tell you what those results really are.

Here is the great work of the home Societies, to collect and diffuse information, to create and keep alive a warm sympathy with the work, to find, and send out men and money, books and tools, and whatever else may be needed abroad. It is a cruel thing to harass a man's mind when he is abroad with questions of home organization, or if he comes home for rest to make him feel that the very existence of his mission depends upon the number of sermons he can preach, and the number of speeches he can make, with just that selection of subject and anecdote in each which shall fit that particular audience. We are quite ready to work abroad—it is your posts to work at home.

But don't let us call our home organizations Missionary Societies unless we clearly understand what we mean. Our great Societies were associations of men who felt that there ought to be missions, but as a body had no intention whatever of doing the work themselves. It is our shame that they all had at first to go to Germany to find men for the work. Now, thank God, the Church has men of her own, and it is time, now, that missions should be really missions, complete entities in themselves, with full power of self-development. Missions sent out by a Society in England, and managed by a Committee at home can never be quite satisfactory. A man sent out to a particular work feels that he has that work chiefly, or only, to do, and to do it to the best of his ability, his conscience tells him that his direct duty is to satisfy his Society.

But it cannot be that people at home, some of whom, perhaps most, have never seen a station among the heathen, can be awake to all the opportunities and dangers which would be evident on the spot. A great opening may close before the news of it gets home. An emergency may become a failure before anyone is awake to it. It is the glory of our Universities Mission that we led the way in what I think is generally admitted to be the true idea of a Mission, and I do not think that our secretaries and committees at home feel that they have nothing to do.

THE RELATIONS OF CHRISTIANITY AND CIVILIZATION ON MISSION WORK.[1]

In Mission work, our civilization could not but have produced a great effect among the uncivilized people with whom

[1] Speech at Oxford, Conference on Missions, 1877.

we come in contact. It was of immense value in every respect; in some sense it stood in the place of miracles, exciting wonder, and a feeling of something to be learned that was well worth learning. We can confer inestimable worldly advantages on savage nations, raising them by degrees to a position like our own, introducing among them the blessings of medical skill, and through commerce arousing in them a sense of beneficial wants. But the civilization is not all gain. We suffer from it ourselves for taking up Mission work in the midst of a web of social duties. We find it hard to enter into it with the simplicity it requires; and there is a proneness to put the supply of physical wants before the teaching of the Word of God; as might be exemplified by supposing such a case as building a church, parsonage, and schools, without at the same time taking pains to instil an adequate spiritual teaching into men's hearts. We should consider such questions as, "How should the Missionary touch the heathen's heart?" To which the answer might be given by the single word, "sympathy." But how can we in our elaborate refinement sympathize with savage tribes? We have much to unlearn; but we must try and feel that we are one family throughout the world, and not be too much impressed with the idea that we must in everything bring ourselves down to the level of the savage; remembering that there is nothing higher than sincerity, which is not always found in civilized society.

In some ways civilization is a positive hindrance to the Missionary, from the very comforts which it teaches him to consider indispensable.

It is of the earth, earthy; and tends to make us too ready to forget the life beyond the earth: so that while we thank God for its blessings we must always bear in mind that there is one thing better, the knowledge of the Gospel. Civilization is then a great and powerful instrument put into our hands for the benefit of those who are now outside its pale, but it is an instrument only, and one that is capable of working fearful mischief if we make it substantially our object to raise a civilized nation, rather than a holy Church.

The one thing is that simple sincerity which can make

itself at home with simple natures, in that oneness which embraces black and white, Indian and Englishman, because they are all redeemed of Christ. With this, civilization is one of God's greatest blessings.

While the Bishop is in England, we may mention a feature of the Mission which seriously increased its difficulties, and added to the labour and anxieties of its head.

We refer to the absolute necessity, as a rule, of each European returning home for a year in England after some three years' life in the enervating climate of inter-tropical Africa, to recruit and recover blood and nerve, muscle and tone.

This necessity is not confined to Missionaries. Consulates and mercantile houses feel its burthen. But it involves a cruel dislocation of all missionary work. Fancy if most of our parishes were to lose their incumbents every fourth year, what a disturbance it would make in all parochial and diocesan affairs. Still more must it add to the cares and work of the Bishop in the case of a Mission with growing and expanding work, such as the Universities' Mission was at this time.

Look at the state of things in 1877. Mr. Woodward, who has since proved himself so valuable a Missionary, returned home sick before his three years were expired. Mr. Randolph, who ably acted as head of the Mission in the Bishop's absence, followed soon after the Bishop's arrival in Zanzibar, and Mr. Farler also; and while the Mission gained much by their earnest advocacy of its claims in England, their absence made a serious gap in the staff in Africa. Mr. Capel and Mr.

Beardall left the Mission about the same time, and Miss Bartlett returned home on sick leave. On the other hand the Rev. F. Hodgson (now Archdeacon of Zanzibar), with his wife joined the Mission, together with Messrs. F. G. Williams and Newham, Miss Thackeray and Miss Hinton. And of course it took some little time for them to become acclimatized, and to find their special sphere of work. In fact, for a time, the stations round and about Magila were left with no Missionary in priest's orders, nor on the Island had the Bishop any but deacons to aid him. In the meantime, during the absence of the Bishop, how was the Mission faring? Was there any tendency to collapse when his strong hand was withdrawn? or had the machine been so well and soundly constructed that it would run smoothly for some months at least without him? It must have been with some anxiety that he looked around him on his return. He found much to encourage him. The work in the Island of Zanzibar, both in the schools, the Mission Farm, and the Town house, with its Infirmary, Infant School, Choir School, and general business department was all flourishing. To the north, the Mission stations at and around Magila showed a steady progress, while to the south, the released slave village at Masasi was becoming widely known, and Mataka had sent a special embassage enquiring when his promised missionary was coming. During his absence also an event, unique, we think, in the history of Missions had occurred singularly creditable to its promoters, and a significant testimony, both to the practical character of the work of the

Mission among the African people, and to the constant spirit of self denial by which the members of the Mission were animated. A subscription of some £120 had been raised and sent to the acting head of the Mission by people of all classes and nationalities in Zanzibar itself, with a note to the effect that it was offered, lest in view of the increasing expenses of the Mission not having been met by a proportionate increase in its funds, the European staff should be induced to forego many little necessaries and comforts essential to health in that trying climate.

Here is a picture drawn by one of his chaplains, of the Bishop on his return :—

I have a very vivid remembrance, [writes Archdeacon Hodgson] of the first visit paid by Bishop Steere, after his return from England in November, 1877, to Mbweni, the Mission station of which I was then in charge.

The Bishop had been absent from the diocese for several months, hence we were all anxious, English and natives, to give him a hearty welcome, and perhaps also to appear at our best on his arrival. He walked out to us early, for a 7 o'clock celebration, from the head-quarters of the Mission on the Old Slave Market in Zanzibar. Most of us, in going backwards and forwards, made use of the steed of the country, an Arab donkey—some kept a private horse—but the Bishop would never mount either quadruped ; he would take a boat, when there was no great hurry, but otherwise he always walked. A walk of five miles, and then a service before breakfast, is no slight exertion, with the thermometer over 80° ; but those who knew Bishop Steere will not be surprised to hear that he was never late on these occasions. It was each month his practice to spend one Sunday morning with us, and the first morning I ever had to wait for his appearance was the very day on which he died.

Few strangers would have taken for a Bishop the solitary

foot-passenger they might meet at that early hour, wearing a mushroom-shaped pith hat, and carrying a white-covered umbrella, though the length of the white coat, and the rather incongruous black trowsers, might seem to denote an ecclesiastic.

Thus had he arrived well before the hour for service on the day I am speaking of. The celebration was in English, the Bishop being celebrant; and then we returned to the Mission House for breakfast. The members of the Mission and the children of the Orphanage all had their meals in one room, the former being accommodated with a high table at the end. On this auspicious occasion the children had, of course, all turned out in Sunday best, and were waiting round the hall-door for the Europeans and the Bishop to go in first. We were just going across the courtyard towards the hall, when the Bishop's eye fell on a tub used for catching the rain-water under one of the spouts from the flat roof. This same tub had been carelessly handled, and two of the iron hoops had been allowed to get loose and come off. There and then, regardless of hunger and fatigue, the Bishop must needs point out the impending dissolution of an article not easily replaced in Zanzibar; and, resolutely deaf to all protestations, that it should be attended to immediately after breakfast, insist on restoring with his own hands the rusty hoops to their original position. Our feelings, during this scene, can be well imagined: it certainly was a very practical sermon against carelessness; and though at the time we may have thought the lesson rather severe, we learnt not to consider any useful work beneath our dignity.

This incident has always seemed to me very characteristic of Bishop Steere. He was intensely practical, and, no doubt, owed much of his success in life to his constant exemplification of the good old maxim, "If a thing is worth doing at all, it is worth doing well." Certainly, whatever he did take in hand, he did it with all his might; and again and again we had cause to feel ashamed of ourselves for thinking beneath our notice what he would pay most serious and painstaking attention to. When he had any building in progress—which, at Zanzibar, was nearly every day of his life—he was to be seen on the spot first thing in the morning and last thing before the workmen left, and frequently for hours in the day, directing all the details of the work. If any Bishop has a claim to be represented in a stained glass window, with a model of his cathedral in his hand, surely Bishop Steere has; for he was not only architect, but builder, and clerk of the works of the noble Slave Market Church. He was as ready to see the mortar mixed properly, as to trace out a symmetrical rose window. He himself planned the scaffolding and cording, besides seeing nearly every stone into its place; he had even to teach his masons to distinguish a straight line from a crooked one. Nor was work of this sort, in his case, all-absorbing; otherwise, he could hardly have left behind him, as he has done, a legacy of dictionaries and grammars in African languages, besides translating, himself, into the chief of them, all the Prayerbook, half the Old Testament, all the New Testament, 180 hymns, tracts, grammars, arithmetics, geographies, and spelling-books, in almost endless variety. At the hours of prayer his regularity was most exemplary. His sermons and charges were equally effective, whether delivered in English, before an educated and critical audience, or in Swahili, before the lowest specimens of African humanity. Lastly, as head of the Mission, we could always ensure his attention to the simplest details of our work, when we sought his advice, as well as to intricate problems. In fact, he was equally ready at any moment to write an answer to a question, whether it concerned admission to Holy Baptism, the management of a refractory child, or the planting of a hedge. He had great faith in letter-writing; living at five miles distance, I have often had as many as three letters from him in the course of a single day. Thus those of us who had the privilege of living near him were able to consult him, rather as very young curates might consult their experienced vicar, or as members of a family might apply to a very practical father, than as clergy applying to their bishop; and we could feel sure that on any given subject his advice would be valuable. It was almost a proverb amongst us: "Don't you know? Ask the bishop—he is sure to know." And really his knowledge did seem inexhaustible. One theory on the subject was, that he had found himself reduced to an Encyclopedia as his only literature for a long sea voyage, so had quietly set to work and learnt it by heart. Whether this were so or not, it is certain that those of us who made a hobby of botany or conchology would apply to him for the Latin names of our specimens; if a hymn was to be translated, he could re-arrange the tune without spoiling it;[1] while in drawing or illuminating he could give useful hints; and in fact appeared to have an acquaintance anything but amateur with nearly every art and science. Languages he acquired easily, both modern and ancient ones, civilized and barbarous; and perhaps none of us knew exactly how many he was acquainted with. Books he read in a marvellously short time, and yet remembered better what he had read than others who had studied carefully what he apparently had only skimmed. With this natural genius, added to intense energy and abounding patience, it was no wonder that he succeeded in what he attempted.

In this year the traveller Stanley arrived from the Cape after his great discovery of the Livingstone River, and his successful crossing of the continent. Amongst the guides was Robert Feruzi, an old pupil of the Mission, who had been chosen for his trustworthiness, with two others to push on and fetch up provisions, when the whole party were almost exhausted on approaching the west coast.

In this year the great Yao chief Matola gave permission for a branch station to be opened at Newala, some fifty miles distant from Masasi in the direction of Lake Nyassa, and a vivid word picture of Masasi, taken from Mr. Maples' journal,

[1] This is probably "the statement" to which Archdeacon Maples "demurs," page 186. We can only point out, that of the two, Archdeacon Hodgson lived in close intimacy with the bishop from 1877 to 1882, as against Archdeacon Maples in 1876.

may help to at once bring that place before our eyes, and to illustrate the Bishop's wisdom in the choice of it for his freed settlement. " I could not admire too much all that had been done in so short a time. The substantial buildings that had been begun and completed ; the extent of ground that was under cultivation ; the sprouting fruit trees ; and above all the pretty little church with its stone chancel— the first church in these parts, and for a distance round which can be counted almost by thousands of miles. But the place itself and the surrounding country is like a scene of enchantment—the gentle slope to the water, the cassava field on either side of the wide road, with the picturesque houses of our people snugly nestled in it, the bright-coloured leaves of the few trees which here and there are left standing, the mountains rising just beyond the water, their hues, their lights and shadows, ever varying from sunrise to sunset in one continued course of changes right before our eyes. Again, the wide stretching bars, reaching in one direction, they tell us, to the very shores of the Lake itself, and spread out before us like a great sea with unlimited horizon. Again, the two great rocks on either side of us, always lovely to look upon, and most lovely perhaps as they rise up tall, grim, and awful in the silence and stillness of a moonlight night. Certainly we are situated on a most glorious spot, where nature has been lavish of her beauties, and where the earth with a loud voice ' showeth His handiwork.' "

But it is full time to return to headquarters at Zanzibar, where the year 1877 was fitly closed by a service (Swahili Matins) being held in the yet roofless church in the old slave market on Christmas Day.

A considerable number of townspeople [wrote the Bishop], came in to listen. I preached to them on the great event of the day, and the strangers listened most attentively. One felt the size of the church when about two hundred of us were packed into the shady side, and the canticles and hymns went most gloriously. One could not but think of the first Christmas day here, when Capt. Prideaux would not let me speak to the people for fear of creating a riot among the Mohammedans.

CHAPTER XIV.

1878.

THE WORK OUTGROWS THE INCOME.

THE long anxious years of the infancy and early growth of the Mission were now practically over, and it was the privilege and happiness of Bishop Steere (to quote words applicable surely to him as a faithful servant of his Master) "to see of the travail of his soul and to be satisfied."

The Mission grew and expanded signally in these later years of his life.

If the great impulse was given in the year 1875, when eighteen Europeans were added to the Mission, yet, notwithstanding the loss, temporary or permanent, of some of them, the numbers continued gradually to swell and grow. Nor did the work more than temporarily flag at his death. His memory lives on. And his able and judicious successor, Bishop Charles Alan Smythies, rejoices in a still larger expansion of its numbers and of its usefulness. We are bound to add, that our gratitude for the past cannot blind us to the truth that our Church and nation have not yet risen up to the true recognition of the value of the Universities' Mission as the best agent of civilizing and Christianizing the peoples and nations with which it comes in contact in the dark continent.

What though, when Bishop Steere sank to his last rest, he left behind him thirty-four European helpers, as well as a large force of native Christians to carry on the work to which, with one fellow helper and five starving slave boys, he had eighteen years before set his hand? What though, at the present time, Bishop Smythies has a staff of sixty-two Europeans, and some twenty-five native catechists and school-teachers? It is but a poor instalment of the debt that England owes to Africa, and a very inadequate occupation of the opportunities still open to her of repaying it.

England may have forgotten, but the African only too well remembers, the English pirates, who came to prey upon the Portuguese commerce, and left behind them no honourable memory of Englishmen and Christians. After them came slave-dealers of every nation, but the most eager of them our own countrymen, all professing the utmost benevolence, seeking only to get the people, and most of all their children, into their power, and then they fastened them below hatches and sailed away. Here is an evil name that has been most justly earned, a long series of evil doings which have to be atoned for. Surely an Englishman and a Christian cannot rest under such a burden as this. Many thousand Africans have died in miserable slavery in order that Englishmen might make fortunes and build up families; and if we could but realize the debt that we owe them, and give but one tithe of English lives for the lives that Africa has given us, we should send out missionaries, not by twos or threes, but by hundreds and thousands. So might we hope to wipe out the reproaches of the past, and show these nations that Christianity is something better than a hollow name.

Again, in Central Africa *we are fighting against time.* On all sides we are met by signs that the stagnation of Africa is past. The various trading, exploring, and missionary expeditions that have penetrated into all parts of Central Africa, have opened the eyes of the natives to their ignorance, backwardness, and weakness. Even the very antagonism of the Mohammedans to Christianity has done good in its way, by arousing the natives out of their lethargic state with regard to religion, and making them enquire into the differences between Christianity and Islam. The whole future of Central Africa is trembling in the balance. The Africans will not remain as they are; they are seeking for a religion, and they will have one. They are calling to England for teachers, even begging for men to teach them the faith of Christ. The false faith of Islam is at their door, they have not yet accepted it, but if through lack of men with the apostolic spirit, the English Church is unable to answer their appeal for missionaries, they have no alternative, they must accept Islam, and in all probability be lost to Christianity, civilization, and freedom for ever. For, as so unbiased a witness as Mr. Palgrave wrote in the "Cornhill Magazine" for August, 1878, "Sooner or later the nation that casts in its lot with Islam is stricken as by a blight; its freshness, its plasticity, disappear first, then its reparative and reproductive power, and it petrifies or perishes."

We proceed with such extracts from the Bishop's letters as may show him to us as he lived on in his multiplying labours.

If his bodily health was not what it had been, and if Archdeacon Maples found him a changed man, may it not have been that the climate and the wear and tear of work, on the one hand, had taken some of the bright sunshine out of his manner; and, on the other, because the full-charged mind was intensely fixed upon the ever-expanding details of the creative and sustentatory labours of the Mission, and because the calls upon that mind were constant and exhausting?

In February, 1878, the Bishop paid a visit to Magila.

We were delayed [he writes] in getting a dhow to Pangani, and so did not arrive until about 8 a.m. on Sunday morning, just as Mr. Farler was returning from the river, where he had baptized a number of converts. I addressed them after Matins. Monday was spent in looking round at the buildings, which are much more solid than our first erections, and will, we hope, be permanent. They are of stone, cemented with puddled clay, and in part plastered with lime. The roof is a flat one of stone for coolness, protected from the rain by corrugated iron. There is yet much to be done, and the temporary church is yet of mud. It was necessary to get part of the house done first, as the large thatched one built by Mr. Midgley, which is threatening every day to fall, stands on the site destined for the permanent church. On Tuesday morning a party of about twenty assembled in the church, where I confirmed them. Thus the church at Magila is at last complete on its lay side. The catechumens are kept a year before baptism, and then another year before confirmation, so that although there will be some instability, I think Mr. Farler has done all he could to guard against it. On Wednesday morning I celebrated the Holy Communion, and admitted Mr. Yorke as Reader in charge of the out-station at Umba, where the majority are very favourable to our work, though there is a small knot of Mohammedans who work against us. There had been a great debate as to whether the church should be built in the village or outside. It was carried, however, in our favour that it should stand inside, and a native is now at work as a sort of contractor erecting it.

Umba is a place of great importance as the chief place on the way to the coast, which must be the door to admit or shut out Mohammedan influences.

I was more impressed than ever during this visit with the bright, intelligent look of the Bondeis. They are so different from the slaves one sees at work near the coast. Our influence here increases steadily, and though Mr. Phillips is as good as gold, it is hard to leave only a deacon in charge of the Magila Mission, as I must when Farler goes home for rest.

And of Mbweni he wrote by the following mail :—

Our Christian village at Mbweni is a matter of great interest to me. Its expenses will be diminished by the starting of Mr. Clark's party, unless we have a large inflow of released slaves, who are, of course, all quite helpless at first. The estate is looking very lovely, with its broad, well-kept roads, and we have been planting extensively cocoanuts and cloves, which add to its value, though not, alas, to immediate income. We have a very promising crop of rice coming on in one part of it. I get over one Sunday and two Thursdays in each month, when I celebrate in the chapel, and preach to the people. They are very attentive, and Clarke and John Swedi keep up their regular prayers and preaching. Miss Thackeray and Kate Kadamweli have put great vigour into the school, and Cornelia is being brought forward as a teacher.

We have put shades to the schoolroom windows, which make it quite cool, even in the afternoon.

At Kiungani Mr. Farler has just conducted an examination of the boys' school. His results show very great improvement on the past year, and a healthy tone in the boys' answers. Swahili reading is the best subject, then Scripture and catechism, writing, spelling, and English reading.

Arithmetic is best in the younger boys, who, of course, are the best representatives of last year's teaching under Mr. Wallis. The rise of particular boys above their place at the last examination is very satisfactory.

For myself, I have just gone over the proofs of the eighth chapter of the Acts in Swahili, and we have added the Athanasian Creed and the Office for Confirmation to our translations. I am now in the middle of a little First Geography in Swahili. I have just been getting the marble shafts on either side of the chancel arch of the church well in their places. One of them had been broken before sending out from England, and joined together with sunken clamps. It was very generous of the maker to charge us nothing for the iron.

So that, "all round," the Bishop, on his return, was cheered by signs of life, and growth, and vigour.

His long and anxious laying of the foundations with Bishop Tozer, Mr. Alington, Mr. Midgely, Mr. Fraser, Mr. West, and others, seemed to be giving way to happier and more promising times.

Nor was it in Africa alone that he now saw much fruit of his labours.

By the very next mail after his return from Magila he was "immensely interested to hear from a missionary to Asiatics in the London Docks, that he saw every year nearly 3,000 Swahili-speaking people, and read the Bishop's books to them, an extension of our work," said the Bishop, "one had never thought of before."

In this strain of hopefulness, cheered by signs of life everywhere, the Bishop opened his letters from home about Eastertide, to find an urgent letter from the Committee in London, stating that the expenditure had so far exceeded the income that some serious reduction of the work was necessary, and recommending either the closing of the Mission Farm at Mbweni, or the withdrawal, for a time at least, from Magila.

What! was it come to this? Was his life and work then a failure? Were all the self-denying labours of his predecessors and fellow-workers in vain?

Was the cross of Christ to retire beaten and dishonoured, in order that the crescent of the slave-dealing Mohammedan might take possession?

And in the meantime the prosperity of England had been advancing by leaps and bounds.

Was the old country deaf to the cry of down-trodden Africa, and blind to the gallant efforts of the "forlorn hope" under their brave leader?

As if to fill his cup of trouble to the full, it became clear to the Bishop that his day for taking long journeys on the mainland was over.

His illness of the year before, while leaving his mental powers, if possible, brighter and riper than ever, had weakened his bodily powers seriously. He was growing old before his time. In returning from Magila he had to be carried all the way down to Pangani, the point of departure by sea for

Zanzibar, and wrote: "I fear that my mainland journeys must be very few and careful; I keep well by doing little."

The following letter is, in part, on matters financial, after the appeal issued in May by the Home Committee, who were straining every nerve to bring the needs of the Mission before the Church at home; but it embraces other topics, and seems to call for insertion here :—

July 26, 1878.[1]

Your letter gives one great encouragement. Any prudent person, of a calm and indifferent judgment, might say that what is amiss with us is that I have been trying to do too much; but somehow, although I too am very prudent in theory, it always seems possible to do just a little more.

I am afraid I should be ashamed of myself if I did not keep the tether tight, when one has all this land before one.

We want money just now most of all, because we want people.

The best helpers we can have are people who, when they leave us, will not want further help. A man who has nothing cannot be just sent home and done with. Otherwise I find the people who have nothing are easier to manage than those who think they are conferring a favour on the Mission by doing a little, and criticising very much.

If I had not had the best set of men and women possible, we could never have done what we have. The labourer here is eminently worthy of a great deal more than he is likely to get.

The Committee being very prudent kept warning me not to spend till I asked them what I was to do, and then they said give up Magila and Mbweni.

A definite proposition like this sets one thinking what it really all means, and then I am sure if one can only set other

[1] To Miss L. K. Stopford.

people thinking too we shall not have occasion to give anything up.

We are, however, running very close.

Masasi is our great effort towards the Nyassa, and the work hangs now upon Mr. Maples, who writes:—" The behaviour of the newly-baptized is really excellent. One seems to see in them every sign of the inward regeneration. Their baptism has had a great effect upon many in the village, who are all looking forward to becoming catechumens, and I may tell you joyfully that really the people are improving. The bad people are driven more and more into a corner, and wickedness can certainly no longer *triumph* in our midst."

So at Magila and Umba one hears of increased attendance; and here, in Zanzibar, Mr. Johnson and Miss Thackeray are making the adults and the girls into real Christians, I hope.

Miss Allen has in town her Mother's Meeting of some dozen or more Christian mothers, and a large practice among the small ailments of the townspeople, as well as her visits to the Arab ladies.

Miss Hinton has the infants of our mothers, and is general prescriber for babies, as well as taking a few obstinate cases from the boys' school, where Mr. Williams is working harder than a man ought at school and household, and Mr. Geldart has just paid me over £20, *profit*, for work done by the printing-press, as well as giving us the Acts of the Apostles printed in Swahili. He has on hand a new edition of our hymns, about seventy-three now, and a new series of Swahili tales.

The Epistle to the Romans has been translated, and is now being finally revised.

We want a devout priest to give a tone to the boys, and, sooth to say, to ourselves also.

Please to remember me kindly to your sister-in-law and her daughter. I hope Bournemouth may be all she wants. I should not wonder if people with weak chests found out, some day or other, that this place would suit them well; we have no cold, and none of the intense heat I hear of in England—say from 75° in winter to 85° at the hottest.

To see wider and wider fields ripening for the harvest, and to know that labourers, many and able, were in England, if only they would give themselves to the work—and yet that they did not come, and that funds were slack—all this must have added much to the Bishop's anxieties. It was a brave heart, and a strong will, and well-seasoned faith and hope, which carried him and the Mission through the trying period of upward and onward growth, beset by difficulties on all sides.

The steady progress of the work during the rest of the year was his comfort. It will be sufficiently gathered from the letters given below :—

August 13, 1878.[1]

We have just sent off another party of freed men to Masasi, including my young Yao chief, who came down with Mr. Williams. He says he will bring his wife and child down, and stay a year at Kiungani, to go on with his learning there.

Two of our elder lads have gone on board an English ship as interpreters, and another has joined one of the C.M.S. parties going up to Unyamwezi. We have taken into the school entirely a lad of about fourteen, a very pleasant fellow who has attended, off and on, for a year past.

He was claimed as a slave, but there seems to be no clear proof either way, and so we think we may adopt him altogether now.

I was on the roof of the church in the old slave market, looking on at the work, yesterday, when a party of twenty women, each with a baby, came up the street. Babies are so scarce in Zanzibar that all the masons and workmen ran to the side to look at them. They had come from Mbweni to ask about what was to be done when the mothers went to work.

[1] To Miss Randolph, Dunnington Rectory, York.

Mr. Johnson had proposed they should leave their babies in charge of someone, and they had a wild sort of notion that perhaps he wanted to take them away. Already we want an infant school at Mbweni; Miss Thackeray has some with her girls, but she has not room for thirty new ones in a batch, nor could Miss Hinton take any more in town; besides that, hers are mostly orphans.

So here is a new want, a sort of *crèche* and infant school for children born amongst us. The mothers and fathers at Mbweni are just getting off our hands, but will not as yet be able to pay much, though they are now paying rent for their land and houses. So we must try and get a resting-place for the little ones while their mothers are out. It is curious how English wants and difficulties grow up with us.

Kate Kadamweli is an admirable second mistress to Miss Thackeray, and I think, if we had anyone here who understood infant school work, there are two other of the old scholars who would soon make good mistresses.

Mbweni is now a village, free and independent, the houses are all numbered on little plates of tin in green paint, and the shop stands at the cross-roads; I see all sorts of articles going out to supply it—salt, soap, grain, dried fish, and so forth. Robert Feruzi, who went across the Continent with Mr. Stanley, is chief manager, with a man named Sadiki under him.

September 30, 1878.[1]

I am very glad to hear of your getting help from local converts, by all means develop this as far as you possibly can. Steady work within a moderate circle is the most likely to produce solid work; above all, get the natives of the place to work with you as far as possible.

I should very gladly see native Readers in the villages. I should have no objection to pay a native teacher; but one must try all one can to get support for him from the taught. I should like to bear about half the cost, if it can be so

[1] To Rev. H. Woodward, Umba.

arranged. The great instrument of knowledge is reading, and this must be the first item of school teaching.

There has been a great discussion about Mission schools in India.

There seems to have been a system of teaching all as if they were Christians. It has a good side, no doubt, chiefly as showing what we deem the most necessary knowledge of all, and in dissipating absurd prejudices. It has also its bad side, and needs very careful guarding. May God be with you.

October 18th, 1878.[1]

We had a very pleasant day on S. Bartholomew's Day, though it rained so hard in town that our friends there bemoaned over our bad day, while we were enjoying ourselves, only two miles away, in glorious sunshine.

We had, at our early celebration, a Chaldee priest gathering alms for his church. I got him passed on free, and the good people here gave him eighty rupees. He said he had never seen among the English anything so like his own country; I suppose in the native dress and language, and perhaps in our singing without an instrument.

The Admiral brought up the Bishop of Mauritius on a visit on his way to Mombas. He looked us round very thoroughly, and praised everything. One question he asked me was, "How do you keep all these people from quarrelling?" However, we looked well.

Our baptisms on S. Bartholomew's Day were typical of our work. One was the child of a slave woman, who died shortly after we had taken her in; the second, the child of a woman educated by the Church Missionary Society at Mombas, and now living at Mbweni; and the third, an old native woman, taken in in charity by one of our old scholars, and adopted as his mother. Shortly before I had baptized one of Livingstone's porters, and he has married one of the Mbweni girls.

Mr. Johnson has about forty adults, mostly men, nearly

[1] To Miss Randolph.

ready. He is doing a great work at Mbweni. His classes, catechisings, and visits are endless. The natives call him "the man that never sits down."

I do think our children are very happy, and yet what miseries many of them have gone through!

They will sometimes talk of the days when they were seized and carried off, and it seems strange to hear from living mouths the same horrors which one used to read of about slavery. One told me that her father was taken with her, but he was ill, and could not keep up with the gang, so he was killed there and then. Another, that her little brother was thrown into the sea. Then they talk of the numbers of children and babes who were killed and thrown into the grass by the side of the road on the march. And now, when one sees them playing about well, and happy, and cared for, or kneeling by the wall in the long dormitory saying their prayers, one cannot feel too thankful for being allowed a share in their upraising.

November 10th, 1878.[1]

The four weeks since I last wrote have been very full of incident. In the first place, there was the confirmation at Mbweni on the Sunday after I wrote. Three men and one woman were confirmed. There were several others whom Mr. Johnson would have presented had I not promised him another confirmation before long.

Then came another party of slaves, taken, most of them, at Uzi, a small town on the island of Zanzibar. It had come to be known that small parties of slaves had been carried across to Uzi, and one of the "London's" boats was set to watch. Late one night the officer got information that a party of nineteen had just been landed, and were at a place mentioned. He set out with a party of his men, and arrived in the dark at a hut where the slaves were. As soon as he approached he was fired upon, and an Arab came towards him and made a cut at him, which tore his coat, but did not wound him. He closed at once with the Arab, threw him

[1] To Rev. R. M. Heanley.

down, and made him prisoner. One of the bluejackets stumbled into a deep hole, and, being attacked, saved himself by shooting his assailant. The rest drew off, and the slaves were brought out, and carried down to the boat under a dropping fire from the bushes.

These nineteen, with other small parties, amounting to thirty in all, were sent on to us.

Among them was a Zaramo lad, taken in the petty war now going on close to the coast opposite Zanzibar. He had hardly been a slave a week.

There were five boys among this party, the rest were all adults.

A father, mother, and daughter formed another group. The two former were quite old people; they had been practically free for a long time, but an old claim had been raised against them, and they were on their way to die at Pemba when the "London's" men captured them.

A man came to me a few days since to ask for shelter. He said he had been a slave when a boy, and sold to a Muscat man, who took him on board a dhow to go to Muscat. He got on shore and ran away, and from that time to this never heard of his master. He is afraid now that he may be kidnapped some day, and sent to Pemba. He has been working for us on the church, and I think he and his wife will build themselves a house on our land at Kiungani.

The walls of the Slave Market Church had been raised to their full height, and a specially designed roof—Bishop Steere's idea—spanning the church in a series of arches cemented together, was now a chief object of interest, not to say anxiety.

The Bishop continues:—

The next great event of the month was the removal of the centreing from the first portion of the vault of the church.[1]

---

[1] When the church was finished, with its arched roof, and the centreing and scaffold poles were removed, the native mind was much exercised. "Why doesn't the roof fall, there

It was an anxious moment, but there was not the slightest hitch, and the second ten feet of roof is nearly covered in. The roof is a plain-pointed barrel of twenty-eight and a half feet span, and the centre line is exactly sixty feet from the pavement. It is made of pounded coral, with a certain proportion of Portland cement.

On All Saints' Day there were two weddings at Mbweni among our old scholars. Almost the whole boys' school was asked over to the wedding feast; and Miss Hinton took over her infants, now seventeen in number. It was a very successful day in every way. Early in the morning Mr. Joseph Williams made his final start for Masasi. The dhow had left the town the day before, and anchored for the night off Mbweni, so that he was able to communicate with us just before starting.

A few days before I had sent off our traveller, Daudi, with money and stores for Magila. Before the end of the week, however, he came back, arriving late at night in a very dilapidated state, to tell us that his dhow had been wrecked off Pangani, and three of the men on board her drowned. He had escaped by clinging to the captain. The money and everything else was lost utterly. So I had in hot haste to raise some more money, and send another messenger to Magila.

Last Monday a great treat was given to Miss Hinton's infants by the American consul (Mr. Hathorne) and Mrs. Hathorne. They were most sumptuously regaled, and provided with swings and games, and waited on by the young men of the house.

---

is nothing to hold it up?" At last one of those who remembered the laying of the foundation stone made up his mind what it was that kept the roof in its place. He accordingly asked the Bishop what had been placed in the cavity when the stone was laid. The Bishop replied that a parchment with a record in Arabic and English of the object of the building had been put in, with a few coins. "Nothing more, Bwana?" "No, nothing more." "Ah! you won't tell us! But I know why the roof does not fall. It was the very powerful *medicine you put in that stone!*"

They distinguished themselves by the most admirable behaviour, taking to the novelties of the table arrangements with the greatest ease and propriety. It was a most enjoyable day for them, and not less so for their very hard-worked but very untiring " Mama."

I should have mentioned that before we removed the centreing of the church roof we finished roughly the western gable and set up the cross. It is more than seventy feet from the ground, and one of the most prominent objects in Zanzibar.

It has been proposed—and a strange proposal it is—that Alington should join the Zulu Mission to ours, seeing that he is 2,000 miles from us, and not 200 miles from Pretoria or Maritzburg. If the Mackenzie Memorial Mission is taken to represent Mackenzie's first love, which he left reluctantly for Central Africa, then things are right as they are; and this view of things is the true one of Miss Mackenzie, his sister, whatever may have been the case with the Bishop himself.

We have preaching excursions now to various villages on the island, both from Kiungani and Mbweni; and I have suggested to some friends at home, as a special subject, the raising means to build small houses near the church to let to Christians, who want to live there, and cannot get lodgings. We have the land, and a church without a parish is scarcely a church at all.

The following letter is a striking instance of the watchful interest the Bishop took in all that concerned the Church at home, in the midst of his own labours.

Dec. 10, 1878.[1]

Many thanks for your letter and all its news. The papers this month seem to me very dull politically, but exceptionally full of practical matters. I see Ince is taking a new line in his Oxford lectures, and will, I hope, give his own University a character like that given to Cambridge by Lightfoot.

---

[1] To Rev. W. F. Norris.

I fancy his implied criticism that Cambridge is drily historic, and we want a constructive theology, is true enough. Oxford seems to me to have no theology at present, and the Theological men I have here do not shine in Theology either. All the leading men of Oxford seem to me to represent tendencies rather than opinions, much as Mozley's Sermons are helps to thought rather than teaching.

I think this state of things leaves many men at the mercy of a party leader, and of course gives power to the great party leaders who come from Rome.

We want very much indeed a good line of definition to show how we stand with Rome. I find a great many men have no guiding principle now, except that everything said against Rome is false, and everything in favour of it is true. On the other side Low Churchmen must be feeling that they must have something to save them from a mere disorganized nebula of views and tendencies. We are all getting sick of the suggestion that practically there is no error, and if anyone can help us to a definite truth or two, he will do wonders for the University.

There have been a number of captures of small parties of slaves; we have taken all of them in as yet.

Mr. Johnson has been wonderfully active at Mbweni, and in the country round. He has thirty adults now ready for baptism, and large classes behind. I hope to ordain Mr. F. J. Williams from Warminster deacon this month, he has been very active in the school. I see that the Dorchester College has been opened—they ought to call it S. Birinus.

We are taking the centreing out of the second compartment of the roof of the Slave Market Church now, and opening the round window. One of our masons had a wonderful escape a short time back. He was at work on the very top of the north wall, finishing a sort of turret on the north end of the west gable, when he suddenly fell off down to the ground, some forty or fifty feet, through the roof of a neighbour's kitchen.

He picked himself up, and walked out and said he had bruised his shoulder, and rubbed some skin off his heel. He went home and stayed at home the next day, which was

Saturday, and on Monday came again to work as usual; his name is Hatibu.[1]

The man who was working with him says he was very drowsy, having been at a dance all night. Suddenly he saw him start up and he was gone. Hatibu himself says the devil took hold of him; anyhow, he sprung off just far enough and not too far. There is a small wall about five feet outside the church wall, and another wall about six feet beyond that. He fell on the thatched roof between the two, and the thin poles, though they gave way beneath him, saved him.

We have had a series of accidents, as became a great work, but no serious hurts. First, a scaffold blew down, but no one was on it.

Then an arch, built during the rains, one of the large side arches, fell in, and people were on the scaffolds on each side, but the arch fell simply down, and the scaffolds stood.

Then in the taking out the centreing of the western arch it slipped and overbalanced the scaffold, and all came down with a crash together, but the masons had just time to scramble on to the side walls; and now this tumble of Hatibu's seems to have done him no harm at all. I see no signs of failure in our roof arch, and am beginning to get less timid about it, but it is risky work.

I am very glad they carried your motion[2] at the Oxford Conference. I have no doubt that the extravagant things which have been said about the relations of Church and State have their effect for good. It would be a wonderful thing if the Liberation Society ended by liberating us—we have seen less unlikely things happen.

---

[1] One of the Bishop's quaint anecdotes arises from this incident. "I went the next day to call upon our neighbour, and to say how sorry we were for the damage done to his house. With true native politeness he expressed himself glad that his roof should have been in the way of the falling man. He was very glad *in any way* to oblige the Great Father."

[2] That it is desirable to establish a great Central Conference, consisting of delegates from the several Diocesan Conferences.

I am not sure that hard times are bad for the church. I suppose no decree of any General Council on matters of faith is valid, unless it is generally accepted by the faithful laity. I am afraid of legalism.

It seems to me that over and beyond the laws and rules of the Church, the Holy Spirit works by modes that we cannot judge of, and have no general right to apply. Thus the regularity or irregularity of a proceeding is a reason for doing it again in the same or in a different way, but is not conclusive as to its validity. A thing may, I suppose, be wrong in the doer, and right in the permitter.

When will these questions end? Meanwhile the general motion seems to me to be by right means to right ends, and so we rejoice.

P.S.—I see the small country benefices are being noticed. I take it, all union of benefices is an unmixed evil, but there ought to be some way of uniting parishes.

Two parishes with one priest and two churches, and two sets of parochial organization, I take to be an abomination; but one large parish with several chapels, seems to me a totally different thing. So that the union of parochial organizations is what is wanted, not the union of benefices.

Then we must have men who maintain themselves by lay work, to serve the chapelries, and mission rooms, call them what you will. I should say make them deacons.

It is monstrous to say that it is impossible to live by one's own work and to be like an Apostle. Anything grosser in its way than Brook Lambert's assertion that a man cannot properly do a priest's work unless he is a rich man, I never remember to have seen. A similar thing has been said at some Conferences—that lay deacons, *i.e.* Deacons maintaining themselves in the world, would secularize those who meant to become priests. I think it would be altogether the other way, they would shame them into earnestness.

Sunday December 15th was a grand day at Mbweni. No less than thirty-one adults were brought forward by Mr. Johnson for baptism before giving over his charge there, and returning to the mainland. Nine boys were also baptized a few days afterwards at Kiungani, and on S. Thomas' day Mr. F. J. Williams, their indefatigable schoolmaster, was ordained deacon.

On Christmas Day, Matins were held again in the Slave Market Church. Some 400 at least of the townspeople were present, and a crowd of Arabs gathered round the great west door to read an address which the Bishop had posted up in Arabic. All were orderly and reverent, and the contrast, to those who remembered the old sad associations of the place, the unspeakable sorrows and wrongs that were so long wrought there unchecked, was almost overpowering.

A curious incident that happened in the afternoon, is worth recording as evidence of the practical outcome of the Bishop's work.

"Dr. Kirk," says the Bishop, "was walking home from Mbweni, and sat down under a tree; by-and-by, a man came out of a hut suspected of being a drink shop, with a bottle, so Dr. Kirk sent after him to look at the bottle. The man gave a sort of smile and said, "I am not one of that sort, *I am one of Bishop Steere's men;* it's American oil," and so it was.

The following extracts from a letter of the Rev. E. S. Randolph, who rejoined the Bishop in the first week of the new year, after a few months necessary rest in England, will fitly conclude our account of the year 1878:—

I found the Mission party as a whole very flourishing, particularly the Bishop, I am glad to say, though he is not without traces of fatigue, which would be unlikely at the least ; still, however, he is tolerably well.

The work he gets through is something marvellous, and to help him he has ordained one man Priest, and two others Deacons, and has kept one of each only to help him ; the others are up country. He is burning to secure more land about the church, and little bits are for sale, of which he has acquired one or more, and paid for himself, I believe, which is noble of him.

I can only say that not one half the truth of the work being done here has been spoken of in England, and we suffer from the ignorance that prevails. You can have no idea of the progress made, and appreciated by those around us here ; and with no contentment indeed by the Mohammedans, who, I believe, are seriously uneasy at the signs of our growing power.

It seems of the utmost importance that now Bishop Steere, with his experience, and the foothold he has gained, should be supported with all the Church's power, and that no longer his work should be done in a corner. I am fairly astonished at the signs I see of advancement, the result of self-denial that the present dearth of funds has compelled to be increased ; hence, perhaps, the wonderful progress, and prosperity of the Mission.

CHAPTER XV.

1879.

THE year 1879 was one of great progress in many ways. First of all it included the ordination and appointment to a mainland station of the first native clergyman of the Mission, the Rev. John Swedi.

Secondly, the taking up and settling down to a well-ordered life at Masasi, of some sixty more adult freed slaves, who had been received at various times from Her Majesty's cruisers, cared for and educated in Zanzibar.

Thirdly, as the natural outcome of their Christian lives, the application of several chieftains in the neighbourhood of Masasi for resident Missionaries.

Then in the Usambara country, the signs of a firm rooting of the Faith among the people of the country themselves became so clear that the church there deserved and required a fixed head, and the Rev. J. P. Farler was appointed Archdeacon of Magila.

And lastly, to sum up the Bishop's own personal work for the year, we may note the completion and printing at the native press of the translation of the New Testament into Swahili; the completion of the Prayer Book in the same tongue; the completion of the outer fabric of the church in the slave market, and its opening on Christmas day; the commencement of a permanent stone church at Mbweni; and during the very last week of the year an expedition by the Bishop into the Zaramo country, which lies due west of Dar es Salaam, some forty miles south of Zanzibar, where he had long desired to plant a station, as being in the direct line of what then promised to become a great trade route between Zanzibar and Lake Nyassa.

There was no more distinguishing feature of the Bishop's character and work than the relations which he always maintained with those who were engaged in the home work of the Mission. Under his guidance the Mission was made to be a Society of Missionaries rather than a Missionary Society. "Do not think," he said to us at home, "that you are without a share in the work, or that we only have it to do. We are indeed the hands by which this Church of ours ministers to those that are in want; we are the tongue by which this Church at home speaks in a strange language to those who have never heard of such a place as this in which you live. We are indeed the hands and the tongue; but then what are the hands and the tongue unless there is a whole healthy body to give power to both?

"Missions can never be, and can never prosper, unless there is the healthy life in the whole Church behind. For what is the Church? Is it not the Body of Christ? And what is the Spirit that lives in it? Is it not the Spirit of Christ? So that you in your parts, and we in ours, each one of us, have the very work of Christ to do as we are His members: we are each one "members in particular," moving as the Spirit emanating from the Head directs."

And so it was, as the following letter will show, that he was just as ready to advise and counsel a home worker as any one of his staff more directly under his personal supervision in Africa.

Feb. 4, 1879.[1]

Looking at things from a distance it appears to me that everybody in England is talking in superlatives, and that oldish people have seen worse times. It seems to me that the Opposition blunder in everything they put their hands to. It is curious that the old contest between the Court of Queen's Bench and the Court of Arches should have revived, and the parties seem to behave very much indeed as Lord Coke and Dr. Cowell did in their days. However, a Chief Justice's publishing a pamphlet in defence of a judgment of his own seems to me a very indecent performance.

I am anxious to see how the proposals at S. P. G. will show themselves. I think that a man approved by the Bishop should in ordinary cases be allowed by the Society. They could always act in special cases, and withdraw their grant.

The most dangerous thing is to try and trim a balance, and carefully avoid being anything. Of course safe men give the least trouble, but they are the least worth having, and bring least support. S. P. G. can never get the thorough support of low churchmen, she ought to be very careful not to offend the high.

For ourselves, I am not inclined to spend money on deputations. I should like to work the Press thoroughly, and let what we do, and wish, appear in as many periodicals as possible, but I should rather fail by relying on volunteers than scrape on by large home expenditure. Better pay for advertisements than for deputations. . . . There really seem

[1] To the Rev. R. M. Heanley.

to be great things doing in a Missionary way in India, and even in China. It seems that the world will have to acknowledge Missions after all.

The scrap-books are lovely, they will be a wealth of delight to the children, only if you can do so without offence, just hint to the senders that they should not mix sacred and secular subjects, and that robins and snowballs are unknown mysteries to the African mind.

Here is a specimen of a note sent out to one of his staff at Mbweni immediately after the mail had come in. It was his habit to gather up and pass on to his fellow-workers at such times all news of general interest that he had received in his own letters.

Zanzibar, 4th March, 1879.

You have, I suppose, heard most of the little news there is. Canon Lightfoot gone to Durham, and Prof. Stubbs to S. Paul's. Thirty pounds have come for Johnson from Canon Linton. In the last six weeks of the year £2000 came on for us, so we did exceed the year before. Mr. Farler is persuaded by his friends to remain in England for the whole of the London season. There is a talk of extending very largely the Ladies' Association. Mr. Sayers and Miss Bashford sailed on February 20th, and Mr. Rankin and Mr. Bellingham are to come this month. Twenty guineas have come from Mr. Causton's father. Marshal Macmahon has resigned, M. Grevy is now President, and M. Gambetta President of the Assembly. Some 12,000 troops have been sent to Zululand. Stanley has hired a steamer for nine months, and is coming to give the Belgians a lift. O'Neil of the "London" is to be Consul at Mozambique. The "Daphne" (Capt. Selby) found the steamer abandoned which Mr. Randolph saw on shore, and towed her into Aden harbour. They expect a lot of money for salvage. Has Miss Fawkes a proper pattern for kisibaus? If not we must send her one. A parcel for you is said to be in a box. Thanks for Miss Randolph's letter. You can tell people of several special objects. The church in town is poor. The houses in town are poor. There is a very great want of a church at Mbweni. A special want just now in several houses are some good sized hand-bells to ring for school, meals, etc. I am inclined to think that £3 worth of these would be the most immediately useful. Good soap is not to be had here, I should like some hundredweights. "Store is no sore." I am glad you are well and so do not get outings like the sick ones.

Writing on April 30th, 1879, the Bishop says:—

Mr. Sayres and Miss Bashford arrived just in time for Holy Week, and Mr. Maples being down from Masasi with his party for confirmation we were able to keep our commemoration of the crucifixion in a somewhat worthy manner. Our great day was on Easter Monday, when one adult and twelve children were baptized. All through this month Mr. Maples has kept up special daily matins and evensong with his people from Masasi, to the great edification of the neighbourhood and of ourselves, for the hearty service so heartily joined in by our own people could not but excite our own devotion. These candidates from Masasi were all confirmed by me on April 25th, and with them a lieutenant on board H.M.S. "London," who has become acquainted with Swahili whilst serving here, so that he was able to join in the service and follow the addresses. Nothing could exceed the devoutness of the whole party. . . . On the 1st May they all received from me their first communion. This was also the first occasion on which the whole of the liturgy was used in Swahili, Mr. Goldfinch having by great exertions got a sufficient number of proofs ready. We have also completed S. Paul's Epistles in Swahili. The Catholic Epistles are in type, the Apocalypse ready for the printer; this leaves only S. Mark, which is in hand now. The church is now more than half roofed. The masons have been trimming up and pointing the western gable, which in true Zanzibar fashion they had got to lean over nearly a foot, but they have straightened it now very cleverly. The Sultan has signified, through Dr. Kirk, his intention to present us with a clock for the turret, and has promised a free passage to Lindi to Mr. Johnson and his party of fifty natives, which latter will be a great boon.

This clock arrived in due course. There was a great discussion as to whether it should keep Arab or English time, and the townsfolk were delighted with the compliment when the Bishop decided that it should keep Arab time, according to which the day begins at our six o'clock of the evening. But the great event of the year, so far as the Mission Schools were concerned, was undoubtedly the ordination as Deacon of John Swedi, which took place on June 8th, Trinity Sunday, 1879. He was one of the first five boys given to Bishop Tozer by the Sultan shortly after his arrived in Zanzibar in 1864, and was brought by him for a short time to England in 1866. The chief portion of his probation however was spent in Zanzibar and latterly at Mbweni, the home for adult freed slaves, amongst whom he made himself both respected and beloved. When new arrivals of poor creatures just rescued came in, John Swedi was there to receive them, and was most useful in making them understand the circumstances under which they found themselves in the hands of Europeans, and the difference between this and the sad destiny that had seemed to await them before they were rescued from the hands of the slave-dealers. The settling down of these new comers, and the providing them at first with food and shelter, was always his work, and their wants were attended to in a way which sometimes entailed great self-denial. He constituted himself at once doctor and nurse in the case of many who were ill; and when the time came for him to go up to Masasi, this was specially remembered, and all said the sick would feel his departure most, whilst the sick themselves lamented it with tears. It was a fact that when the actual time of departure came very few were there to witness it or to say a last "good bye;" and when one of the European members of the staff expressed some surprise at this apparent neglect, answer was given that it had been said the day before, and they would not come out to see him leave for they could not bear it. Later news spoke of his having a school of some twenty children in a village a few miles from Masasi, and of the good effect produced in Masasi itself, not only by his pastoral work, but the example of his well-ordered house and family, for he had been married for some years, and had three children.

The importance of this step, wrote the Bishop, can hardly be overrated. The permanent success of our ministry depends in no small degree on its acceptance of all the marked outward features of the native life from which it springs. The heathen cannot suspect Christianity of being a crusade against all they hold dear on seeing that the preachers of the new religion in no way differ from themselves save in the purity of their lives and steadfastness of their faith. For the missionary himself there will be no new language to acquire, no acclimatization to undergo, no strange modes of life to encounter. He will be intimately acquainted with all his people's characteristics, their modes of thought, their likes and dislikes, their superstitions, their national habits and customs. Nor will his own conversion to Christ have made any very great outward change in his daily life. Possessing the pearl of great price, all things, in one sense, will have become new, and yet outwardly the things themselves will not be different. His hut, his goods, his dress, will all be as that of those around him, and if these external circumstances are but the accidents of a Christian man's life, in no way affecting its truthfulness or reality, why should they be thought inconsistent, or even unsuitable, for such as are admitted to Holy Orders? Surely nothing can be so false as to suppose that the outward circumstances of a people are the measure either of its barbarism or of its civilization. For instance, there is nothing higher than sincerity, which is not always found in so-called civilized society. The chief ornaments of the Apostolic Church would certainly be regarded as uncivilized in the present day, and probably we shall ourselves appear so to those who come after us. But the Church of Christ is not affected by distinctions such as these. She has no commission to bring all nations to any other uniformity than that of the faith. She can leave national habits and customs alone, sure that the indwelling Spirit will, in His own good time, work out in any particular national church that special form of civilization which is best suited to the nation.

Perhaps the following letter from a sailor, a Welshman and steward of an American merchant vessel, that happened at the time to be in the Port of Zanzibar, is the most extraordinary specimen of the multitudinous notes and calls upon his time that the Bishop was constantly receiving:—

Zanzibar. August 15. 1879.

My Revrent Sir and Christian Brother, You are Sir my Superior, I am your humble sarvant, and I ask you if with your beter judgement you will take the love and plesure of Reading and Explaining to the Barer of this note and others from the Acts of the Apostles the 8th chapter, touching on conFirmation and Simon the Sorcery, and Philip his sermon.

Also on the first book of Kings, of Elijah killing the prophets and the little cloud he prayd into a storm. Also on Matthew 21 the first 11 verses, and chapter 28. the resurrection and the last 3 verses. Dear Sir your conversing 5 minutes with this young man will oblige. I see that he have the belief of the Supreme Beene, but not of the Savour Jesus Christ.

The apostal Paul greats the saints of the church, then let us great the sinners into the church, Until all the World has learnt Messiah's name.

and the God of love will give you the Works of your labour, and you will pray for me . . But let us all pray the Lord of the Harvest to send more Larbrors into his vineyard. I am yours most obidiant sarvant of the Church in Newport. Monmouth. Wales.

One can feel no doubt of the readiness with which the request would be granted, and how tenderly the Bishop would deal with the young man's difficulties, smiling withal at the sailor-like touch about the storm, and not failing to note the nationality of the writer, as evidence that the Church in Wales is not so weak as some would have us think. The note itself was carefully preserved inside one from the Bishop of Pittsburgh, written for the anniversary of his consecration, and dated from the house of the Bishop of S. David's, in the previous year.

Meanwhile cheering evidence was not wanting that the work was telling upon the natives in the town of Zanzibar itself. Under date of July 25, 1879, the Bishop wrote:—

Dr. Kirk, a few days since, was surprised, in passing through the town, to hear a group of natives discussing the doctrine of the Holy Trinity with a good deal of intelligence and interest ; but as he went further he met others, and found that they had been listening to a discourse of Mr. Goldfinch, who is, I hope, regularly to preach in the further part of the town.

So also Miss Bashford, who looks after the town school, was teaching a soldier who came to learn to read, and when she asked him if he knew anything of God, he took out of his cap a copy of a hymn, written out by Miss Allen, which he was carefully keeping and studying.

We are also trying to form a Temperance Society here, the first man to come forward being a Sierra Leone man, and we hope to bring in a Krooman or two, as well as our own and the C. M. S. people. Drunkenness is just as crying an evil here among the Mohammedans as with our Christians at home, only it is kept more out of sight. Our traction engine, too, is doing a good work in its way, and I am very pleased to have it. The Seyed has been to see it, and is so delighted that he says he shall get one [1] of his own. So we are doing something for civilisation if only we improve the roads and bring stone into the town in waggons instead of on women's heads. The necessary consequence of using people as beasts of burden is to degrade them to the level of beasts of burden; and so the Arabs regard them, but we cannot. Again, the expense and slowness of this kind of labour hinders all progress, and makes much possible trade impossible. Practical works of this kind constantly come to us to do, and there is no one else to do them. There is the labour of a life needed to adapt our civilisation to the wants of the people, and bring them to understand and use our improvements, just as there is the work of a lifetime in the creation of a vernacular literature. Here we have had to do all from the very beginning. And so we feel that in making carts at Mbweni, and teaching oxen to draw them, and now in using our traction engine, we are doing a very real missionary work.

As to the printing-office, the Bishop adds, under date of October 15, 1879:—

Owen Makanyassa is now entirely in charge of it, and has had to print the menu and musical programmes for the entertainment the Seyed has been giving to the Portuguese Governor-General of Mozambique and the American Commodore, who are both here just now. He has done them very well.

[1] He has three at the present time.

I am hearing good news of several of our boys lately. Ackworth is with a surveyor in the town, who speaks highly of him. Captain Foot has just been praising William Senessi, who was with him, and Ali Katia, who is with the elephant expedition, is also very well spoken of.

We have had a slight shock of an earthquake here, very much like those in England. I did not perceive it myself, but some people in the town here say they did, and it seems to have extended to Magila. About twenty years ago there was a shock which, they say, broke some crockery in a few of the houses; but no severe shock is at all remembered.

The Seyed sent us word that he would come and see our printing-office, as he was so pleased with the work we had just done for him. So I went over to Kiungani and set up a little couplet in the Arabic, that he might print it himself if he chose:—

"There are many writers who have passed away and what they have written remains.

Write nothing save what, if you see it at the last day, you will be glad to have written."

He came at about half-past four in a steam launch with a party of about a dozen, all of them men of learning and devotees. I suspect they thought printing an uncanny art, and he wanted to show them what it was.

Christense was printing off some of the book of Genesis, and went on like clockwork, and then they came and looked at the type and read the couplet, which comes out of the "Arabian Nights," and approved of it highly, and saw another of our printers setting up type.

Then they went out and would stay for nothing more. I reproached him rather with going away without taking anything, so he said he would take a flower, and chose one off the table.

Another scheme is half proposed by the Seyed, and that is to add a general hospital to his soldiers' sick-house. I told Dr. Hague that we would get him out nurses if the scheme was to come to anything.

Christmas Day was a special time of joy this

year, as being the opening of the great church in the slave market, the outer fabric of which was at last entirely completed, though much remained to be done inside.

First the Bishop celebrated the Holy Communion, at eight o'clock, in the little school chapel opposite the church. And as soon as breakfast was over they began preparations for the morning service in the church. It had been beautifully decorated the day before by some of the Kiungani boys, under the direction of the Bishop and Miss Mills.

The scaffold poles still needed at the east end had been masked with palm-branches, till they looked like a decorative screen. In front of this, where the altar was to be, a cross was set up about twenty feet high, covered with mango boughs, relieved with white and red flowers. The walls were hung with banners of most effective design, and the floor was swept and laid with mats.

There were a few benches and chairs carried in for the use of the Europeans from the town and the members of the Mission, but all the natives sat on the floor. The girls and women were on the north side, the boys and men on the south.

All were in their holiday dress, white relieved with scarlet prevailing, the girls in particular looking so well in their white dresses and scarlet headkerchiefs and scarves. Black skins are ever so much more effective and picturesque in a mass like this, than white ones.

English people may laugh at this, but if they had seen that congregation on that Christmas Day they would have agreed that it was so.

And one thing is certain, that no English children would have been so reverent, or have entered so heart and soul into the service, as worship of Almighty God, as did these, by some despised, black children.

One could not but think, as one looked at them, of the groups that might have been seen upon that very spot, not so many years before, when it was the slave market. Groups so similar, but assembled for how different a purpose! And to heighten the resemblance, there were at the west end of the church, in the ante-chapel, a number of Arabs and Swahilis, some of whom doubtless had, in former times, come to that very spot to choose a slave, now listening, with these once slaves but now free indeed, to the glorious Gospel of Christmas Day.

The church proved all that could be wished for sound, the voices clear and resonant without any perceptible echo, and the chants and hymns, all in Swahili, rolled magnificently under the vaulted roof.

They sang "While shepherds watched their flocks," and "Hark the herald angels," and the Bishop preached a beautiful sermon on the love of God shown in the condescension of the Incarnation and the Birth on Christmas Day. Nearly all the Europeans resident in Zanzibar were present, about 250 of our own people from Kiungani and Mbweni, and some 200 of the townspeople besides, so that it was in every way a grand "Sala," and Day of Thanksgiving.

Only pause for a moment and compare this

peaceful orderly place as on the Lord's Day morning, with no sound of labour, but all gathering in their best into God's house to sing hymns of praise in their own tongue, and hear, it may be, one of their own countrymen expound to them the great gift of their salvation—compare this with the open slave market, rows of men, women, and children, sitting and standing, and salesmen passing in and out amongst them, examining them, handling them, chaffering over them, bandying their filthy jokes about them, and worse scenes still going on in all the huts around—there is Africa as heathenism and Mohammedanism have made it; in Christ Church, Zanzibar, one may see a glimpse of what Christianity can do for it.

The style of the church is a mixture of Gothic and Arabic, with windows very narrow but of great beauty, and very thick walls.

The roof is a plain-pointed barrel of twenty-eight and a-half feet span, and the centre line is exactly sixty feet from the pavement.

It is perhaps the greatest evidence of the Bishop's skill. Wood could not be used because of the white ants, nor iron because of the heat of the sun; he therefore resolved to build it of concrete, over a wooden centreing, which was afterwards removed, and now it stands a solid stone roof, covered over on the outside with sheets of corrugated iron.

There is a fine semi-circular apse with a bishop's seat or throne in the middle behind, and the Bishop himself lies buried between the altar and the throne. It is not without a deep significance that the altar itself occupies the site of the whipping-post of the

CHRIST CHURCH, ZANZIBAR.

To face p. 252.

old slave market, thus carrying the mind at once to the Crucified, by Whose stripes we are healed.

The Bishop always celebrated in each of the chapels in the Island at each great festival of the Church, and so the next day (Friday) he was at Kiungani, and on Saturday at Mbweni, where he traced out the foundations for the beginning of a permanent church. On Sunday he was in town again, so he had his time fully occupied till Monday, December 29, when he was at last able to set out on his long promised, long hoped-for expedition to the Zaramo country.

Before entering upon this little journey we add an important letter of the Bishop's, closing the story of 1879, and opening out wise and far-seeing visions of the future :—

January 9, 1880.[1]

I send you a copy of the year's accounts for 1879. I think we may safely say that it has been a year of much prosperity, though chequered by many disappointments. I am specially cheered by the sympathy and encouragement one gets from the Europeans who are living here.

As to the question of the C. M. S. Bishopric in Eastern Africa, it is a mistake to deal with it as a question of the starting of missions by particular societies, it is only a question as to the boundaries of the episcopal jurisdiction.

I have come to the conclusion that there are really four centres of work here :—
1. Mombas, and the triangle between the sea and the Masai and Wakwasi. There need be no other barrier laid down, this is the old C. M. S. field.
2. Zanzibar and Pemba, and the tribes opposite, *i.e.*, Uzaramo and Usambara.

[1] To the Rev. J. W. Festing.

3. The northern lakes, lying north of 7 S. latitude. The centre of communication with this district is at Mpwapwa, where the C. M. S. has a station.

4. The Nyassa district south of 7 S. latitude.

I have asked the Archbishop to allot to me the second and fourth, and to give the Mombas Bishop, when there is one, the first and third.

In time there must be four bishops at least. All questions of detail should be settled by consent, or by the Archbishop. I do not think that any scheme will work better than this.

I am very glad that you are going on pleasantly in your own work ; may God be with you.

CHAPTER XVI.

ZARAMO AND 1880.

SIR T. FOWELL BUXTON, Mr. W. Mackenzie, and some of their friends, in their anxiety for the civilization of the East African, commenced in 1879 a road into the interior from the Port of Dar-es-Salaam, due south of the Island of Zanzibar, and forty miles from the city of that name.

The reports which had been brought by Livingstone and other travellers of the great chain of lakes extending for 1,000 miles, where all had been regarded as desert, filled many persons with hopes of boundless mineral and metallic wealth to be brought to light in the unknown regions, especially as copper and iron had been seen in more than one district, and gold certainly in one.

And as nothing could better extinguish the slave trade in the interior than more profitable trade of a legitimate character, it was a work of true philanthropy to seek to open up the country for legitimate commerce.

If Zanzibar had proved itself to be the chief port and emporium for commerce, would not a good road into the interior from a convenient port near to it prove to be the best handmaid of the Christian Missionary?

The north of Lake Nyassa was not more than 400 miles, as the crow flies, from Dar-es-Salaam; Lake Tanganyika was from 180 to 200 miles further. At all events it was desirable that a start should be made, and the road was begun, Mr. Beardall, who had done good service as a member of the Universities' Mission, being engaged as engineer.

While the road was in progress the well-known expedition of Mr. Keith-Johnston for the Royal Geographical Society to the Central Lakes was undertaken.

It started in May 1879, and returned in July 1880 to Zanzibar, with the sad loss indeed of its leader, but having been admirably conducted by Mr. Joseph Thomson, a young Scotchman, who was geologist and naturalist to the Expedition.

He subsequently conducted a search for coal on the Rovuma River for the Seyed of Zanzibar, and a still more important expedition to the Lake Victoria Nyanza, through the Masai country, for the Geographical Society. Some persons were surprised that he was not chosen as Leader of the Relief Expedition to Emin Pasha, rather than Mr. Stanley.

But, however this may be, he passed over the Zaramo district a few months before Bishop Steere took his last walk on the mainland of the Continent, and we note a few particulars of the country gathered from the book he published on his return to England.

Zaramo is about thirty miles square, bounded on the east and north-east by the ocean, on the north-west by the river Kingani, and on the south and south-west by a strip of desert. The whole of the country is a comparatively level plain, being in fact an elevated sea-beach, and scarcely more than 200 feet above the sea, except where a few more important towns have been placed; they stand nearly 400 feet high.

We fear that this fact alone would make the Zaramo country dangerous to the lives of Europeans, unless the fine ranges of the Usagara mountains can be relied upon to send down cooling breezes from the N.E.

The country looks tame in the absence of hills. Gently undulating slopes or sandy ridges prevail, covered with matted bush and monotonous stunted trees. Streams flow, some to the north, to Dares-es-Salaam, some to the south to the great river Rufiji, some to the east to the ocean.

The land is chiefly cultivated on the sides of the ridges.

The hollows are occupied with filthy marshes,[1] where only spear grass and huge sedges find a congenial soil among the rotting vegetation which fills both water and air with noxious and malarious gasses.

There is more variety about the villages, where groves of cocoanut, mangoes, oranges, and jack-fruit trees have been planted.

---

[1] "To the Central African Lakes and Back," Sampson Low and Co., 1881. Mr. Thomson writes feelingly, having twice fallen over-head into marshes of this character.

In the wet season, the country is submerged except the ridges, and becomes almost impassable. In the dry season, owing to the sandy soil, the country seems scorched up.

The people were peaceful and unassuming, hospitable and friendly, and quite eager to barter.

The stoppage of the slave trade has much improved their condition, as there is a steady demand for indiarubber and gum copal, both of which abound.

Mr. Thomson concludes his remarks by saying that Sir T. Fowell Buxton's road "will not bring 'unspeakable riches' from the central highlands, which consist chiefly of districts of cold clay, slates, and rocks of a granitoid character, but that it has developed more steady and industrious habits, produced greater peace and security, and otherwise given a distinct impetus to material advancement, and the work of civilization."

Though the road has for the present not been carried far inland, we are happy to think that it has not been undertaken in vain, and when the happy day comes for a *native* Missionary party to advance into the interior, the Zaramo country is ready, and they will be following in the steps of Bishop Steere.

With this preface we proceed to draw a picture of our Missionary Bishop setting forth on his journey into the interior.

First of all he had to provide himself with a light fold-up bedstead and a blanket; nothing more would he take, neither sheets, nor pillow, nor mosquito net.

Then food must be carried with him, as well as

means of cooking and eating it. So a couple of small iron cooking pots, or "sufaria," as they are called, were bought, and also a small kettle for boiling water, and a tin pot to serve as teapot or coffee-pot.

Next in the way of utensils came two iron plates, one iron mug for water, and one earthenware one for tea. Two knives and forks and two spoons, and a native wooden spoon for the use of the cook. For where everything has to be carried every step of the way, one limits oneself to the barest necessities.

For food the Bishop took a dozen small tins of preserved meat, half-a-dozen tins of cocoa and milk, and half-a-dozen small loaves. Nothing else except a tin of tea, and one of sugar. Rice he would have, because the men that accompanied him had rice provided for them on the way, and when they cooked theirs he had a small quantity of it.

He also took a lantern and a few candles and matches. He wore a large shady pith hat, and carried an umbrella and a waterproof coat, but no arms or ammunition of any kind. His faithful travelling servant, Daudi, and a couple of natives as porters, accompanied him.

The dhow which was to take them across to the mainland had been ordered for ten o'clock, but as a matter of course the captain and his men found means of delaying the start, in true African fashion, till well on into the afternoon, which lost them the best part of the breeze, so that they did not reach Dar-es-Salaam until nearly midnight.

Dar-es-Salaam, formerly called Mzizima, was planned out by the late Sultan Seyed Majid as a secure place from sea attacks. He feared his brother Thuweyne at Muscat, who had often threatened to make a descent upon him, and he would gladly have been a little less in the power of the English shipping, so one of the shrewdest of his advisers suggested a new town on the mainland at this place, which has a wonderful natural harbour, a great land-locked basin, entered only by a narrow passsage, but with plenty of water for any class of shipping. The old name Mzizima means "very still," referring to the perpetual calm in the harbour.

The town was begun on a grand scale, but Majid died before it was nearly finished, so that now there are only a few large stone houses complete, and long rows of large buildings raised to the level of the first floor, and broad streets laid out with the beginnings of long ranges of shops: only two streets have now any inhabitants.

It was Sultan Majid's intention to have brought all the caravans from the interior to this spot. And the road of which mention has been already made, tends to bring this scheme to a reality. The natural facilities are as great as well may be.

The journey was a successful one from every point of view. The Bishop reached a point some five and thirty miles inland, and found the country well populated and cultivated, whilst the people seemed not averse to listening to the Gospel message, and quite ready to welcome a resident teacher. One young man, indeed, came down to the schools on the Island after a time to learn more of what he had heard from him, but from one cause or another, chiefly lack of men and means, the Bishop was never able to carry out his long cherished scheme of planting a station there.

Amongst his letters on his return the Bishop found one from Lord Shaftesbury, as President of the Bible Society, requesting his acceptance of the post of a Vice President.

Whilst very far from agreeing with those who regard the Holy Scriptures as "God's one Sacrament of Life," the Bishop had long learnt that which so many Churchmen still fail to perceive how *without the generous aid of the Bible Society it would be utterly impossible for the Church to carry on her mission work efficiently;* and there was no place where he was more gladly welcomed, or felt himself more at home, than in his visits to the Bible House. There is something so characteristic in the modesty of his letter of acceptance, that we cannot withhold it from our readers :—

Zanzibar, January 5th, 1880.

Allow me to thank you and through you the Committee of the Bible Society very much for the honour you have done me by proposing to add my name to the list of your Vice Presidents. If I can be in any way of use to the Society, I have long wished to do what I could for its cause. My only hesitation lies in the fact that the obligation is all on one side, and that side mine. I would gladly assist by money gifts, or personal advocacy if I could, but I am here in no position to do either. I feel here that our work must be all unsound without a Vernacular Bible, and this the Society has made possible to us.

Under the date of May, 1880, a very interesting testimony from an outsider, not a member of the Church of England, reached us to the following effect :—

I think you should know that all sorts and classes of people are struck with the reality of the work here. There is no show or sentiment, it is just real ; for instance, the other day a Colonel Harrison, returning from the Zulu war, called ; the Bishop asked him to stay and look through. He did, and the next day sent the Bishop a cheque for £25, and such a nice little note. The Mission-house is just what it ought to be, open to every one, a bed always ready. If any one likes to come out and share a meal with them the Bishop welcomes them most heartily, but they must take them as they are. They live very simply, and have nothing in the way of luxuries. Wine and beer you never see on the table ; they are all teetotallers.

Here is a glimpse of some of the varied incidents of Mission life in Zanzibar taken from the Bishop's letter of the following month :—

I have just bought three more plots of land, one just to the east of the church, and two to the south of it. They cost together £320. The price of land is increasing terribly, even in our unfashionable part of the town. A piece of land just outside the town, which a Hindi bought a few years ago for £300, he has just sold for £1,000, and it will probably be worth £2,000 before long. Seyed Burghash has asked us to metal for him the road between this and Mbweni, and Bellingham is using the engine and the trucks for it. Stone we have of our own in any quantity, and the payment is to be £100 a mile. It is, in fact, doing our own work, as much of it must have been done in order to get the engine along. One of the women at Mbweni made away with a little daughter of hers a few days ago under circumstances suggesting strongly that she had sold her. So we took possession of her other children, and sent her off till she could bring back the missing one. Thus a little boy is added to Miss Mill's charge, and possibly a child or two may be added to Miss Thackeray's. A still better addition is a young man named Mwinyi Kondo, whom I spoke to in the Zaramo country, and who has now come down on his own account to be taught by us at Kiungani. So you see that though we cannot yet get on, the Zaramo Mission *will not* let itself be given up.

There were eighteen baptisms on S. Bartholomew's Day, August 24th, four of whom were adults from Mbweni, who had been admitted as catechumens twelve months previously, and been under Mr. Hodgson's care in the interval; the rest were children, seven boys and seven girls.

A severe strain was put on the resources of the Mission in October by the arrival of the largest party of freed slaves that had been received for years, seventy-nine in all. We quote from a letter of Archdeacon Hodgson's, who is in charge at Mbweni:—" I got a scrap of paper on the morning of October 25th from Lieut. Smith, saying he had ' caught a mob,' would I care to come off in the cutter he had sent with the bearer and see them in *statu quo?* Of course, as I had never been on board a slave dhow, I was very glad to take the opportunity. It was, I suppose, about forty feet long, had no deck except a few feet at each end, and the bilge water was flowing about the large stones in the bottom, which did duty for ballast, in a manner perceptible to more senses than one. A cocoa-nut thatch served for awning, and when boarded all the slaves were crammed together out of sight under this. When I got on board I found Smith at the rudder very well pleased with his prize, and men, women, boys, girls, and infants swarming all over the craft, most of them very dirty and with little or no clothing on. I was most struck, or fancied that people unaccustomed to Central Africans would be most struck, with the utter absence of anything like excitement in the expression either of the Arabs or their slaves. Both might have been entirely unconcerned. They went on their way to Zanzibar, where it turned out that there were no less than ninety-nine souls on board the vessel, small as it was. The dhow was confiscated, the owners got a year in the Sultan's convict chain-gang, and, lastly, the slaves were handed over to us. The same evening, just as I was taking a funeral at nightfall, the long troop came marching in; two or three had been left at the small boys' school in town, ten at Kiungani, the rest, twenty-nine men, twenty-three women, eleven girls, and four babies, had come on to us, and had then and there to be provided with food, lodging, and every requirement for passing the night. Fortunately that does not imply as much here as in England, and they had each had a garment (about two yards of calico) given them before starting. The new house which is in process of building here was called into requisition for the men, the women were divided between the sick house and the women's house, and the girls taken into the large schoolhouse. We gave them old matting to lie on, and had a lot of rice put on to boil. When this had been served out to them (in buckets!), and water to drink, they soon made themselves at home. When I went in to look at them the last thing at night the men were all stretched out, or sitting down on their mats, down the long room. Some were singing and some few passing round a pipe to take in turn very homœopathic whiffs of tobacco. Next day I had them all up before me to take down their names and tribes, giving them each ten pice, a day's wages. These men had suffered but little, and very soon were able to work for themselves. No one works for us unless he likes, but if he wants a day's work he comes to the 6 a.m. service, after it receives a ticket, and gets his wages on producing the ticket at five in the evening. Most people work every day, or at least five days a week. What sort of work? you will say. Well, at present we have:—First, two sets of masons, one set building alternately at the church on this Shamba and at the stone house above mentioned; and the second set at stone cottages, a shed for the engine, and circular saw, &c. As each mason requires five or six assistants, this gives employment to a good number. Then, secondly, there is always a gang, chiefly of women, hoeing, clearing grass or weeds. Thirdly, roadmaking, and the various jobs connected with the engine, the bullocks, carts, &c., take a number of hands. And, fourthly, quarrying stone and lime burning, as it is the most remunerative to us, so it brings in the largest wages to the man employed. These are the chief occupations, and the lowest wage is ten pice per day, about threepence halfpenny.

"But to return to the new comers. They were not very long before they wanted to marry and have houses of their own. Every married couple here has a house and a quarter acre of land to themselves. I am very anxious to get all the houses built of *stone*, so as to be lasting, clean, and healthy, none of which can their mud huts be in any great degree. However, this takes time and money, so we must also have mud ones as makeshifts. We have thirty or forty stone houses already, and build about two a month; if any one likes to subscribe for this special purpose, about £5 will build a real "model cottage" for Mbweni requirements. With these last people, what I did as soon as a man had pitched on a ladylove, which they often do before they know her name, was to set them to work on a quarter acre measured out for them, give them poles, cord, and grass, and made them build for themselves. When the house was finished I registered them as man and wife (not being Christians, of course), with mutual promises of fidelity, and allowed them to enter on their occupation. Thus having made provision for their external welfare, the next thing is to enforce as far as possible morality, and endeavour to inculcate Christianity. With a view to the latter all are supposed to attend one service on Sunday; no work is allowed on that day, and I have a class every afternoon of the week after the day work is over, to which I try to persuade all new people, and old ones who are still only hearers, to come. When they have attended some little time and appear interested, they are publicly admitted catechumens, and, after a full year, if they have attended classes regularly and led respectable lives, they are baptised. At present I have here thirty-eight adults baptised and sixty-six catechumens. About the real spiritual work I do not find it easy to write; you will know how it is little more than the external statistics which one can give of work in an English parish even, and here, where the government is necessarily more paternal, these must count for less. Still the work gives me encouragements no less than discouragements, and very much in the same way as in England. On the one hand, one feels how little one can tell how much of their old superstitious belief or practice of witchcraft, magic, &c., remains under the exterior of Christianity, whilst on the other, every now and then one is surprised with unexpected fruits of Christianity in apparently barren stocks, or with the return of those whom one had thought to have hopelessly gone out from among us. We had, for instance, a fight between two of our men this morning. One of them was a communicant, and yet what do you think his reason for the row was? 'Some relative of his had been bewitched by some one connected with the other man'!!! This seems to me the great difficulty here. A native is quite ready to receive all you teach him, and has no previous religion to prejudice him, but witchcraft, magic, divination, charms, &c., are so thoroughly a part of his nature that, after years and years of apparently accepted teaching, the old superstition will come up to the surface again and again in most unexpected ways."[1]

[1] Nor is it yet quite dead after centuries of Christianity in

Of Kiungani the following report is condensed from various letters of the Bishop :—

Mr. Geldart managed the whole place alone for two or three months in the year, until joined by Mr. Lowndes, and now carries on the school with a freshness, effect, and vigour which never flags except from sheer illness. He has complete command of Swahili, knowing it thoroughly as spoken by the boys. This alone would make his addresses tell even if they were not, as they are, full of thought and depth and earnestness. His sympathy and gentleness makes him firm friends among the boys, while he has firmness and strength to lead them. The school has of course suffered from the great disadvantage of constant change of head. Still, no boy can be long here without a conscience in some degree enlightened, faculties strengthened, habits formed, making it impossible to return quite to the old level, and some Christian ideas of life and living. One old scholar, who had been lost sight of for some time, appeared, for instance, last Christmas at Magila, and asked for a supply of books, as he was engaged in teaching the sons of several chiefs of his own tribe. On the other hand, the provision made for their wants necessarily tends to unfit them in some degree for the rough and simple way of living in their own land and the duty of hard work with their own hands and making their own livelihood. They get a kind of conceit, too, from mere contact with the friendly and omnipotent European. Everything is to be hoped for from a comparatively settled management, and nothing to be feared in the future. What can a generation or two of experiments signify, if one wholesome lesson of success or failure is learnt for the building of the future Church of Africa?—The

---

England. We ourselves were applied to in the autumn of 1887, by an old man, and a communicant, on behalf of a sow that was supposed to have been "overlooked." "I thought mebbe as you would say a few words over her. For I am feared if I was to *draw blood* of the party that had done it, she would have me up before the magistrates."—R. M. H.

printing office, under Mr. Hayman, continues to turn out excellent work, and is fairly besieged by customers from the town, so that we want both more room and more working power. Mr. Ellis has put new life into the carpenter's and other workshops, and the tailors and laundry hold their own.

Of the work in town the Bishop added :—

Mr. Jones Bateman is doing really great work in town and harbour. He has charge of the professing Christians in town, now numbering nearly a hundred, and has brought in already eight new catechumens. Every Sunday afternoon he goes to a distant part of the town, where he preaches under a spreading mango tree. He has besides daily a class of beginners of various nationalities, and the four sons of an Arab who was in his time the chief man under the Seyed here, but yet he is besides able to give a little thought to the crews of the merchant ships that frequently visit the harbour. Miss Bashford has gathered a good many women together, and a catechumen's class has been formed out of them. She has thirty-one on her books altogether. Miss Allen has been able to relieve great numbers of ailments by her medical skill, and to diffuse among the Arab ladies some knowledge of our faith. The better to do this she is diligently applying herself to the study of Arabic.

CHAPTER XVII.

DAILY LIFE IN ZANZIBAR CITY.

1880.

A singularly interesting letter from Miss Allen, a daughter of the late Archdeacon of Salop, gives a graphic picture of the Bishop in his inner home life in the Island, and we therefore give it here, premising some account of his outer life, and a description of Zanzibar as it appeared to the late Consul Elton.

"Before[1] breakfast on the 9th of March we sighted Zanzibar. It was a dead calm, the sea like molten glass, the distant hills of the mainland quivering in the hot atmosphere, and the tree-fringed promontories of the Island standing out against and above an indistinct horizon, in distorted mirage, as we steamed past Ras Kizimkasi, sending long rocking waves to glitter in the beating sun-glare, and ripple and die away upon the narrow strip of sandy beach.

"Beyond these arose, in perhaps too great profusion and monotony, shadowy clumps of graceful cocoanut palms, intermingled with groves of clove trees, and faced by a tangled wild foreground of fantastically matted and labyrinthine tropical vegetation. One or two clumsy dhows, with their

[1] "Lakes and Mountains of Africa," p. 33.

broad white lateen sails shining in the sun-way, relieved the calm purple tone of the misty horizon, and faint curling columns of smoke ascended through the brilliant green forest-colouring that covered the land. A hot, dreamy, tropical landscape, a languid idle atmosphere, a day upon which it was a positive punishment to move about more than was necessary, and almost too much exertion to think, a day upon which the dull heavy thud of the screw propeller, and the vibration of the steamer, persistently combined to be perseveringly annoying in asserting claims upon your unwilling attention.

"Past some coralline and water-worn islets, fringed at low water by narrow strips of bright sandy beach, and densely covered with entangled brushwood, and here and there a dwarfed baobab tree, past one of Seyed Burgash's dismantled frigates, stranded during the hurricane of 1872, and we make the anchorage and Zanzibar city, a white-washed, mildewed, oriental town, of flat-roofed and many storied abodes, with high wooden look-out stages and turreted walls, a pointed temple of Hindoo architecture, consular flags of many nations drooping over the houses, the Seyed's red standard fluttering over a white green-jalousied, weather-stained, irregularly built pile—the palace—with a delapidated saluting battery facing the sea, a town vividly recalling to memory the orthodox and conventional oriental port, at once picturesque, strong flavoured, highly conservative, and best to be admired at a distance."

Such is the utterly un-English frame-work of the picture.

In such weather, in such a city, amid such surroundings, Bishop Steere passed more or less upwards of eighteen years of his life.

Take such a morning as has been described, let it be a weekday, if you will, and the first thing that will greet you will be the sound of bells in the church tower, ringing out for Matins at half-past six. At the door of the house are assembling the boys who form the church choir, along with the smaller ones, who have not yet attained to the dignity of choristers, some forty in number, being the town boys' school under Miss Mills' care ; and there, in the road, just ahead, are passing a file of a dozen wee little girls under Miss Bashford's care, coming from the house where she lives with them, adjoining the Mission house. And then from many of the houses built on the Mission quarter, you see men, women, and children, the Christian people who have settled round the Mission House, gathering and moving churchwards.

Well, the Bishop is always present, coming in exactly to the minute, the service begins and the singing is undoubtedly hearty, even if not always quite in tune ; all, of course, in Swahili, so that much of it could be understood by the merest heathen or Mohammedan, who had never seen a church before, and it is wonderful how it attracts them. The grandeur of the building compared with anything they have seen ; the sound of the organ, which in itself is a kind of miracle to some of them, so that they visibly shake when they first hear its sound ; the heartiness of the worship, the prayers and praises in their own language ; all this and other little incidents in connection with the morning and evening worship, make it the greatest testimony for Christ in the midst of a dark world of Mohammedanism and heathenism of all the work that goes on in Zanzibar.

Here in the very *heart* of Eastern Central Africa, those who come and go, and travel north and south, walk this town to see what to them are marvels ; and in the grandest and finest building in it, which towers above the rest, they stand and witness something they have never met before, Christian worship in the Swahili tongue, and they go away and remember about it, and bear witness to others that they have seen another religion professed, and heard its worship, different entirely to the forms of Islam, which for so long have been the only kind of worship of which they knew.

It is good that rough up-country people, after visiting the centre of Mohammedan Eastern Africa, should go home with the story of the wonderful Christian church, and the worship that they all took part in.

Who is Bishop Steere? it was once asked far away in the interior, and the answer promptly came, " He is the man in Zanzibar who prays for all us Africans, and tries in every way to do us good."

And this result is effected (not by having a Chaplain to provide two services per week in English to twenty or thirty English townspeople, as some have fancied), but by having a resident Swahili-speaking Bishop and clergy, a vigorous choir school from which to draw the choristers for these services, and a Christian quarter round the church, lived on by a body of native Christians, to form a congregation, and to be a help to each other by the very force of numbers and living together.

And now we will go out of church, and in to breakfast about 7 o'clock, ourselves at one table and Miss Mills' school at two other tables close by; and after having introduced you to various little luxuries, like delicious pineapples, relegated to the rich alone in England, but worth only a penny apiece here, and having generally finished breakfast, every one at once goes to their various occupations.

At the front door, and even at the windows, have already gathered a number of different people. Here is a sick woman, an Arab's slave, with a terribly bad foot, waiting for Miss Allen to apply her daily course of treatment; and then another, a man with another dreadful ailment, living not far off; and then some of our own people on the quarter with sick children, or babies, or themselves unwell, coming for the all embracing "dawa" *i.e.*, the remedy, whatever it may be, for their special complaint.

As for the Bishop, he is at once hard at work. There is the *major domo*, Ali, asking him for orders about the building, or carpentering, or general business of the Mission, which wants looking after in the town.

After him comes the Banyan carpenter, waiting in turn to be shown his work, as in the carpenter's shop just outside the Mission house they have constantly in hand work for some of the stations, or some of the churches in the Mission, and their work is quite equal to, and much cheaper than the best English work, only they need a great deal of showing and directing.

Next perhaps will come a messenger with a note from the Consulate, requiring instant and anxious thought, and this is scarcely answered before like notes come in from the boys' school at Kiungani, or the girls' school, or the native settlement at Mbweni, dealing, it may be, with the simplest details of daily work, or presenting some intricate problem, on the wise solution of which much depends. In either case they find the Bishop ready to write an answer; for he had great faith in letter-writing; it was the way in which he kept himself, and expected to be kept by others, fully informed of all that went on in the Mission, and those who had the privilege of living near him were able to consult him, rather as very young curates might consult their experienced vicar, or as members of a family might apply to a very practical father, than as clergy applying to their Bishop; and they could feel sure that on any given subject his advice would be valuable.

It was almost a proverb amongst them, "Don't you know? Ask the Bishop, he is sure to know." And really his knowledge did seem so varied and inexhaustible that more than once one has heard the theory gravely broached, that he had found himself reduced to an Encyclopædia as his only literature for a long sea voyage, so had quietly set to work and learnt it by heart.

Here are two notes, which will serve as samples

of the rest, both written to Archdeacon Hodgson at Mbweni:—

My Dear Hodgson,

Mr. Holmwood says he told the man you sent in to come again last Monday to see Dr. Kirk, but he has not turned up. Dr. Kirk is out at Mbweni now, could not you take him to see him there? By all means let Uledi and Margaret marry as soon as they like. He is a Christian, having already fully renounced heathenism and accepted Christ as his Lord. I do not think catechumens can be ineligible as husbands or wives. It is a matter of discipline that they should show themselves in earnest, and be further instructed before they are baptized, but so far as they are concerned, they have already accepted the Christian covenant. Two odd things have just come into my mind to tell you. (1) I don't see why you should turn to the west in saying the Creed at the Shamba church. (2) If I should disappear suddenly, all I have in Africa is left to the Mission, so there need be no sending home. Are not these odd things to come together? But you may as well know them. Is Miss —— going to stay over Sunday?

Yours ever,
E. S.

My Dear Hodgson,

—— has just come over to say he has quarrelled with his wife because she wanted to keep a cat; I told him he had better let her keep a dozen.

Yours ever,
E. S.

This last letter is in its way typical. For in him the natives, as one of them wrote after his death, knew "they had a father, who loved them so that they could tell him all that was in their hearts." Rarely did a day pass without some one or more coming thus to him with their plans and troubles, fancied or real. Any hypocrisy, or attempt at deceit, was dealt with summarily enough, but no trouble that was real to the petitioner, however small in itself, failed to win a patient hearing from the Bishop. Or it might be that Christease or Chuma would come to draw several dollars, or a boy a few pice, from the Savings' Bank that he kept for them, or another seek permission to join an up-country caravan, and whatever it was that he might be doing at the time, it was cheerfully laid aside to attend to the request.

But it is high time to go upstairs. There we shall find Miss Bashford in front of her cases of Arabic type, setting up the Bishop's Arabic tracts, or Swahili in Arabic characters, to be printed off at Kiungani for circulation both in Zanzibar and on the mainland. We shall see her surrounded with book-shelves, filled with the results of the printing-press, not only for our own Mission, but to send in various other directions, to the C.M.S. at Mombas, or Mpapwa, to the L.M.S. at Ujiji, the Primitive Methodists at Ribe, and the Romanists at Bagamoyo. It is rarely that the Bishop does not look in here in the course of the morning.

The school for the boys began at 9 a.m. Their schoolroom is downstairs, and the five biggest of them are rapidly developing into efficient teachers for the smaller classes, and can be trusted to insist on the order of the school, and see that the rules are kept. It is nice for the Bishop, remembering as he must the five wretched little naked boys with whom he began his schools in 1864, to go down after school has begun, perhaps to give some message, and find school going on under these other five big boys in just the same way as if Miss Mills was there, while she may have been called away elsewhere by the imperative demands of one of her baby charges, or something else.

And yet, with all these calls upon his time, before it is noon, the Bishop will have found time to work at his translations in his own room. It is not much like an episcopal library. The walls are simply whitewashed; there is no glass in the windows, though they are furnished with wooden shutters to keep out the sun, through which the inquisitive Java sparrows poke their pretty coloured heads; there is no carpet on the floor, but one or two of those grass mats, which the natives weave so well; and the floor is laid *uphill*, with a hole at the lower end right through the wall of the house, and when it is washed, a bucket of water is poured out at the upper end and swept out down to the ground below. It is furnished in the simplest possible way, just a table and a chair, some cupboards, and a bed with the inevitable mosquito net.

Here, too, at this time of day, perhaps, a traveller is received, who has an appointment for his Swahili lesson, which language he is studying before going into the interior of the continent. For the Bishop was always ready to assist in imparting such knowledge.[1]

---

[1] "In making our calls we did not neglect to visit that genial and laborious gentleman, Bishop Steere, whose life for the last sixteen years in East Africa presents a record of travel, and of literary, philological, and missionary work,

At twelve o'clock there is a short service in the little chapel in the house, and then comes dinner directly after, for they keep terribly unfashionable hours in Zanzibar.

In the afternoon the Bishop is supposed to take a rest, but it is often broken in upon, perhaps like this.—" Two grand Arabs have just come in; the younger is very tall, with a melancholy face. His white kanzu reaches nearly to the ground; his black cloth 'joho' is bordered all round with red and white embroidery; wrapped round his waist is a costly shawl, in which is stuck a splendid dagger, all sparkling with jewels and silver mountings. Resting negligently against him is his sword, a perfectly flat straight weapon, about four feet long. It is held by a silver ring and leathern band round the waist. His turban is red and yellow, and if unrolled would probably be six yards long by three broad, and of a substantial stuff, too. The other and older man is dressed precisely the same, only that the trimming round his 'joho' is all white and silver down the seams. He is paler than the Bishop is, but his companion is very dark.

"They both sit in chairs, but gradually draw up their feet until they are in a more congenial position, sitting on their legs. Their sandals are left at the door. They have come to see the Bishop, who is

so vast and varied in character."— THOMSON'S *Through Masai Land*, p. 15.

" To the acquisition of this language, then, we devoted our mornings. In our studies we were materially assisted by Bishop Steere, who is universally recognized as the best of all Swahili scholars."—*Ibid.*, p. 30.

telling them a story in Swahili as rapidly and as fluently as if it were English." And after the interview, with courteous and formal salaams in due Eastern style, they leave him.

Nor must we forget the packing or purchasing of all manner of supplies and wants for the up-country stations. It is not the least remarkable instance of the Bishop's manifold gifts that he was able to the last to retain all the financial management in his own hands, signing every cheque drawn on England, and distributing himself to each of the stations, according to its needs. Not a request for anything from England, except to private friends, but it passed under his eye, and received his sanction. Up to the end of 1880, even the packing of goods for the mainland was done under his immediate superintendence, if not always with his own hands.

To take this one thing alone, the careful execution of orders from the mainland is one of the most exacting and responsible tasks of its kind in the Mission, involving constant perambulation of the shops, selection of goods, bargaining as to prices, and so forth. To this must be added the ordering and receiving goods from England, passing them through the Custom House, opening, unpacking, sorting, repacking them under strict limits as to shape size and weight, so that they may be carried on men's heads, of cases of the most heterogeneous articles, in a cellar with the thermometer steady at 80°, and moreover registering and cataloguing the whole. How much longer the Bishop could have continued to bear this burden, it is impossible to say, but certainly after his death it was soon found that no other single person could perform it, and the money matters of the Mission were given over to a treasurer, whilst two other members of the Mission generally shared the labour and responsibility of the "Agency" work.

When the visitors are gone, he will get a little quiet time again for his translations before giving a final look to the workmen outside, and when at last the Bishop comes in late in the afternoon, there is some tea followed by Evensong at sunset, which is much the same in every way as Matins, only on Fridays the Litany with an Address is substituted for Evensong.

Bishop Steere once gave up this practice for a short time, but he was met in the road by a stranger who was a regular listener at the window outside in the then temporary church, who said, "Why have you given up preaching on Friday nights?" So since then it was recontinued.

Soon after this the bell rings for supper, there are prayers in the house chapel at nine, and for the rest of the evening Bishop Steere will generally remain in the sitting-room talking and looking at papers, or it may be clearing off letters for England which he was unable to despatch by the last mail. And so ends the daily life in its outer aspect in the Mission house at Mkunazini.

Miss Allen shall now take our sketch, and in her hands it will be transformed into a picture:—

"In asking me to write about our much loved Bishop Steere, you have set me the most difficult task possible.

"Again and again during the four years that have past since he was taken from us have I thought of trying to put into words my recollections, and each time it seems more impossible than ever. It is just because his memory seems to pervade everything here that I find it so difficult to define and describe my thoughts about him. Whatever happens, I find myself thinking—I wonder what he would have said to this? If I learn a new word in Swahili, or come upon an instance of an idiomatic use of a word already known, my first thought is a longing for his sympathy and pleasure at the increase of our knowledge of the language of the people for whom he lived. If I get hold of a new book I long for the way in which he used to devour and *digest* a book in little more than the time it takes me to cut the leaves and glance at the headings of the chapters. He used to give one some trenchant criticism on the book that seemed to lay open its purpose and meaning at once.

"If I am weeding the little patch of ground in front of the house, I am longing for his appreciation of the plants and flowers there, and I recollect with a smile how he himself dug over the whole of it, because, he said, the natives would not know how to get it level. How amazed the dignified Arabs used to be when passing by they saw him, whom they all looked up to as a man of much learning and piety, thus engaged. This often furnished me with an excellent text from which to enlarge on the dignity of labour, when the Arabs argued that they must have slaves, for how else could the work be done? 'An Arab cannot dig,' they used to say;

then I used to take such delight in telling them how our great Bishop could dig.

"That is another way in which I constantly miss him. With all his great gifts he was always ready to turn his hand to the meanest occupation, if he could thereby do anyone a service. Oh, how I miss his ready 'Can I help you?' in any difficulty. It did not matter what the obstacle was, he was always ready to help you over it. If it was some difficulty in our life as a community here, he would give one some pithy saying which made one ashamed ever after to have thought of the difficulty as a trial at all. For instance, we were speaking one day of the forbearance which is certainly occasionally required to enable five or six persons who are no relations, to live together harmoniously in one house, and some one said it was quite different from doing parish work at home, where one met one's fellow-workers in district or school work only, and then went home to one's own family. 'Yes,' said the Bishop, 'half-Christians may do for that, they won't do for this.'

"Or again, whether the trouble was a lamp that would not burn, he would have the chimney off and trim the wick, with the sort of unerring skill with which he seemed to do everything, and the lamp would burn as it seemed never to have burnt before.

"Even if he saw one try more than once at threading a needle, his 'Can't I help you?' never failed.

"His quick observation, too, seemed always to shew him who needed a helping hand, even in such trifles as the assistance of his arm upstairs if you were not quite well.

"The readiness, too, with which he always lent us any assistance we asked for from the work-people outside the house, whether to alter the position of a door or window in the fabric of the house,—or only to send any of them on a special message in any direction that might be convenient,—it gave one a sense of everything being done that could be done to make the wheels of life run smoothly, which was worth far more than the actual service rendered.

"Thoughts of him are of course indissolubly connected with every corner of our beautiful slave market church. Few have any idea of how much thought, and pains, and watchfulness, he bestowed upon the laying of almost every stone. How he would stand patiently watching the native workmen till he thoroughly understood their methods of working, and had thought out for himself the practical advantage of the different proceedings, for which they themselves would give no reason beyond saying that it was the custom; then, having mastered their methods, he was in a position to carry out his own ideas safely and satisfactorily. So well did he do this that even the Seyed himself said to him one day, 'Can you tell me why it is that when I build, my buildings tumble down, but what you build never falls down?' It is quite true that there are frequent accidents to the buildings the Seyed puts up, but work done under Bishop Steere is conspicuous for its stability. There is not a building in all Zanzibar or its neighbourhood at all approaching the slave market church as a triumph of architecture. The grand vaulted roof is a feature quite unparalleled in Zanzibar architecture. I remember when nobody believed so bold a design could be accomplished, when the Mohammedans said the whole structure was only standing by miracle, until the day when the building should be opened and it should be full of the Christians, and it would then fall and crush us all; and even some of the Bishop's best friends amongst the Europeans in the town shook their heads and said they didn't think they should like to be under that roof when the supports on which it was built were taken away. Now people will hardly believe that they ever doubted its stability.

"It was one of Bishop Steere's characteristics, that he threw himself so entirely into whatever he undertook. 'Whatsoever thy hand findeth to do do it with thy might,' was indeed his practice. I remember he had been laying out a scheme of water-courses to carry off the streams of water from the town that flooded our premises whenever it rained heavily. Soon after the work was completed there came on a heavy downpour of rain. I was expecting the Bishop in from Kiungani, and looking out was much amused to see him calmly standing out in the pouring rain watching with satisfaction the success of his plan for carrying off the flood of water that was racing past him.

"It was in the course of this very undertaking, that having to make a pavement past a couple of houses that did not belong to us, the Bishop went out of his way to pave right up to their doorstep.

An Arab passed by and said, 'Are those houses yours?.' 'No,' said the Bishop, 'but they are our neighbour's, and if I don't carry the pavement right up to their doorstep they will have a pool of water left there when it rains.' The Arab looked at him, shrugged his shoulders and passed on, remarking as he did so, 'We should not do that.'

"It was just by this sort of practical Christianity that he won the hearts of the natives. I was told once in the the town that we were called the 'Islam' Europeans, 'to distinguish you,' said my informant, 'from the other Europeans, who come here to make money; now you do nothing but improve the place; you read, and you teach, and you build, all for the good of the people.' The Bishop was much pleased at hearing this, and said, 'You see it is a title we can hardly wish to repudiate, because ' Islam' means ' Peace.'

" His sermons were always deeply interesting and full of instruction. I used especially to like to hear him give one of his masterly analyses of character. As for instance, of Jacob and Esau. I have heard him bring out in startling manner the likeness of Esau to the frank pleasant country gentleman, who has everybody's good word and is fond of sport, but who certainly would not value his spiritual privileges above a good dinner. Then, on the other hand, frankly acknowledging that Jacob would be a much less pleasant acquaintance and neighbour, his faults just those which the world scorns, as those of Esau such as the world most easily condones, he would shew that the point to be noted throughout Jacob's career is his belief in the supernatural; his very crimes even were to obtain a supernatural privilege which he saw that his brother despised. But the sermons I liked best of all were on the rare occasions, such as the ordination of one of his Missionaries, or the day of Intercession for Missions, when he seemed to pour out his whole heart with a depth and fervour of spirit, that few suspected him of who did not know him intimately.

"In some respects he was remarkably unreserved. Anything that was communicated to him as head of the Mission he felt would interest each one of us as much as himself, and he shared with us unreservedly the failures as well as the triumphs, the disappointments as well as the joys of the work.

"There was something very helpful and very bracing in the entire confidence with which he treated us. I am persuaded it did more than anything to unite us closely as members of one community, amongst whom the failure of one was a grief to all, and the success of one the triumph of all.

"He was a man with whom all he came in contact felt it impossible to take a liberty, and yet his manner was completely frank and unassuming, but his ready wit always gave him the complete ascendancy in any company in which he found himself. His power of ready repartee made his society wonderfully invigorating. His sense of humour was so keen that he was always ready to take up and make the best of one's attempts at fun. I found myself saving up any humorous incident I met with, to tell him when next I saw him, feeling sure of the responsive smile that would light up his whole face. He used to delight in what at first sight seemed like a paradox, but which had generally a fund of practical sense when examined. As when he startled a zealous young Missionary who was inclined to be fastidious about his food by saying, 'I consider a good appetite one of the first qualifications for a good Missionary.'

"One of his pithy sayings I found myself quoting the other day. 'Nothing that was worth doing was ever accomplished unless you went on at it after it had begun to become a bore.' He was very fond of pressing this idea upon us. He used to say the same thing in various ways, 'If you only hold on long enough you'll do something.' 'It is the one who holds out longest who wins.' And other variations of the same saying that he used to bring out on occasion.

"He used to make great fun of anything that was unpractical. I have often heard him laugh at the idea he said some people had of Mission life, 'that it was sitting under a tree talking to a native.'

"At the same time he greatly appreciated those of his staff who had the gift of making friends with the natives. But what he always maintained was that those who were engaged in keeping the stores, and packing, and such like homely practical work, were just as truly engaged in Mission work as those who were more directly occupied with teaching and preaching. He himself was always ready to lay aside even the grand work of translating the Scriptures, to work with his own hands at the most trivial bit of packing or unpacking that wanted doing. At the same time few are so ready to trust others to do anything as he was. He used to say, laughingly, 'I never do anything for myself that I can get others to do for me.' And when I exclaimed incredulously at such a misrepresentation of himself, he added with a humorous side-look, 'I mean if they can do it better than I can.'

"Another saying of his that I have heard more than once was, 'I am *always* ready to listen to advice,'—then with a change of tone indescribably humorous—'but I don't always follow it.'

"I never saw *anyone* so completely at the service of everyone. He was more patient of interruptions than anyone I ever knew. Nothing would annoy him more than to find that you had tried to spare him an interruption, however tired or busy he might be, by sending away anyone who wanted him for the most trivial matter. He constantly took care of the money belonging to the native children in the house, or even of those who were earning their own living; and this, though it entailed his being called upon at all sorts of unreasonable times to give back a part of the trust. He never let them wait or have to come twice, but got up and gave it to them at once, whatever he was doing.

"How often, too, have I been touched by his bright look, and cheerful readiness to help or advise when I have had to interrupt him myself. However busy he might be I never saw the least shade of annoyance on his face, but always a smile of welcome as if he was delighted to be interrupted. It seemed to me as if he never gave his brain any rest. He said his favourite reading for recreation was the Arabic grammar! In answer to one's look of astonishment he said, 'Yes, I think I always find something to interest me whenever I take it up!'

"I had at one time a pet ape, and I used to think she was of great value to the Mission, because the Bishop could seldom resist having a game with her if I let her loose, and in this way one often had the pleasure of seeing him really resting his brain for a brief interval. Without professing to be what is called fond of animals, he was like all heroic characters, very tender and pitiful to anything that was weak. Many a time have I seen him take a journey across the house to his own room to get some water for the ape, and he would himself stoop down and patiently hold the saucer for the creature till she had satisfied her thirst.

"He said to me once, 'A man is never less dignified than when standing upon his dignity.' That he certainly never did. We have in the employ of the Mission a certain Mohammedan servant, who on state occasions, such as a visit to the Seyed, etc., used to walk in front of the Bishop with an air and manner so completely in contrast to the bearing of his master that one was always greatly amused at seeing the two together. I said so to the Bishop one day, and he laughed and said, 'Yes, I think it is very fortunate I can get the swagger done for me, I think it is cheap at 8$. a month, I am sure I couldn't do it for the money.'

"He used to say it was a great advantage for the Mission to have 'roots,' as he expressed it, in the place. He did not agree with those zealous young

Missionaries who, when fresh from England, would say we ought to employ none but Christian servants. He would say, on the contrary, if you make the Mission a mere excrescence that could at any time be swept away without anybody outside of the Mission perceiving themselves to be the losers, you are liable to be thus swept away, so that the more people you can employ outside the Mission itself, the better. He was also very anxious that everything about the Mission should be as open to the inspection of outsiders as possible. We lived with our front door open all day long, and he wished everybody to feel at liberty to walk in, and almost all over the house at any hour. He said there were sure to be absurd stories of all kinds told about the Mission, but that the best way to refute them was to avoid the slightest appearance of mystery or concealment."

CHAPTER XVIII.

Finance.

IT is necessary to refer to matters financial, both because they added very much to the Bishop's anxieties, and because they show, as we have already mentioned, his command of figures and details, as well as of the larger question, namely, proportion in expenditure, not only as between the money raised at home and the expenses proper to the Mission, but also the proportion, as between the various branches of the Mission, of the limit of the expenses which each ought properly to incur.

What we mean is this: the Mission is one to "Central Africa." Important work was being done, say in the year 1879, in the Island of Zanzibar; important work was being done also to the northwest of Zanzibar in the missions round Magila; and the village of freed slaves at Masasi was second to none in importance as the half-way house to Lake Nyassa.

It required a clear head for business, and a master mind, zealous yet cool, to hold with a firm hand the financial reins of all the varied parts of the Mission, and to regulate fairly and wisely the limits beyond which each must not pass.

And to the last the Bishop kept the supervision of the whole in his own hands, distributing to each station as he might in fairness to the rest, and initialing every order for goods from England at the Mission's expense, before it was sent to the Secretary at home.

In the early days of the Mission Bishop Tozer had had difficulties of a very different order to contend with.

The Home Committee, in 1867, while giving him absolute power to remove the Mission from the Shiré, recommended rather its transfer to Zululand, under the double feeling of doing honour to the memory of Bishop Mackenzie, and because plausible reasons were assigned in favour of that country, as affording a better approach to Lake Nyassa than "the principal *entrepot* of the slave traffic between Africa and Asia, and the capital of a Mohammedan power."[1]

Many persons at home took this view, and the "Mackenzie Memorial Mission" had its rise accordingly, and has had a useful and honourable, if chequered career; but whilst experience has abundantly confirmed the wisdom of Bishop Tozer's action in moving the head-quarters to Zanzibar, there can be no doubt that in the eyes of many the real work of the Mission was, if not abandoned, at all events indefinitely postponed, when, *in their opinion*, he "withdrew altogether from the district;" and the funds which came into the hands of Bishop Tozer became seriously lessened in consequence.

[1] "Colonial Ch. Chronicle," June 1867, pp. 237-8.

To add to the other financial troubles, the Home organization was on so costly a scale that the disproportion between the Home expenditure and the annual income, was excessive. It was therefore determined, in 1867, that the Mission should throw itself on the unbought services of those who were prepared to return to a more wholesome if less ambitious mode of acting.

In the first place the system of a paid organization was abandoned, the Home officers all becoming honorary. To the two original honorary secretaries a third was added—the Rev. W. Forbes Capel, who generously undertook to devote his whole time to the work of supplying the place of the Organizing Secretary, the Rev. W. J. Halcombe, and by speaking, writing, and working in its favour, to steadily extend the area of the Mission's interests at home.

Diocesan secretaries were also generally appointed, and many kind friends consented to act under them as local secretaries in their various neighbourhoods.

The next important change related yet more closely to the finances of the Mission. Formerly the responsibility of administering the funds rested wholly with the General Committee. And yet, from the peculiar circumstances of the sphere of operations, it had been impossible for those in Africa to act otherwise than independently of the Committee in the matter of expenditure. The Committee felt therefore that the wiser course would be, after discharging such small claims as must necessarily arise in connection with their body, to place the whole of the remaining income of the Mission at the absolute disposal of the Bishop, and such clergy in priests' orders as might be with him in Africa, on the understanding merely that an annual statement and balance-sheet should be sent home to them in England.

Henceforward, in very truth, The Universities' Missionary Society became a Society of Missionaries selected by the Church at home to dispense her bounty in the propagation of Christ's Gospel amongst the heathen; whilst those at home had the keen satisfaction of knowing that the great bulk of the subscriptions would find their way to the hands of those who were actually bearing the heat and burden of the day.

Nor must we omit to add that Bishop Steere, on his consecration, took a yet further step of asking for honorary workers in Africa also, and at the present time not one of the members of the Bishop's staff in Africa is receiving any stipend beyond the modest allowance of £20 a year for clothes and other like things, which could not be provided in kind. All other necessaries are provided from the common fund of the Mission. Thus rich and poor live and work together on equal terms.

The third great change effected by Bishop Tozer was that by the kindness of the S. P. G. the Home business of the Mission was transferred to their house, where, for the small sum of £50 a year, a room was placed at its disposal, together with the services of a clerk. Nothing could exceed the kindness of the venerable Society, to the Mission in this its day of small things.

In 1876, after nine years of devoted service at

home, Mr. Capel resigned his office in order to undertake more direct missionary work in Zanzibar itself, and no one being found to carry on the work as he had done so generously and effectively without remuneration, the Rev. Cecil Deedes was appointed an Organizing Secretary, the only paid officer besides the Bishop, who in the same year had a stipend of £300 a year assigned him by an arrangement with the Colonial Bishoprics' Council. Mr. Deedes' health breaking down under the work, the compiler of this Memoir succeeded him in the following year, holding it till laid aside by a severe accident in 1880, when he was succeeded by the present Secretary, the Rev. W. H. Penney, in whose care, under God, the interest at home has so widely expanded that it has now become necessary to have an additional Organizing Secretary for the Northern Province.

The year 1877 closed the career of the Rev. W. H. Bullock, the much esteemed Secretary of S. P. G. He had been a member of the Committee of this Mission from the very first, and his advice and warm sympathy were of the greatest assistance on many occasions.

With the appointment of his very able successor, the Rev. H. W. Tucker (the author of the Memoir of Bishop Feild, and of the Life of Bishop Selwyn), it was, perhaps, not surprising that the Mission should be regarded with other eyes than those of Canon Bullock.

In the year 1877 the income of the General Fund of the Mission had amounted to £4,100, in round numbers.

In 1879 it had risen to £6,000.

And in 1881 it exceeded £8,000.

These sums were largely supplemented by various Special Funds[1] which did not pass through the S. P. G. books, the grand total for 1881 being all but £12,000. So that the Mission, important as Prebendary Tucker knew it to be, was, perhaps, not unnaturally regarded by the Secretary of the great Society possessing its Missions all over the world, somewhat in the character of a young cuckoo growing too big for the parent nest. Anyhow, the room in 19, Delahay Street, which had been so generously accorded to the use of the Mission was required by the Secretary, and the Mission removed to an office near at hand, grateful for the kind fostering care with which its weaker years had been tended in the S. P. G. house; and Prebendary Tucker retired from the London Committee of the Mission.

But when the Committee of the venerable Society proceeded further to pass a resolution against undertaking to receive any Mission funds of which they had not themselves the administrative control, it became necessary to speak out plainly in the cause of missions as against missionary societies. And the following letter from Bishop Steere lays down principles of so much importance to all who are concerned with missions and mission work, that we are bound to reproduce it here, not only because it

[1] Notably the "Children's Fund," which, by the devoted efforts, first of the Rev. Vernon Musgrave, and later of Miss Randolph and Miss Burrows, has been, and is of the greatest possible value to the Mission, both at home and abroad.

shows the subject of this Memoir wielding his powerful pen in very nervous English, but because it is not an ephemeral brochure, and must in time, in its main positions, commend itself to the good sense of English churchmen, though the mode of application may vary in different times, and in different regions :—

SPECIAL MISSIONS AND S. P. G.
From "The Guardian," 8th June, 1881.

SIR,—It has come as a surprise upon me, among the letters I have just received, that the secretary of the Propagation Society has in effect declared war against special Missions, and has put our own among the chief offenders. I feel bound to say a word or two in reply, as to the position we and the Society really hold.

It has always seemed to me a misnomer to call such societies as the Society for the Propagation of the Gospel and the Church Missionary Society *missionary* societies. They are not missionary at all. Their managers have no part in Mission work. Very generally they neither have gone, nor have ever thought of going upon any foreign Mission themselves. What are they then? They are societies for the encouragement and support of Missions. Now, what are Special Missions? They are the very things these societies were formed to encourage and support. Our Universities' Mission is not a society to encourage and support a Mission to Central Africa; it is an actual Mission living and working in the country itself; and the Society for the Propagation of the Gospel, after many years of hesitation, during which we had paid for our accommodation at their office, at last took up its right position in regard to us, when it made us a grant specially to enable us to extend that branch of our work which Mr. Johnson has just carried to the Nyassa Lake. We are as far as possible from any design of rivalling the old Society; we are doing its work, and I think I may say, in proportion to the extent of our Mission, doing it better; we interest more and better men to the extent of getting them actually to engage in Mission work, our papers are more full of details and interest, our home workers are more zealous and successful. I do not see how a Mission can possibly compete with a society for encouraging Missions. The Society for the Propagation of the Gospel has, I know personally, realised a good deal of money out of the interest excited by ourselves and our work. I wonder what some of its speakers would have done without Bishop Mackenzie. But what has not passed through their hands has still been employed in their work, and in helping on their ends and objects. We are quite willing that the Society for the Propagation of the Gospel should reckon to its own honour and encouragement every worthy life and death that has been found among us. If need be, I think we might claim that the funds of the Society for the Propagation of the Gospel were subscribed for our support, and that we have a right to share in them, because we are really doing the Society's work in the Society's way.

There is, indeed, a view of the Society's nature and work to which we are a living contradiction and rebuke. It has been the custom far too much to think of foreign missionaries as of an inferior set of men, sent out, paid, and governed by a superior set of men, formed into a committee in London. Of course, then, you must have examiners and secretaries, and an office, to see that the inferior men are not too inferior; and you must have a set of cheap colleges, in which the inferior men may get an inferior education; and, since they must be ordained, it was provided further, that they should get an inferior sort of ordination, which would not enable them to compete in England with the superior men, out of whom the committees were chosen. It is well known that at first, Missions from both our great societies were worked by Germans and other foreigners, who formed a perfectly distinct class from the heads of the societies, and who wanted overlooking. The manners and talk of secretaries, as well as far too much of the ordinary English notions of Missions, have been formed on this tradition. Thank God, our special Missions are breaking it up. I have men under me of whom any diocese in England might be proud, and we are gradually proving, what indeed is really self-evident, that a half-taught man, such as the so-called Mission colleges generally used to turn out, is much more likely to be useful as a preacher in England, where he will address people who share his ignorances and his prejudices, than among nations whom the cleverest of us can only imperfectly understand. Only let us ask ourselves the simple question, Is it easier to preach in English or in, say, Tamul or Swahili? We must then see at once which branch of work demands the better-educated man.

But the moment you have a set of missionaries who are the equals of any home committee in every other respect, and their superiors in zeal and local knowledge, it is evident that they ought not to and will not allow themselves to be dictated to by a secretary and his clerks. The Church has been a missionary body from its foundation, and its Episcopacy are, by the very nature of their office, the chiefs of its Missions. Of course no one pretends to special knowledge over more than a limited area. Hence it follows of necessity that real Missions must be Special Missions, and that any society really aiming at missionary work, and not at the greatness of its committee or its secretary, must encourage and support Special Missions.

The late Bishop of Capetown was a man of power and influence, with a tale to tell of actual wants and work. It was impossible for any secretary or committee to restrain him from asking for what he wanted. How much more proud everyone must be now of having helped than of having been jealous of him. No one has done the Mission cause, or the old Society itself, more real benefit than Robert Gray. Bishop Patteson, again, belonged to a Special Mission, and the Society for the Propagation of the Gospel is surely the better for his life and death. Honolulu has depended on the Society for the Propagation of the Gospel and is Mr. Tucker's example of decadence and poverty. I had hoped that the system of block grants for colonial dioceses was the beginning of a new system by which the Episcopal system of the Church was at last to be recognized, and Missions were to be governed by missionaries. The Church Missionary Society has a character which the Society for the Propagation of the

Gospel has not. It is not a Church society, but an association of a section of Churchmen to whom their specialities appear to be matters of vital importance. They have, therefore, an unction and a party sympathy which a more broadly constituted society is likely to lack.

There is, however, a grand field for a real propagation society. Its first work must be to collect information. For this they should send men, call them travelling secretaries if you like, to see what Mission fields and Mission works really are. We have now no independent witnesses who can tell us what is being done or what wants doing. Our Mission (Church Missionary Society and Society for the Propagation of the Gospel Missions included) are started separately, and no committee in London can of itself know anything about the comparative state of various places; they have only local and personal reports to go upon. A society would be invaluable which could give us from actual inspection a summary view of the whole work, and let us see what sort of proportion there is between wants and working. The information we have at present is altogether partial and inadequate. The Society for the Propagation of the Gospel has given us papers for Africa, for India, and so on, but they fail because they are merely the reports of particular people in particular places—a style of information always unsatisfactory and very likely to be misleading. We want to know from an impartial witness how much remains to be done and how much is being done, not by one society but by all Christians of whatever name. The Scotch Kirk and the London Society have already done something in this direction. I can vouch for the missionaries that they would welcome everywhere a genial, sympathising visitor, and gladly tell him all they know. When this information is gathered, the next work is to put it before the Church. For this the diocesan and parochial organisation of the Society for the Propagation of the Gospel is admirably adapted. Do let us put the gathering of money in its proper place, which is the last. When the Church is told what is wanted money is sure to come in, some labelled specially, some trusted to the discretion of the Society. Here the committee, with their special information, will be able to do great service to the Church in distributing its funds with discretion, and all missionaries will rise up and call them blessed. I want the Society for the Propagation of the Gospel to rise to its opportunities, and to make all missionaries of the Church its missionaries, and all Mission work its work. I want it to encourage men who are on the ground by visits on the ground, and to make it unnecessary for missionaries or Bishops to come home and beg, by letting all their wants be inquired into on the spot, and then fully and fairly laid before the Church at home. It is because this is not done that special organisations have become necessary. Surely this is a great deal nobler work than to send out paid servants to work under directions from home, and to ignore everything outside the petty circle of work of those paid servants. Above all, let us have sympathy, and let the missionaries feel that they are treated by the committee and secretaries at least as equals. Let us copy the Church Missionary Society in its personal devoutness and spiritual sympathy.

I see gladly that missionaries are coming freely from our best-educated men, and that Mission colleges are raising their level of teaching. Warminster, for instance, is, I hear, now affiliated to a University. It will follow as a consequence that men must be left more and more free to manage their Missions as local experience dictates, and their freedom will be more and more a means of getting better service work done. If the result is that special Missions take more and more the form of missionary brotherhoods, I should rejoice, and I think the Society for the Propagation of the Gospel ought not therefore to refuse them aid, or to insist upon their not pushing their special claims at home. We are full of good wishes for the old Society; but we are not going to be silenced, nor are we at all inclined to depend only upon a grant made by some committee in London. I should like to know how much it is supposed that our annihilation would add to the funds of the Society for the Propagation of the Gospel. I think that it would be followed by a heavy fall in their receipts. The distress of Honolulu is a distinct discouragement all along the line, and there is such a solidarity amongst us that we cannot help assisting or depressing one another. We have paid gladly all that was asked of us, and were willing to have paid more. I quite agree that Special Missions ought not to be a drag on the Society for the Propagation of the Gospel, and I think the Society ought to charge a reasonable per-centage on all moneys going through its hands. If the Society derived a small profit from this branch of their work, over and above the interest on balances, it ought not to be grudged them ; and it would be better for the cause, as a whole, that they should gain, say, £100 a year by our business going through their hands than that we should be driven to pay four or five hundred a year for worse accommodation elsewhere. Is it even yet too late for some new agreement to be made between the Special Missions and the Society for the Propagation of the Gospel on such a basis as this?

      EDWARD STEERE, Missionary Bishop.

It would be unsuitable to the plan of this Memoir to do more than add here that the matter was formally brought before a large general meeting of the S. P. G., when the action of their Standing Committee was confirmed by a majority of those present, and subsequently the " Central Agency for Missions" was established by an influential body of Churchmen, in order to secure to such Foreign Missions as might desire it, a central house of financial business in London, where funds can be received, and transmitted at the senders' option. It will be a happy day, in our opinion, when the venerable Society finds itself able to undertake this portion of its work again.[1]

[1] It seems right to mention that the S. P. G. gave a grant to the Mission of £300 for each of the three years 1879-1881. It was then withdrawn, and has not since been renewed. Otherwise the work which would naturally have fallen to

the lot of the S. P. G. (and in the earlier years of the Mission it was more than once proposed to merge the Mission into those of the Mother Society) has been wholly undertaken by the Universities' Mission. And deeply as we must regret, for the sake of the S. P. G. itself, that it should no longer be taking any part in so necessary, and so noble a work, it is certainly well that this proposed *amalgamation* never took place. It is due to the memory of Dr. Livingstone and of Bishop Mackenzie and his fellow martyrs, and to the great cause of christianizing that part of the dark Continent in which slavery and the slave trade have been rampant, that the Church's forlorn hope should have been managed by a Mission worked on the lines indicated in the Bishop's letter. We have the pleasure of numbering among our supporters many of the tried friends of S. P. G., and we are sure that all wish us well, whether directly aiding us or not.

CHAPTER XIX.

Mohammedanism.

THE prominence that the Mohammedan controversy has lately assumed in consequence of the paper read by Canon Isaac Taylor at the Wolverhampton Church Congress, seems to require that we should devote a chapter to it at the risk of interrupting somewhat the thread of our story.

It is true that Canon Isaac Taylor has since stated publicly that his remarks were not intended to apply to the field of labour occupied by the Universities' Mission, or indeed to any part of Eastern Africa, lying south of the Equator; and that he regards the Bantu races of Southern Africa as presenting more hopeful openings for Christian Missions than the degraded tribes of Nigritia; but inasmuch as the Official Report of the paper still contains (page 326) these words, "the faith of Islam already extends from Morocco to Java, *from Zanzibar to China, and is spreading across Africa* with giant strides," without any qualifications such as could lead an ordinary reader to understand that Eastern Inter-tropical Africa was to be omitted from his sweeping charges; it cannot be without deep interest and benefit to the Church at large to learn the deliberate opinion of Islam formed by the master-mind, zealous, yet cool, of one who for eighteen years lived and worked, till death took him at his post, in the earnest conviction "that he had a message to the Mohammedan as well as to the Negro," in one of the chief Mohammedan cities of the world.

From a letter to Lord Justice Fry, written in December, 1864, only four months after his first arrival in Zanzibar, we learn that his keen mind was already occupied with the question, "I am teaching an Arab English, and so am picking up a little Arabic myself. If I can learn that, Hebrew will need little work, but the Arabic pronunciation is horribly difficult. They have three *t*'s, and four *th*'s, to say nothing of strange sounds which one must choke oneself to imitate. The Arabs who are now arriving with the northerly monsoon are keen-looking, dark, slim men. I look upon them with great interest, as a race that has done more, and is less known than any other in the world."

How this interest grew and deepened with passing years, and how completely he won the respect of the Arabs, may best be gathered from the fact of the present Sultan, Seyed Burghash sending to England in 1879 for a clock to adorn the tower of Christ Church, Zanzibar, though a most rigorous Moslem, and his mourning for the Bishop "as though he were my brother," at his death in 1882.

In the following utterances of the Bishop the question falls under two heads, first that of Islam as taught by Mohammed himself, and as it appears in the Koran; and secondly Islam as it appears in practice, in the daily life both of the Arabs and the African converts.

In a paper read by proxy before the Croydon Church Congress in 1877, the Bishop thus expresses his view of Mohammed's personal character and possible "mission."

I think the lowest explanation we can give of Mohammed's preaching is that he was a man possessed with a great zeal for God, and a great hatred for idolatry and injustice. He was eminently an Arab, and it is of and to Arabs that he is always speaking. He may have persuaded himself that he was led of God ; we know that he had strange sensations, whether we call them epileptic or not. It is not at all a hard thing for men possessed by a powerful impulse to persuade themselves that it is divine. The moment he began to gather followers their enthusiasm would necessarily react upon his, and we may very well ascribe the littleness and unworthiness of some things in the Koran to the littleness and unworthiness of their thoughts and motives acting upon the mind of Mohammed himself, and helping him in a way, which all men are ready enough to go, the way of self-exaltation, of tyranny over the fallen, the glorification of mere success, the smoothing down of strict obligations, the putting of personal desires and hates among the class of divine virtues. I do not think we need suppose any more conscious hypocrisy than the vague feeling that a character had to be supported, and that any strong impulse might be accepted as divine.

There is another possible view of Mohammed's mission, which I should very gladly see treated by some competent theologian. It is that he had really a divine commission to call back the Arabs to the faith of Abraham that they might be so prepared for the faith which is in Christ.

There is no doubt that there was room for such a work, and to a certain extent it has been accomplished : the Arabs could hardly turn to anything else now except to Christianity. The Koran is so eminently Arab in itself, and claims so specially to be a special revelation in the language of the people themselves, it fits in so special a manner Arab customs, Arab climate, and Arab thought, that a wise instinct has prevented its translation, and wherever it has been accepted, the language of the country has become more Arabic, while old national characteristics have been more and more suppressed. All this shows a special local and national power, from which it may be possible to infer a Divine purpose.

The attacks upon Christianity in the Koran seem to me to show, either that the author was utterly ignorant, or more probably that he had in view some debased forms of Christian doctrine, which were real enough to himself and his contemporaries, though they have only left a few traces on general Church history. The Arabs have always been a nation apart; they have always been intensely proud of their own language; and one may say that the rest of the world has been exceptionally ignorant about them, and about that language of theirs, which yet has been and is so rich in itself, and so powerful in its influence upon other tongues. There may have been forms of Arab Christianity about which we know absolutely nothing. The Koran accepts many fables about Christ; of most of them we find traces in the Apocryphal Gospels and early heresies. The Koran denounces Christian doctrine; but it is manifestly not our doctrine which is denounced, as when the doctrine of the Holy Trinity is spoken against, it is not obscurely intimated that it was understood to mean the joining of our Lord and S. Mary with God as objects of worship. The orthodox doctrine of the Incarnation, the union of the Divine and human natures, the perfect God and perfect man, was as little before the mind of Mohammed and his Arabs, as the Divine Unity which makes it impossible even for them to worship God, and not to worship the Word and the Holy Ghost. Indeed the idea of the Holy Ghost seems to be mixed up with the person of the Angel Gabriel.

Even that special assertion aimed at our faith, that "God neither begets nor is begotten," manifestly meant to Mohammed and still means to all his followers, what we ourselves should be as ready as they to assert, namely, that carnal generation is altogether repugnant to any true idea of the Divine nature. I was once asked by some Mohammedan doctors to give my sense of the saying that man was made in the image of God, and they were quite astonished to find that I did not attribute to God body, parts, and passions.

The next few paragraphs seem to furnish the true answer to the plausible arguments of those who, whilst allowing that in themselves Christianity and Mohammedanism cannot be compared as rival religious systems, yet seem to hold that Mohammedanism may be the more immediately suitable to the African, simply because it presents a less exalted ideal of moral progress and civilization.

It has often been remarked that Arabs and Mohammedans generally are ludicrously ignorant of history and chronology. It has not so often been remarked that Christianity is the only faith under which there can be any rational history. Our theory of the world begins with its creation and ends with its extinction, and through all this there runs a thread of Divine purpose, developing itself slowly to our apprehensions, but probably rapidly to some other observers. One generation is not as the one before it; there is a Divine germ of life, evolving patriarchs and saints of ever-growing and improving types. We have thus a work to do which must modify the spiritual life of the ages to come, and history is possible because God's work really progresses.

This is one great reproach of Mohammedanism. Instead of looking forward it looks back. Instead of encouraging growth it petrifies. The faith of Abraham is its conception of perfection; Moses, the Psalmists, the Prophets, OUR LORD Himself, are recognized, but their work is ignored.

The feeling it suggests is that the religion of the world was once perfect, but that innumerable attempts have been made in vain to bring it back to the patriarchal standard. How different from the tale told in the Bible of ever increasing light, and continual falls, each one giving occasion to some distinct advance! On the Mohammedan theory history can be nothing but a weariness, and of this the history of Arabia itself is a very complete illustration.

The Mohammedan doctors have made a special difficulty against themselves, by teaching that the Koran was written from all eternity in heaven, whereas the Koran itself bears traces of growth, for there are contradictions in it, and the very men who say the whole book is eternal, say also that what was first uttered by Mohammed was abrogated by a later revelation. Men may try to persuade themselves that the world stands still, but it moves on notwithstanding.

The Bishop then passes to Islam as seen in practice, and suggests how the Church may best lead the Moslem on to the Christian faith.

We have heard a good deal about a Mohammedan's toleration. He tolerates other men much as we do the lower animals; they are at liberty to live and do what they please, so long as they make themselves useful in their places, or at least do not excite the anger, or the cupidity, of the superior race. Beyond this toleration or contempt, no thorough-going Mohammedan can ever get; that he or his should ever have anything in common with non-Mohammedans seems to him in the first place impossible, and in the next so utterly flagitious that it must be put down by a general massacre. Non-Mohammedans have no rights, but outside of Arabia they may be allowed to live if they pay a tax for permission to do so. A just man will be just even to an infidel. This is the sum of the doctrine of the Koran itself.

Once within the Mohammedan society, a man can only escape from it by death; if he shows any signs of renouncing it, it is the duty of every true believer to kill him.

Here is a great reason why the Church has done so little against Mohammedanism. A convert can only escape with his life through the fear of some external power. The late

Sultan of Zanzibar told one of the European consuls that if the Missions made any converts, there were many people in the town who would consider it a duty to cut their throats, and he could not protect them.[1]

As things now are, anyone under the protection of any great European Power has very little to fear from open Mohammedan violence, but that very exemption makes Mission preaching more difficult; for converts cannot claim it, and all officials will direct their utmost energies to prevent the possibility of any disturbance, and therefore will stop all controversy with Mohammedans if they can. There is, too, this thought which may hold one back, viz., that one is bidding another to endanger his life, while one's own is in perfect safety.

Like all similar powerful organizations, however, Mohammedanism is in most danger from within. There are a great many in India and Turkey who have no real faith in their religion. It is simply impossible for a Mohammedan to go with the stream of modern education. Already in India they are falling behind the Hindoo, who is himself leaving his old religion far away, or sentimentalizing it into a hazy deism.

There is likely to be a growing laxity of opinion and practice among Mohammedans, until the stricter try to stir up a persecution against the lukewarm, or it may be, against some of their people under Christian influences, and find how few they themselves really are.

It may be that, more or less openly, Mohammedanism may be reduced to what its European admirers dream of it as being—a simple system of colourless theism; that the fables and superstitions of the Koran may be laid aside, and the

---

[1] This actually happened in the case of the Arab gentleman, Abdullah Bin Mahomed, mentioned at the beginning of this chapter as learning English from the Bishop. A few weeks after the Bishop's death he entered the Slave Market Church, and knelt down bare-headed with our Christian people. He was immediately seized and imprisoned and kept there for four years, untended and uncared for, except

grosser traditional stories openly derided. The Ramathan fast and the public devotions, which are the substance of practical Mohammedanism — may be etherealized as the prohibition of strong drink very frequently has been, until the whole fabric falls to pieces. It is just possible that the growing strength of Christian nations may convince the Eastern mind that the doctrines of Mohammed have not the Divine approval.

There is even now but little inner life in Mohammedanism. It satisfies the religious instinct, and its forms enable a man to feel as if he was serving God, but there is no *grace* in it. A man wants not only a good moral code, but he wants a new life, he wants an inner power stronger than himself. "Do this and live," say philosophers and Mohammedans, but they cannot tell us by what power to do it. "God is merciful," they say, and say it so often, that it undermines their sense of justice. Sin and wrong seem to them things that can be wiped out by a word, and they must be very grievous sinners indeed if an orthodox profession does not win them forgiveness.

They have never learnt that all forgiveness implies sacrifice, that a debt when forgiven is in fact paid by the forgiver, that a dishonour borne with is really a dishonour voluntarily accepted from some stronger motive ; and, therefore, that if God forgives us our unpaid debts, He must take them upon Himself; that if He forgives us our want of reverence, He must willingly accept disrespect. He must do, in fact, what the Gospel tells us was done in Christ. Without this doctrine justice becomes revenge, and mercy weakness or indifference.

The Church may operate in several ways against the great evil of Mohammedanism. First of all by direct preaching, and in this we shall probably find at once the most effective

---

by the Mission, bravely refusing to recant his belief in Christ Jesus, and so win his freedom, till death put an end to his long trial in 1886. May God, Who is not bound by His own Sacraments, of His mercy gather him in His own way into the fold of His Church, that he may be saved " at that day."

and kindly way is to build upon the truths which are acknowledged in the Koran itself, and to encourage the study of the Bible, which must in the end make its superiority felt.

Then we want a great many tracts in Turkish, Persian, the Indian languages, and above all, in Arabic itself. We want a central depôt where all these could be found, and an organization for their circulation. It would be a new light to many Mohammedans to hear that there could be any controversy at all about their faith, and if we drive their learned men to write books against us, we have opened a door for the truth.

At home we must try to understand better what the controversy really is, and so to put an end at once to ignorant denunciation and sentimental admiration.

We must press on the European Governments that converts to Christianity must not be murdered, and we who have so many millions of Mohammedans whom we protect, ought to be the first to compel the Mohammedan Powers really to tolerate Christianity.

As a first step towards direct work I would suggest that the S. P. C. K. should open a special branch of their Depôt, at which or through which any and every book and tract on the Mohammedan controversy should be procurable.[1]

---

[1] Something has already been done in this direction, especially in the publication of a volume of 120 pages, entitled "The Apology of Al Kindy," a condensed translation by Sir W. Muir of an argument against Islam, written by a Christian courtier at the court of the Caliph Al Mamim, 830 A.D. The arguments are singularly bold and telling, and coincide, many of them, with those of our own day. It is in Sir W. Muir's opinion absolutely unique of its kind. In antiquity, rhetoric, daring, and power, we have nothing in the annals of the Mohammedan controversy at all approaching it. Thus our great Master, Who left not Himself without witness, even in the heyday of their early triumphs, has preserved this remarkable witness to our own time, and will, we doubt not, aid the Church to win new triumphs for Him, by means of a wise use of its arguments in the future.

In the next place, S. P. G. might open a special fund for Mohammedan Missions, and so collect the small and scattered offerings towards the cause, which are now lost to it.

In the last place, men and women too should be invited to offer themselves for the special work of study, and of direct intercourse with Mohammedans, and if there is any difficulty in finding a place where pure Arabic can be learnt, and unmixed Mohammedanism studied, I can offer some a home in our house in Zanzibar. There we have Arab, and Indian, and Persian Mohammedans, and at least five distinct sects meeting in that one city. The people of the coast are orthodox Sunni, the Persian soldiers and settlers Shiayi, the ruling Arabs Ibathi, the Indian immigrants are some Sunnis, of a different school from that of the coast people, and some Khojas, representing the ancient sect known to us as Assassins, and some Bohras, another sect of Indian origin. But wherever the work may be begun, it should be taken up speedily and systematically.

It did not come within the scope of his Congress Paper to deal with the special evils connected inseparably with Mohammedanism, the slave trade, and polygamy with all its accompanying degradation of women.

Nor is it necessary to repeat here, or enforce by additional evidence the undoubted fact that as regards the former, that "open sore of the world" remains open in Africa chiefly because Mohammedans support and practise it.

But, inasmuch as, apart from the horrors of the slave-gang, we are told by Canon Taylor that domestic slavery "in the hands of Moslems is a very mild institution," we must turn to the speech delivered by Bishop Steere at Liverpool, in June, 1882, to show conclusively how wide as the poles asunder are the teaching of Mohammed and the practice of Moslems, in this matter. True it is that Mohammed enjoins the humane treatment of slaves; that he encouraged emancipation as a religious duty. The Koran *says:* "Though a man is your slave, yet he is your brother;" he is to have the same food, and the same clothes as his master. " He who ill-treats his slave will not enter paradise." But let Bishop Steere tell us what the Moslem *does :—*

It is often said that slavery has its advantages, as, for instance, when a man is sick, his master is bound to care for him. It may be so in theory, but it is not so in practice. In point of fact the master *does not care for him.* I could give you a case where a man was comfortably situated, being overlooker on a small plantation. His mistress died, and he was taken over by another man. He fell sick and one of our people took him in and nursed him through his illness, until he recovered again. His master refused to give him any help. When he had recovered, the man who had nursed him went to his master, but instead of offering any reward, the master said, " What are you going to pay me for having had my slave in your house all these months?" The slave himself was grateful enough for everything that was done, and in many ways has done something to repay it; but this is the sort of way in which Arab masters take care of their slaves in sickness. I might add a number of cases of those who have been turned out altogether, because they were so sick as to have no prospect of recovery—cast out to die by the roadside. Our work is to bring them into our houses, to give them better food than they could have anywhere else, and medical attendance such as they never had elsewhere. Some may recover, and to those who do not at least we can give a decent and orderly burial. Thus we are a continual admonition to all slave-masters that they ought to behave well to their slaves. When they see us, and the way in which we have taken up, without any profit to ourselves, the work of educating and doing good to all these people that were utterly lost and forsaken before, this in itself is something of a lesson ; but when a slave is ill-used, he immediately comes off to us and asks to be received as one of our people : we inquire into the case, and find sometimes it is merely a case of idleness ; but if it is a real case and the master has ill-used his slave, we can send him on to the English Consulate and secure that he shall have a hearing, and in many cases we have gone from the Consulate to the Sultan, and the slave has been released and has come to live with us permanently. We have been the means of releasing a number of slaves who have been oppressed by unjust and cruel masters. And the mere fact that we have done this has had a powerful influence in protecting a much larger number.

Again, in view of Canon Taylor's extraordinary assertion that "Islam has abolished drunkenness and prostitution," we feel bound to give a portion of a letter written by the Bishop to a naval officer in 1880, though the horrible nature of the real facts forbid its insertion as a whole.

I have often heard before that Mohammedanism had a more practical influence than Christianity, because there were no immoral women in the streets as in London. I think, on the other hand, that Mohammedanism deliberately sanctions a much worse state of things. The streets are empty of these women because the houses are full of them, and there is no scandal because there is no shame. . . A man can go to the houses where women are kept for sale. . . buy as many as he likes, and need not keep one of them an hour longer than he pleases. . . These women have no choice or hope of escape. They have been taken as young girls, not unfrequently taken by force out of a Christian home, and whipped and starved into learning their lesson. Henceforth the only thing the woman has to think of, is how to please the man. When she is young she may take the fancy of a rich man who will pet and pamper her, then she will pass to poorer men and rougher usage, until at last she is handed over to some slave who will soon make her the drudge of some younger and more attractive woman. If she is fortunate enough to bear to one of her masters a son whom he will acknowledge, she may hope to be pensioned off for life. On the other hand, she may at any time be maimed for life, or tortured to death, and no one will take any notice, or so much as ask why.

There is nothing worse than this in English life in what is scouted and condemned, but here it is all right and proper, and what a religious man may do. This is the kind of slavery which English officials are recommended not to interfere with.

Again, polygamy and divorce have made Mohammedan marriage something lower in the scale of morals than even illicit connections in England. A man may get rid of a wife and take another, and take back the old one, and change about indefinitely much more easily, and with less sense of shame and scandal, than elsewhere he could get rid of a woman, not his wife, with whom he was living. A married woman knows that she can only keep her husband by the same sort of arts as those by which an immoral woman can keep her lover, and she avowedly uses them. Thus the whole tone of thought goes down. . . . You may find even in Lane's books about the Egyptians a woman held up as a model wife, because when she grew old she spent her private fortune in keeping her husband supplied with attractive mistresses. In Shakespeare's time they would have called such a woman by a pretty plain name, and I do not know how else to describe her; but here it is a known, and quoted, example of moral and wifely excellence. What sort of man is he likely to be who lives all his private life among five or six, or it may be twenty slaves and freed women trained in such schools as these? It is not without reason that Mohammedan nations crush up like an apple with a rotten core. There is hardly a street-walker in London who has not a higher and better ideal of life than the great Mohammedan ladies; she does know that her mode of life is not reputable, and has generally a wish, a hope, or an intention some day to quit it. . . . Of course many Mohammedans have but one woman, slave, or wife. It must be so with poor men everywhere. The system is based on the cynical avowal that vices are for the rich. When one man has twenty women, somebody must certainly go without. . . . Of course, a fair proportion of Mohammedans are better than their creed, just as many so-called Christians are worse than theirs. . . .

The result of the Mohammedan system seems to me to be a hopeless depravation of the standard of *men's* thoughts.

Again, as to drunkenness, which Canon Taylor says "Islam has abolished," Bishop Steere wrote to the compiler of this Memoir in 1881 :—

Drunkenness is just as crying an evil amongst the Mohammedans here as with our Christians at home, only it is kept out of sight. When a Mohammedan is seen drunk in the streets, they say, "He has left Mohammed and gone to Jesus," not because he is drunk, but because he is *publicly seen* drunk.

It remains to speak of the Bishop's evidence as to the true nature of the spread of Mohammedanism among the natives of Eastern Africa.

Writing to the Home Committee of the Mission in 1876, he said of Shambala tribes :—

The more thoughtful have unavoidably looked hitherto to the coast Mohammedans as the only people who had a religion to give them. The coast people baptize them by dipping in a river, give them Arab names, charge them not to drink palm wine, not to eat pork or the meat of any animal not slaughtered with the invocation of God's name, teach them an Arabic formula or two, fix them in the professed belief of one only God, and leave them all their old charms and superstitions. The best taught learn very little, and seldom understand what they learn.

It is especially acceptable to the natives as giving them a recognized civilization. One can see in a moment what an immense social advantage it is to be admitted into such a community. A Mohammedan feels himself at once a man; the rest, as the Zanzibar men say of the negroes, are merely like sheep and oxen. The grand kind of Freemasonry of Mohammedanism, especially valuable to merchants and travellers, helps to win it acceptance with Africans and the Malays.[1]

But with many, their nearer acquaintance with Mohammedans has bred no liking for them. The greediness and treachery of the coastmen and the open violence they use when they dare, give great point to the objection to their religion generally, that it tries to prove itself by mere brute force. Those who go in terror of their lives and liberties from the Mohammedans can understand that a prophet of God should come with some other message than a sword.

I heard myself a Mohammedan who was vapouring about their achievements in war silenced by the answer that there was war enough in the world before without God sending a prophet to teach men to kill one another. A series of ready answers to Mohammedan cavils and self-recommendations is a necessity wherever traders go, and most of all among natives who are conscious of their old inferiority and want to get civilized connections by the easiest road. Some, as for instance, that the enjoyments promised to the blessed in Paradise are exactly what are condemned on earth as sins, are obvious enough. Others need more elaboration, and we hope to get out a series of tractlets in Swahili, in Arabic characters, which will be valuable along the coast, as well as for our own and other missions in the interior.[2]

---

[1] So again in his account of his walk to Mataka's, near Lake Nyassa in the previous year, he had said, "It seems to me morally certain that the Yaos will be Christians or Mohammedans before very long, and I think the question will turn a good deal upon which is the first to write and read their language. The Mohammedans have the advantage now, and we must work hard to win it from them."

[2] The following letter to Lord Justice Fry, written Jan. 29, 1880, will serve to show how this hope was fulfilled :—

And finally in his speeches at Liverpool and at Willis's Rooms in June, 1882, in summing up the results of his long labours, he said, in dealing with this subject :—

We were buying a house at Pangani, a town on the coast a little while since, and found a good deal of difficulty in making the purchase. Some of the Mohammedans said, "We know perfectly well what you will do. You will buy a house, and then buy another, and then you will build a church, and make Christians of all, and then we shall be turned out of our own town." And, please God, it shall be so. It has been so to some extent already.

At Umba there was a Mohammedan mosque. We planted a Mission there because our Africans were propagating it themselves, and as things went on it happened that the Church grew up and the Mosque fell down. Now lately, the man who had had the greatest influence in building the Mosque, came back and complained that it had fallen down; but the people treated him with scorn, and when he was troublesome and tried to get up a riot, they had a meeting and said : " It appears to us that what he wants is to turn the Christians out of the country. Most of us are Christians, and those of us who are not, like it better than anything else ; let him go himself." So that, instead of the Christians being turned out, the Mohammedan was turned out.

" I have been very busy lately with Mohammedan ideas. I printed some little papers for the people here, and sent a copy to Dr. Muhleisen Arnold at the Cape, a great Moslem Missionary man, and last mail I got a little English pamphlet, " Kind words and loving Counsels to the Malays and other Moslems." The first half consisted of my tracts with a few alterations, which of course I do not consider improvements. The only acknowledgment was written on one ' With Dr. J. M. Arnold's best thanks.'

" So he evidently thought them worth using.

" I am trying to form an opinion as to what Mohammed

In the same way, a great many people in the Usambara district were beginning to feel themselves the utter darkness and insufficiency of their own heathenism, which is indeed a belief in God, but underneath, and subject to it, a much more present belief in the power of evil spirits. A large portion of them were listening to the Mohammedans on the coast, finding them more advanced in civilization than themselves, and several professed themselves Mohammedans, and so when we came to the country, they at first looked with suspicion upon us. But they soon began to find out that what was best in Mohammedanism was to be found in us, so they joined us to a man.

They said, "We have heard the coast people say a great many things, but find that they do not do them; we have listened to you; you say better things still, and you do them, so we have come round to you."

In this way the best preachers are not merely our words, but our lives; and our deaths, if need be, are better preachers still.

---

really knew of the Gospel. His professed extracts are either from apocryphal sources, or from his own invention.

"I do not think that it has been noticed that the Christians he would meet with, say from Abyssinia, were almost certainly deniers of the Human Nature of our Lord. His notions were evidently so carnal, that I am inclined to think that in relating the miraculous conception of our Lord, he thought he was proving that God was not his human Father.

"Meanwhile, I find abundant texts in the Koran to show that it was intended for Arabs and Arabs only; to them, it seems to me, that it has some ground for claiming to be a Divine message."

CHAPTER XX.

LAKE NYASSA, 1880-1.

IT will be remembered that Bishop Steere's title as Missionary Bishop was *Bishop of the Mission to the tribes dwelling in the neighbourhood of the Lake Nyassa*, and to all that was involved in such a title he was anxiously alive.

Like David waiting patiently for the time when *someone* would build the Temple in the sacred hill, he made his preparations in Zanzibar, and thought out the plan of work, and longed for the time when the advance could be made into the great continent before him, content to be misunderstood at home, in the conviction which experience only the more thoroughly confirmed that Zanzibar, though an Island outside it, was the true capital of East Africa, and the centre of all its trade, and therefore the true headquarters of Missionary effort; that the best way in the end would not be to attack the interior directly, as before, but by the gradual process of a siege in regular form.

And although immediately upon his consecration, in 1874, he had asked for volunteers to commence the Nyassa work, and himself advanced as far as Mataka's in the following year; although he had successfully carried up a body of adult free slaves and formed a Christian village at Masasi in 1876; although it had prospered beyond his hopes under the able management of the Revs. W. P. Johnson, and Chauncy Maples; yet he was far too careful of those that worked with him, and too anxious to make his footing sure as he went along, to be led away by the desire to get all at once a long way into the interior.

We are, he wrote, for those who would have urged him forward, in all our mainland stations, between two enemies, the heathenism of the interior and the Mohammedanism of the coast, and these two are ready enough upon occasion to join hands against us. If, therefore, we can find the great point of communication between the coast and the interior, we want to put a force there to bar the progress of the coast enemy. This is what has been done with great effect in our Usambara Mission at Umba. On the Masasi line a somewhat similar post offers itself at Abdallah Pesás. Nothing has been done yet for the Mweras, who have a very fine country, very accessible from the coast, and are untouched by any propaganda or any civilization. We should not be led away by the desire to get all at once a long way into the interior; it involves enormous difficulties, and leaves Mohammedanism a free track behind it. I am not in favour of the scheme of making many small stations. I would rather have a compact station made as comfortable as possible, in a plain way, in food and lodging and the ordinary details of life. All this is more likely to be attained in a well-ordered central station than in a small location. Many men want change, and for this a six months' stay at an outstation, varied by a month at the chief place, would often serve well. It is very desirable that more than one man should know something about the people at each place, and be known, more or less, to them; occasional changes of men are therefore a gain to all. This is why I should wish to see the station at Masasi enlarged and improved in every possible way. I should like to see permanent sub-stations at Abdallah Pesá's, Machembá's, Mayeye, and Newala, each of them occupied by a man from Masasi, but not always by the same man, and as soon as possible a native catechist and schoolmaster put in charge, and the European to spend a week from time to time with him, as an Evangelist rather than a pastor. As our men increased in number, or (rather and) as our native catechists improve, it would be easy to enlarge our operations, and almost immediately Evangelistic tours might be made among the Mweras to the north, and among the Yaos on the west, as far as the Lake itself. In these journeys endeavour should be made to bring back to Masasi for definite instruction, not boys, but young men, and, after a while, their wives with them.[1] Boy teaching is

---

[1] These words are few, but they tell a tale of many years' faithful schoolwork, honestly and steadily carried on, and often disappointing in their direct results.

Slavery carries with it a poison (especially in the slave-gang) which eats quickly into the roots and fibres of character. For one John Swedi, or Cecil Majaliwa, the failures are many—failures, that is, in successful training for the high office of the Ministry.

Nor was the experiment of sending such youths to England to complete their training and education there so satisfactory as was hoped.

Contact in England with western civilization created new wants and desires, and the loss of the means of satisfying them on returning to Africa led to discontent and failure to keep up to the highest standard of conduct. "Where is the sugar?" asked a returned native youth when the European missionary on the march produced the cocoa and compressed milk for their evening meal. The question was a deeply suggestive one.

They miss the "sugar" of Western life. Whether a change of students between Kiungani, the Zanzibar Theological College, and Chota Nagpore, in India, where the native life is simple, might not give each the wider views of life, which preparation for the Ministry seems to require, may be

eminently unsatisfactory in its ordinary results. Youths and adults are much better worth the labour of instructing. By these means chapels may be built, and public worship, in some form, maintained over a much larger extent than European work purely could hope to reach to. Of course there are other places opening to us. Thus the proposed Uzaramo Mission might probably enough extend itself, in a south-westerly direction, along the line of the proposed road to the Lake and Mr. Thomson's explorations. The Ubena people seem to be a fine race, and on the high plateau near the Lake, and onward, are many others, some, I hear, very hospitable, and neat and orderly in their own ways. All these, in time, we may hope to reach, but we must not beat out our gold too thin, and it is to the work of the young men of the land itself that we must look for permanent progress.

But though the Bishop would not be led away by the desire to get all at once a long way into the interior, yet when it appeared that time and opportunity favoured the advance, he heartily encouraged Mr. Johnson in making an effort to extend his work to Mwemba, the capital of the Yao tribe, which lies nearly 250 miles beyond Masasi, and not far from Lake Nyassa.

The return of Mr. Maples to Masasi, after a visit to England, with a considerable party of clergymen and lay-helpers, enabled him to make this effort. So, taking with him five freed men, and two lads who had been educated at Zanzibar and employed as sub-teachers at Masasi, Mr. Johnson set out on his long contemplated journey to Mwemba, Mataka's town, which he reached on All Saints' Day, 1880; having spent some time in becoming acquainted

worth consideration. Chota Nagpore is mentioned because friendly relations between that Mission and one of our older Missionaries have already been commenced.

with the country and the people on the way, with a view to future settlements.

It was a perilous venture, and in nothing more so than in its success, inasmuch as the founding a Mission station in the midst of the heathen must of necessity raise numerous questions as to the true relations between the Missionaries and the civil powers of the land.

But the Bishop had no doubt as to the right course to be pursued, as it had been long and anxiously pondered over and considered in all its bearings. The lawyer, the moralist, and the Divine shew themselves in the following observations :—

A Missionary has no right to go with arms in his hands, and force his way into or through a country where he is expressly forbidden to enter. Into such countries he ought to go, but only with words and deeds of peace, ready to give up his own life for the faith, but under no circumstances to take the lives of others. Why should modern missionaries consider it such an immense evil to be killed? Is not a death for the faith the greatest blessing a man can meet with? Next to this to suffer wrong and be evil entreated was to the Apostles a subject of thankfulness. We can never preach effectively the Gospel of Christ, Who suffered of His own will for us, until we too are willing to suffer for His sake. Asking for the punishment, by the secular arm, of those who persecute us for our faith seems to me to be a denial of that faith itself; yet there are plenty of missionaries, and still more of the nondescript people who send out missionaries and do not go themselves, who talk as though without some sort of secular support Missions would be impracticable and almost wicked.

In going into a foreign country the first object of the missionary should be to make his converts good subjects of the State to which they belong. We find, in only too many places, that, instead of this, missionaries aim at forming independent communities. S. Paul taught the slaves whom he converted to serve their masters, especially bad ones, better than they had ever been served before. There have been modern missionaries, on the other hand, who proposed, in all good faith, to open a refuge for runaway slaves, and to put arms into their hands to shoot their old masters with. Missionaries ought to form a Church ; what is sometimes formed is rather a Statelet. Forming a Church they have only really power to censure and to expel from communion ; but this involves any kind of punishment which will be borne willingly rather than suffer expulsion. In this way it is possible to punish offences against Christian law by fines and stripes. The offender can always leave the Church if he likes.

The cases of thefts and murders, and such like, stand on quite a different ground. People's words are open to great misconstruction when they say of Mohammedans and heathens, that "their crimes are not our crimes, their view of right not our view, their laws are not ours." Of course, in the sense that Christianity forbids many things which heathen laws allow, this is true ; in the main, however, it is inexact. All modern European law is based upon the law of heathen Rome, and I can say, as a fact of my own knowledge, that Mohammedan and heathen African law are, in their great features, identical with English law. I have been surprised to find how many of what we used to think refinements of the English common law are regarded as a matter of course in an African village. One of the first duties of a missionary is surely to teach his converts to obey and respect the laws of their country in all cases, unless they directly contravene the laws of God, and then with sorrow and reluctance is he compelled to disregard them.

Polygamy and slavery are two points often mentioned ; but no law in the world commands a man to marry many wives, or to keep slaves; it is lawful for him not to do either, and, in fact, everywhere there are many who do neither. It is no part of Christianity to interfere with heathens or Mohammedans who do either, except by showing them a better way ; and it is not necessary for a second wife that she should be divorced, or for a slave that he should be set free, before she or he is baptized; in either case, as a Christian, she or he will be bound to perform whatever the law of the country declares to be a duty with more exactness than before.

That there is in Central Africa such a thing as a "No man's land" is an error which needs everywhere to be strenuously denied. Every inch of land in Africa is subject to law, and to law which has the same substantial principles with European law, only that it recognises a number of social customs which are very un-European, and some of them very nasty and very wrong. These social customs the missionary must fight against; but one great reason why Mission converts, of the nominal sort, so often turn out utter reprobates is that they feel themselves freed from native law, without being really under the power of Christianity.

Our great effort ought to be to build up a native African state by supplying the great essential, so often wanting where Christianity is not, of a body of sober, God-fearing citizens. In my judgment missionaries ought to be absolutely forbidden to hold land except under some native authority, or to take the law into their own hands in any case of theft, or murder, or fraud, or violence. The law of all Africa clearly forbids all these things, and punishes them in a way which native opinion supports. The only capital punishment in the hands of a missionary is Excommunication; lesser punishments are penances endured willingly, or they are not true Christian Discipline.

A European blunders into the midst of a state of things of which he knows as nearly as possible nothing, and having set all law and order, as the natives know them, at defiance, complains that his goods are pilfered and that he can get no redress. You are likely to get scant justice anywhere if you begin by insulting the judge, still more if you take the law into your own hands, and happen to flog the wrong man.

It is a sore temptation to a missionary to see an opportunity, as he thinks, of obtaining a great slice of the country and governing it on Christian principles. We see in the Blantyre[1] Inquiry what the result is likely to be. And here

---

[1] The Scotch Kirk Mission at Blantyre got into trouble by punishing a murderer with death. Mr. Chirmside, an English

let me say that all missionaries owe a debt of gratitude to those who, like Mr. Chirmside, call attention to the mistakes and failures of Missions, and still more to those who, like the Scotch Kirk, inquire into such charges thoroughly and take sound measures of cure and prevention. Nothing is worse than a hidden sore, or a wound deceitfully skinned over, or to cry " Peace, peace," when there is no peace.

Surely never were wiser or abler words penned than these! And if they shew in their pungency no loss of vigour, no failing powers, but rather the bursting forth of righteous indignation, it must not be forgotten that when any band of Missionaries, who plant themselves down in a heathen land with no doubt an earnest desire to do good, but equipped somewhat slenderly with principles of jurisprudence, or of international morals, make mistakes analogous to the Blantyre mistake, they do afford tempting handles to the enemies of all Missions and Missionaries to attack the whole system of Christian effort in their Master's cause.

Few things vexed the righteous soul of the Bishop more than these unnecessary and gratuitous blunders. Missionaries have troubles enough to bear without making fresh ones for themselves,

traveller, happened to be near the place at the time, and made a public complaint at home. The Kirk of Scotland very wisely sent a responsible Commission to make full enquiries on the spot, and while giving credit to the full to the desire on the part of the Mission authorities, to act according to what was best in the interest of the natives, shewed their sense of the mistake which had been made by recalling one or two members of the Mission from Africa, and laying down rules which would prevent such errors in the future. The Bishop was one of those whose advice they sought in so doing.

and dragging their brethren after them into the discredit which ensues.

The course of events soon justified the foresight of the Bishop, and showed the wisdom of his counsel. Mr. Johnson quickly found that the slave dealers were doing their best to prejudice Mataka against him : little by little, owing to his conciliatory action, these prejudices seemed to have disappeared. But it happened that one caravan which came down from the Nyassa district met on the coast the captain of an English man-of-war, who took possession of some 1,500 slaves belonging to it. The news of this capture went up to Mataka's, and there was an explosion.

"This Englishman," they said, "has been communicating with his people, and this is the result." But again it seemed to have passed over, and Mr. Johnson went on quietly with his work, till one morning when out on his rounds he met with the intelligence that his house had been plundered. It seemed that the people from whom these slaves had been taken came back, went and demanded compensation, and made a rush upon his house, till everything belonging to him was either stolen or destroyed.

He waited till he had ascertained that all the people connected with him were safe, and then he made his way to Masasi, whence, finding supplies unequal to his demands, he hurried down to Zanzibar, where he spent S. Andrew's Day, taking part in one of the Bishop's first ordinations in the slave market church ; Mr. W. D. Lowndes being made Deacon that day, in order to return to Magila in time for Archdeacon Farler's Advent and Christmas work.

Mr. Johnson was soon refitted, and joined by a brother missionary, the Rev. Charles Janson, pushed straight on to Lake Nyassa by another route, the result of which, under God, has been the present vast extension of the Mission's work in that district, which, however, Bishop Steere did not himself live to see.

Indeed, Mr. Johnson became swallowed up in the Nyassa, Yao, and Gwangwara districts, exploring the Rovuma and Lujenda rivers to their source, and following up the valleys made by two of the most promising feeders of the latter, the Luchingo and the Masinje valleys, ascertaining the heights of the chief mountain ranges to the S.-East of the Lake—penetrating to the homes of the dreaded Gwangwara, and even far north, to the Wabena or Wajinga, of whom the Gwangwara were in fear. He made friends wherever he went, accepting the native food and hospitality, and bringing back, not only Geographical information, which would have warmed the heart of Livingstone (as they said in the R. G. S. office when they saw his maps), but the most encouraging prospects for the future of the Mission, and a warm sense of the brotherly love of the Scotch Presbyterian Missionaries at Livingstonia, who more than once nursed him and set him up when worn out and exhausted by the climate and the want of ordinary food.[1]

---

[1] An account of seven years travels in the region East of Lake Nyassa appears in the proceedings of the Royal Geo-

In the meantime his friend and brother Missionary was left behind. He lived to dip his feet as we may say in Lake Nyassa, and died on the shore on the 21st February, 1882. His life was a singularly holy one, he hallowed all he undertook and every place he dwelt in. He had long wished to devote himself more completely to the Nyassa tribes, and after the very happy Christmas at Masasi, when all the Nyassa party met, he was much pleased when the choice fell upon him to push on with Johnson to the Lake itself. Whilst not rejoicing in the unbounded physical strength of his friend, he had wonderfully recovered from the ailments caused by the climate, and though not over strong, neither he nor any of the party felt any alarm about him until a very few days before his death.

His memory is preserved in the name of the "Charles Janson," the Missionary Steamer happily established on the Lake, which was purchased by a special fund raised in his honour, in which his friend Mr. Johnson often sails to and from the head-quarters of the Nyassa Mission, the Island of Lukoma, nearly opposite his resting place.

We cannot close the record of the year 1881 better than by the insertion of the following letters from the Bishop, the latter probably received by Mr. Janson shortly before his death. They touch upon a subject, which was referred to by the Bishops of Bombay and Colombo at the S. P. G.

graphical Society, with an excellent map, for May 1884, pp. 512-536.

gathering on occasion of the last Pan-Anglican Synod, which has more than once lately been publicly urged for adoption amongst the heathen of our great cities at home, and which must necessarily take a prominent place in the action of the church in the future, both at home and abroad.

My dear Brother,

The races of tropical Africa, being amongst the lowest of the human family, need very special self-sacrifice as the instrument of their elevation. Amongst their most prominent defects are the love of capricious self-indulgence, working itself out into idleness, gluttony, drunkenness, and uncleanness, whilst slavery, the worst scourge of these races, helps to make labour distasteful, and, therefore, progress impossible.

It is necessary to hold up before their eyes the spectacle of constant self-denying labour, gladly undertaken for Christ's sake, and after His example, before they will be able to comprehend the first elements of the work of redemption.

In order to do this no way could be more effectual than the establishment of something akin to the monasteries, to which Europe owes its Christianity, its peace, and its civilization.

Brethren are wanted, who to a life of prayer and orderly self-denial, will add manual labour, general instruction, and zealous preaching.

There is scarcely a single act of life in which the Africans do not need a better example than any now before their eyes, while the dangers of the climate make it necessary that men who devote themselves to this work should live in the remembrance that heaven is their home, and death is not, in itself, to be dreaded.

The general idea of such a Society as is wanted would be embodied in some such prospectus as this :—

Scheme of day.—Weekdays—3 a.m., First Bell; 3.30, Matins; 4.15, Celebration; 4.45, Prime; 5 to 9, outdoor work; 9, Terce; 9.30, Breakfast; 10 to 12, indoor work, school, etc.;

12, Chapter and Sext. ; 12.30 to 2 p.m., Rest ; 2, Nones ; 2.15 to 5.30, Work ; 5.45, Evensong ; 6.30, Supper ; 7.30, Compline ; Silence from Compline till Prime ; Special refection after Prime and after Sext., at the discretion of the head of the house.

Feastdays—4 a.m., First Bell ; 4.30, Matins ; 5.30, Prime ; 6 to 8, Reading, Music, &c. ; 8, Terce followed by meditation ; 9, Celebration ; 10, Breakfast ; 11, Sext. and Sermon ; 12 to 2 p.m., Rest ; 2, Nones ; 2.30. to 5, Teaching ; Reading and Litanies, &c. ; 5, Evensong with Sermon ; 6 to 6.30, Meditation ; 6.30, Supper ; 7.30, Compline.

These hours are planned with reference to the necessities of a tropical climate, and practice would soon show what modifications might be needed.

(1) Europeans will, as a rule, be able themselves to work out-of-doors in the early morning, and at other times teaching and indoor work will be quite possible for them ;

(2) The first work of Europeans will be to learn what they may of the various languages, and to make translations and original works in them.

It will be necessary, for the sake of the natives in the house, to have Evensong, and the lesser hours daily, and the Sunday Celebration and the preaching, in the Vernacular. Special addresses to members of the house can be made at the daily Chapter.

(3) The education of children will be a great work of our Societies.

It is hoped that many of the native children may become Brethren, or secular priests and preachers.

(4) Building, planning, cultivation, road-making, and all the best kinds of handicrafts will require attention.

(5) Each house should aim at being as nearly as possible self-supporting.

(6) Natives should be encouraged to settle near our houses, subject to general rules for good conduct, and, at least, the profession of a desire to hear the Gospel, coupled with the regular attendance of their children at the Mission schools.

Sisterhoods will be needed, and can at once be established in or near the coast towns.

Zanzibar, December 19th, 1881.[1]

It seems to me that there is room for two kinds of Community: one aiming at influencing others, of which I take it that the Oratorians and the Jesuits are the chief types, and the other seeking to set up a standard of holy life free from the chief temptations of the world, of which perhaps Trappists, *i.e.*, Cistercians, *i.e.*, Benedictines and Carthusians, are the chief types, the latter being more of the eremitic, the former of the coenobitic character.

It is of the essence of a community that a man once joining a community should be secured from any further anxiety, knowing that he has a home for life, and that "for better for worse" he and his brethren will share together.

The tendency of our age is all for external work and for influencing others; there is a great deal too much of the tacit assumption that ourselves are capable of being a fountain of life to others, but how far is this from being true! A little acquaintance with the personal character of Missionaries, who are, in a sense, picked men, soon tells us this. I should be sorry to think that I aimed at making men like myself. Then the busy eagerness of life amongst us needs a corrective, and one cannot but sympathize a little with Rosmini's doctrine that even our works of charity should be brought to us by God rather than sought for by ourselves. One cannot but tremble for a great preacher's own soul. It is already complained at home, that a Mission preacher does not always show to advantage in his own parish. And yet one dreads the artificiality of a mere preacher, who has no commonplace work to steady him, and give him sympathy with his hearers.

Then again there is a great difference between a place where there is a recognized standard of religious life, as in a Christian country, and where there is a merely ascetic one, as in India, or none at all, as in Africa. In India mere asceticism would be a language at once understood by the people, but possibly they want more examples of self-denying *usefulness*. In Africa the very first links are wanting.

I confess if a healthy spot could be found I should dearly like to see a brotherhood on the Benedictine model, cultivat-

[1] To the Rev. C. A. Janson.

ing the ground and singing Psalms, and content to wait till hearers came to be instructed. I do not think they would have to wait long.

It is probable that the strict discipline of a house, which leaves scarcely anything to the discretion of its junior members, might be the very training for our unstable Africans. I am afraid their vanity is easily puffed up when they find themselves teachers.

I do not know how far I ought to attribute to physical causes the feeling of utter weariness, which makes one work on, as it seems, only because to work is ours, and all else is God's. It does sustain one when exultation and almost hope seem to be banished.

I feel as though PEACE were far too little valued by any of the prominent factors of our church life, but perhaps it is the necessary background of them all.

You see what it is to be a good listener, but I hardly know where to stop. It is manifest that in Mission work an orderly life is of great value, and yet it must not hinder any suddenly occurring call for work. I wish the early morning hours could be so occupied as not to leave one weary for the day. But in the position where you are all rules must be held binding in principle, and dispensable in detail.

"Peace!" "utter weariness!" The yearning of the true-hearted warrior of Christ has been heard above. And in a few months that noble heart will cease to beat on earth, and that strong brain will be at rest.

CHAPTER XXI.

1881.

IT may perhaps be of service to our readers, as enabling them the more readily to gather up the various threads of the work of the Mission, if we commence the record of the year 1881, by reprinting the following letter from "The Times" of January 5th, 1881, on the occasion of the Mission entering upon its twenty-first year.

Sir,
You were good enough to mention in a recent number of "The Times" that a large number of slaves of various ages, lately captured by an officer of Her Majesty's ship "London," had been handed over to Bishop Steere, and by him distributed among the several institutions in and near Zanzibar which are connected with the Universities' Mission to Central Africa.

Will you kindly allow me space for a few lines, before your columns become too crowded, to call the attention of your readers to the following facts?—

1. The country very properly pays Her Majesty's cruisers a bounty upon each slave captured, but (not so properly) leaves the slaves, when brought to land, almost entirely to the mercy of the charitable.

2. The Universities' Mission to Central Africa has now been established for twenty years, Bishop Mackenzie having

been consecrated on the 1st January, 1861; and after the expenditure of many lives of devoted men, and much money generously given in the cause of Christian liberty of the slave in Africa, the Mission has passed through its infancy and long apprenticeship, and is fairly engaged in its good work.

3. In the past year eight new missionaries have joined Bishop Steere, including a Senior Student of Christ Church, and six other graduates of Oxford or Cambridge.

4. None of the Mission Clergymen receive any stipend. It is their privilege to work for the love of God and of man. A sum of £20 a year is granted towards clothes, and they have their passage out and home provided for them, but no stipend.

5. The experiment has been made of founding a Christian village in the heart of the slave district, near Lake Nyassa, within fifty miles of the highest point on the Rovuma River, reached by Dr. Livingstone and Bishop Mackenzie when sailing together. This settlement at Masasi has been in operation for several years, and is eminently successful. The Rev. Chauncy Maples, M.A., who has lately returned there after a year's recruiting at home, finds the Mission not only prospering, but promising to act as a centre of Christianity and civilization in all the districts around it. Bishop Steere has work for many more men in that promising field of labour, and they will doubtless come forward. The days of generous chivalry in a good cause are not over.

6. But all Mission work in a new country, and especially in Central Africa, must be costly until that native ministry is trained and in action, which it is the dearest wish of Bishop Steere's heart to see flourishing. One ordained Clergyman—the first fruits, I hope, of many—is happily and actively at work in a village near Masasi. "John Swedi" was one of the six little slave boys presented to Bishop Tozer and Bishop (then Dr.) Steere by the Seyed of Zanzibar, in 1865, and at his baptism took the name of John from the present Bishop of London. Others are in training, but Bishop Steere most wisely refuses to "lay hands suddenly" on any, and there are many disappointments.

The conclusion to which I venture to think these facts point is that a Mission of this character deserves generous support. Surely it is not too much to ask that the £6000 of last year may be doubled in 1881. To keep all the varied agencies in active operation we ought to have an assured ncome of £10,000 a year at least. If these few lines should induce any person to seek further information, it would afford me much pleasure to give it.

WM. H. PENNEY
Organizing Secretary.

Writing under the date of May 2nd, 1881, the Bishop said :—

Events have crowded upon me so much that I have almost forgotten that Easter had to be included in this mail. We had a very large baptism on Easter Monday, thirty-four in all, and SS. Philip and James' Day Miss Mills' boys, to the number of nine, were baptized in the slave market church.

The attendance of women at the catechetical class continues to increase, and Mr. Bateman also has classes here at Ng'ambo for men.

On April 24th, Dr. Kirk sent us fourteen more released slaves, six men, four women, three boys, and one girl. The printing work goes on briskly and well; we have just begun printing our new edition of hymns, it will make a book of about 170 in all. . . .

The following extract from the Bishop's letter in August will also give a fair idea of the general activity of the Mission in Zanzibar, in 1881.

We are at great expenses now with all our new people, for there has been a great revival of slave captures, and our houses are getting so full that we are very glad that Mr. Farler should wish to take a few, as he does, up to Magila direct.

On August 1st, nineteen released slaves were sent to us from the Consulate. One girl went to Miss Thackeray, one very little girl to Miss Bashford's nursery, two very little boys, one less than two years old, to Miss Mills, three boys to Kiungani, one man and nine women with two children to the Shamba at Mbweni. Miss Mills's baby is the quaintest little fellow possible, with a great idea of taking care of himself, and an answer for everybody.

On August 8th the goods for Mr. Johnson were sent off with Peter Sundi and his wife, who had volunteered to join Mr. Johnson at Mataka's.

August 9th.—Mr. Farler returned from his cruise in the "Ruby" much restored in health, and almost at the same time came another party of slaves. One man and eight women went to the Shamba at Mbweni, two little boys to Miss Mills, three boys to Kiungani, and two girls to Miss Thackeray.

August 11th.—"The dhow returned with Peter Sundi and the goods, having lost its mast in a squall. Peter said they were all very sick, and thought they should be lost, and that was all he knew about it.

On Sunday, the 14th, I made Mr. Bellingham a Reader at Kiungani, partly in acknowledgment of the admirable way in which he has managed matters at Mbweni during Mr. Hodgson's absence.

On Monday the dhow having got a new mast, sailed again.

August 16th.—We buried a catechumen named Kalinganisa, a soldier in the Seyed's army, who was the acknowledged leader among the freed slaves in the town here, and exercised over them a wonderfully good influence. He died of small-pox, to the great grief of Mr. Jones-Bateman, who had found him a most valuable ally and friend, and of Mr. Matthews, who commands the Seyed's army, and told me that he would rather have lost fifty men. We used some prayers, and sang his favourite hymn over the grave.

On the 18th the admiral arrived; the 21st was the Sikuamwaka, the first day of the Swahili year, and on the 21st the mail came in during the time of Evensong, bringing Mr. Wallis and Acland Sahera.

On the 24th we all went over to Mbweni to keep our feast-day. I baptized seven girls and three boys. Several other boys and infants were not well enough to appear, but I hope to complete the number in a week or two. The new church at Mbweni is rapidly taking the place of Mr. Randolph's old preaching shed. Four out of six bays of the wall are built and a temporary roof thrown over them, and over the western apse, in the centre of which the font is placed. The unfinished part was covered for the day with an arrangement of mats and cocoanut leaves, so that the whole space of the old shed and apse, and half a bay beyond were available, and all was quite filled. Archdeacon Farler said the prayers, and I baptized the children presented by Mr. Phillips and Miss Thackeray. Miss Mills' two smallest boys will probably be baptized in town on the Sunday after next, and very shortly I am to make a Reader of Michael Gudula, who is now senior scholar, and two new native teachers have been put on the list. On Monday we all go in state to pay our respects to the Seyed. On Wednesday Farler will sail for Magila with Mr. Wallis and Acland Sahera, and Cornwallis Penyewe, some of the new-come boys, and several adults, taking Geldart with him, to show him a little mainland life. Mr. Bradley has kindly consented to stay a little while and take Mr. Geldart's work here, and then he is to go to Masasi, and Mr. Wilson, who is having great success at Umba, will come down to put the organ together, and proposes to bring a party of his people to Zanzibar. Archdeacon Farler hopes with Mr. Wallis's help to open a new station at Mkuzi, on the Pangani road, whence the people came who stopped his building, a very appropriate revenge.

Towards the end of October Messrs. Litchfield and Pearson of the C. M. S. station at Uganda, stayed a few days on their way to England, and a young man named Duta, whom they had brought down with them, remained at Kiungani to be educated there.

As coming from the outside, the following extract from the letter of another visitor,[1] not a member of the Church of England, will be read with interest. "It is impossible to be in the presence of Bishop

[1] Mrs. Pringle, author of "Towards the Mountains of the Moon," 1884.

Steere and Miss Allen without feeling the one great motive that influences them; self is entirely forgotten, and their bright Christian life, and sympathy with their fellow-workers and those around them, is visible in all their actions. We were merely passing through Zanzibar to and from our Scotch Mission at Blantyre, and our visits to the Mission house greatly cheered us. All we heard of the work, not only from the residents in Zanzibar, but from people whom one did not expect to have much sympathy with Missions, was most favourable." And again,[1] "I think it must have made an impression upon anyone to have seen so many young men as we did on arriving at Zanzibar, some of whom were giving up University Fellowships, and all kinds of prospects in the way of 'careers,' while others had ample means of their own. Besides, they were going, not to follow each his own devices, as if they were all bishops, but to work unostentatiously in any place and in any manner that might be prescribed, and that, too, as long as life should last. Neither could I see that they were ascetics, or in any respect enthusiasts.

"While making these observations, I do not need to be reminded that in the details of what is called religious persuasion most of them probably differ from me more or less. But I am sure no one who knows really what they are doing, can dispute that the course of life they have chosen is a most rational one, and a wise one. In view of all that came within my own observation, *it appeared to me that theirs was the most suitable tribute to the cause*

[1] Dr. A. Pringle, in Preface to the above-named book.

of Christianity I could see coming from the British Islands."

The Bishop's own description of the system upon which the Mission is worked may fitly follow this kindly worded comment on its results.

It has been a speciality of this Mission from its beginning under Bishop Mackenzie not to pay stipends to its members, but to supply them with all necessaries.

It was hoped thus to cut off many temptations, and many suspicions which have attended on the old plan of individual salaries.

It is not intended chiefly to save money, though no doubt it does, but in the first place to raise the tone and position of the Missionaries themselves.

There is an universally recognized distinction between a man engaged at a salary to do a work, and a volunteer whose expenses only are paid. In point of fact we do find inferior men rebel against our system, and hanker after a something they could call their own. It was never supposed that our missionaries could do without food or clothing, but it is an important point that all should fare alike, that we should not have a rich man keeping a sumptuous table, and a poor man keeping a very poor one, one man saving money, and another running into debt.

We endeavour to make all feel as brethren, and therefore do not allow any of the members to make private arrangements for themselves, either with a view to what is called better fare, or in order to make savings for some private purpose of his own.

For these reasons we allow all to draw only a small sum in money, just what may reasonably suffice for clothes, writing materials, and any extras such as wine, or stimulants of any kind, which his constitution may make necessary.

The Mission is not bound to provide stimulants, except under a direct medical order, and nearly all our missionaries find they can do very well without.

No one except the treasurer knows who draws his money

allowances, or who does not, by which means shame of poverty and pride of riches are alike excluded.

In point of fact a great many do not draw any money, but on the contrary, during the past year, more than £1,000 has found its way into the Mission funds from the direct and indirect gifts of its missionaries.

It is left to the honour of each not to draw what he does not want, and this confidence is not abused.

We flatter ourselves that we have hit upon almost the only plan on which rich and poor can work well together.

The Bishop, the Archdeacon, the richest men and women amongst us, all eat at the same table, and lodge in rooms furnished on the same scale with the poorest. Everything like distance or separation is carefully avoided, with our black as well as with our white fellow-workers, and the community of feeling thus engendered is the greatest safeguard we can have against selfishness and private ends.

We live as brethren and sisters, and those who will not are soon discerned, and seldom wish to stay.

Our standard, both of life and work is fairly as high as it can be made, and we think we have done something towards showing that a Mission worked by the missionaries themselves as a community can take a higher line, and waste less, and live more happily, than one where each depends separately upon some home committee for funds, and for directions.

We are very glad to see other Missions working in a similar manner, some day perhaps all will.

If any further comment is necessary upon the line of life and work thus laid down by the head of the Mission, it may perhaps be fitly found in a letter of about the same date from one whose unvarying kindness, and readiness to help in every possible manner, for a long term of years, is beyond all power of acknowledgment on our part, and who is without doubt the greatest living authority on all matters connected with Eastern Inter-tropical Africa—Sir John Kirk,

K.C.M.G., Her Majesty's late Representative at Zanzibar.

"There is nothing, I assure you, would give me greater pleasure than supporting the claim of the Universities' Mission, or testifying to the admirable work done under the direction of Bishop Steere.

"It is, I think, little known how greatly this Mission has acted with the British Government in the case of freed slaves. Without the Mission I do not know how otherwise I could have provided for the welfare of the many poor slaves who, when freed, fell upon my hands.

"They had to be taught what freedom was, how it could be defended, and how as free men they could live.

"All this has been done under the Mission, and now a large and influential class has grown up in Zanzibar, looking to the British Agency and the Universities' Mission for protection and advice.

"Apart from this, much good has been done on the mainland; and then again I have often been indebted to it for early information that has enabled me to act against the slave dealers, and to prevent native wars. The Bishop's work in reducing the languages of the coast to a system, and the books published by him, are no doubt well-known in England, although more fully appreciated abroad by those who feel their use.

"Having seen so much of the work of the Mission, and having been from the first[1] so closely connected

---

[1] Sir J. Kirk is referring to the kind medical aid he rendered to the first mission party on the Shiré River after the

with it, I shall always have the greatest pleasure in doing what I can to aid the Society."

In view of all that has lately been said and written about the rarity of converts from Mohammedanism to Christianity, we will conclude this chapter with a letter from Archdeacon Farler to the Bishop under date of November 9th, 1881:—

> We have another notable conversion this month, Mzee Semakuto. This seems to have been brought about by the direct working of the Holy Spirit. He himself declares that God changed his heart. Four years ago when his son, Alfred Makuto, was baptized, his father was a devout Moslem, he had learned the Sala (form of prayer) and received Uhaji (baptism) from a Zanzibar man, and has been recognized on the coast as a believer, so that the Waislamu (Mohammedans) ate with him. He was furious with his son, threatened him with dire punishment unless he gave up Christianity and conformed to Islam. It ended in Alfred being turned out of the house and having to go away and live with his mother's relations. Lately they have been reconciled, and Alfred has never ceased to entreat and argue with his father to become a Christian. Last week Semakuto came down to me and said, " I want to follow Jesus Christ ; what must I do?" I had a long talk with him, and he told me he had repented of all the evil that he had done us and the persecution of his son. He said that his son was constantly urging him to become a Christian, but the chief thing that had changed his heart was the constant abuse by the Mohammedans of our religion ; they were always talking about dini (religion), but they were mere empty words, they acted badly, they cheated and lied. When he looked at us he saw that we practised what we professed, and we were known throughout the land as "watu wa haki" (people of

---

death of Dr. Dickenson. He was then attached to Dr. Livingstone's Expedition.

justice). Every one believed our word, for we cheated no one, and so he felt he must join us. He had told his friends at the coast what he intended to do, and they had driven him away and refused to let him eat with them, but he did not mind this, he was determined to seek after God. This man is an Mzee (Elder) and a man of some importance; he knows some Arabic also. As far as I can see it is a real conversion of the heart. He says his son Alfred is determined not to marry until he can find a wife who will promise to become a Christian, and he approves of this decision.

CHAPTER XXII.

LAST DAYS.

EARLY in 1882 the Bishop fainted during divine service, and the medical men on the spot augured gravely. It was thought right that he should visit England, and he consented the more readily as all was going well with the Mission, and his next mail brought the news that Mrs. Steere[1] had been taken seriously ill and required his presence. Full of loving care for her, he at once set out for England by the return boat, and arrived in March, bringing with him a precious treasure in the corrected and revised version of the complete New Testament in the Swahili tongue, but certainly not to get anything like rest.

The last visit of Bishop Steere to his native land will ever be remembered as a bright spot in the history of the Mission. Although evidently broken in health, he was in excellent spirits; he visited the Universities of Oxford, Cambridge, and Durham; he attended meetings, preached sermons, poured forth addresses, answered questions on all matters missionary and extra missionary; and

[1] Mrs. Steere did not long survive her husband. She died at Lincoln on April 6, 1883.

evoked a fresh interest, not only in his own Mission, but in the extension of our Master's kingdom generally, at home and abroad.

One interesting feature of his stay was the visit he paid to the homes of each of his missionaries, as showing the personal fatherhood which he felt for them, one and all.

Few who heard it will forget his sermon in S. Andrew's, Wells Street, or the address he gave on the 23rd of June to a dense mass of the friends he had made, concluding the weightiest words in the same matter-of-fact way, watch in hand, as the train had to be caught which was to take him to the steamer, and so back to Zanzibar.

It was a grand and a truthful, unvarnished story of an enterprise greatly blessed in its career, but blessed especially by the raising up of his clever, steadfast, pure life, to marshal its forces for so many years—all who looked on him that day must have felt as much.

He had had at one time but one fellow worker in his mission field; he spoke that day of his staff of thirty-four Europeans, and nearly as many native helpers, all of whom had once been slaves.

It was the means of opening the eyes of many at home to a clearer perception of the true principles of mission work amongst the heathen, and the proper relations of missions and missionary societies.

It was the record of the establishment, on a broad and deep foundation, of a great indigenous Church in Central Africa, not a feeble copy of our own Anglican Church, but a genuine Native Church.

It was the history of the foundation of civilisation, of all the freedom and liberties which are dear to the Englishman's heart.

He had formulated a language, so that not only future colonists and teachers might make themselves at home, but that the deepest theological truths might be clearly stated.

He had, to a marvellous degree, won the respect of both Arabs and natives, and rolled away the deserved reproach that hung over the English name there.

He had devoted himself, as Sir Bartle Frere testified that same day, with, perhaps a little pardonable exaggeration, more than any other man he had known or read of, in times past or present, to give the Word of God to the people in their own language, to make every one of the numerous tribes with which he dealt, able to hear the words of the Gospel in their mother tongue.

When he first arrived in Zanzibar he had found there the largest slave market in the world : he had made that same spot the Christian quarter of the largest city in the world south of the Equator, save Sydney and Melbourne, with its noble church, built in great measure with his own hands, an infirmary, mission house, printing-press in active work, crowded schools, and a settlement of native adult Christians, once slaves.

He began his work with five little slave boys, naked and starving, in a half-ruined house ; but before his sun had set he had the satisfaction of having restored numbers as Christians to their own homes, and having formed three great centres of work upon the mainland, many hundreds of miles apart, and knowing that at the antipodes of his vast mission-field his young clergy could grasp the hand of the missionary of the Free Church of Scotland on the shores of Lake Nyassa, strong in the trust which man has for man engaged in common cause; and no testimony was more warmly offered to his worth and goodness, than that which was uttered by members of the Bible Society's, and the Church Missionary Society's Committee, who had come to bid him God speed on his departure.

A small party went down to Charing Cross to see him off, and one remarked, " We have come to see the last of you, Bishop." With an accent upon the word that yet lingers in the memory, he replied, "Not *the last*, I hope," and then, turning round, characteristically busied himself in arranging not his own, but his travelling companion's wraps and parcels.

Their voyage out was a trying one. Through some misadventure of the mails there was a delay of nine days at Aden, spent by him in the hot, stifling town, as each day it was expected that the vessel would be ready which was to take him on to Zanzibar. It undoubtedly undid most of the good he had gained from his voyage to England, and stay there.

S. Bartholomew's Day, however, the eighth anniversary of his consecration, saw the Bishop once more at home with his flock, and his presence supplied all that was needed to make the festival a bright one.

He had set himself to finish his translation of the book of Isaiah into Swahili by that date, and it was completed two days before. He had resumed his multitudinous[1] correspondence with the members of his staff, on all the details of their work, and visited both Mbweni and Kiungani ; he had married two couples of his old scholars, and given all the children their presents ; and then the call came to him, just as he would surely have desired it, in the midst of his work, at what to him was " home."

"I was rather hurrying back from Kiungani," says Miss Bartlett, " on the afternoon of St. Bartholomew, and the Bishop said, 'Wait a little bit, and we will both go together.' How glad I am now that I had that walk with him. He told me many of his plans and arrangements. He was expected at Magila, and he intended going as soon as the mail left.

"But the mail having been put off made it difficult to go and return before the next mail would have been due, and he said he did not quite see how to arrange it. And he never had to. We got back to Mkunazini about 4 o'clock. The Bishop at once went to look after the work-people. When he came in he had a cup of tea and talked cheerfully, and did not seem so very tired. At 6 o'clock he went to church. While he was away the English letters arrived, and we had sorted them before he returned. He had just carried all his into his room as usual. Soon the supper bell rang and we all went down. The Bishop did not come, so we had the bell rung again. He did not come, so we thought he was engaged with his letters and did

---

[1] See a most valuable letter on the management of the Boys in the Appendix.

not wish to come just then, and we began, as he always said we were to do. When he came down he asked why there had been no bell. I am afraid some of his letters had distressed him.

"On Friday he was a good deal in his room, writing letters and doing accounts.

"On Saturday afternoon he took his letters to the post himself. He generally sent them the day before the mail left.

"After tea on Saturday a number of mail boxes arrived, and the Bishop was busy unpacking them.

"After supper he sat most of the evening in the sitting-room, talking and looking at papers. Before going to bed some one asked him if he were not going to Mbweni in the morning, and he said, '*Perhaps.*' He said good-night to me in an especially kind way, such a bright, kind look on his face. That was the last time he ever saw me."

Our report is now continued by another hand.[1]

"We met in the Private Chapel at Mkunazini at 7 a.m., believing the Bishop to have gone to Mbweni. I had returned to my room, and was on my knees preparing for the celebration of Holy Communion in the church at 7.30, when Miss Bartlett came in sore dismay with the news that the Bishop's door was fastened and the Bishop not gone. We knocked and knocked, but could get no reply, and hearing his hard breathing, at last broke in by main force; I rushed to the bed and found the

---

[1] The Rev. W. H. Penney, Organising Secretary of the Mission, who had gone out, at his own charges, to pay a short visit to the Mission-field.

mosquito net quite undisturbed, so we think the attack must have come during sleep. We did what we could till Drs. Bartholomeusz and Gregory were fetched, but our good Bishop was quite unconscious. Bleeding was tried, at first in the arm, but in vain; ultimately an artery in the temple was opened. When this had been done such of us as could be spared went to church and pleaded in the Master's own appointed way for relief to our distress. A little later on leeches were freely applied, but no sign of any return to consciousness. There was for a few minutes a return of natural colour, giving ground for our ardent hope that he might at least recognise us, and speak one word. I left the room for a few minutes, but was quickly recalled by the news of a fresh seizure, and from this time hope died away. It was a sad blow. Those not actually tending the Bishop joined in loving prayer and intercession. The doctor promised to tell us when the end was quite near, and about 3 o'clock all those who could be there were assembled. Archdeacon Hodgson led our devotions and commended the soul of our dear Father-in-God to the good Father in heaven. At 3.30 we on our knees around the bed gazed on that strong frame and massive face as the last breath was drawn, and the soul fled away. A few moments of silent prayer, and then we had at once to arrange for the last sad rites, which could not be delayed beyond the morrow. We decided to bury the Bishop in his own grand church behind the altar at the foot of the episcopal throne.

"During the rest of the afternoon there were

heart-breaking scenes of woe as the children came in from Mbweni, &c., to take a last look at the 'Bwana Mkubwa' (their great Master), whom they knew loved them so well, and had been such a protector to them. Poor Cecil Majaliwa became almost unconscious. He said they had lost their Father, and had none now to understand them. The Bishop was lovingly prepared for burial by the ladies' own hands. He was dressed in his scarlet robes, and his massive hand grasped the Guild of S. Alban cross that he had worn in life for more than thirty years, and a copy of the Swahili New Testament was placed at his feet. Far into the night the lights burned in the Church for the grave to be dug, and all night through the carpenters were at work on the coffin, which they finished just at daylight. We kept watch by turns throughout the night, and at 7 we placed the Bishop in his coffin and carried it down to the Private Chapel, where we had a Celebration at 8. The funeral was fixed for 10, but long before that crowds of people of all ranks began to assemble. The Captain and Officers, with fifty Blue Jackets, attended from the 'London,' and eight of them carried the coffin; the rest lined the nave of the Church. The Consul-General attended in full dress, the Sultan sent a representative and some soldiers, and consuls of other nations joined us in paying the last tribute of respect. The service from end to end was in Swahili. On leaving the house we sang 'O what the joy and the glory must be.' Our order was:

>   CROSS BEARER,
>   CHOIR,
>   PASTORAL STAFF,
>   THE BODY,
>   NATIVE READERS,
>   CLERGY,
>   LADIES OF THE MISSION,
>   CONSUL GENERAL,   CONSULS,
>   OFFICERS OF THE 'LONDON,'
>   MEDICAL MEN,
>   REPRESENTATIVE OF SEYED BURGHASH,
>   People of all creeds and nations.

When in our places, the service was for a time drowned, as was also the sound of the organ, by the sobs and wailing of the densely packed congregration. At length we were able to get a comparative quiet, and the service proceeded. And so we laid the wise master-builder to rest within the temple that his love and skill combined to raise, and we returned home singing,

'Jesus lives! no longer now, can thy terrors, death, appal us.'

"Late in the evening we made search for any directions the Bishop might have left about the conduct of the Mission. Though no word was spoken, yet the Bishop must have had some feeling that he was not long to be here. He had carefully in the cash and cheque books stated how much of the balance belonged to himself, and how much to the Mission.

"On the table in his room lay the last corrected proof-sheets of his translation of the book of Isaiah, done up and directed to the printer at Kiungani; and side by side with them the following unfinished letter to the Home Committee":—

INTERIOR OF CHRIST CHURCH, ZANZIBAR.

Gentlemen,

I am sorry to have to tell you that I feel myself more and more unable to fulfil properly the duties of my office as Head of the Universities' Mission. I can reckon upon fair health so long as I stay in Zanzibar, but I cannot undertake journeys to and upon the mainland, and without them the Mission cannot be adequately superintended.

I find also that I cannot bear up against the ordinary anxieties and petty cares which are continually arising, or deal with them without more of irritation, and mental disturbance than is good, either to the Mission or myself.

I feel bound therefore to put in your hands the offer of my resignation. I should not have hesitated about retiring at once had it not been that there are still some things in which I think I could do the Mission good service.

The first is by completing the translation of the Bible into Swahili. I think I could do this more quickly and probably better than anyone else, and if so I certainly ought to do it.

Another thing I should like to do, is to carry further the little series of papers on the Mohammedan controversy, which I have already begun.

I think, too, that I might be able to assist my successor in a great many matters, which come within my own knowledge and power.

These things make me reluctant to leave Zanzibar, for the present at least. I should gladly have resigned all my income and offices, and remained as a private individual, but I am under various money engagements, which would prevent my doing so.

What I should propose is that I should remain here as an assistant to whomsoever you should choose as the new Bishop, on the understanding that I am not to be called upon to leave Zanzibar, and am to make the completion of the Bible translation my first work.

If you think it better that I should retain the title of my office, I am quite willing to give up half its income to assist in finding a younger, and more active, and sympathetic man to undertake the necessary journeys, and to form a judgment of the wants, and proportionate claims of the various branches of our work.

I beg you to understand that I put myself in your hands unreservedly, only protesting that I am unable to do anything like what I see ought to be done, and that the consciousness of this inability prevents my doing even as much as with a clearer mind I might———.

These words, so touching in their utter abnegation of self, remind us of a conversation held with the Bishop during his visit to England in 1877 :—

A Missionary *Priest* may well return and take up work at home, often it will be his duty to do so, but if he accept the office of a *Bishop* it should be for life ; he may often do more from his arm-chair than a new man who does not know the country ; and if it should be necessary to resign, a Bishop should be the servant of all, and can therefore be the servant of a successor. England may be the easiest place in which to live, but Africa is just as good to die in, and his death at his post may do much more than his life. What England wants, and what Africa wants, are many such deaths. Why should it be thought so great a thing to die in the best of services?

There is a passage on page 256 of the first volume of his "Sermon Notes," occurring in an address on "Coveting God's Best Gifts," which seems so exactly to represent the rule of Bishop Steere's life, that we make no apology for reproducing it here :—

For the body, seek health and strength, rather than ease or pleasure.

For the mind, try after sound knowledge, cultivate the memory, keep open the eyes and ears for better information, be patient and persevering in all your pursuits.

Guard your character in your own eyes, rather than in other men's.

Be sincerely good, and never try to seem better than you are, or seem to consent to what you cannot really approve.

Such was his life, and we know it was by such a life only that he thought the work of the Church could be brought to bear on the "servants of servants" in Central Africa. They are to be brought out of darkness and the shadow of death "not [1] by wisdom. This work is not done by words; it is done much more by *living*. Though a man might preach with all the eloquence of men and angels, there is something more powerful still, and that is the preaching of a *life*. This life of quiet perseverance, this going about unacknowledged and unreceived without any thankfulness of men, this going about doing good, this hiding oneself rather than coming forward to be seen, is the very thing that has opened, and does open, the souls of men to receive the Gospel; nor is it enough only to live, but one must die also—the most blessed of all things is not only the life, but the death in this great service."

Little we thought at home, as we listened to the words in the first lesson that Sunday evening of August 27, 1882, that "*the Lord was indeed taking our master from our head that day*," or that we should so soon require the consoling thought that he himself had given us of another, but three short months before, bidding us "remember that the prayers of a saint in Paradise are worth more than all the work he could do upon earth."

"But [2] for him whose toil is over, and whose joy

---

[1] Last sermon in England on June 23rd, 1882.
[2] Bishop Steere's "Sermon Notes," vol. i. page 64.

is come, how can we love him, and yet grudge him his peace?

"The angels rejoice, the spirits of the just are glad, and how can we be grieved? Lift up the desponding heart, lift up the tearful eye, open the dull ear, listen to the songs of Paradise. See the bright gleam that shoots forth as the gate is opened to receive him.

"Know that we have a friend nearer God, and that if we too gain an entrance, there will be one to welcome us, whose love we have felt already.

"Call up the sound of that voice, telling us in the silence of the inner soul what a just spirit desires for those it still loves, what he is now wishing for us, and then sorrow and mourning will begin to flee away, even before this vale of tears is passed."

And the fittest remembrance of him is to think once again on his own words, spoken the very day that he left England, and to which, perhaps, some intimation of his approaching end lent much of their impressive earnestness.

"The martyr's life," he said, "is not lost, nor is the life sacrificed for love of the brethren in the Master's cause a life that is lost. It is the opening of glory, it is the very entering within the veil along with our Lord Himself. It is following Him not in life only, but following Him through life into Paradise, through life into Eternity.

"If we would indeed see what is blessed, the most blessed of all things is not only life, but death in His great service."

APPENDIX.

Part I.

MANY of Dr. Steere's papers and letters have been placed in our hands, which were hardly suitable for insertion in the body of this Memoir, and indeed would have too much overlaid the thread of the story of his life in any case.

And yet they present so vivid a picture of the many-sided character of the great Bishop that to have wholly omitted them would have been unpardonable.

They are therefore placed in an appendix, which, for convenience of reference, has been divided into two parts—the former consisting rather of what may be termed "set papers," the latter of his "letters of counsel and advice." The division is doubtless in some degree arbitrary, but we venture to think that it will be found useful.

We would suggest to the careful reader that he should note the dates of the several letters, and then, on comparing them with the corresponding portion of the Memoir, they will often be found to throw an interesting side-light on that part of the Bishop's career.

May we add but one word more? It shall be a

saying of the Bishop himself: "It is not what we read, but the use we make of what we read that is the great thing."

On S. Matthew xviii. 17, "Tell it unto the Church."

26, Chancery Lane, December, 1850.[1]

The use of the word *Ecclesia* in S. Stephen's defence, in the phrase "the Church" which was "in the Wilderness," would alone suffice to show that it was no new thing with the Jews to talk of the body of God's people as a Church.

In the sixteenth chapter of S. Matthew our Lord had announced His intention to found a Church, and to found it, as I understand the text, upon the confession that He was the Christ, the Son of the Living God.

We know that this confession has been in all ages the basis of Church doctrine, the great bond of Church fellowship.

I think the difference of gender is sufficient to show that Peter was not that rock. It is true the Aramaic may make no such distinction, but that would only create an ambiguity which is cleared up by the fact of the Gospel having been handed down to us in Greek.

S. Matthew, xvi. 17-19, might be most literally translated, I think, somewhat in this way: "Blessed art thou, Simon son of Jonah, because flesh and blood hath not 'enlightened thee, but My Father, Who is in the heavens. And I say to thee that thou art a man of the rock, and upon this rock I will build up My Church, and the gates of hell shall not prevail against it. And I will give to thee the keys of the kingdom of the heavens, and whomsoever thou shalt bind," &c.

The "Μου" seems to me strongly emphatic. The kingdom of heaven is, we are told, like a net bringing up good and bad, like Peter's own net, and really his when he became a fisher of men.

[1] To Mr. E. Fry.

These good and bad then are those who have been admitted by Peter and his fellows; who by baptism received them into that Church which was founded on the rock of a true confession.

I think in all these cases *we should look first at facts*, and then apply ourselves to interpret our Lord's sayings.

There was a Church, containing good and bad, into which Peter and his fellows had a power of admitting or refusing to admit, and in which they had a power of directing, and of expulsion if their directions were disobeyed.

This Church was founded on a confession of Christ, that he was the Lord, and Peter personally was the first to admit both Jews and Gentiles; and the first, if I remember right, in the cases of Ananias and Elymas, to reject them.

This Church some parables show to have been, sometimes at least, intended by our Lord in using the phrase "the kingdom of heaven."

Come now to the reading of the text with these impressions, and I cannot but think it tolerably clear; the essence of it being a prophecy of the new Church, "Μου την εκκλησιαν," as distinct from God's old national "εκκλησια"; and a declaration that admission and expulsion upon earth, where the binding and loosing were to take place, should be of effect, not there only, but in heaven.

An awful doctrine, which must of course be so understood as not to assert that S. Peter had power of his own mere motion to exclude from heaven, but only that he should be God's minister on earth to pronounce on earth, in God's stead, that sentence, which by the law of God had already been prescribed; that his power would be the power of the judge to pronounce the sentence of the law, which God the Sovereign would assuredly see carried out, while, as is the case here on earth, God will of course preserve and exercise that power of pardon and commutation when the judge is mistaken or corrupt, which is the distinction between a Sovereign and a Bailiff.

As earthly judges are God's ministers, "bearing not the sword in vain," whose sentences are declarations and forerunners of God's judgment in temporal matters, so in spiritual matters did Christ appoint His judges, saying, "Whosoever sins ye remit they are remitted."

Why, then, was this said here to Peter only?

Because Peter only had confessed Christ, and also because it was a prophecy, not a giving of power—a prophecy fulfilled when Peter with the rest received authority to absolve in Christ's Name and as His minister. (S. John, xx. 23.)

As I believe that God will punish carnal sins chiefly in a carnal manner, and spiritual sins chiefly in a spiritual manner, so it seems to me natural that He should appoint and allow two sets of judicial governors wielding His swords of temporal punishment and spiritual condemnation, in both cases the ordinary foretastes of that punishment, which God's other ministers, being evil, delight to inflict.

If, then, a Christian offend against his brother, and will not hear him, or the one or two brethren who go with him, his offence is to be declared to the Church, and there to be inquired of; if he will not repent at the call of his brethren, the judge's office, left in the Church, must be exercised; and being cut off from the Body of Christ he becomes a heathen man and a publican.

It is clear that the Church is in this case to exercise a judicial power, for the supposed offence may be disproved, and then the Church will not censure him.

In what maner the Church is to speak is not here specified, but in the passage we have been examining it was foretold who would be one of those, who were to exercise the judicial function, that, as when a crime is declared to the nation, the criminal is tried and sentenced according to the law of the nation, so a sinner may be tried and sentenced according to the law of the Church, whose judges, appointed by the King of the Church, have power even to remit the sin.

SOCIALISM.[1]

Augt. 15th, 1857.

If we investigate the matter to the bottom we shall find that in very truth we have nothing which we did not receive.

[1] To a member of the Guild of S. Alban.

It is no merit of ours that we were born of Christian parents ; it is no merit of ours that we have a quicker apprehension, a more retentive memory and a juster judgment than others ; still less is it a merit of ours that we have been to better schools and stayed longer at them, and have read more books, and seen more places than some other people.

The poor are but the younger sons of the same family with ourselves, we have the estates and advantages which birth to a better property generally brings, but we have no right to regard them as presumptuous when they treat us as we should deem it natural for younger and portionless brothers and sisters to do.

If all the property goes to one son, it carries with it the duty of being a father to the rest. If he take all and refuse to acknowledge any obligation to his brothers and sisters, society frowns upon him ; if they call him hard and unnatural, we should not condemn them ; if he gives them the merest parings of his abundance, and expects them to be very grateful, we feel that he adds insult to injury.

The moment he does these things the younger ones begin to stand upon their dignity, and to say " We are children of the same parents, it is a mere accident that one of us does not stand in his place ; nay, perhaps some day one of us may," and so forth.

And we all think it a very natural feeling, and rather admire the spirit of it.

But when a man, the circumstances of whose birth and education enable him to make some hundreds or thousands a year, wishes his poorer brothers and sisters, who can scarcely with greater labour make twelve shillings a week, to be very grateful, because he spares about a hundredth part of his income for their relief, immediately we say, " Well, it is enough to make one leave the poor altogether to themselves to see how impertinent they are, and how they seem to think they have a right to our money." Let us speak freely before God, they have a right to more than most of us give them, and they can only be blamed for resenting our neglect upon the principle that we ought to suffer patiently, and not to be angry with those who are unkind to us.

When we say that the poor have a right to share our property, we mean that it is impossible to regard the world as God's world, and deny them that right. *Politically* they have no right, because if we view society as a human institution it finds men unequal and must proceed upon the assumption of this inequality; nay, one of its great objects is to secure men in their property, *i.e.*, in their inequality, but when we go back to the *religious* idea of the world we find men equal, and can see that the origin of their inequality lies only in the free grace of God, Who gives them property, talents and health, not for their own immediate benefit, but that they may so use them as to promote His glory upon earth; by which they may secure to themselves the largest and most real benefit their nature is capable of, when hereafter He will reward them in heaven according to their doings here.

As citizens then we must maintain that what God has given to any man, no one else has any civil right to take from him. As Christians we must admit that when we give alms we do but distribute the funds of which we are trustees, to those for whose benefit God gave them into our charge. The only thing a man has strictly of his own to give to others is the good or bad purpose of his heart. Being merely trustees, we have no right to claim the gratitude which belongs to the Founder of the trust. As trustees we must not be surprised if it be hinted that we are bound to discharge our trust fairly. Let us feel this, and act and think as such a conviction requires, then shall we find that he which humbleth himself will be exalted, the merit which we do not claim others will unhesitatingly give us.

September,[1] 1857.

The great source of the intellectual difficulties men urge against the truth of religion is a misapprehension of the nature and objects of the present life. We find the existence

---

[1] To a Member of the Guild of S. Alban, who had inquired how he might best deal with objections against Christianity, raised by those amongst whom he was working.

o God denied or doubted on the ground of the evils which prevail in the world, the doctrines of the Church are denied because the evidence of them is not written on the heavens, and the duty of holiness cavilled at because rogues sometimes prosper.

All these objections derive their force from the idea that men have a right to expect perfect satisfaction in this world, that this life ought to be a state in which man could desire to abide for ever, whereas it is evident that if this were so death would be a much greater evil than it is, and we could not think it far better to depart and be with Christ, as S. Paul says it is.

It is evident to the most careless observer that our life here is in fact transient, that we are passing away to something else ; be it life immortal, or be it death eternal, we do but pass through life in this world ; and further we do not pass through life unchanged, our characters, tempers, feelings, abilities, are changing every day. What we could do yesterday we cannot do to-day ; what we were inclined to do yesterday we would not by any means do to-day ; and on the other hand, what we refused a year or two since we now most earnestly desire ; what we could not have aspired to then we have now within our grasp.

There is nothing substantial and abiding in this world, but things only have a permanent being so far as they leave permanent traces of their effects upon the characters of the beings who pass through them.

There is to us no *end* in this world—happiness and misery, wealth and poverty, sickness and health, friends, family, and oneliness are all transient, all mere *means*—means to some end which is determined by the effect they have upon our moral characters—means it may be to procure us everlasting life—means, it may be, to plunge us deeper into hell.

It follows that nothing is to be dreaded in this life, nothing is to be sought, *in and for itself.* So soon as we begin to fear and desire in this world, we make means our end, and we ensure to ourselves disappointment ; for what we long for, even if we get it, we can never keep.

Away, then, with the love or fear of earthly things. Come

joy come sorrow, come sickness come health, come poverty come riches, come friends come solitude, let it be all one to us; these things can none of them abide with us; our home is not with them. Whatever God gives us we must use it to the same one real end, the only end we can attain, the object of our being, the promotion of His glory, by ourselves becoming such that, when all transient things shall fade away, we may find ourselves by their means become permanently holy.

This is what we want to make men feel and strive for. If we aim at anything lower, we shall only prepare disappointment to ourselves, and shall find our arguments much more difficult to handle.

The first thing, then, we have to do, is to persuade men to argue upon facts, not upon theories; to view things as they are, not to dream about things as they ought to be.

The religion of Christ is a fact, a great fact; view it how you will, no infidel can deny this. It stands upon distinct external authority; it has been received by very many persons of good sound intelligence as a message from God to man, to declare to him his duty, and to explain so far as is practically necessary, the economy of the world, as the moral and religious creation of God.

It is important to dwell upon this, that the Bible does not intend to teach natural philosophy, or to instruct us in secular history.

If it is objected that the Old Testament writers speak as though the sun went round the earth, no discussion should be allowed on such a point. It is evident that such a mode of speaking is generally intelligible, and that whatever moral deductions could be drawn from the sun's really going round the earth, can be drawn with equal propriety from his seeming to do so, or from the truth that the earth goes round on its own axis and round the sun as well.

The object of the historical and prophetic books of the Old Testament is generally to give an account from a moral point of view, of the Providence of God in relation to the family, whence the greatest Person in the world was to be born.

No reasonable man can deny that the life and death of the Man, our Lord Jesus Christ, have been the most important events in their bearing upon the world generally, and upon our part of it in particular, that have ever happened.

Chronological and historical difficulties are therefore beside the mark, except so far as the chronology and history have a practical bearing upon ourselves and our conduct, that is, these difficulties are worth the investigation of those who are convinced that it is God's Word, and that no part of God's Word can fail to be instructive, but are of no practical importance to the general question whether Christ was sent of God to teach us, for that is proved, though the record contained twice as many blunders as have ever been alleged against it.

This brings us to the question what sort of evidence we must expect in matters of religion.

Now if the world is God's world, and the Church is God's Church, we must expect His Providence in regard to each to be of a piece with, and similar to His care in respect of the other.

You will find it of immense advantage in arguing to have a stock of common things quite within the experience of those you are addressing, in which doubtful evidence is acted upon ; and things apparently inconsistent, which are, notwithstanding, both true, to allege these will be the best answer to any similar objections in religious matters.

The idea that the world is governed by fate or chance is easily refuted in this way. A man's work is not done for him by fate, and nobody ever yet had the food leap into his mouth by chance, unless he put a hand to help it there.

The more familiar the illustration the better, for often the occurrence of the common thing you allege, will bring back the memory of your arguments at a time when the mind is better prepared to accept them freely.

Christianity then being propounded upon evidence well deserving consideration, how does its teaching about the world square with what the world really is?

The Gospel teaches that this life is a state of trial and

education, according to our behaviour, in which we shall be placed eternally.

This solves the greater part of the objections we ordinarily meet with.

If we are here but a short time, and those profit most who most improve in goodness, it is evident that a bad man who prospers has not so desirable a life as a man oppressed by troubles, who is thereby exercised in patience and all virtue.

If the Church hold the truth, we are never to judge of things by their present appearance, but always by their future tendency.

This changes the whole face of affairs; and in this view there is no evil in any of the external things men think evils, they are but incentives to, and opportunities for improvements in virtue.

We cannot talk of good or evil till we come to a permanent state; there is nothing here which may not be either to us, according as we handle it.

The existence, therefore, of God and His goodness is not to be denied because there are apparent evils in the world. He never intended us to stay here. He will soon take us hence, and then none of these things will any longer affect us; the moral character we have here formed will alone remain with us.

How childish and unmanly then it is to dwell on troubles which cannot possibly last long, and how foolish to call medicine an evil because it has for the moment a bitter taste.

The analogy of the education of children may here be used very forcibly.

The doctrine of the fall of man, of his declension as a race from the purity of one of God's immediate creatures, by means of an exercise of his innate free will, explains the immense amount of sin and consequent misery in the world, and then Christ's Passion shows why heaven is offered to sinners.

The reason why Christianity is not offered on irresistible evidence is that man is not a mere thinking machine. We are moral beings, and in this, as in all other matters of religion, the truth and our duty are so propounded to us as to call our moral faculties into play.

We are not compelled to believe, because there would be no advantage to us in an involuntary belief, it would be no improvement to us in goodness, as a belief founded on spiritual experience and candid inquiry always is.

The necessity and merit of faith may well be illustrated by the exercise of faith, which is always necessary in everyone who learns to read and write ; he cannot at first see exactly how all he is told to do is necessary to bring about the end intended.

A good general argument to prove the existence of God may be drawn from the infinite multitude of things and persons there are in the world, and the nice adaptation of the whole, as well as the continual superintendence of some vastly superior power, without which the world could not continue in existence. Millions of beings, all pulling in various ways, could not make up one continuing whole without a God to direct and govern them, any more than they could at first have come together, or had any existence without a Creator.

The probability that man is immortal, or at least that he will exist in some future state may be deduced from the fact that nothing satisfies him. We often think that what another has would satisfy us, but in point of fact no one is satisfied, so that probably we should not be so if we had all we wish for. And however this may be, it is certain that the power which directs all things does not allow us to be satisfied in this life. Men all make plans for their life, and accomplish them, but just in time for their death. There must then be some mistake here, and it is far more probable that it lies in our expecting to live *here* than in our expecting to live somewhere. Our desires, our anticipations, our wishes, all point to life, and there is no evidence that death is not the entry on a new life.

The necessity of a Revelation is proved by the darkness and obscurity which surrounds our fate without it. If we take the highest view of natural religion it proves that there is a God, that He is holy, and we are corrupt. How, then, can we hope for anything or expect anything at His hands but punishment? Revelation, then, is necessary to give us hope.

If we take the lowest view of natural religion—that all certainty is excluded—that there are some arguments to prove the existence of a holy God, some to disprove it; and as to our immortality and the other points, just light enough to show us the intensity of our darkness, then much more is Revelation necessary to enable us to see our way through the world at all.

There is nothing *unnatural* in the idea of a Revelation. Our education is one long course of revelation. Language is a revelation to an infant, and a revelation imperfectly understood by most of us to the end of our days. The whole course of conduct and the amount of knowledge necessary to our life in this world is a revelation. All knowledge communicated to us by another is a revelation.

Revelations, too, received upon authority, and proved by miracles, and which profit those only who have faith.

For we accept the teaching of our parents and masters without being able to see the whole of its connection with the objects it aims at. We receive it in faith, because we believe them able to teach us; if we had no faith, and would believe nothing that we could not prove to ourselves, or did not fully understand, we could never learn.

And we receive it on the evidence of *miracles*, for a miracle to us is a thing which we ourselves have no power to do, and the ground an which we obey parents and teachers, and listen to them, is that we see them do what we cannot. What more incomprehensible doctrine to a child than that labour is the means of happiness?

It is a doctrine which all of us are illustrating one way or the other. It is but another form of the great Christian doctrine that self-denial is the road to heaven. Yet men who will descant eloquently on the necessity of young men's following some occupation, will ridicule the practice of fasting and voluntary poverty, in the most happy ignorance of the fact that they are directly contradicting the principles of their own teaching.

With these illustrations I must leave the further prosecution of the subject to your own taste and diligence, simply assuring you that you will find devout meditation upon the facts of human life and the bearing of men's habits upon their success in this world, as compared with the facts of this world and the next viewed as one whole, and the bearing of men's modes of life here upon their everlasting life, an almost inexhaustible source of consolation and guidance to yourself, as well as a rich storehouse of most persuasive arguments wherewith to convince gainsayers.

ON WESLEYANISM.

Dec. 6, 1857.

The Wesleyan Body grew into existence, and if it ever be reunited to the Church it must be so, as a Guild or Brotherhood. John Wesley desired to unite into one well organized society those members of the Church of England who had been awakened to a peculiarly vivid apprehension of the great work done for them by Christ, and of the duty incumbent upon all such of giving themselves to good works and the awakening of others. The body is in an anomalous and indefensible position, the moment it is separated from the Church. Its rulers, who claim implicit obedience, have manifestly no direct authority from God to demand it, and therefore cannot oppose the secession of those who became united to the body by no act of their own, but simply because they were born of Wesleyan parents. As a voluntary society, leaders chosen by consent may be absolute without unlawful assumption, but the Church of Christ is not a voluntary society, and therefore is not the Wesleyan body. There are two questions to be settled with all Dissenters—that of heresy and that of schism. As to the latter, it can be healed only by unhesitating and unconditional submission; the Wesleyans must cease altogether from their unauthorized ministry, they must receive the Sacraments at the hands of the Church's priests only, and no one of them must presume to preach without the license of the Bishop; these rules must be clearly laid down in any agreement for reunion. As to the other question, of heresy, it is heretical to maintain that the order of Bishops is wholly unnecessary in the Church. Saving this, there is no clear heresy maintained by the community, and John Wesley himself was clearly and intelligibly orthodox. Upon the question of what has been called the second birth, no one denies but that sudden renewals of spiritual life may take place, and the mere fact of joining the Church would withdraw the taint of heresy that lies about the assertion that sudden renewals are necessary to all.

But while upon all questions of heresy the Church is bound not to yield in the smallest degree, it will be equally necessary for Churchmen to beware of allowing their prejudices to hinder them from tolerating religious associations of a character and extent to which they are unaccustomed. The Church of England has been far too much the Church of good taste and refined feeling. Protestant dissent has been too often condemned merely because its teachers were cobblers, and Romanist dissent, because its decorations were tawdry and pretentious. But in spite of all that can be said and written, the Church, which is to be the Church of the multitude, must not be so high in feeling as to pass over their heads without touching them. There cannot be a worse fault than to laugh at earnestness. Earnestness is always ridiculous in some things to those who are on the watch for an object. It is of the essence of earnestness to pursue its purpose regardless of the impression it produces on others, and of the external circumstances by which it is surrounded. The Apostles were a set of rough-looking fishermen, and when the Holy Ghost descended upon them, they were so strangely excited that men laughed and said they were drunk. Try and realize a love feast held by such men, and attended by others who were not sincere, as we know that many of their first converts were not, and you will feel, with the polite heathens and the formal Jews, that these men are the dregs of the people afflicted with the fanaticism not uncommon in the ignorant. You must not expect a labourer to talk like a nobleman, but he has as much need of a Saviour, and can as little help talking of his religion when he really has it. Conversion to Christ does not teach grammar, or correct a Yorkshire dialect, but it does prevent a man turning religion into ridicule because it is uttered by the mouth of an ignorant countryman; he, therefore, that laughs at or despises words which are drawn from the heart, because they are adapted to the comprehension and feelings of a less educated class than himself,—such a man is not yet really a Christian, however he may wish to be, or perhaps feel sure he is one. Wesleyanism was an effort to rouse the lower classes; its manners and phrases belong to those classes; very carefully therefore must we be on our guard against condemning it for being rude and noisy and in bad taste. A man of coarse manners will be coarse in his religious expressions, but it is a mere accident of time and place that makes those expressions coarse; one word is as good as another in itself, and manners and pronunciation change daily. We shall find that if we are to have any share in the evangelization of the multitude, we must be content to put up with a great many things that will shock us at first; and we must get rid of a great deal of reserve and shyness in these matters, the want of which offends us in others. But while all this must carefully be allowed for on our own parts, those whom we strive to have sympathy with must remember on their parts that words are not feelings, and feelings themselves are not religion; and that a man cannot be sure that he is saved because he feels bursting with praise and thankfulness to God, and ready to do or suffer all things for Him. It may be that he is only excited as people are when they read a novel or see a play, and it will take years of perseverance to give him real grounds of confidence. If he think this, he will be certainly more quiet in his manner, and more careful in his expressions.

A Pastoral Letter on Public Worship, Offices and Ritual.[1]

Zanzibar, Oct. 25, 1880.

As we have just received from the liberality of the Christian Knowledge Society a complete translation of the English Prayer Book, and it is inevitable that we should in some way abbreviate and alter the forms in our practical use of them, I think I ought to lay down the principles on which I am prepared to sanction such alterations.

I take the substantial part of the daily Morning and Evening Prayers to consist of the Psalms and Lessons, with such Versicles and Prayers as are included between the first petition, " O Lord, open thou our lips," and the third collect. If the Office is confined within these limits I should be entirely satisfied with it. As to additions, the Confession and Absolution might I think be very reasonably used at Evensong, when the sins and shortcomings of the day naturally demand some remembrance. I had rather they were not used in the morning. The Sentences and Exhortation I do not think many of us would desire to use at all. They are adapted to a congregation of hereditary Christians, but not to one of new converts. After the third Collect, the prayer for All Conditions of men and the General Thanksgiving might be employed constantly, the former in the morning, the latter in the evening, as well as the Collects for Ember days and special occasions, as the occasions arise. The Prayer of St. Chrysostom, or one of the Collects at the end of the Communion Office, with the Apostolic Benediction, would make a natural conclusion. I think it is very undesirable to use the same forms morning and evening where it can be avoided. If therefore the prayer for All Conditions of men and one of the final Collects are used in the morning, it would be well to use the General Thanksgiving and the Prayer of St. Chrysostom in the evening.

I do not at all like the custom of singing a hymn after the

---

[1] To the clergy of the Universities' Mission.

third collect—that is, practically in the middle of our intercessory prayers. I suppose the anthem was appointed to be sung there, as the special note of the day with which to conclude the service. But we have now no anthems, and no special memento of the day giving a tone to its psalmody, as the ancient anthems were intended to do. If a hymn is desired near the end of the service, I think it should be followed only by the final Collect.

The best place for a hymn is, however, immediately before the Psalms, where it may give a tone to them, and for this purpose I should be glad to sanction the omission of the Venite, and the insertion of any appropriate hymn for the season in its place, and even the insertion of one in the same position in the Evening Service. Hymns before and after preaching are of course at the discretion of the preacher.

I should be glad to allow the largest possible liberty in the choice of special Psalms and Lessons. My predecessor sanctioned a shortened form of Matins and Evensong, in which special Psalms were allotted to each day of the week; I have no wish to withdraw in any way that sanction, but wherever the larger part of the congregation can read, I should be sorry that they should not join in singing the entire Psalter in regular course. The Te Deum is sometimes found too long to repeat daily; if so, I must sorrowfully allow a hymn in its place.

The Litany should, I think, be said every Friday, and, if so desired, may be made to end after the Lord's Prayer. I do not wish to make its use on other days obligatory. Sermons should, I think, in missionary work precede the devotions of the congregation, and not follow them as is usual at home.

I have no objection to the use of newly devised forms before or after preaching, or catechizing, or of extempore prayer, or the insertion of special Collects after the third Collect in the daily Offices, but the prayers should be such as are specially called for by the place or circumstances, and not a mere addition or supplement to the authorized forms, as though they were incomplete without them.

The Occasional Offices and the Form of Baptism are all,

I think, already in use, and I am not prepared to recommend any alteration in them. I do not think that unbaptized persons should be invited to be present at any of them, but I am not disposed to prohibit their appearing altogether except at the Celebration of the Holy Eucharist.

As to the Office, which is by way of distinction the Liturgy, I would gladly have said nothing, as any kind of controversy about it is in the last degree painful to me. I am afraid, however, it is my duty to speak.

I think the custom which has prevailed so long and so generally of wearing a surplice only and standing at the north end of the Holy Table is an ample justification for those who continue to do so, but there are many who do not, and who claim the sanction of law for other usages.

I have no doubt in my own mind that the decisions which forbid the use of the vestments and ornaments mentioned in Edward VI.'s first book are mistaken in law, and will in due time be disowned by the Courts which pronounced them. I cannot therefore pretend to object to the use of chasubles or copes, or to the two lights on the altar. Nor do I object to a cross, though I do see many objections to a crucifix. In English usage after the Reformation the cope was practically adopted as the exclusively Eucharistic vestment, and the candles were not lighted. I would gladly have seen these customs authorized, and I intend to follow them in my own practice. One vestment is in itself as good as another, and a candle lighted in the daytime is to my mind an appropriate symbol of superstition, but certainly not of light. The mixing of water with the wine is so plainly a primitive custom, and is so far from being forbidden anywhere in the Prayer Book, that I should like to see it universally adopted. I think it is clear both in law and in history that any kind of bread is allowable, if only it be the best that can be got.

As to position, we are bound honestly to obey the rules of our church. A man must, in some sense which he can in conscience defend, stand at the north side of the Lord's table at the beginning of the Office, and break the bread and take the cup into his hands before the people. I am not anxious to enforce on any one the exact use I think myself best warranted in adopting. Private acts of devotion, of whatever kind, on the part of priest or people are to be regarded in the most kindly way. Only we must remember that the true Priest is in Heaven, and that His presence with us is a joining of our offering with that in Heaven, and though there is a real, yet there is not a *local* or *exclusive* presence of Christ in, with, or under, either element or communicant. As an object of worship He is, as ever, in heaven. The priest ought not to use any private forms in so marked and constant a manner as to make them part of the Office, no matter what liking he may have for them, or what authority elsewhere and at other times may have belonged to them. We must not brand our Church forms with a mark of insufficiency. Partly for this reason, and partly from mere reverence, I do not think it right to insert hymns, or canticles of any kind into the body of the Office. I hope that all our clergy and congregations will do all they can for the beauty and order of this chiefest of our acts of worship, and will exert the best of their musical skill in rendering the formulæ which are authorized, especially the Gloria in Excelsis. A psalm, or hymn, before the Office commences cannot be reasonably objected to. I hope also that all our clergy will be careful to teach their people that those who are present without communicating miss the chief end of Christ's institution, and do not give Him the honour which is His due. In the same way, I hope the rule that none should eat before communicating, will be treated as what it is—a godly and reverent custom, and not an absolute inflexible obligation.

The appointed days of fasting and abstinence are to be observed as the conscience of each member dictates and his health permits; they must neither be altogether disregarded, nor so observed as to unfit the observer for his duties.

Within the rules here laid down, the senior priest, or first in dignity in each station of our Mission, has the right to give such directions as he will for the conduct of Divine Service, and his juniors are bound to comply with them, only remembering to do all things in a spirit of love and of Christian liberty, that authority may not degenerate into tyranny, nor freedom into disorder.

ON MISSIONARY COLLEGES, AND ENGLISH PARISH PRIESTS.[1]

Mission work is certainly attracting very much more attention than it did formerly. Nothing shows this more clearly than the foundation in many places of special Colleges for the training of men for Mission work abroad. Nor is there any lack of men to come forward to be trained. It is much more difficult to say what training means.

Practically, men are taught, in as complete a way as time and their own abilities allow, those portions of a University education which are specially needed in order to pass the Bishop's examination for holy orders. To this is added—in various places—a little medicine, a little printing, a little joiner's work, and so on. Sometimes, a little teaching in some foreign language.

The chief teaching, however, of all Mission Colleges is directed not to make men specially Missionaries, but to qualify them for ordination. Practically, it is confessed that thoroughly educated men are not to be had for Missions; and, therefore, Bishops must be contented to ordain for that work men who have had a less expensive training. Happily, education is not the most necessary qualification for holy orders, and truly Christian and earnest men do make good Missionaries and good Clergy without the best possible education. Still, there is something wrong in a system which does in effect make Missionary work an easy mode of access to holy orders.

Missions to the heathen do not require inferior men, they require very superior men indeed. There are many who have got through a University course, and are fairly useful among their own countrymen, who would be a mere hindrance to a Foreign Mission. If you take a number of average country Clergy in England and compare them with the same number of average Colonial Clergy, you will see at

---

[1] Found in MS. amongst the Bishop's papers after his death.

once a very great difference. If you were inviting a dinner party, you would choose the English; if you wanted any kind of work done, you would greatly prefer the Colonials. There is a knowledge of the world, a readiness, a business-like activity, a sense of being at work, a disposition to adapt themselves to other men, an absolute refusal to sit down and wait, or to stand on mere dignity and lawful rights, which are all necessary to Foreign or Colonial work, and are often sadly wanting in England. I have known an English clergyman who thought himself entitled to take the curacy of an adjoining parish because his own people did not come to church. "It does not matter," he said, "when I hold my own services, for nobody comes. I don't think there is a church person in the parish." Now if you could imagine this temper among the Missionary Clergy, one man would soon suffice for all the Missions in the world. The fact is, Missions must have activity and zeal, and they must get them where they can find them. In England, more has been thought about education and social *status*. One sees English parishes overrun with dissent and palsied with decent indifference, while Missions have won themselves attention even from the heathen and the foreigner. The real use of Mission Colleges has been that they have furnished an opening for zeal and devotion which the Church could not afford to lose. I quite feel that the time is not come when we can do without these special and extra means of introducing salt into the Clerical body. As a matter of fact, however, Mission Colleges are machines for helping men to ordination, and such ought not to be their special character.

I hope to see the day when a very large proportion of the Clergy of England have not cost several thousands of pounds to educate, and have no special claim to rank as gentlemen. The majority of English benefices are worth less than £300 a year, and the enormous majority of the parishioners have much less. It does not commend practical religion to the multitude that a poor gentleman should be all but starving on an income which to most of them would be a very good one indeed, the special work of the said gentleman being to preach the gospel to the poor. Some patrons, shall I say specially Episcopal patrons, try to remedy this by carefully choosing gentlemen of private means. The effect of this is to diminish yet more the class out of which Incumbents are chosen, and therefore to diminish the proportion of really zealous and effective parish Priests, for a class can only yield as many as it contains, and if you want more you must take inferior qualifications. No doubt the parishioner prefers a rich man, and still more a man of gentlemanly manners; but this, a good deal, because he likes to be treated well and not to be called upon to do too much himself; besides, when he wants mere religion, he can always go to the chapel. Things go smoothly enough where the clergyman is a quiet man who pays for everything himself; but, for the sake of the Church, a parish had better get a Christian than a gentleman, when it must choose one or the other. It is all very well for the Clergyman and the Dissenting Preacher to stand on different levels, provided that the Dissenter does not get his influence from his religion, and the Parson his from being a gentleman. There are thousands of men in England now—zealous, active, eloquent—who could beat the Dissenter and the popular infidel with their own weapons, to whom £200 a year would be a good income, and who would be gladly ordained if only the way were opened to them. Why are they not? Because, in the first place, they have not the means of going to College; and, if they did, they would get a varnish of breeding, and learn to be ashamed of their present standing in life, and so be spoiled utterly. There cannot be a greater mistake than to suppose that the Church of England gains anything by its Clergy being all supposed to be gentlemen. It excites the bitter envy and hatred of the great mass of Dissenters; it destroys the sympathy that should be between pastor and people; it makes a man talk and act as though he and his people had little in common; it makes upstarts and prigs seek ordination as a means of rising in the world, and it makes necessary a style of house and housekeeping which cannot be maintained upon the ordinary endowments of our benefices. The Church does gain immensely by having many gentlemen among her Clergy; they would have the same social position, and in every other way very much more influence and respect, if poor parishes had, as a rule, a lower class of men for their Priests. There used to be a class of Curates, in many districts, who were notoriously of a lower standing in society than the run of beneficed Clergy—a sort of non-commissioned officers in the Church staff—the most distinguished made their way upward; the mere ordinary man lived, and was contented, on a very small income. His Church standing gave him respect and importance, and enabled him to place out his family rather better than the mass of his parishioners, but still he was essentially one with them; and though, of course, treated with special courtesy by the gentry—for his office sake—he was decidedly not one of them, still less were his wife and family expected to come up to any artificial standard. He married a woman who knew how to manage a cow and make profit of her poultry, and so could spare something to help those in real distress; and could receive gifts from the farmers and the squire without any loss of dignity. Easter offerings made under such circumstances were a reality. One thing Missions have learnt everywhere —the advantage, if not the necessity, of a Native Clergy, and it would be well if England learnt the same lesson.

The next letter deals with the ever-recurring difficulty of the Church at home arriving at a really just estimate of Mission work. It will be seen that the Bishop points to a system of *Missionary Inspectors* as the only satisfactory remedy, and many of our readers will note with special satisfaction the step that has lately been taken in this direction by Mr. Wigram of the C. M. S. in his newly-accomplished Mission tour.

We hope the day may not be far distant when lay members of the Church will devote some of the time they now give to yachting tours round the world, or shooting excursions in distant lands, to fairly examining and reporting upon the Missionary work of the Church. We can assure them of a warm welcome in Eastern Africa.

October, 1881.

The reading public of England has special difficulties in arriving at any fair judgment on the subject of Missionary work. Any man is a bad witness in his own cause. The accounts of "Missions by Missionaries" have been discredited. It has even been asserted that they have made what were actually false statements in some instances, but this is a charge that has seldom, if ever, been substantiated.

It is much more true that they dwell on favourable signs, and ignore the unfavourable. In this matter Home Committees seem often to look on the raising of "money" as the one thing necessary to the success of a Mission, and to sacrifice all to that. I suppose every Missionary has been told over and over again : "You must send us something interesting." He, poor man, is struggling against manifold difficulties, the people he is sent to are carnal and indifferent, and he himself is worried and unwell, he wants sympathy and encouragement. And, under these circumstances, he is told to write so as to raise "Money"!

Of Missions as they actually existed, little was known till quite lately, even by the members of those Committees who were supposed to be directing them. The Church left the duty to them, and they left most of it to their secretary. He it was who had the chief voice in determining what was, with any sense of the difficulties to be encountered, to be published. Some pious and good men, like Mr. Bullock, of the S. P. G., were so anxious not to publish what was not strictly true, or mere sentimentalities, that they reduced their reports to dry hard skeletons, which could interest nobody very warmly. Others were very fond of anecdotes of travel and of Eastern customs, while others devoutly prized pious ejaculations and tales of death-beds.

Meanwhile, the story published had unintentionally become materially different from that sent home, and without being actually false, it was in reality, very often, not a little distorted and misleading.

It is not easy to determine exactly how far one should go in suppressing scandal. This is not always the fault of Home Committees. Missionaries do not always report fully and faithfully what occurs. The authorities at home ought at least to know of the weaknesses of the men they are maintaining. Such cases as these occurring and being smoothed over, help to excuse, in some way, the utter contempt in which many seafaring men hold "Missionaries."

It is unfortunately true that the greatest obstacle to Missionary work (as, indeed, to Church work at home), does not lie in the hostility of the natives, or in the presence of Missionaries of other denominations, but in the occasional personal squabbles and bickerings of the Missionaries sent out by, perhaps, the same Society.

Much of this is never reported, even to the Home Committee. It is, however, perfectly well-known to the outer world, and helps to form their false estimate of Missions in general. It is a marvellous thing, no doubt, that Christian Missionaries should quarrel with one another, but emphatically they do. And it would perhaps be well if those intending to go abroad were warned more often and more carefully of the great temptations and dangers to which they will be exposed in this direction.

From the Missionaries themselves people will naturally turn to European residents, and ask of them, first, what their ideal of Missions is. You will generally find that the European resident's ideal of the functions of a "Mission" is that it should furnish them with good servants. There is a great deal of the "Planter's ideal of Native Races" prevailing abroad.

This is that the special function of coloured races is to furnish labour for European speculations. If they do *that* they are good; if they do not they are bad. A native Christian, as a rule, has a keener idea of his rights, and a more bitter dislike of European oaths[1] and abuse than an untaught native. He is more apt to compare his master with what he was taught a Christian should be. It is no wonder that many residents should say that all Christian natives are insolent and worthless. When you see English sailors rolling about the streets of an Eastern town in a state of riotous drunken-

---

[1] As, for instance, when Mr. Thomson himself records that his native cook, a boy trained in our schools, reproved him for swearing violently.—*To the Central Lakes and Back*, vol. i., p. 280.

ness, and when one of them catches a native Christian in a lie, you will find that he will dilate by the hour upon the utter worthlessness of "Missions," and will declare that they make the natives worse than they find them. As a fact, most Europeans start with the idea that non-Christians are *utterly* bad. They soon find that they are not so; on the contrary, the decencies of life and the ordinary proprieties of behaviour are perfectly well understood by them, and truth and honesty are well-known virtues. . In some cases the European's own religion goes very little further; but however that may be, the great majority jump to the conclusion that the heathens are every bit as good as are the "Christians," if not better.

There is a third stage, in which language and inner lives are better understood, and in which one begins to feel again how necessary "Missions" are; but to this even some "Missionaries" seem never to attain. To take an instance. It is a painful thing to hear English oaths and curses coming from native lips, and if the native has ever been connected with any Mission, or even if he has not, the fact is put down to the Missionary's discredit.

But in heathen and Mohammedan countries a perfect acquaintance with the language will generally disclose an amount of filthy allusion and profane blasphemy of which the average European resident has no idea whatever; on the contrary, he would probably tell you that he never heard an improper word uttered, simply because he did not understand the allusions, even when he knew the words!

There are, of course, those who never care to inquire about Missions, and will gravely tell you that they never heard of any, when, in fact, they have lived for years close by one or more of them!

In a class by themselves should go the tales brought home by sailors, whether officers or men. The wonderfully superficial view a sailor gets of places where he has often been, the exceedingly narrow circle of his acquaintance with natives, and the exceedingly worthless classes to which they often belong, is only equalled by the positive and sweeping manner in which he tells of them, and the pure good faith in which he retails mere current shipboard stories as being a certainly true and fair account of what they refer to. I have myself traced a scandalous story of some Missionary all round Africa, and through several generations of messes, till it was lost, long ago, somewhere on the West Coast!

And this same story I have myself heard told as a present and very grave impeachment of all Mission undertakings!

We come now to travellers who, at all events, have seen Missionaries at their homes. Upon the whole they are much fairer in their accounts, but they are sadly apt to invent, or at least to generalize on scanty premises.

Mr. Thomson,[1] in one of the liveliest books of African travel I have ever seen, relates a visit to a Mission under my own charge, and gravely talks of our Missionaries walking through the bush in long priestly garments and shovel hats.

I happen to know all about what he did see. A man in charge of a station some eight miles off came in in considerable *déshabille*, and put on a cassock as the best means of making himself decent to meet the visitors. Thereupon they concluded that he had walked all the way in it, and invented the shovel hat out of their own consciousness. There certainly never was one at any of our stations. The same traveller, who is so good tempered and hearty that one can forgive him everything, singles out for special praise an undertaking of which he had seen nothing at all, and which is just now in trouble for importing such an inordinate amount of gunpowder, guns, and ammunition. Thus one sees that Missionaries are not the only people who make their stories picturesque at all hazards.

But the main defect of travellers' talk about Missions is that they can only tell what they saw. Now there are two very distinct systems of Mission working. One is to take the natives into tutelage, and make them live and move by order, and work when and as they are bidden.

This system, well worked, produces fine plantations, good cultivation, well-kept houses, and a most respectful demeanour.

---

[1] "Through Masai Land," p. 51.

The other system aims at giving the native independence and force of character. It leaves him free to cultivate and build and live as he pleases, subject only to instruction and a moderate amount of Church discipline. The strong point of this system lies in its development of a really native, home-grown Christianity, with a principle of self-improvement which works slowly and from within.

It is morally certain that nine travellers out of ten will report better of Missions on the former plan, and, therefore, will say that Roman and Moravian Missions are more successful than any others. I doubt the fact. On one Mission I know of, managed on the tutelage system, gross cruelties and irregularities have lately occurred, which will very possibly be never heard of at home.

Many people have special crotchets, which materially affect their estimate of what is done. Many treat the idea of converting the adults as chimerical, some seem to think it positively wicked. Some say that we should try first to make people more moral rather than to make Christians of them. Others affirm that we ought to begin with civilization. Missions ought to be self-supporting, says one; the really important element, says another, is the industrial. And so they condemn and approve according to some abstract principle, and distort all they see by some antecedent bias.

One man, high in authority, told me that he thought Missions very mischievous things. "Why, sir," he said, "you aim at making the people of one religion. If the people of India were all of one religion, they would chase the English out of the country in a week. I will never give anything to any of your Missions."

Surely some means of securing good information should be attempted. We want periodical accounts from some one living ordinarily at home, and who sees with English eyes, but who is too well acquainted with the history and objects of Missionary work to be blindly led by any private fancy, and whose first aim and invariable rule is to tell the truth, alone and entire, and not just so much of it as is likely to increase the subscriptions to some special scheme. It is very desirable that we should be told of what has *not* been done, as well as of what *has*, and all sects and sections of Christianity should have fair mention.

If our great Societies cannot find men to go on such a round of visits, possibly the proposed Board of Missions might do it even more impartially. At all events, the wretched system of compelling Missionaries abroad to puff themselves and beg and scheme for their own bread, ought to be altogether abolished, and with it the miserable narrowness which ignores everything not done by the special agencies of a single Society.

PART II.

LETTERS OF COUNSEL AND ADVICE.

As has already been noticed, Bishop Steere had great faith in letter writing, and any Memoir of him would be most incomplete without some selection from his letters of counsel and advice to those with whom he had to deal.

He was equally ready any moment to write an answer to a question, whether it concerned admission to Holy Baptism, some deep point of doctrine, the management of a refractory child, or the planting of a hedge. And when occasion seemed to demand it, he would write a reproof, so plainly moulded on the strictest principles of self-sacrifice and truth, as to generally ensure so hearty a reception of it by the person to whom it was addressed, as would naturally be obtained by letters of appreciation of good work, or consolation in sickness or trial.

Of open praise, however, he had as great a horror as of lengthened apology. If he said, "I am satisfied," or "I cannot resist the pleasure of telling you that I hear well of you," one felt that it was praise indeed; and, "For myself," he says in one of his sermons,[1] "I have no liking for apo-

[1] Vol. i. p. 125.

logies and acknowledgments of faults. It is very often that a new quarrel grows out of them, and precious time is always lost in waiting for them. Do not make many words about any wrong you have done, but watch your opportunity, and make it up by good; so both parties will be gratified. If you have been injured, beware for the future, but bear no malice; meet your enemy with a smile, and shame him by kindness."

Fuss he utterly abhorred. One reason why he had such a great power of helping others was, that in listening to troubles, or even complaints, he never underrated difficulties or disagreeables. That curious argument of so many good people in such cases, "*I* should not mind that," whence follows in their mind, "*you* should not," never formed his way of counsel. He would rather say, "Yes, I know this or that, this person's ways, or that circumstance is very disagreeable or trying," or "is disagreeable, I see, to you, but you know a Christian has no right to be angry, and do wrong because another is disagreeable. Why do you let people have that power over you, that their conduct will make you do wrong? If, when we were vexed, we would think, not what would so-and-so do, but what would Jesus Christ do if He were in my place, I do not think we should so often go wrong as we do."

HOW BEST TO DEAL WITH OTHERS.[1]

We are all ignorant of many things, and perhaps in all created things there is nothing more difficult thoroughly to understand than the course of another's thoughts and the working of another's affections. Long experience and observation of men and their doings will be of great assistance, but the one royal road to a discerning spirit is to understand oneself—not to have a general idea that one is hot-tempered, or reserved, or irreverent, or fond of some particular pursuits, and apt to fall into certain sins, but a nice and exact discrimination of the motives which habitually urge us into action, or keep us back from it, and how we should judge of any other person who stood in our place and did what we

[1] To a member of the Guild of S. Alban, February 18th, 1857.

have done ; how those motives may be weakened or brought into stronger action, and what natural limits we find to our powers of self-control ; how far we are swayed by our position in life, how far by a real judgment and determination of our own in the matter.

Such an examination as this will open to most people an entirely new view of things ; they will often find themselves strangely and startlingly like some whom they have always felt bound strongly to condemn. Those who blame others for thoughtlessness and want of kindness to themselves will often find that they are, in other matters, or perhaps in the very same, careless and perverse themselves ; those who condemn one act of irreverence in others, will find some other of their own strangely similar in its general features.

In fact, we may accept it as an axiom that, as we have all one common nature, so have we within ourselves the germ of those same faults, ignorances, and imperfections, which we deplore in others ; if we are unconscious of this, it is only an illustration of the fact that self-deceit is a very common failing.

Here, then, is our book ; we must read out of ourselves and our own inner experience how to deal with others ; when we have done this, we shall find intercourse with others a most valuable means of self-improvement. When we hear a pernicious opinion expressed, or see a vicious action done, we must ask ourselves, Why do I not hold this error or do this wickedness? It will not be sufficient to give some general reason, as most of us do, amounting in fact to this, that we are better and wiser than our brethren, and therefore do not fall.

It is God's grace and His Providence that has really made us different, and the problem for us is how to supply the defects which have ministered occasions of evil to others. . . . God has given us the power to do much, and we must not be slack in using it.

Thoughts like these will make us feel kindly towards our neighbours, and impress upon us the necessity of understanding their circumstances and temptations before we attempt to lecture them into goodness. We may take it as a rule, that if we see no excuse for their faults—in the sense, we mean, of a special reason for their falling in that particular way—then we have something yet to discover, either in our idea of what is natural in men, or in regard to the particular circumstances and trials of the people we are thinking of. Better it is to say two words to the heart, than to deliver whole homilies to the ear only.

LAY HELP IN CHURCHES.[1]

My dear Sir,

No one would deprecate more than myself any confusing in men's minds of the essential difference between the spiritual and lay characters.

But is it true that preaching and saying the prayers are characteristic parts of the clerical office? I believe that it is a Puritan error to say that they are.

The great office of the clergy is to administer the Sacraments, which, as they derive all their efficacy from the ordinance of God, can only be properly administered by those who have a special commission from Him to thus act in His Name.

But our Prayers are notoriously a re-arrangement of the Monastic Offices, which were first put together by and for laymen; and as to preaching, take it in its essence, it is an exhortation to holy life, or an explanation of God's Revelation, which derive their value chiefly from the understanding, zeal, and eloquence wherewith it has pleased God to endow the speaker. If God has given these gifts to a layman, He has pointed him out as a fitting preacher.

The Church has always held that a layman might preach, and there were few cases only because persons able to preach, and fit to do so, were in most instances exactly the persons fit to be ordained.

The Deacon's duty is clearly to do zealously after his ordination such church functions as he might by license have

---

[1] To Mr. J. W. Lea, November, 1859.

performed before; and his new and peculiar office is to assist and wait on the Priest when he officiates at the Altar, to read the Gospel in the Communion Service, and to baptize in the absence of the Priest.

But the Puritan notion was that preaching was the great clerical function, and so the office of a Deacon came to nothing—either he had a license to preach and was as good as a priest, or he had not and was no use in the Church.

After a while people found by experience that laymen could preach, and did preach, as well and better than many Presbyters. *This* lowered their notion of the clerical character, and always will do so until preaching is no longer deemed so great a part of that character as now. There is nothing injures a cause more than to stand stiffly for what one has no right to, and this is very much what has happened in regard to preaching.

It is a monstrous perversion to say a man whose heart God has touched, and to whom He has given great power to touch the hearts of others, shall in no case be allowed to use his power till he has learned to construe Greek with tolerable facility.

As the law of the Church now stands this is so, and all are bound by that law; but it is a law vastly to be regretted, and speedily to be amended, for it has no ground in God's Word nor yet in primitive example.

Let it be freely acknowledged that he to whom God has given the gift of preaching may, upon proving that he has this gift, be regularly admitted to exercise it by the Bishops of the Church, and you will cut away the ground from all really evangelical dissent.

The Sacraments would be much more respected if we ourselves made more of them, and did not rather choose to say our office consisted in preaching, than to profess the truth, that what distinguishes us from laymen is that we have authority from God to bind and loose, to give and withhold His great Sacramental gifts.

Dissenters may outpreach us, but our authority they know they have not. The more strictly we maintain that we alone have a right to preach, the more clearly we put ourselves in the wrong with those who *know* that others are more effective preachers than we are.

I am convinced that in principle it is wrong to challenge the right to preach as belonging exclusively to the clergy, and I think I see many evils which have resulted from it.

Some would allow laymen cottage lectures, but in my opinion it would be much more dangerous to allow them to lecture outside the church than within its walls, for it seems to tend to schism in a much higher degree to gather people to what is exactly an imitation dissenting service.

I cannot now go into the question of what help the Clergy have most need of. I do not know what my brethren in large towns may feel, but for myself, when I am responsible for three full services and the proper superintendence of Sunday schools, they make my Sunday harder work than is either right or good for one's voice or health; and in places where two or three small churches are under the care of one Priest, I cannot but think a lay service would be the very thing for all parties.

This is part of a letter written with reference to the Union of Benefices. It is given here as strikingly apposite to the appeal lately made by an English Bishop for a Priest *possessed of good private means* to come forward and occupy a benefice, the income of which had totally disappeared under the pressure of these hard times in the agricultural districts.

"If a large parish has a small endowment, what is to be done? What is done in the colonies where there is no endowment? What is being done in many places in England? Let the Rector do his duty, and let the Church maintain him.

"The Church will never rise to its duty so long as Bishops and dignitaries check the liberality of churchmen by cutting and contriving an income for poor incumbents out of pluralities, whether legal or illegal. If a re-arrangement of endowments is necessary, let it be made by some authority which will consider first—I should like to say *exclusively*—the welfare of the souls of the parishioners.

"But better a great deal that a stingy parish should be without an incumbent at all, than that it should be taught to be content with the lesser half of a non-resident one because he costs them nothing.

"There are many country places where the so-called church people would maintain that one service a week was quite enough. What has become of the majority of the parishioners? Dissenting chapels and local public-houses could tell.

"I pray God that English churchmen may soon be heartily ashamed of thinking small endowments one of the chief hindrances of church work in rural parishes, or anywhere else. The true endowment of the Church is to be found only, and may be found abundantly, in the awakened hearts of its members."

A LETTER TO THE ——— DISTRICT OF THE GUILD OF S. ALBANS UPON THE BEST MANNER OF SETTLING DIFFERENCES AMONG MEMBERS.

April, 1860.

It is with the very deepest regret that I have observed of late the prevalence of a spirit of disunion and insubordination among the members of the ——— District, and of your brotherhood in particular.

We are called, brethren, to peace, and love, and mutual helpfulness, and not to bickerings and recriminations. Our minds and thoughts should be raised above the possibility of petty dissensions.

You have professed yourselves willing and desirous to serve God in the society called after the first martyr for the truth in our native land; let the remembrance of him, and of the long train who from that time to this have been willing to lay down their lives in the cause in which you are engaged, continually serve to remind you that the servant of God must not seek his own pleasure, or think himself worthy of any honour or consideration. We are not so good as they, and yet God suffered them to fall into the hands of wicked men. Shall we, then, deem it a hard thing if we cannot procure our own way, or lead the minds of our brethren in the direction which we wish?

Thus much is common to you all, Master and brethren alike—bear your cross as the Great Cross Bearer shall appoint, think very humbly of yourselves, and do not murmur that others should think humbly of you also.

Nevertheless, as it is of the essence of all organized bodies that the parts and members should be in due relation and subordination each to other, it is very necessary for you to remember that you are not many masters, but rather to look upon yourselves as the eyes and senses which are to inform, and the hands and feet which are to act, upon the direction of him whom you have chosen to preside over you.

I am sure there is no danger of your so misunderstanding me as to suppose that I would have you mere blind machines, but it seems almost certain that you have forgotten that deference and respect to the authority of your head which is implied in the very notion of a Society, and most of all in a society of soldiers—soldiers of Christ as we are—who have volunteered to bind themselves by a stricter discipline than anyone could have imposed upon them without their free consent, for the express purpose of presenting a more compact and unbroken front to the common enemy.

Let me then briefly tell you how I would urge upon all our members to act in case of difficulty.

In the first place, it is the duty of all Masters and Stewards to be very careful and thoughtful in all they say and do, for upon them lies the chief burden of responsibility for all that, as a Society, we do. It will happen that some of the brethren will not agree with them in judgment upon some things they do and say. What then? Shall those who differ at once rise up and complain? By no means. It is their duty to consider whether the matter is of serious importance to the Society. If not, they are deserving of censure who make it a subject of complaint. But if it seem to them dangerous to pass the matter over unnoticed, it is their duty, in the first place, to lay it before the Superior himself in as inoffensive a manner as possible, and if he continues in the same mind, to think it over with themselves again.

Should they still feel that it ought not to be left, it is then their duty to lay it before the Provost or Warden, not by way of formal complaint and demand of judgment, but by way of information and request for advice. The mere idea of imitating legal proceedings is one to be scouted and abhorred.

We are a Society of friends, and must speak and write always in a friendly manner. It is only in extreme cases of what amounts in some way to wickedness, that we should lodge formal complaints and wish for formal adjudications. A litigious spirit is very easily aroused, and it is a wicked spirit that we should all agree in striving to avoid.

Suppose, then, that the advice of one of the heads of the Guild has been asked, and he advises the dissatisfied brother to give way, this puts it to him as a matter of duty to submit cheerfully and heartily if he can; and it is my opinion, that if any of us should find the opinion of his immediate superior, of the majority of his fellow-labourers in the brotherhood or district, and that of the heads of the Guild, opposed to his own, he ought either to give up his opinion and submit to that of the Master or Steward, or else to request the Warden to remove his name from the list of members.

This may seem an extreme measure, but it is evident that either the dissentient brother is wrong-headed and perverse, or he is opposed to some prevailing feeling in the Society, which will prevent his working cordially with his brethren, and make his union with them a source of annoyance and weakness instead of comfort and strength.

But woe be to him who cuts himself off from such a Society as ours on any mere private fancy or petty disappointment! God does not command any man to put his hand to our plough; but if, when he has done so, he looks back, I tremble to think what peril he must be in.

And now, brethren, apply these principles to your own case.

Are the causes of your differences really deep and great matters? If so, let them be brought as soon as possible to an issue, and be once for all decided by the heads of our Society.

But if, as I feel no doubt is the case, these are matters, all of them, of mere expediency and personal feeling, then let him who is on the weaker side accept his disappointment as a golden opportunity of pleasing his Divine Master by silent submission, and let all the brethren firmly determine to put down, and put an end to, all future dissensions and divisions.

It will be well for the Master not to act on his own discretion merely, if he does not feel sure that all think with him, but to ask the advice of the rest, and adopt, if possible, the opinion of the majority. When, however, the Master has decided, there must be no more disputing, and no attempt to evade or oppose his decision.

The Warden or myself will be ready to hear and attend to what any brother feels it his duty to say, and will take all proper steps to amend what is faulty, invoking, if need be, the help of the Provost's Court; but, in the meanwhile, the aggrieved brother must not make his grievance a matter of common remark, or act in open opposition to his Superior.

If he feels that his conscience requires him to make a public and decided stand against those whom his brethren have elected over them, he has no choice but to withdraw from the Society, so soon as he finds private remonstrance useless.

I have been anxious in writing to you to lay down the principles which ought to guide us in extreme cases, because by them it is easy to decide smaller matters.

I have a good hope, however, that your past differences have mainly arisen from that want of a habit of self-denial and self-control which marks us all at the beginning of our Christian course.

Remember, all of you, that the way to make your brethren agree with one another is for you to take the lowest place yourself, and not to press your own wishes any further than your position in the Brotherhood may compel you to do. I would take occasion to suggest that you should introduce the 133rd Psalm after the Psalms for the Office when you pray together, and I pray God to shed abroad His Holy Spirit of peace and love in your hearts.

NIGHT SCHOOLS IN ENGLAND.

November, 1861.

My dear Brother,

As we are all now about to engage in our great Night School work for the season, I should be glad to be allowed to say a word or two about the spirit in which that work should be undertaken. I shall be delighted to be corrected where I am in the wrong, and I beg to ask the special prayers of all engaged in the work, that we all may both think and do those things that be rightful.

It has many times occurred to me that the motives which urge us to this work are not quite what they ought to be. Why do we spend our evenings in instructing poor lads and men? Is it because we hope thereby to attach them to ourselves? Is it because we hope to attach them to our party in the Church rather than to any other? Is it because we hope to attach them to the Church and so preserve them from Dissent? Is it because we hope by secular instruction to gild the pill of religious teaching? Or is it because we think all honest knowledge better than ignorance, and are therefore anxious to impart it?

Very possibly a little of every one of these designs has entered into our thoughts. Which is the one that should be the chief and central motive? I venture to think our chief motive, as in all work, ought to be a direct one. We ought not to exhibit ourselves before our scholars as wishing one thing, while all the while we care very little for that, but are really aiming at something else. Why do boys and men come to us, but because they feel the want of secular knowledge and are anxious to have it supplied? Do we meet them honestly with the wish to supply it, or do we propose to them terms of barter, something after this fashion—you want to read and write, we want religious disciples; you listen to our catechizing, and we will teach you what you want to know? Of course we do not use such words, but is there not the feeling in the hearts of a good many that we care very little what sort of scholars we turn out, if we gain Churchmen; and that, in fact, our time is given to make Churchmen and not to make scholars? When this is the case, we scarcely seem to act fairly by our pupils. We go, in fact, a long way to justify the suspicion felt by many of the poor of charitable schemes, as though they were only baits, which must have a hook in them somewhere. We are in great danger of finding ourselves at cross purposes with our pupils, they attending to one branch of the instruction, we to another, and each party, day by day, growing more dissatisfied with the inattention of the other, and less disposed to adapt themselves to their wishes. Many night schools have come to nothing through the growth of a silent discontent of this kind, and in many cases those only remain who would gladly have attended our avowedly religious class. There is great danger of both secular and religious teaching falling into a dry formality, unless the teacher's heart is going along with his scholar's. Dry schoolmasterism is a dreary thing, but dry formal Office-saying and Bible-reading is a great deal worse. If a man feels that he cannot throw his whole heart into anything but religious teaching, his right course seems to be to open a religious class, and he may depend upon it that if his zeal is sincere, and he has anything sound to impart, God's blessing will sooner or later rest upon his labours; what he does will be done in the spirit that wins, because it deserves respect; and his pupils will really get good from him because they will come properly prepared to receive it. It is, as I think, greatly to be lamented that, besides our Sunday schools, there are so few avowedly religious classes, and associations, and periodical meetings of a really edifying character. We want men who will be in earnest about such things, and compel respect by their indisputable sincerity. I do not think that our quasi-religious night schools are sincere, or that anybody thinks them so, and probably it is for this reason, that they have less effect than they ought to have, a chill restraint lies upon both teachers and taught, neither dare speak out their whole feelings, and so the coldness of one side increases the chill of the other.

But, it may be asked, what would be the good of such schools at all, unless they were the thin end of the wedge to open a way for Churchmanship. Who would spend his winter evenings in merely making clever villains out of ignorant rogues? The answer is that we are doing so now, and that a gloss of religious knowledge, with a seasoning of half-hypocritical compliance, makes the clever villain none the better. But it is not true that this would be the effect. Is the power of self-denying love to count for nothing? Are the mass of mankind so hardened that they can take at your hands all they want, and give you back nothing—no honour, no deference, no respect, no gratitude? Do we not all understand the difference between being trusted and being watched—between acting upon an agreement and being left to our sense of honour? Should we not be more to be trusted if we were trusted, than if something were enacted by way of security? And now, in night schools, the prayers, and hymns, and religious instruction are far too often, on both sides, regarded as a sort of balance to the reading, writing, and arithmetic. This is not the way to win souls to God. Physicians do not make Christians by tending the sick, but Sisters of Mercy do; and why, but because the one have their reward, and the others have not. And the Sisters themselves convert, not by talking, but by nursing lovingly. We must do good for doing good's sake, and then it will work like leaven in the hearts of those we benefit. Why does our Lord say that Pharisaical prayers and almsgiving have no reward of God, but because they have a reward from men; and so our scholars too often feel as though they had paid us because they have acquiesced in our devotions. Every one can understand our working to bring men into our Church and party—it is outward work for an outward object, and so they are not impressed by it; but work which aims at no reward, and hides itself in a manner from reward, this is godlike and heavenly—this is startling to men and well-pleasing to our Heavenly Father.

So, then, I conclude that our chief motive as teachers should be the same with that, which obliges the compassionate to relieve sickness and distress. Christian love that cannot be repressed, and will not have any good thing without giving of it freely to others. How wretchedly selfish was Dives, who feasted while Lazarus starved! And what else are those who, having knowledge, will not impart it freely? Is there any sensible man that does not love knowledge even as he loves life? Shall he not burn to share it with those who have less? Would not a man deserve public execration who brought up his children in utter ignorance? And how do we love our neighbour as ourselves, if we are contented to see him in ignorance as deep? But, then, knowledge may be misused. And may not life? Do we keep our food away from the hungry until we are sure their lives would be valuable to the community, or do we ask first in sickness, will this man be a blessing to his neighbour, and leave him to die, unless we are sure that he will? Such thoughts would be horrible, and so it is to withhold knowledge from the ignorant, for knowledge is the food and clothing of the mind, and ignorance shuts up every avenue of good, as well as some of ill. The glory of our charitable schemes for men's bodies is the physical relief administered; the tarnish upon them is hypocritical religion exhibited by "*Soupers.*"[1] So the glory of our schools is the actual knowledge acquired in them, and not that little show of outward conformity which is too often the whole of their religious fruit. If we heal the sick and feed the hungry, and clothe the naked, and teach the ignorant, and bury the dead, because we are Christ's disciples, and love our brethren as He loved us, He will work in their souls for His own glory. Very possibly we may never see the work, but it will be real, and will stand the judgment fire. The curse of this age is not irreligion, but hollow religion; and the way to remove this curse is to live in the real spirit of love, asking nothing, and giving all things; while the way to increase it, is to make temporal advantages a bribe for outward compliance.

[1] A name given by the Roman Catholics in Ireland to those who sought to win over some of their body by doles of food.

THE BIBLE A CRITERION, NOT A TEACHER; A RECORD OF THE PROCLAMATION OF A REVELATION, NOT A REVELATION ITSELF.[1]

Little Steeping, July, 1869.

I suppose all earthly Revelations are made to man, and published by man. I do not see any reason to believe in the Revelation of a Book. I see only a call to man, and a commission to man.

In the Gospel I see Christ and His Apostles gathering a Society, teaching all that will listen, and bringing them into a society for conserving and propagating that teaching.

All teaching and Sacraments seem to be but little more than empty forms, unless they bring about a personal communication between God and the disciple.

The Church, then, is the body of those who are, or who profess to be, in special relation with God. The history of this Church is the history of Christianity, and it was in, to, and for this Church, that the Revelation was made.

But as all things human corrupt and fade, so the history of the Church shows that the knowledge and appreciation of the Revelation made to it became corrupted and changed also.

How shall we be sure about the Revelation that comes to us through such channels?

By observing what kinds of changes have been made, and checking our present doctrines and practices by our historical knowledge of their origin, and that we may do this the more certainly God provided that records of the beginning of the Church should be provided for us, in which we may see its first life.

In these we see what did occupy the minds of those to whom the Revelation came most directly, and what we do

---

[1] To Mr. E. Fry.

not see clearly there, we may be sure they did not think very much about.

But no one of us is without prepossessions, or was ever meant to be. The Bible is a criterion, and not a teacher. The teacher is the living society of people calling themselves Christians.

It is by them, as a matter of fact, that doctrine is shaped and practice moulded. We all, as a matter of fact, get hold, from tradition or reading, of a set of notions which some of us try, and all might try, by the Bible, and find some compatible with it and some not.

It was thus with Christians who lived while it was being written, and will be so with men till the end of time. And what is universal must have been Divinely intended.

The Bible, then, I suppose, ought to be viewed as not a Revelation itself, but a record of the proclaiming and receiving of a Revelation, by a Body which is still existent, and which propounds the Revelation to us, namely, the Body of Christians commonly called the Church.

Manifestly, then, small critical questions about Inspiration are curious rather than unsettling.

Those who treat the Bible as a direct Revelation in itself must always be perplexed with questions as to the limits of its divinity, and its claims to authority, and how such and such books came to be accounted part of it.

The Christian Body has a history, and an account of the Revelation of its own, and one that can lend authority to the Bible, since it in no way depends upon it, but existed before the first book was written, and long before the whole list of books was put together as a Bible.

In truth Christianity and the Bible must both be first propounded by a sufficient authority, and shown to be reasonably supported by historical testimony before either can be a subject of argument at all. Then it must be examined, and this is the point at which internal evidence becomes the main thing.

No external evidence can perfectly prove its truth, but without external evidence there would never be any examination at all.

Those who build on internal evidence exclusively are like those who plan an upper storey without relation to the lower, their edifice may be very good and beautiful, but there is great uncertainty as to its being practicable.

Our moral sense and reasoning faculties are perfectly fitted for trying what is propounded to them, but they are powerless to discover, or to give authority to an imaginary scheme of doctrine.

It is thus that criticism could pull to pieces the old Roman history, but failed altogether in building up a new one.

It is thus, again, that Christian consciousness can try schemes of Theology, and reject, and approve, but can never itself construct anything save an airy web of possibilities which no man's faith can hang by.

A good many difficulties seem to me obviated by these notions of mine, but I ought to apologize for wasting so much of your valuable time.

On Loss of Interest in Work.[1]

1878.

"I do not know what is the matter with me. I used to get up in the morning, feeling as if I liked so much everything I had to do, and now I cannot." The Bishop answered, "Well, there was no merit in it then, there may be some now." He paused a moment, and then said very gently and gravely: "You know it would be nothing to offer one's life, if it were no sacrifice.

And in a day or so he wrote and said : "It seems to me that you want a warmer faith in the continual love of God towards you. Do not try to go alone at all, but lay your

---

[1] Reminiscences of a conversation with a member of the Mission, who at the end of about a year went to tell the Bishop of a want of the former feeling of interest in the daily round of duty ; and parts of a letter written subsequently to the same person. A few deep loving words of fatherly counsel ; an echo of some chapters of the "Spiritual Combat."

plans and efforts entirely in His hands, and be quite sure that He loves you infinitely, and cares for you all day long. It would be a sad thought that we had our own way when it was not God's way. Do not think of your own work as a separate thing, for it is not, and cannot be alone, and so while you are careful to do your best, seek your consolation and rejoicing, rather in what is done by others. We know that we can judge of their work much more fairly than we can of our own.

"If others take your work out of your hand they take from you the fearful responsibility of it; it is not a loss to be delivered from care. So we must feel our work most blessed when it helps on the efforts of others, just as our lives are most blessed when we are a comfort and a happiness to others. We need never desire to be first; it is much happier to follow and to co-operate, than to direct and to lead. And to get tranquillity we must rest in a Love which is continually with us in our faith and falls, just as much as in our successes. For He never changes. When we sin, God does not condemn us, He goes on giving us His blessings, He is kind to the unthankful; and He would not have us condemn ourselves as though it was a wonderful thing that we should fail. The wonder is when we do well. I do not think you want penances, you want to feel that you are loved and cared for, and that all that vexes you is really done and permitted in love. Believe me, it really is so."

The Greatness of the Humblest Work.

If there was one thing more than another which Bishop Steere desired to impress on the minds of his fellow-labourers, it was that what some would call the merely secular work of the Mission, was just as important, and just as much Missionary work, as the preaching or teaching which are popularly supposed to be the sum of a Missionary's labours.

Here is an instance in answer to one who had charge at

the time of the Printing Office, and had asked for "promotion" to the mainland :—[1]

I should certainly like you to occupy a post of honour and importance, and certainly you now have one. When I came out from England as a priest of some standing, I found such work as yours was necessary, and I devoted myself to it, not doing it so well as you can perhaps, but as well as I could. Bishop Tozer took for his share exactly what Mr. —— is now doing.

If either of you turned out incapable, I should look out for some other work for you, but certainly not by way of promotion. The printer preaches to many more than any speaker can hope to reach.

As to Ordination, I have generally wished for two years experience of a man's powers and steadfastness. I have constituted you and Mr. —— Readers, and I wish you to share the Offices and preachings, and catechizings in the school Chapel and elsewhere. I am watching to see how far you both can discover and use opportunities for speaking a word for Christ. I take for granted that you wish to help on the conversion of Africa in the way which best suits your special powers. In the matter of printing you surpass us all. I should hope well for the future if I had a priest working amongst the carpenters, and in whatever other workshop there may be, and learning there to sympathise with his fellow-helpers, and how to speak best to them of the great motive of his own life. One who lives and works among the natives is doing a great work by his simple zeal and diligence, and no one will be likely to make so effective a preacher, or so wise and discreet a spiritual adviser. I would never have a man to teach any kind of work as a mere lay occupation, I should prefer a priest, but at least I hope for a candidate for holy orders. A man who would do nothing but preach I should get rid of as soon as possible. We are here something in S. Paul's position, and he earned his own living by

---

[1] The dates of this and the following letter are for obvious reasons omitted.

what people call secular work. He was all the better preacher for it, and it would be absurd for us to praise him, and not to try and imitate him. I wish we could, every one of us, find work to do, which would earn enough money to feed us. Our position would then be greatly better than it is in all respects. The preaching of the Gospel ought not to depend upon how much money can be gathered at home.

On Working Pleasantly with Others.[1]

"I am afraid you have not yet learnt how impossible it is for you to do everything yourself, and how very necessary it is for you to make working with you agreeable to other people. You are in a post of great responsibility, and you cannot afford to quarrel with any of those who have to work with you. I have had a great deal of experience of the annoyances you are likely to meet with, and I can assure you that a pleasant temper and bearing towards people who do not do as you wish, is very necessary for your own sake, as well as that of the work. It is very easy to find an excuse for being out of temper, but the problem you have before you is how to get the most and best work out of your coadjutors, and for this much kindliness, and a firm resolution never to take offence is most necessary. Please to let me know if anyone does not please you, and in the meantime to treat him with the politeness which is always due from one gentleman to another, not to say from one Christian to a brother in Christ. If you will let your troubles go through me, I think I can arrange that they shall disappear; but you must not expect that men who are in every way your equals will bear to be spoken roughly to, or treated with a silence that may seem either sullen or contemptuous.

"You should talk over your plans freely with your companions, and hear what they think. You will generally find that they either agree with you, or are quite ready to conform to your wishes. If there remain any difficulty, I am at hand

[1] To Mr. ——.

to settle it. You must not take upon yourself to give orders to your fellow-workers. You should never put your wishes in a stronger form than that of a request—you are a leader among equals, not a master over inferiors. And if you try from this day to make yourself thoroughly agreeable to all who are with you, I will answer for it that your troubles will disappear, and I am sure that a great deal more and better work will be done. Think how God bears with all our perversenesses, and you will feel ashamed of resenting those of your companions.

"I have thought a great deal about your troubles, and I have no doubt that they are of your own making, and that you could put an end to them in five minutes by merely doing to others as you wish them to do to you. However, I daresay they are real troubles to you, and I do not want to hold you to an engagement which has become irksome to you, only, in justice to the Mission, we must have time to write home, and see if we can get some one to take your place. I propose, therefore, if you are of the same mind, say in four months hence, to send you home then."

We need only add that this member of the staff cheerfully remained at his post till ill-health drove him home some two years and a half afterwards.

A letter showing the Bishop's power of entering into the minutiæ of the mysteries of the kitchen, and the care he took of the health of his staff.

December 18th, 1880.

My dear W——,

Do not aim at too much, and insist on having good food somehow. Have a man up from the coast if no one in the country can be found to cook properly. Do not be content with bad food, or allow your cook not to do what he is told. Possibly ——'s Swahili may be bad, and his ideas of cooking vague, so that he may perhaps puzzle a native more than he instructs him. The housekeeping is always best done by the head of the house. The head is the only one who can care equally for all. He should not think of himself, but should consult the wants and wishes of the others.

I should recommend a stew of fowls and viazi,[1] or of Indian corn and preserved meat, or goat. Mind and skim the fat off any preserved meat you use. A fowl stewed down to make a good soup and thickened with rice makes a good dish, if well-seasoned with salt and pepper and a touch of red pepper. New half-ripe mtama is also very eatable.

All these things are nice when done nicely, but not at all nice if you are careless. In cooking meat of any kind remember to put it in cold water, then it will stew and make soup and be tender; put it into hot water and it goes hard directly. But green vegetables generally want hot water.

Do not think that keeping —— in health is unimportant work, and remember that the chief cause of weak stomachs and diseased livers in Africa is alcohol.

A letter to Archdeacon Farler when ailing, urging him to take a short or long voyage, or go to England, showing, too, how anxious the Bishop was about the result of a promising scholar's English training.

May 25th, 1881.

I am very sorry that you do not get stronger, it must be a sore trial to you to slip back so often. You are, I hope, founding a Church which will outlast us all. Do not let your troubles and loneliness overcome you, and do not try to do too much at once, but organize your work as well you can to bear the strain when you have to leave for refreshment.

As you know, I am not fond of half-measures, and if you and the doctors think that a trip to Delagoa Bay and back, where it is winter, or to Bombay and back, would not be likely to set you up, then I see no remedy but a voyage home. Indeed there are some things to recommend this, and at once, before the summer is over in England.

I am specially anxious that you should have the starting of

---

[1] Sweet potatoes.

X—— [a Native]. It is an experiment in which I think you would very likely succeed, whilst I am sure that almost anyone else would fail.

Nothing would be worse than for you to hang on here until he was ready to come out, and just at that moment go home.

I cannot bring myself to think of using you as a stop-gap for any work here in Zanzibar, even if I thought you likely to gain strength here, which I do not. If you go home by this mail you could take X—— under your wing, and judging for yourself of his tone and progress, might be able to bring him out already ordained a Deacon, that is, if you were entirely satisfied and confident. I have no doubt he wants a great deal which no one could give him so well as yourself.

Of course you would always be useful to the Mission in England, as elsewhere. Don't think twice about the expense. I'll take the responsibility of that.

———

October 19th, 1878.

My dear W——,

If I were you I would do as little as little as I could in the physicking line. It is a very hazardous thing. Pains in the chest, such as you speak of, are almost always better for a mustard plaister or a blister, and I should never myself trust to books. The symptoms of chest diseases are a great deal too obscure for an unprofessional person to have much of an opinion upon them. I had a great deal rather trust in God's Providence than in untried drugs. Go by experience as much as you can, and not by books.

I do not see how there can be any harm in people living near a Mission if they get nothing by it. If they were fed gratis it would be quite a different thing. The common story of criminals often escaping to Missions I do not believe; the right of sanctuary ought to secure a fair trial, it was never intended to do anything more. . . .

I take it that what is chiefly intended by the letter you send is, that if you aim at a brotherhood for the sake of forming a brotherhood, it will probably come to nothing.

If you are so zealously occupied in any one thing that others draw round you to join in it, then a real brotherhood will grow up. The first thing to think of is the work to be done, and the best way of doing it.

Rules for a community must follow the gathering of the community, and not precede it. The first communities arose out of the feeling that it was impossible to live in the world without sin ; thence, first hermits, then all communities, have begun with one man, who set himself to the work, and was compelled to admit others.

Later societies have originated in a want felt for some work such as teaching children, tending the sick, preaching in neglected places, and so on. One man has set himself to the work, and others have gathered round him.

If the object is felt to be of overwhelming importance, men will submit to the restraints of a community life, but, as a rule, not otherwise.

You are quite right as to the use of a daily meditation ; this is always useful.

November 15th, 1879.[1]

I am afraid it is impossible to expect much increase in the number of our Missionaries. If you remember how much has been done by men who were quite alone in a heathen country, you will feel how much is yet possible.

The company of Europeans keeps a man separate from the natives, and no one will ever be a good missionary who cannot be happy among the natives. It is very foolish of —— to talk as he does of isolation, especially as he is within a day's walk of you all at Magila. There are five of you, and there are but five clergy in some dioceses to a district half as large as England. I assure you we shall expect great things.

The following is a sample of the way in which the Bishop kept himself in touch with all the daily work of the Mission in the Island of Zanzibar :—

[1] To the same.

My dear ——,

I send suggested versions of the hymns for comparison with your own draughts. I have my doubts about the intelligibility of "Shadows of the evening steal across the sky." It has an air of mere prettiness. It is not at all true that beasts sleep at night, as we know them; and the line "Soon will be asleep," strikes me as bathos. The whole hymn has, in the English, rather an air of being *written down* to children. The boat seems to have had quite a series of adventures. Please tell —— that all the window-frames, except one, are supposed to be made to one measure, and were intended for the upper rooms. The one for the lower rooms is smaller than the rest.

To A—— F.[1]

November 28th, 1881.

The more I think about it, the more it seems to me that the Mfunti people have a right to interfere with the burning of lime in the Nyika near them.

In England the neighbouring occupiers always have rights over the adjoining wastes. I should think there is no doubt that the Mfunti people have a right to cut wood and to cultivate the ground where you have been burning lime, and could and would exclude any Majila people who proposed to occupy the place.

H—— says the lime lies within a gunshot of the actual present clearings of the Mfunti people.

Anyhow, it must be within the possible area of cultivation.

If anything like this is true, I am sure that we ought to make an agreement with them, and satisfy all reasonable claims, especially as we are bound as Christians not to stickle for our rights, or to resist even if we suffer wrong. I think the only reasonable course is somehow to get together the chief men of the villages which border on the Nyika, including Semkali, and to get yourself represented as well as

[1] The rights of the natives are sacred.

may be, and then and there to settle a compensation, and pay it.

There is no difficulty about money, but there is evidently a charge of injustice lying against us at present, which must be removed.

To a member of the staff who had suggested that a horse would be a useful adjunct to his work.

June 7th, 1881.

I have a very strong objection to people's riding about at all, unless it is a case of absolute necessity. I do not think we are justified in taking the money of poor people and spending it on horses or carriages, or in any other kind of luxury.

I know it is difficult to draw a line between what is necessary and what is not, but I would always rather miss what might have been an advantage, than run any risk of exceeding.

I am intensely disgusted at the spirit of self-indulgence which seems to be more and more the spirit of the age, and am, I daresay, inclined to go unreasonable lengths against it, but still I am so inclined.

To a Member of the Guild of S. Alban on his offering himself for the Mission.

71, Euston Square, October, 1874.

My dear Brother,

I thank God that He has put it into your heart to give yourself to His service, and I ask His blessing for you always.

I shall be asking our medical adviser to see one or two who hope to join us, and should be glad if you could see him at the same time. I will send you word when we are able to make an appointment; in the meantime, give double attention to your present duties, as I have many arrangements to make before our plans can be matured.

I should like you to join us as a candidate for Holy Orders, giving your time to native languages and private reading, as far as you are not required in the immediate work of the Mission, in which you would, of course, be always ready to assist. Men usually find their employments of a more humdrum character than they expected, but there is nothing which is not holy when done for God. The great thing is to be able to throw oneself heartily into the work of the present, and do the little things well, then a man is surprised to find how great the estimation is in which others hold him.

To a Father of an Intending Missionary.

Zanzibar, May 2nd, 1879.

My dear Mr. Z——,

Thank you very much for all the kind expressions in your letter, and for the gift you are so generously ready to offer through us.

The first thing your son has to do is to get as good a degree as he can. He will never be able again to win so much of a permanent honour.

The secret of success in serving God is to do the work of the hour with all one's might. After that, it will be a question whether he had better have a year here or in England before Ordination.

I have, of course, a bias towards a year or two among ourselves, but I could not object to a year of good real work in the North of England. I think better training is to be had in the North than in the South.

The advantages of being ordained in England are so obvious, that you would probably be wise to secure these for him.

If so, he could return, say at the end of two years, and serve a year in England. I think some of the English Bishops, if not all, would then ordain him priest for foreign work.

I am myself anxious to see less distinction made between home and foreign work; they are in essentials one.

Our Secretary will give you an introduction to our consulting physician. The special thing to be looked for is any weakness of heart or brain; general lowness of vital power is often greatly helped by the steady temperature of this climate.

Please to let me hear all you fear or think. We are just now flourishing greatly, thank God, in every way, and continual openings beckon us on.

To a Missionary.—Deferring Deacon's Orders.

March 1st, 1881.

Thank you very much for your openness in all matters. You are very right and good in all that you say, but one cannot help feeling that you have not yet thought sufficiently over the very solemn thing that life is, and how much depends upon the choice of one's lifework.

I do not think that I ought to let you bind yourself for life to the work of the Ministry, until you have somewhat more maturely considered what the nature of that work is.

Many a young man has drifted into Holy Orders, and not really understood what it all meant until it was too late for him to draw back.

One must take one's whole life, and one's pleasures and one's pains, one's hopes and fears, and lay them upon God's altar, and then he may be a good Christian; but for a Priest one must do more.

One must have an inner zeal for God's glory, and a desire for the salvation of one's fellow men, at the cost, if need be, of one's own life.

One must study to understand the intellectual and moral difficulties of others, and know how to help them to meet them.

You have evidently never thought over the great problems of God's existence, and of our own, which are the questions of the day.

It seems as though you relied upon a merely traditional belief, even in the Being of God.

Now when the civilized world is claimed as being largely Atheist, and Mohammedanism and Buddhism are habitually praised at the expense of Christianity, one must have an opinion on such subjects, and be ready to give an answer to those who ask us a reason for our faith. It would be a terrible thing after one's ordination to wake up to a world of doubt.

So, again, it is very right and amiable to go as one is led, while one is young, but when one is about to take upon oneself lifelong engagements one must have a set and serious purpose of one's own.

Of course, one must do as one is guided, but the reins are in one's own hand, and woe-betide him who does not determine what he wishes until the moment for action comes and passes.

You have been already six months at least under the direction and guidance of a priest who has a great reputation for activity and success. But what have you done?

I will ask him to take you under his charge for at least six months more, and to introduce you to the great questions and difficulties which beset a clerical career, but it is upon yourself that you must after all depend, you must set your own mind to grapple with the great questions stirred by Mission work, and determine not to be guided merely, but to be a guide and teacher.

You will soon begin to feel that a great deal of work, and serious application, among both books and men, is necessary to qualify you for all this.

You have been a boy hitherto, you must now begin to be a man—one upon whom others may lean, and who can, and will, help them all out of his own experience and thought and acquired knowledge.

We all love you dearly, and only wish you to be as strong as you are well-principled and well-meaning. May God supply all your needs.

March 4th, 1881.

I am very glad that you have taken so kindly all that I have felt it my duty to say. As to books, their use is to tell us what others have thought, and to guide us into thinking for ourselves. The right way to regard a standard book is not to take it for an infallible guide, but to think that thus and thus men of wisdom and reputation in their day have thought, and therefore, in some sense or manner, there must be truth in what they have laid down.

It is quite possible that their arguments will need entire reconstruction to meet the wants of the present day.

In any case one must think the matter over for oneself under their guidance if one can.

Thus Pearson on the Creed gives one the whole of what one may term traditional theology, in its strictest dogmatic sense; and Browne on the Articles gives one a compendium of general theology, determined as to its arrangement by the 39 articles. Almost any Church history will do to start one on the right lines. I think Robertson is at Kiungani. I should on no account wish you to give more than an hour a day to actual reading; it is of consequence to think a great deal more than one reads. Read one article out of Browne's book, and then think it well over; consider why it was thought of importance then, and how far it is of importance now, and what corresponding questions are likely to meet you in life.

If you feel difficulties write of them in full to me. Only one caution—do not get entangled in the controversies of the day. Such doctrines, for instance, as that of the Sacrifice in the Holy Eucharist you had better not try to have an opinion about, till you have a grasp of the great fundamentals of all religion, and a pretty clear idea of the history of Christianity itself. Religion now-a-days is too often made to consist in taking a side in Church Politics.

Let me give you one word of advice. Never say, "I can't."

TO THE FATHER OF THE ABOVE-NAMED MISSIONARY.

March 4th, 1881.

My dear Mr. Y.,

I am afraid that you will be disappointed that after all, having talked over the whole matter with your son, we have come to the conclusion that it would be desirable for him to take a further time before binding himself by Ordination.

His extreme goodness and candour make him loved of all who know him, and Mr. M——, who was kind enough to give him a paper on the Greek Testament reports exceedingly well of his knowledge of that, but he himself feels that as to the special work of a clergyman he has never yet fully realized what it is, nor have his thoughts or studies been much directed that way.

I am hoping that he will be able to give himself an hour or so every day for reading, which, with as much original thought as may be, will very well suffice for abstract theology, and that under Mr. F——'s immediate eye, he will be well introduced to the practical part of his profession.

The main thing he seems to me to want, is to have some idea that it is his business in life to work, and open his eyes to what wants doing, and set his energies to do it. He seems up to this time to have been content simply to follow when led and to obey when bidden. Of course this cannot last. He must begin sooner or later to think and act for himself. I have very little doubt that he might have been ordained in England, but I have much less that it would not have been a good thing for him.

I am not at all sure that he has any real vocation for Holy Orders at all, and if not it would be a cruel thing to ordain him merely because he was modest and obedient.

These are not times in which a man should bind himself to the priesthood, unless he has great resolution, and a strong desire of his own to live and die in it. Any way he is so young yet that a little prolonged preparation will certainly be to his advantage. He has been so well cared for hitherto in all ways, that independent life is yet strange to him.

To the Same Candidate a few days before his Ordination.

November 24th, 1881.

My dear Y——,

This is the first day I have had clear of the many engagements that have come upon me, to give a little time to you.

In these few days you should take a review of your past life, and humble yourself for any shortcomings, and of course still more for any actual faults or sins of which you may be conscious.

And for the future you should consider the serious vows you are to take upon you. You must not look only upon the questions and exhortations in the Deacon's Ordination, but you must look on also to those in the Priest's Ordination, of which this is a shadow.

You have, of course, read over these Offices carefully, you cannot do so too often, especially with prayers that you may be able to fulfil the pledges you are giving.

For practical considerations the old series can hardly be surpassed.

(1) Man was made for what? For God's glory.
(2) What hinders his attaining his object? Sin.
(3) What is Sin? Indifference to God and selfseeking.
(4) What is the end of Man? Death, Judgment, Heaven, or Hell.
(5) The great fight—on one side, Christ and all holy things. On the other, the devil and all evil things. Resolve to choose and hold a side.

These will branch out into innumerable other thoughts, if you seek throughout a personal application.

The two spiritual books I most value myself are "The Imitation of Christ" and "The Spiritual Combat." I recommend both to you.

Have you any choice as to the place of ordination?

He was ordained in the Slave Market Church on S. Andrew's Day. He returned to England after his three years in Africa, but was not allowed by the London Physician whom he consulted to go back to Africa.

ON MARRIAGES AMONG NATIVES IN THE MISSION.

August 7th, 1878.

My dear J——,

I am glad to have your account of the men and the women they desire to have as wives. The question as to long courtships is a difficult one everywhere. At what time a man should be allowed to take to himself a wife is one that must be answered according to the moral status of the man and the woman. In the case of men and women settled in the same place, I think your rule is a good one (of a month's courtship), and in any case you are quite right to deprecate and, so far as you can, to prevent hasty unions. It was very right that a man should tell you at once that he thought he had met with a woman who would suit him, and equally right that you should tell him to wait a bit.

We have, of course, neither the right nor the power to say to two people, you shall or shall not marry, unless they are under some previous obligation. In this case the men have been here more than a month and are likely to be only the more unsettled by prolonged waiting.

It is easy enough to delay marriage, but the moment the delay becomes irksome, there is almost a certainty of mischief resulting. I am clear that in England, when two people have made up their mind to marry, it is better for themselves and the community that they should do so, and I have seen many grievous evils come of delays.

Here the scandal of a number of single men and single

women living on the same shamba is sure to be great, and I look upon hasty marriages as a less evil.

We are not dealing with the case of born Christians, or of intelligent thoughtful people, we are dealing with the case of heathens, unaccustomed to restrain their passions, and barely just beginning to comprehend the existence of a law of self-restraint, and to get a glimpse of spirituality. Surely it is a very heavy burden to take upon one's own conscience for you or me to say, "You shall not have a home nor any lawful union with the other sex until an indefinite period shall have elapsed, and I have been thoroughly satisfied with your conduct."

It is a tolerably well-ascertained fact that no power on earth can *compel* to chastity. While, therefore, one does all one can to fence it round with helps, one must remember that one has to do with human nature, and with a very degraded sensual type of it.

Now, what is God's remedy against unchastity? It is marriage. However hasty, however imperfect, or insufficiently thought of, marriage, openly and deliberately entered into, is the one hope of escaping innumerable and nameless mischiefs.

Everything that makes marriage difficult helps to make unchastity excusable to the mind of the man or the woman who is tempted. I will not for one, when a man and a woman come to me and say, we have well considered it and wish to become man and wife, take upon my soul the responsibility of saying, you shall not. I shall always, as I always do, lay the whole matter clearly before them, and give them such time, as they will consent to take, to consider of it. But, if they are determined, I feel that the matter belongs to them and God, and that I have no right to put my ideas or feelings in their way, knowing how easy it is to fall and how hard it is to stand. Certainly incontinence is not a reason against marriage, seeing that marriage was appointed specially as its remedy.

In the two first cases you bring under my notice, I have no doubt we ought to encourage the men to marry.

The third is a more difficult one. The man has a wife,

who for a long time past has lived very badly. In England he would have got a divorce, as a matter of course, and might have married again the next day.

I am clear that among *non*-Christians a man is not bound to such a woman, and I think not even among Christians. It is a case as to which I, as the Ordinary of the place, should, according to old English customs, have been the judge, and I think I should have set him free.

If, however, the woman he proposes to marry is a slave, she is liable to be reclaimed by her master, and so the marriage would be liable to be broken off at any time. Such a marriage I think we ought not to sanction. If I could, I should like to purchase her freedom. If the woman is a fugitive and escapes to Masasi, I think she would be safe, and I think we ought rather to help than to hinder her. We submit to Arab law, but we decline to enforce it.

OF MARRIAGES OF NATIVE CHRISTIANS WITH HEATHEN WOMEN.

May 30th, 1879.

My dear W——,

There is no objection to a Christian marrying a catechumen, but they cannot be married as Christians, unless both have made some kind of a profession of Christianity.

Where there are no Christian women, a marriage according to the custom of the country may be tolerated, and the Christian is not guilty of fornication, though he is guilty of irregularity, which will be more or less serious in proportion as he is more or less under necessity in the matter. A Christian is not bound to celibacy, and it is a question of conscience and prudence how far his circumstances excuse an irregular marriage. Such a marriage is subject to local law so far as the non-Christian is concerned, but the Christian is bound by Christian principles. If mutual divorce is allowed by local law, he cannot divorce, she can.

TRANSLATION OF A PASTORAL ON POLYGAMY SENT TO
THE BONDEI CHRISTIANS, IN AUGUST, 1878.

To the Bondei Christians and Catechumens, the mercy and blessing of God.

My brethren, I hear that there are doubts among you regarding husbands and wives. According to your ancient customs men have married two, four, or many wives, but by Christian law a man can have one wife only.

It is unlawful for a man to marry a second wife while the first is alive.

Our Lord Jesus Christ has told us that if a man marry a second wife, even if he leaves the first, he commits adultery (Matt. xix. 9). And the Apostle S. Paul saith, "Happy is he who does not marry at all, unless he desires a wife for the sake of remembering the things of God."

However, for other people, it is better that every man should have his wife, and every woman her husband. "One, not many."

And this is the law of God from the beginning. For our forefather Adam God did not create many wives, but one only, who is our mother, Eve.

Again, to this day, when children are born, the number of males and females is equal, but those who are a little in excess are the males, not the females.

Thus God teaches us that men should take one wife only.

We know also that a man is unable to love well more than one wife; and if the wives are many there is much quarreling, and the children do not love one another, but each wife wishes to surpass her companions, and the children to inherit their father's property.

Now a man of true knowledge does not marry more than one wife; but there are men who married in the time of ignorance, and having many wives, before they knew the truth—what shall they do?

Our elders have decided they may be instructed that they choose one wife, and put away those who are left.

If a woman have no home, the man shall give her a house and food, but shall not go near her again.

However, if a man does not put away his former wives, he has permission to pray with us; he may call himself a Christian, but he is not allowed Baptism, nor the Mysteries of the Church, except at the time of death.

Let him not be driven away, but we do not count him to be perfect yet.

And this is our advice for these days: If a man do not leave his former wives he is a catechumen only, until death.

If a man who is baptized returns to his former wives, he removes himself from the number of Christ's people; he makes himself again only a catechumen.

If he follows with other women he is not one of us any more, nor is he even a catechumen, but a heathen (kafiri), nor has he any life unless he repents. And these words are true. And we pray God that He may keep you from all evil and mischief, for the sake of our Lord Jesus Christ.

I who write this am Edward Steere, Missionary Bishop.

To One in Charge at Kiungani.

May 19th, 1880.

My dear G——,

If you have any reason to think that wrong things are going on in any house on our land, you will of course call the owner to an account. The first thing to ascertain is, who lives in the house. I think it ought to have its regular tenant. The man came long ago as a refugee and catechumen; his wife came out of a dhow, with others who are at Mbweni. I have an idea that Abdallah, possibly, and Granville and Caroline are living in the house; if so, they ought certainly to leave it. Granville ought to live in the great house; Abdallah might possibly lodge there, but not if there is a female lodger.

Please do *not* bring strange work*men* on to the premises. . . . I have been pleased to see that only our own people were at work on the houses, and I wish this very much not to be changed. I have never noticed any strangers amongst them.

It is impossible to work without women, unless you employ little boys and girls; and I have been very pleased to see our own women at work, instead of lolling about indoors, or gadding off to town.

Of course that man and his wife are, as catechumens, under our charge, and are not to be sent away hastily. If they do or encourage any wickedness, then of course they must go. Their house must no doubt be rebuilt as soon as possible. Please to see that it does not harbour a nest of lodgers. It is, of course, neither more or less dark than every other house in Zanzibar. Don't pay attention to vague suggestions, but try to stop any definite sin.

Three wise and able papers follow, upon a subject very dear to the Bishop's heart—the boys and girls in school, and on leaving school:—

ON THE ELDER BOYS.[1]

As regards our elder boys, several are now on their own account in the world. There are plenty of means of living in the town here, and though one would of course wish to see all our boys grow up into saints, it would not be reasonable to expect it, or even to be surprised at a larger proportion of them turning out badly than is usual among English lads.

We do not of course intend to maintain them all their lives, and I am very glad to see among them some independence of feeling I cannot consent to spend time in lamentation over failures, it can be much better spent in work. Think of the millions of Africans, and one has no time for regrets.

All our boys are the better for what we have taught them, and the best are so much better, that to turn out one of them would pay for many years' labour.

[1] To the Rev. W. J. Festing, 1873.

As to industrial work, it must be remembered that our boys are better able to teach us agriculture than we them; they could, any of them, get a living at that at once. Do not imagine that any of them are as helpless as English boys of eighteen or so without a trade.

Life is so simple here, that no elaborate training is necessary; and really the best thing for any boy is to cultivate his intelligence as much as possible, keeping alive, of course, his physical powers. An intelligent boy can hire himself out for a year or two to a native workman, and he takes his place at once as a master.

If a Christian village is thought of, our boys are quite fit to shift for themselves in it. . . . I must, however, express a doubt as to the policy of trying to isolate our scholars. We teach them to know God's will, and we cannot hold them in bondage; they must go out into the world, and fight for their Master there. We shall produce nothing but hypocrisy if we try a sort of Christian communism, and endeavour to enforce religion by the power of the law.

For myself, I think that to desire anything for our boys—except those with a special vocation—than that they may get an honest living in the fear of God amongst their equals, is to expect something unnatural. I do not think that Zanzibar would be so very much more likely to be Christianized by planting in it a facsimile of your own parish, for instance, as a whole, nor would an English country village be at all to the native heart what a pious missionary and a few real converts would be.

One sort of European work, however, which we must introduce for the general work of the Mission, is the art of printing. We have an influence on the heart of East African life by our books and our conversations in Zanzibar; and our mainland stations, if they succeed in Christianizing what exists, will have done much more sound and real work than the formation of an artificial semi-European village.

If one must speak of oneself, I claim to have done really more for East Africa by my works on its languages, and my translations, than has been done by the French Mission altogether.

It might disappear to-morrow, as such Missions have disappeared, but sound vernacular work among the natives never disappears.

The weakness of Roman Missions, with all their many excellencies, lies in their artificiality and dependence upon foreign influences; the strength of Protestant Missions, with their innumerable defects, lies in their putting a new power into native hands. Witness Paraguay and Madagascar.

I do not mean to decry our French neighbours; they are excellent men, working admirably; but one cannot help seeing the influence of their system, and how it excites suspicions against them, and hinders them from their rightful power.

I doubt whether their establishment at Bagamoyo comes up to Captain Fraser's plantation at Mkotoni; and it is wonderful how many men mistake Europeanization for real improvement.

I do not see what we should gain by introducing a travesty of European dress, language, and manners; the natives are going in that direction only too fast, and the first result is moral degradation.

On Difficulties in the Management of Boys.[1]

Zanzibar, August 9th, 1882.

I am very glad that you realize so well some of the problems you have to meet. Your difficulties are, of course, those that have always met us all, and which we have tried to meet as best we could. You will have to do the same. I should like to tell you what has been done, and what I think should be aimed at.

Bishop Tozer inclined to keep them always (by force, if necessary,) under our control, but it would not answer at all.

My own wish is of the very strongest possible kind that no senior boy should leave Kiungani. I wish it were pos-

---

[1] To the Rev. J. Kingsmill C. Key, then in charge of the Kiungani School.

sible to make them feel that they are in very deed our own children, and that if they are only reasonably well behaved no possible circumstances could occur to cause them to be driven out. I feel myself that wherever they go they are still, as it were, part of me, and that wretched want of confidence in our intentions towards them distresses me exceedingly.

In theory a boy ought to become so attached to his companions and teachers that he would look upon our houses as his permanent home, and wish for nothing better than to stay among us. This is the case with the best, and nearly all of them dread being sent away so much, that they determine, if there is a chance of that happening, to take themselves off in good time. It is the fear of being sent away that most unsettles the boys generally.

We must, then, look forward to their having a will of their own as to their own disposal. Boys who desire to be independent cannot be retained, only they must be kept in strict order while with us. Boys like discipline if it is firmly and genially enforced. . . . I think a great deal of mischief is done by letting a boy have much liberty while we are clothing, feeding, and perhaps paying him for work. . . . We have to train all of them into habits of neatness, promptitude, industry, and general good order,—all most contrary to their natural dispositions, but all indispensable. We cannot trust to a boy's honour ; he understands that to be a licence to do what he pleases. We have not, as in England, the influence of a thousand years of Christianity to fall back upon.

There is no difficulty whatever about any boy earning his own living anywhere ; they can all do that with only too fatal facility. He has to work a great deal harder at Kiungani, lax as the work may be, than he need do, or probably would do, outside. Nor is there any difficulty in our finding an outlet for them. The Europeans in the town would like us to provide them with good servants and competent overlookers ; but boys whom we are disposed to part with are not, for the most part, of sufficient age, or at all willing to work as hard, or to take abuse so quietly, and do not, of course, know the town and its ways so well as those who have lived in it all their lives. A curious result of going into European service is a strong tendency to Mohammedanism, resulting partly from the pressure of other servants, and partly from the indevout habits of their masters, and the distance at which they are necessarily kept. I used to give papers to boys leaving us to look for service, but I found that they were counterfeited and transferred, so I had to give that up.

Another outlet is sea service, in which many have done tolerably, but generally acquire a habit of drinking and riot on shore. Several have been apprenticed to trades ; the masons have done best. But the ideal of most of these boys is to travel about as a caravan porter, as a good many are doing, and some doing well. Some, as you know, have settled in a little colony on their own account at Dar-es-Salaam.

As to sending such restless boys to our mainland stations, I know it is the fashion to represent up-country life as freer from temptation than town life ; people used just in the same way to imagine that country villages were better and purer than towns. We know very well that it is not so in England, and my experience does not show it to be so here. Drunkards and fornicators are just as plenty up country as here, and thieves too, where there is anything to steal. The only real difference is, where you find a man like Farler, who takes hold of a boy's respect and liking by his decision and sympathy ; otherwise, Masasi and Magila are just as bad, or worse, than Zanzibar. Farler has taken a very large share of the bad boys from Kiungani, and done most (not all) of them a great deal of good.

Let me, in conclusion, give you a few hints as to managing the boys.

1. Take care to see and know all you can about them and their doings in a straightforward way.

2. Never let any distinct fault pass unpunished, or at least unnoticed.

3. Having punished, let all be as though it had never been, except, of course, by way of caution.

4. Always punish on the spot, and never defer it or threaten without doing.

5. If you tell a boy to do something, and he will not, give him his punishment, but do not repeat the order, at least not for some days after.

6. If a boy is obstinate or sulky, no punishment will cure him ; a little ridicule in *play time* may do him good, but it is far best to leave him alone till he has tired of his own way.

ON THE MANAGEMENT OF THE GIRLS.

September 13th, 1879.

My dear Miss T——,

It is perfectly useless to try to discover what all are agreed to hide ; you can do nothing but show that you have observed, and are angry about it. Do not speak of it again after the first day. . . . Do not allow any impertinence to pass unnoticed, but do not for one moment expect that you will not meet with it, or that moral persuasion will have any effect at all unless there is a firm hand behind it. At the same time, beware of anything like favouritism, and be very glad to accept anything like a plausible excuse from anybody. It is curious how a sense of injustice, or the pretence of one, lies under almost all rebellion. If you allow their wrong-doing to vex you, you give them a power over you which they will not be slow to use. Why should it vex you that they want correction? If they were good, you would not be wanted at all ; it is because they are bad we are here ; do not therefore be surprised if they are naughty. *We* go on all our lives sinning and suffering ; it is no wonder if school-girls go on wanting and getting punishment. The true discipline is to know that disapprobation and punishment are ready, and pretty sure to come. It is your duty to enforce order, and therefore it ought not to be painful. All this naughtiness will mean nothing if you take it as a matter of course, but as a matter of course to be put down.

On Ritual.[1]

Zanzibar, 1878.

As you are to celebrate to-morrow for the first time at Kiungani, it is perhaps necessary in these days to say something about Ritual.

I expect a man honestly and fairly to take the English Prayer-book as his guide, and not to treat it as an imperfect document, which has to be supplemented out of Roman or Mediæval uses. I fancy the key of the present position lies in the attempt to introduce a local adoration.

I have no hesitation in saying that *local* adoration is in the nature of idolatry. We cannot worship a thing or a presence, we must worship a Person. We offer special worship to our Lord sacramentally present, but He is in and during the whole Eucharist primarily and locally, in the only possible exclusive sense, in heaven, and therefore our worship to Him must be addressed primarily and locally to Him in heaven.

The Presence in the Holy Eucharist is especially non-exclusive and supra-local. If you are careful to teach and practise worship addressed to our Lord in heaven, you will be Catholic and orthodox.

I do not want any answer to this, I only want to let you know in good time how I think.

As to the rest, whatever an honourable and straightforward man can do you are at perfect liberty to do.

On Privy Council Judgments.

November 16th, 1881.[2]

I cannot imagine anything less likely to help the perse-

[1] To the Rev. E. H. D——.
[2] To the Rev. W. Foxley-Norris.

cutors than the imprisonment of Mr. Green, or anything more foolish than the talk about Royal Supremacy, such as I saw in "Church Bells," "the Queen's decision is law," meaning, I suppose, that the decision of the Privy Council is law. But no court can *make* law, and I am very sure that the decision against the vestments is not law, and no judgments in the world could make it so. It is the more disagreeable, because our friends do do other things which are unlawful, and foolish into the bargain; but "Magna est veritas, et prævalebit."

ON THE GRAHAMSTOWN CASE.

Zanzibar, December 20th, 1880.

The gist of the Grahamstown case seems to lie in the settlement of the property upon "Bishop Armstrong and his successors, Bishops of the Church of England, nominated by the Crown."

Bishop Merriman was not nominated by the Crown, and has disclaimed the title of the Church of England for himself and his followers. Therefore, said the Chief Justice, he is not the person named in the deed.

But I think one of the judges held a sounder view in law, when he thought that Dean Williams, having come in under the new state of things, could not object that the bishop he had so long acknowledged was not his bishop, on the principle on which a tenant sued for rent cannot dispute his landlord's title.

ON THE PROPER SWAHILI WORD FOR "SOUL," AS THE WHOLE IDEA OF IT IS NEW.

July 29th, 1879.

My dear W——,

I heard from Mbweni just before I had your letter that the people understood "roho" to mean "the heart." I did not know it before. However, I suppose the heart is a very fair analogue for the soul. It is certainly a very great deal better than "kizuli," "the shadows."

Of course people believe in apparitions after death, but one must not make these do duty for immortal souls.

I take it the whole idea of a soul is new, and has to be taught, and then the word it is tacked on to gets a new meaning, as "roho" and "πνεῦμα," both of which mean simply "breath." It must have been a puzzle at one time how the breath could be immortal. But the "kizuli," like the "shades" of old classical times, seem to be thoroughly and hopelessly heathenish.

On Confirmation as Completing Holy Baptism.

July 4th, 1881.[1]

The following little paper will, I hope, help you in your difficulties about Baptism and Confirmation.

There is nothing in the whole world without God, and therefore nothing without the Holy Spirit, for God cannot be divided.

We read of the Holy Spirit working in the creation, and speaking by the Prophets. All the wisdom and goodness of the heathen world we must attribute to the action of the Holy Spirit.

When, therefore, it is said in the Gospel, "the Holy Spirit was not yet," it is evidently to the special and avowed manifestation of the Holy Spirit that it refers.

In Holy Baptism the laying on of hands is the completion and confirmation of the Sacrament. In early days they almost always went together. The apostles at Samaria put their seal upon the baptism given by the deacon Phillip. So S. Paul at Ephesus baptized those who had received John's teaching, "and when he had laid his hands upon them they received the Holy Ghost." Manifestly the laying on of hands was connected with a special gift of the Holy Ghost.

The Holy Spirit comes to us in innumerable ways and by innumerable instruments, no one of which can at all exclude the others.

[1] To Mr. Z——.

In fact no grace is so tied to any form or sacrament as that it cannot be given without it; witness the outpouring of the Holy Spirit upon Cornelius and those with him, without laying on of hands, or even baptism.

It would be very rash to say of anybody, heathen or Christian, that he had not in any way received the Holy Spirit.

The desire to be joined to Christ's Church is certainly always to be attributed to the Holy Spirit. It is thus easy to construe any texts by reference to the special object to which they are directed.

There is always a sense in which one can say that any particular thing is or is not, according to the object we are aiming at, as one may say of a beggar that he has nothing, when he has certainly a good many things notwithstanding.

On the Effects of Original Sin.

My dear W——,

There is a very nice distinction to be observed as to the effects of Original Sin. So far as it makes us hateful to God, it is washed away in Baptism; but so far as it involves a sinful tendency it is not washed away, only a promise is given of sufficient grace.

Thus it is that baptized people so often grow up just as bad as the unbaptized, and the Church will not baptize any of whom it is not assured that they will be taught to ask for and use the grace promised.

There are two results of the Atonement and Incarnation:—

1. The forgiveness of actual sins, and of innate alienation from God.
2. The implantment and development of a new nature.

For this last the co-operation of the human will is necessary, so soon as it can work at all. Our unrenewed will would make heaven itself a place of unhappiness, and man is not—without saying whether he could be, which we do not know—converted without his own consent.

This letter on the Holy Eucharist illustrates and confirms the words of Archdeacon Maples in Chapter XI. as to the teaching of the Bishop on this great central doctrine of the Church.[1]

"I hold for myself that in the Holy Communion there is first a commemorative Sacrifice when Bread and Wine are offered as the appointed symbols selected by our Lord Himself as memorials of the great Offering of His Flesh and Blood : this may well be the Pure Offering spoken of by the Prophet Malachi. By the act of consecration the elements are in a mysterious and sacramental manner united to the great realities of which they are the symbols, so that the Lamb that was slain, and is now, as it were, still on the Altar before God, is on our altars to be our spiritual food and sustenance, and is verily and indeed presented to all, and received by all worthy communicants. But I hold that our Lord gives us Himself that we may receive and feast upon Him, not that we may gaze at and adore Him. Christians were forbidden to eat of things offered to idols, because to eat of a sacrifice was to take part in it, and so in the heathen persecutions it was accepted as the same thing in effect to burn incense on the idol altar or to eat of an offered victim's flesh. I do not think that to go and see a sacrifice offered, and to turn away instead of eating it, or to look on while others eat, is any acceptable worship to the Deity, and I cannot but feel that the nearer we are to Christ's Presence the more dreadful must our offence be in refusing to receive Him and in gazing upon what we will not take part in."[2]

[1] To the Bishop of Lincoln (Dr. Jackson), 1862.
[2] See also Sermons, xxi. and xcvii., vol. iii. of "Sermon Notes."

ON THE INVOCATION OF SAINTS.

February 26th, 1880.

My dear B——,

The only objection I see to your form is that it is vague, and hardly direct and explicit enough. It sounds like a wish, or an aspiration. If I remember right, it is the nearest approach to the Invocation of Saints for which Mr. Carter could find any reasonably good precedent.

There is always an awkwardness in asking God to cause a creature to intercede for you with Him, and, of course, that He will receive the intercession.

One must not say that the Saints are more merciful, or more inclined to help us, than God Himself; and it is hard to say that God is likely to listen to others praying for us more than to ourselves, especially after the parables of the Lost Sheep and the Prodigal Son.

We ask the prayers of saints on earth, because to our bodily senses they are nearer to us than God; but we know how easily a reliance on the prayers of some saint or hermit may degenerate, and result in a trust in man rather than in God. One can hardly be definite without being wrong.

The modern Roman doctrine about the Invocation of Saints has all grown up out of pious imaginings and mediæval legends and visions.

The only doctrine as to the state of the departed that can claim to be Catholic, is that after death there is no more passing from a lost state to a state of salvation, but the souls of the departed await the judgment day with more or less assurance of salvation, and more or less light and enjoyment therewith, or else with more or less certainty of condemnation, and more or less of darkness and suffering therewith.

But people were not contented with this, and with the consequent prayer for the departed that they might have present light and peace, and a merciful judgment at the last.

It was argued that very few souls are fit to enter heaven without some kind of purgation, and as S. Paul mentions fire (though he speaks of loss, and not of purification), the idea grew up of a purgatorial fire. Some thought it would burn at the last day itself; but then it was said there must be some sort of separation at the moment of death, and so the doctrine of a particular judgment came into being, involving an allotment of purgatorial pains, and in effect superseding the last judgment, which becomes merely the declaration of a long-since decided judgment.

But then souls that needed no purgation, and those that had been purged, were fit for heaven, and why should they be denied anything belonging to the state of the blessed?

And still more, if any number of souls are fit for salvation, some must have exceeded its requirements, and what becomes of their excess of deservings?

It must be somehow available for the help of sinners, and if so, it must be in the power of God's vicegerent upon earth to dispense it.

Hence arose indulgencies, which are drafts on the treasure of saintly merits for the relief of sinners.

The earliest references to the Saints departed which we have are in some of the oldest liturgies, which pray for them all, including S. Mary herself by name, that God would give them light and peace. This soon changed into commemoration by way of thanksgiving, and thence into praises of them, and thence into a mention of their intercessions, which were supposed to follow from their old charity towards all men; thence to asking God to receive their intercessions for special persons and objects; and thence, lastly, into direct appeals to them to intercede for those who prayed to them for help; and even, last of all, into a direct prayer to them, especially to S. Mary, for gifts and graces.

The earliest trace of the idea of being helped by the prayers of the Saints seems to have come in the form of an idea that prayers made at the tombs of martyrs were in a special way united to the prayers of the martyrs themselves. Images and relics have always been supposed to help invocations.

Of course, the departed are not omniscient. How, then, can they know when they are asked to intercede?

This was got over at first by the awkward expedient of, in effect, asking God to tell them; but as soon as the doctrine of purgatory had got into shape, the Saints were supposed to be in heaven, and to enjoy the vision of God, and in God to see, or rather perceive, all things, and therefore to perceive when their intercessions were asked.

Henceforth there could be no difficulty.

It went one step further when the fiction of the Assumption of the Blessed Virgin was generally accepted. Historically there is no foundation at all for this, and, with the details generally given with it, it is a manifest falsehood throughout.

But it really rests upon the comprehensive doctrine, that whatever grace any saint received, the Lord's Mother must have received more abundantly.

If, therefore, Enoch and Elijah were translated, she must have been so also.

Of course, with S. Mary in bodily substance in heaven, seeing all things in God, and claiming the obedience of her Divine Son, there can be no reason why she should not be asked directly for any and every gift.

Only the whole doctrine rests upon a dream, and ends in idolatry.

I should say myself that it is tolerably certain that the Saints in Paradise do intercede for the Church on earth, and specially for that part which was known to them; that it is tolerably certain that they do not know what is actually going on here, or, at all events, not in detail; that Christ is more easily entreated than Saint Mary or any other; that God is not pleased with those who rely to an appreciable extent on any creature as an intercessor; that the Saints are not now as near to God as they will be after the Resurrection.

From all this it would follow that the intercession of the Saints, and especially of those we have known, may be confidently hoped for, and whether they will be heard depends chiefly on ourselves.

That in Christ and the Holy Spirit we have better and nearer help, and Intercessors Who have power and are sure of acceptance.

Any reference in our prayers to the intercession of the Saints is, therefore, practically of no importance ; it may not be sinful, but it must not be leant upon.

On Eternal Punishment ; a Fragment of a Letter to Mrs. ——.

Eternity, and eternal duration, is Duration.

Eternal being is Being, all else is merely a show of being.

We think of the substance of the world as an entity ; the changing things of the world are a passing show ; but an Eternity of change is no Eternity at all. You cannot make Eternity out of an infinity of time, any more than you can make gold out of an infinity of iron.

If there is such a thing as Eternity, it must be unchanging. If unchanging, there is an end of the question.

The ideas of growing in light and knowledge pre-suppose a want and a goal. If they go on for ever, the want is never satisfied, and the goal never reached ; if so, there is no perfection and no heaven, as well as no hell.

If it is inconsistent with God's goodness that men should be for ever unhappy, it is inconsistent with His goodness that their lot should ever be finally determined.

Unless, indeed, evil is not hateful to Him, but is strictly and only a means of producing good,—if so, it must be lawful to do evil that good may come.

Mohammedanism.

There are two passages in Bishop Steere's published Sermon Notes, which bear so closely upon the Mohammedan controversy, that we venture to reprint them amongst his letters of counsel and advice, as bringing forward a side of the question not always fully realized at home :—

" The distance between God and man is immense. . . . .

Our natural relation ... is as the New Testament describes it, *a slavery*. This is the basis of the ordinary worships of mankind. An awe, and fear, a sense of helplessness, a blind submission, or an abject entreaty, and strange offerings, and self-torture. Sometimes in Africa it becomes a mere dull acknowledgment; sometimes it takes the form of horrible and depraved rites. Upon this Mohammedanism is a great improvement. It shows God as just, and as delighting in just men, and merciful to them. God is no longer a mere master, but a good and just master, not capriciously inflicting evil but judging justly, and forgiving many offences in consideration of zeal for His glory, and exactitude in following His express commands.

"Still God is *a master*, and men are His *slaves;* and the sort of obedience given, and the sort of dependence upon Him, are tinctured by this fact, God is still a God far off.

"But the birth of Christ changes this altogether. Our whole position in regard to God is changed; a filial confidence takes the place of slavish awe. We can now speak of the whole family of heaven and earth and Christ its Head. A new idea has come in now, that humility is God-like and self-sacrifice divine. With this all law and rule is done away, because love outruns the law. A kind servant is better than a slave, but the owner is best of all. The Faith of Christ struggles on against men's evil impulses, but it stirs men in spite of themselves, and so far as it prevails makes earth a heaven." (Vol. i., p. 32.)

"Religion and theology, as most men receive them, are the practical forms of a deep science; the nature of God lies behind it, but its bearing and importance are not recognised. Thus the untaught man thinks of God as of other men; the herdsman as a God of cattle; the cultivator as a God of seasons; the sailor as a God of the sea. It is a great advance when all these are seen to be but different actions of one God. . . . . The wildest savage and the most bigoted Mohammedan and Jew intend to worship the Holy Trinity, however much in words they deny or blaspheme our doctrine. For they intend to worship the one true God.

Whom, and Whom only, we adore. And Christianity may speak to them in the words of S. Paul :—' Whom, therefore, ye ignorantly worship, Him declare I unto you.'" (Vol. ii., page 220.)

INDEX

To the main topics of the Bishop's Letters.

Activity, a too great longing after, the fault of the age, 42, 325.
Admission to a brotherhood, on, 39.
African and European Law identical in their main features, 327.
An address to native Evangelists, 106.
A Pastoral to his clergy on public worship, &c., 376.
—— to the G.S.A., 395.
—— to the Bondeis on Polygamy, 424.
Apologies, his dislike of, 390.

Bacon's Philosophy, 17.
Benefices, the small country, 236, 394.
Bible, the, a criterion, not a teacher, 403.
—— the value of a vernacular, 261.
—— Society, the, 88, 261.
Bishopric, his refusal of the, 126.
Blasphemy against the Holy Ghost, its nature, 12.
Board of Missions the, as Missionary Inspectors, 387.
Boys, on the management of the native, 426, 428.
Brotherhoods, 37, 333, 412.
—— for Africa, 335.
Butler, Bishop, 14, 17.
—— Bishop, the Analogy, 45.

Chalmers, Dr., his estimate of, 12.
Christianity and civilization, 209, 249.
Church, Hear the, 362.
—— and the Slave Trade, 100.
—— Reform, 99.
Churches, lay help in, 392.
Churchmen, over fastidiousness of, 374.
Civil power, the, and Missionaries, 326.
Clergy, a cheaper needed in England, 94, 381.
Colleges, Missionary, 380.
Committees and Missionaries, 299, 384.
Committee, last letter to the Home, 357.

Confession amongst native Christians, 183.
Confirmation as completing Holy Baptism, 434.
Critics and Missions, 383.

Dealing with the faults of others, 390.
Death of Mr. West, 135.
Differences, the, of home and Mission work, 81.
Direct moral influence, what is it? 21.
Dislike of apologies, his, 390.

Endowments, on, 93, 382, 394.
Eternal punishment, a fragment of a letter on, 440.
Eucharistic Doctrine, 180, 379, 436.
Evangelists, address to native, 106.

Fascination of beautiful surroundings, the, 13.
Father of an intending Missionary, to the, 415.
—— of one whose Ordination had been deferred, to the, 419.
Faults in others, how to deal with, 390.
Forbearance, mutual, on, 42, 395, 408.

Grahamstown Case, a letter on the, 433.
Girls, on the management of the, 431.

Holy Spirit, all goodness of the Heathen comes from the, 434.
Humblest work, the true greatness of, 406.

Individual responsibility, 41.
Intellectual Difficulties of belief, 366.
Intercession, a letter on, 204.
Intuitive perception of truth easily lost, 15.
Invocation of Saints, the, 437.

Keys, the power of, and S. Peter, 362.
Krapf, Dr., as a Linguist, 72.

Lay-help in Churches, 392.
Lincoln Theological College, his plan for, 91.
Loss of interest in work, on, 405.
Luxuries and necessaries for Missionaries, 414.

Metaphysical Theology, the danger of, 13.
Missionaries and the civil power, 326.
—— and their critics, 383.
Missionary, letter to a, deferring his ordination, 416.
—— to the same, just before his ordination, 420.
—— Colleges and English priests, 380.
—— Inspectors, the need of, 207, 388.

INDEX.

Missions and Missionary Societies, 207, 299, 384.
—— Special, and S.P.G., 298.
—— and travellers, 387.
Mission work, the practical realities of, 87.
Mohammed, personal character and mission, 307.
Mohammedanism, 219, 305, 440.
—— and civilization, 307.
—— converts from, 320, 346.
—— how the Church should deal with, 310, 441.
—— and drink, 317.
—— its grasp of the Unity of the Godhead, 20, 441.
—— the true nature of its growth in East Africa, 318.
—— and slavery, 78, 314.
—— and its treatment of women, 316.
—— its unconscious worship of the Holy Trinity, 441.
Mother, a letter to a, 39.

Native ministry, the, 245.
Night schools, 399.

Original sin, the effects of, 435.
Oxford, letter to, 113.
—— speech at, 79, 130.

Pagans, the, and their religion, 16.
Pain, the moral influence of, 12.

Pastoral letter to his clergy on worship, &c., 376.
—— letter to the Guild.S.A., 395.
—— letter on Polygamy to the Bondeis, 424.
Personal holiness, the only sure way to peace, 14.
Peter, abbot of Cluny, 43.
—— S., and the power of the keys, 362.
Practical realities of Mission work, the, 81.
Priests, English, and Missionary Colleges, 380.
Privy council judgments, the, 378, 432.

Reasons, his, for joining the Mission, 56.
Refusal of the Bishopric, 126.
Relations, the, of the Church and the slave trade, 100.
—— the, of Christianity and civilization in mission work, 240.
Respect the, due to the rights of natives, 413.
Responsibility of all men for their belief, 41.
Ritual, on, 379, 432.
Rule of life, the Bishop's own, 358.

Schoolmen, the theology of the, 18.
Slave market, the closing of the, 120.

Slavery and Mohammedanism, 314.
Slaves, the arrival of, in Zanzibar, 77.
Socialism, 364.
Soul, the proper Swahili word for the, 433.
Special Missions and S.P.G., 298.
Speculation on the unrevealed, useful, 27.
System of voluntary workers, the Bishop's, 343.

Theological College at Lincoln, plans for the, 91.
Theology at the Universities, 234.
Travellers and Missions, 387.

Universities, the, special duty of, towards the Mission, 113.
Unsalaried Missionaries, 225, 343.

Vernacular Bible, the value of a, 261.
Voluntary workers, 294, 343.

Wesleyanism, 373.
Work, greatness of the humblest, 406, 415.
Working pleasantly with others, 408.

Zanzibar, a description of, 75.
—— customs, 85.

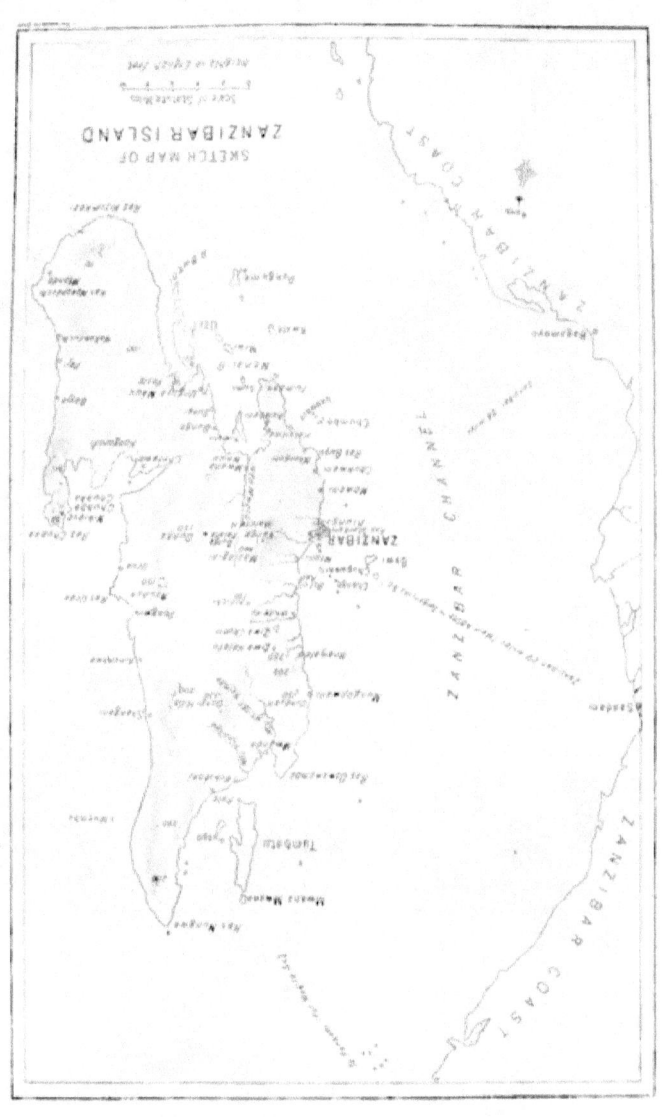

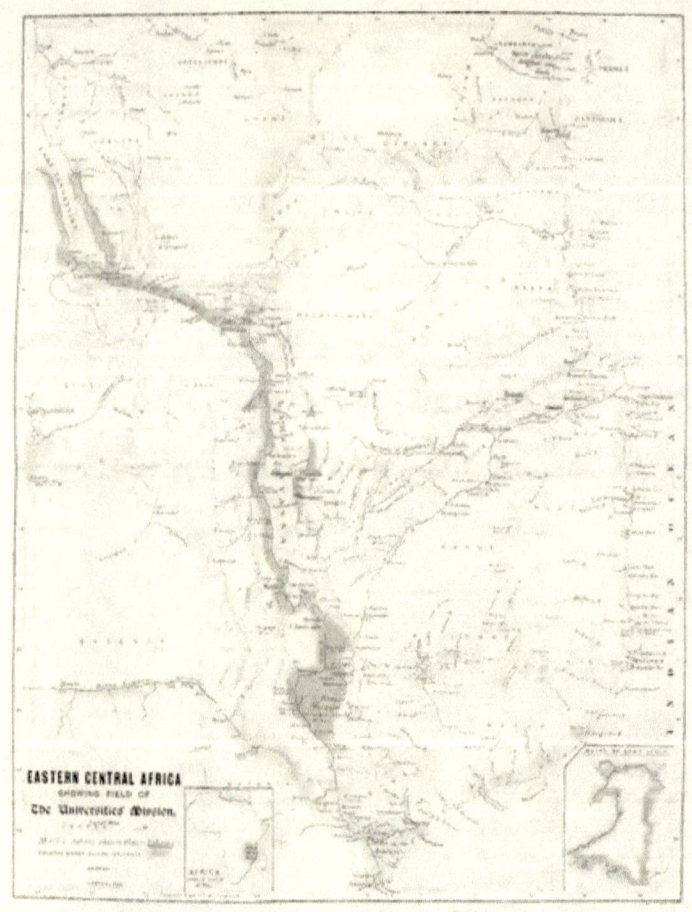

www.ingramcontent.com/pod-product-compliance
Lightning Source LLC
Chambersburg PA
CBHW022105300426
44117CB00007B/597